# Designing Effective Organizations

# Designing
# Effective
# Organizations

······························

## Traditional &
## Transformational
## Views

DAVID K. BANNER

T. ELAINE GAGNÉ

**SAGE** Publications
*International Educational and Professional Publisher*
Thousand Oaks    London    New Delhi

Copyright © 1995 by Sage Publications, Inc.

*For information address*:

SAGE Publications, Inc.
2455 Teller Road
Thousand Oaks, California 91320

SAGE Publications Ltd.
6 Bonhill Street
London EC2A 4PU
United Kingdom

SAGE Publications India Pvt. Ltd.
M-32 Market
Greater Kailash I
New Delhi 110 048 India

Printed in the United States of America

**Library of Congress Cataloging-in-Publication Data**

Banner, David K.
    Designing effective organizations: traditional &
transformational views / David K. Banner, T. Elaine Gagné.
        p.   cm.
    Includes bibliographical references and indexes.
    ISBN 0-8039-4848-4
        1. Organizational sociology.   2. Organizational effectiveness.
    3. Organizational behavior.   4. Social systems.   I. Title.
    HM131.B23   1995
    302.3'5—dc20                                                    94-5921
                                                                        CIP

95  96  97  98  99  10  9  8  7  6  5  4  3  2  1

Sage Production Editor: Yvonne Könneker

# Contents

# Foreword

This book presents an avant garde approach to an important topic about which, to my way of thinking, no one else has written even a contemporary book. What makes this approach avant garde is the metaperspective used by the authors to interrelate a diverse, and often fragmented, literature on organization theory. Their perspective readily allows the reader to comprehend and appreciate what is always present—often hidden and almost always controversial—the *subjective side of organizational life*. Everyone understands that self-interests, personal biases, professional agendas, and limits to consciousness determine what an individual sees inside an organization. And everyone understands that what a person sees determines how that individual characterizes each organizational situation and attempts to get others to respond to it. However, to this point, integrative books on the subject either fail to acknowledge the omnipresent subjective factor or attempt to partition off to the side. They use a "rationalistic" logic that leads people to conclude that organizational behavior is far more rational, logical, and controllable than it actually is.

The rational mind wants to stand apart from organizational events and view behavior as logical, predictable, and under control. Accomplishing this is an objective that any textbook on organization theory is supposed to fulfill—and all do. Such texts take diverse phenomena, put them in comprehensible order, and present what the collective field has discovered and offered as explanation. Nevertheless, every organizational veteran knows that actual events are seldom logically explainable, predictable, or under any degree of tight control. Even when events momentarily seem to fit one person's explanation or model of order, the veterans know that only one thing is predictable: The next moment is likely to upset their experience of that order. Apparent chaos is the norm; it is the individual's mind that needs order and thus creates it. To a large extent, the order created is a function of the mind that seeks it. That is why different people experiencing the same events will see and interpret those events differently. This takes place even when the individuals have read the same organization theory books.

The book you are about to read provides the rationalist and the veteran exactly what each craves most. It provides synthesis and order within a structure that acknowledges the interaction between an individual's motivations and needs and the apparent order that individual perceives. The authors accomplish this, in part, by providing one vignette after another. This allows the reader to experience abstract theory with observables and to reflect on their own experiences to flesh that theory out. The use of cartoons and other "right-brain" highlighters allows readers to look down, as opposed to looking up, to understand and critique the phenomena a theory purports to explain, and to self-reflect on the importance a theory holds for the field.

Certainly, this is a book for the 1990s. It is reader-friendly and is written with a heretofore missing or overlooked theme. Looking back, this seems to be characteristic of the field of organization study—an overlooked theme seems to gain prominence every 10 to 15 years. In the 1960s, it was "the individual." In the 1970s, it was "systems." In the 1980s, it was "contingencies." Now, in the 1990s, it is "mind-set," or, as the authors call it, "paradigm."

*Samuel A. Culbert*
Professor of Management
John E. Anderson Graduate School of Management
University of California, Los Angeles

# Preface

□   □   □

It's the summer of 1988. Driving through the lush hills of Vermont, USA . . . one verdant hill after another reveals itself in this drive north on Interstate 89 to Waterbury. . . . I enjoy the drive. It's kind of meditative. Reflecting on whom I'm going to visit, I invent a picture in my mind of 1964 on Long Island, New York. Two chubby seventh graders are "inhaling" banana splits at a local ice cream shop while their classmates are trying out for the baseball team. Their baggy pants and overhanging T-shirts leave plenty of room for expansion. . . .

I first read about them in a discarded magazine in an airport. These two best friends, Ben Cohen and Jerry Greenfield, stayed in touch with each other through the years. Eventually, their sustained mutual love for *good* ice cream spawned a business that has earned international recognition. Their first investment was a $5 correspondence course in ice cream making. This initial investment in 1978, coupled with an additional one of $12,000 and their own creativity has evolved into a 1987 gross revenue of $31.8 million. Projected sales for 1988 are $45 million. Production of 9,600 pints an hour "when all is working right" can't keep up with the demands for their product!

I'm on my way to visit their plant in Waterbury, VT, now—but not because they make a lot of money. I *am* interested in the *spirit* of their business. The ingredients of their company include elements not all that common in today's corporate scene. They are concerned about how they treat their employees and the surrounding community. Their view of their own salaries doesn't reflect the usual "more, more, more" attitude. To them, bigger is not necessarily better.

They don't just philosophize about these things. They let their thoughts take form. Employee participation is important; production stops for a two-hour staff meeting once a month. Rather than see this time as a great cost to the company, Ben and Jerry see it as an essential investment. Fifteen percent of the company's pre-tax profits is given to charity through the Ben & Jerry's Foundation. This donation is believed to reflect the highest percentage of any publicly held company. Their own salaries are no more than five times the lowest employee salary. The lowest annual paycheck is $15,000. Against the advice of financial experts, Ben and Jerry promoted low-as-possible public stock purchases in Vermont through their "get a scoop of the action" campaign. One out of every 100 families in Vermont owns Ben & Jerry's stock and are they ever happy about it!

The directions that Jerry gave me are great. His "You can't miss us!" was accurate. The new plant he told me about is a combination of fancy and down-to-earth. I chuckle at the life-sized, man-made black and white cows which grace the huge lawn in front of the plant, the same cows pictured on all the trucks and vans. From thirty feet away, I spot Jerry in the parking lot. Even though his back is turned to me and I have never met him before, I would recognize that T-shirt and baggy pants anywhere. As he turns, I call out and introduce myself. We meet. It's the beginning of a genuine friendship.

Ben is away, but in being with Jerry and with David Barash, Director of Human Resources, and by reading additional articles, I learn more about the company and about Ben and Jerry themselves. They seem to have resurrected a primary definition of business: to provide a quality product and/or service. "I think treating the customer right is a really big thing," says Jerry.

They have added some pieces to this definition: first, provide a context for employee growth (I saw the renovation and expansion of the staff area well under way. The 30 or so staff working after 6 p.m. seemed fully "present" and involved in their work in a, yes, *joyful* way); and, second, have a concern for the world outside of their company. Ben once said, "If every company contributed the same percentage of profits to the community that we do and [others do] there would be virtually no social problems in the country because there would be enough money to solve them." Even though it may take more than money to solve social problems, Ben and Jerry demonstrate a rare "giving without concern for results" that will indeed make a creative difference in our world. "We've ended up giving away a lot of ice cream and a lot of money," Jerry says, "always with the idea that it was just something we wanted to do. Not that it was going to be good for business or that we'd get paid back in the long term. We just always felt like it was what we wanted to do." Ben and Jerry don't feel the need to take in a lot more money and to get big just to be big. As Ben said, "I mean, what does that get me? It doesn't get me anything." They are different all right.

In spite of their desire to control growth, Ben and Jerry's company is nevertheless growing at a good clip. They have added over 50 employees per year for the last three years and are building a new plant in southern Vermont. Their organization is feeling the pressure that comes hand-in-hand with such growth. Can they continue to operate in their unorthodox way and survive the competitive business climate of this decade? Will they redefine "survival" and "success"?[1]

□    □    □

---

## Ben & Jerry's:
## What's Behind Its Success?

---

Ben & Jerry's Homemade Inc. is a contemporary organizational phenomenon. Its success is a result of more than merely being in the right place at the right time. Enthusiasm, consistent hard work, and *organization structure and process* have also contributed. This last ingredient is a product of who Ben and Jerry *are*. The question begs to be asked: Why is Ben & Jerry's so different from similar organizations, and what, if anything, do these differences have to do with its success?

The structure and process of an organization are part and parcel of its substance. The study of organization structure and process is called *organization theory* (OT). Organization theory has spawned many theories that attempt to explain why organizations are structured or designed as they are. According to these "traditional" explanations, the success of Ben & Jerry's may be the result of its strategy, size, technology, environment, or power and control balance.

*Strategy.* Originally postulated by Chandler in his classic work is the notion that the strategy an organization chooses to follow will necessarily affect the structure that organization uses to implement the strategy. Viewed from this perspective, the Ben & Jerry's strategy seems to be a moderate-growth, quality-emphasis, premium ice cream approach. They are seeking to expand gradually, and are adding bureaucratic features grudgingly. However, Ben and Jerry both realize that growth leads to the need for increased formalization (even if they don't like it).

*Size.* Another OT line of reasoning argues that all organizations, in their early entrepreneurial stages, have loose, flat structure and, with growth, require increasing levels of specialization and formalization to achieve their goals (hence the onset of bureaucracy). Ben & Jerry's is growing, and new workers, who perhaps do not share Ben and Jerry's vision, need direction in the form of policies, rules, and procedures. Increased size seems to bring on the need for bureaucratic structure.

*Technology.* From the early, pioneering work of Woodward to the Aston and Birmingham studies in England, research has made it obvious that there is a relationship between the dominant (or modal) technology a firm employs and its structural configuration. The dominant technology at Ben & Jerry's is long-linked (assembly line). Long-linked technologies tend to work best with decentralized bureaucratic structures that include a lot of planning and control.

*Environment.* The open systems view, developed by Lawrence and Lorsch of Harvard (among others), argues that the complexity or the relative stability of the environment is a causal variable in determining the structure that will most effectively meet the needs of that environment. The environment in which Ben & Jerry's does business is complex and dynamic. A great deal of competition from other premium ice cream makers (such as Häagen-Dazs), plus the growth of low-fat frozen yogurt alternatives, has required Ben and Jerry to stay flexible and adaptive. Therefore, their market research and new product development departments are organically structured.

*Power/control.* Another view, originated by March and popularized by Pfeffer and Salancik, holds that the demands of the *dominant coalition* (that group of people in the organization who hold the most power) will necessarily shape the structure so as to enhance the power of the coalition and enable it to achieve its collective goals. Ben and Jerry have sought to include representatives from every organizational level and every functional department in their dominant coalition. By building widespread participation into the decision-making process, Ben and Jerry have avoided the typical elitist, centralized power structure of large bureaucracies.

All of the above-described approaches have considerable face (as well as empirical) validity, but the success of an organization like Ben & Jerry's can perhaps best be viewed in light of a new discipline in the behavioral sciences called *organizational transformation.* One transformational author writes:

> The concept of transformation is powerful and complex. It represents a complete change of consciousness from one level of operation to a higher, more integrated level of operating. Transformation implies the awakening of new levels of awareness; a fundamental resolution of the internal causes of stress; the discovery and clarification of essential values; the creation of new goals through which to manifest these values in the world; and the redirection of basic energies toward a higher and more fulfilling purpose.
>
> In short, transformation requires the willingness to explore uncharted territory and blaze new trails, and the capacity to utilize new energies in the realization of stated objectives and goals. It is obvious that something significant must take place to facilitate a process of transformation.[2]

Ben and Jerry seem to realize that their state of consciousness—their beliefs, attitudes, and values—finds form in their organizational structure and process. In that sense, they are part of a new breed in management, the transformational leader. Their priority is to release the innate creativity, resourcefulness, and commitment inherent in the human capacity. This, as CEO Paul Allaire of Xerox has noted, will be the competitive advantage of American corporations in the 1990s and beyond.

## The Design of Organizations (Organization Theory)

Organizations have been studied by social scientists for many years, in part because organizations constitute such a dominant influence in our lives. Understanding how and why organizations are the way they are is a prerequisite to learning how to manage or change them.

OT involves the study of the structure and the process of organizations. Studying the *structure* of an organization means analyzing the following:

- how an organization is put together
- who reports to whom
- the degree of centralization or decision-making power concentrated at the top
- the extent of the rules, policies, regulations, and procedures in an organization

Studying the *process* of an organization means examining the following:

- internal processes of conflict and resolution
- internal politics
- corporate culture
- the organizational life cycle

In other words, organization theory is concerned with how organizations are created and maintained and how they function internally. The unit of analysis is the *whole organization*.

There are two distinct perspectives from which organization theory can be approached: the traditional and the transformational. The *traditional* perspective is that organizations are structured according to the influences of the five variables just applied to Ben Cohen and Jerry Greenfield's thriving ice cream business:

1. the power relationships in the organization
2. the external environment
3. the type of technology employed to do the organization's work
4. the size of the organization
5. the strategy the organization chooses to pursue

In other words, the structure and design of the organization are the results of these five factors.

The *transformational* perspective is radically different. The five factors discussed above are still important, but, instead of being seen as causing structure, they are seen as intervening variables of a more central cause: *the agreement in consciousness shared by the organizational participants.* The transformational approach argues that all external organizational forms are created by internal mental structures in the consciousness of participants. According to the transformational view, the invisible mental and emotional structures that are shared collectively by organizational members (beliefs, attitudes, values, assumptions, and expectations) actually create and maintain the structure of the organization.

Organizational change is viewed differently, too. Under the traditional perspective, organizations change when forced to do so—by external factors, such as the environment, or by internal factors, such as power or strategy shifts. In the transformational view, change occurs first at the level of the mind (the aforementioned beliefs, attitudes, and values). When we change the way we think, the structures we create with our thought forms change as a result.

In summary, the traditional approach sees the organization in a *reactive* posture, trying to anticipate what the external changes will be. The transformational approach sees the external world of the organization as a *projection in consciousness* of the agreement shared by members relating to the nature of that world. In other words, the approaches are exactly opposite. The traditional approach sees the organization as the effect of the external environment. In the transformational view, the external environment is caused (or "enacted") by the shared consciousness of the members.

## What Is Unique About This Book

This book is infused with the transformational point of view. In it, we offer an alternative way of understanding cause-and-effect relationships within organizations. This book is about a new way of seeing organizations—not as independent entities, but as the products of a prevailing or dominant agreement in consciousness, or a *paradigm.*

One of the core assumptions of the dominant way of seeing organizations is that their functioning can be "figured out" with the rational mind. In this book, we will develop a new way of looking at how organizations are created, maintained, and changed. This manner of "seeing" employs ideas and concepts that cannot be totally verified with the mind. Our core assumption is that this fact does not necessarily make the ideas invalid. In fact, we assume that there are invisible factors of consciousness that are central to understanding why organizations are the way they are. These invisible factors play a key role in the creation of the visible factors of structure and process. This is now being widely recognized, as Larry Miller points out:

> The decline of a corporation is often explained by pointing to external events such as competition, technology, changing economic and market conditions. Similarly, some historians have explained the decline of a civilization by pointing to changes in the physical environment such as earthquake, volcanic eruption, or plague, limits on physical expansion or the attack of external competitors. Arnold Toynbee examined each of these (in the fall of twenty-one civilizations) and rejected all external explanations, leaving only the internal cause, the loss of human vitality.[3]

Here is the crux of our argument: The external factors of strategy, size, technology, environment, and power/control are not unimportant in the creation of structure and process in an organization, but they are, at best, intervening variables. The key causative element in the creation, maintenance, and change of organizations is the invisible agreement in consciousness (the collective paradigm) of the organization's members. We explore this argument through a metamodel that unifies superficially disparate approaches to organization theory and provides an explanation of how organizations are created, maintained, and changed. This unifying model, which serves as the foundation for this entire book, is fully developed in Chapter 7.

Throughout this book, we consider the traditional topics of organization theory from both traditional and transformational perspectives, with the goals of sensitizing the reader to the latest transformational research and thought about organization structure/process and of comparing that with the traditional concepts.

## The Macro Versus Micro Distinction

There are two ways to approach the study of an organization's behavior; these can be designated *macro* and *micro*. The study of macro organization behavior, also called organization theory, is the study of whole organizations and their major subsystems. The study of micro organization behavior, also called simply organization behavior, is the study of individuals and small groups within an organization (see Table 1).

People are important in both organization theory and organization behavior; however, they are the major consideration in the study of organization behavior (micro), which focuses on such individual behavior aspects as leadership, communication, decision making, motivation, and personality. The study of micro organization behavior is concerned with cognitive (rational) and affective (emotional) differences among people in organizations. The organization behavior approach predominantly attends to individual and small group processes.

Macro organization theory, on the other hand, is concerned with people aggregated into departments, divisions, and organizations, and with the structure and process issues in these aggregates. Organization theory deals with the *organization,* rather than the individual, as the unit of analysis. It addresses such issues as organizational effectiveness, goals, power, politics, structural conflict, the impact of technology on structure, the effect of the external environment on structure, and similar topics.

Basically, organization theory is concerned with *contextual factors* that help explain organizational reality. Organization behavior addresses *individual influences* upon that same reality. In the study of micro behavior, one looks at individual motivation, the design of individual jobs, role relations, group dynamics, and the like.

In macro theory, the emphasis is on unit tasks, organizational and unit technologies, and their implications for the design of complex organizations. Rather than looking at individual responses to organizational dynamics, macro theory stresses the adjustment processes of systems and their major subsystems to changing environmental/technical/social milieus.

The focus of this book is macro organization theory. However, the human factor will be included in our consideration of organization theory. This is another point where our approach departs from the standard OT approach. The traditional approach sees the collective behavior of individuals as a function of *external influences* such as organization technology and environment and *internal organizational influences* such as power relationships, strategic decisions, and organizational size.

In this text, we will look at *patterns* of social behavior across groups of organizational members as they reflect their *collective* internal mental states. We will demonstrate that these apparent external and internal influences actually are a product of the collective agreement in beliefs, attitudes, and values, and the assumptions and expectations that flow

**Table 1** Comparison of Micro and Macro Views of Organization

| *Traditional (Micro)* *Organizational Behavior* | *Versus* | *Macro* *Organizational Behavior* |
|---|---|---|
| | Issue Emphasis | |
| Structures and processes (cognitive, emotional, and physical) within individuals, small groups, and their leaders, and the linkages among them | versus | Structures and processes within major subsystems, organizations, and their environments, and the linkages among them |
| | Research Focus | |
| Study of the behaviors of individuals, small groups, and their leaders in the laboratory or in relatively isolated or immediate social settings | versus | Study of the behaviors of members of major subsystems, subsystems themselves, organizations, and their environments within their larger contexts |
| | Primary Applications | |
| Individual self-improvement and job design, intervention into interpersonal and group processes, training of leaders of small groups; individual and group change | versus | Design and management of the structures and processes linking major subsystems, organizations, and their environments; organizational and environmental change |

from them. Viewing macro organization theory from this perspective is a radical departure from the conventional thinking in the field.

To summarize, the field of macro organization theory primarily involves two aspects of organization:

1. the *structures* of organizations, which serve to differentiate and integrate the organizations, plus help them relate to their external environment
2. the *processes* of organizations, which include such things as power, politics, conflict, organization life cycle, culture, and strategic planning

Also included in the field are such *contextual* factors as size, environment, and technology.

In this book we consider all of these traditional macro organization theory topics from both traditional and transformational perspectives. The reader will get to see the "old paradigm" and "new paradigm" interpretations side by side. As Gareth Morgan would say, we will view this subject through two radically different "lenses." This will likely stimulate much creative thinking and dialogue. In fact, some who read this volume might see it as "an organizational behavior book masquerading as an organization theory text," as one of the book's reviewers alleged—completely misunderstanding the transformational assumptions inherent in our model. In this book, we will bridge the gap between organizational behavior and organization theory with the metamodel.

---

## Overview of the Book

---

Because we believe people want tools they can use to understand and influence organizations, we employ a pragmatic approach that avoids jargon and favors pedagogical devices that increase student interest and enhance the "real-world" flavor of the book. The extensive use of behavioral objectives, tie-ins with previous chapters, discussion questions, vignettes, our own personal experiences, and cartoons all serve to make the book user-friendly. Chapter summaries, examples, and cases ground the theoretical material in up-to-date situations and circumstances.

### Chapter Sequencing

*Part I: Organization Theory*
*From a Transformational Perspective*

- Chapter 1, "Organizations and Organization Theory": This chapter traces the history of organization theory and discusses the definitions of organizations and the emergence of large-scale bureaucratic organizations.
- Chapter 2, "Of Paradigms and Paradigm Shifts": In this chapter we look at the definition of *paradigm*, how paradigms "shift" or change, and how the collective or shared paradigm actually creates organization structure and process and how our paradigms shape reality through selective perception, the self-fulfilling prophecy, and self-limiting beliefs.
- Chapter 3, "The Industrial Era Paradigm": Here we look at the major beliefs, attitudes, and values that have characterized the industrial era in the

Western world, and we examine the impacts these have had on our organizations.

- Chapter 4, "Transformational Thinking: The Emerging Paradigm": This chapter begins to discuss exactly how the industrial paradigm and the transformational paradigm differ, and what the implications of those differences are.
- Chapter 5, "Creating the New-Paradigm Organization": In this chapter we look at how the new organization might be created. This includes a look at how bureaucracies are created and how personal maturity and willingness to take responsibility play a part in creating organic structures.
- Chapter 6, "Systems Thinking in Organization Theory": Beginning with the early systems theorists in organizations and ending with the latest (Peter Senge), we examine the concept of open systems and show how systems theory is a precursor to the transformational perspective.
- Chapter 7, "The Metamodel of Organization": This chapter introduces the core model of the book, which states that the shared or collective paradigm of the organizational members actually creates and maintains the organization's structure and process.
- Chapter 8, "Transformation and Organizational Effectiveness": Here we look at the thorny issue of effectiveness. No one can quite agree on what it is, but we examine several models purporting to measure it, and we conclude with the transformational perspective on effectiveness.

## Part II: The Structure of Organizations

- Chapter 9, "Macro Structural Variables": We look at the major structural variables in this chapter—centralization, formalization, complexity, integration, and the role of goals in organizations.
- Chapter 10, "The Creation and Evolution of Organization Structure": In this chapter we show how organizations are created, maintained, and changed over time.
- Chapter 11, "Emerging Organizational Designs": This chapter looks at some of the most recent organizational designs (which, according to the metamodel, are symptoms of the paradigm shift), such as the matrix, hybrid transorganizational systems, network organizations, and the organic structure.

## Part III: The Context of Organizations

- Chapter 12, "The Environment of Organizations": In this chapter we examine the traditional and transformational views of the organization/environment interface. In the traditional vein, we look at typologies of environmental complexity and turbulence. From the transformational view, we see environment as a projection in consciousness of our own internal (collective) state.

- Chapter 13, "Organizational Technology and Structure": Here we examine the traditional theory of structure being caused by dominant organizational technology. We define technology, show how different technologies are associated with different structures, and conclude with the transformational view of the technology/structure relationship.
- Chapter 14, "Organizational Size and Structure": In this chapter we examine the relationship between organizational size and structure, citing traditional research, and then we postulate a transformational view of this relationship.
- Chapter 15, "Power, Politics, and Structure": Here we look at the organizational creation and symbolic interpretation of power, how power is used for political advantage, why organizations are not rational, why power is so important in the industrial paradigm, and more.
- Chapter 16, "Strategy and Structure": The relationship between strategy and structure, from both traditional and transformational perspectives, is the subject of this chapter.

*Part IV: The Processes of Organization*

- Chapter 17, "The Organizational Life Cycle": The focus of this chapter is on how organizations are born, mature, and either decay and die or are reborn.
- Chapter 18, "Organizational Culture": The shared or collective paradigm of all organizational members produces the culture. In this chapter, we look at this very important organizational variable.
- Chapter 19, "Structural Conflict in Organizations": Here we examine how the structural arrangement in an organization can cause conflictual situations, and we describe the traditional, interactionist, and transformational views of conflict. We also address conflict resolution.
- Chapter 20, "Facilitating New-Paradigm Organizations": The subject of this chapter is how we might actively foster the growth and development of new-paradigm organizations.

---

## Before We Proceed

---

One final observation might be useful. Macro organization theory, as this topic is sometimes called, can often be dull. But the changes that are occurring in these times in organizational structure and process are anything but dull. In this book, readers will have the opportunity to trace what has gone before and to discern how we have been subtly moving into an era of unprecedented organizational change. Challenges to organizational effectiveness abound, and it is our intention to present a perspective on these changes that will empower readers, as managers or as students of organization, to understand and facilitate this change. An understanding of the metamodel is essential for anyone who is interested in accommodating the massive changes that are affecting organizations today.

## Acknowledgments

We would like to thank Dr. Bob Tomlinson, our tireless research assistant, for his endless hours of enthusiastic support, diligent library work, and keen insight. Bob, you are a gem! Also, we appreciate Becky Armstrong's creative work on graphics design.

Now, get ready to enter a new world . . . literally . . . the world of "new paradigm organizations."

## NOTES

1. T. Elaine Gagné, "Ben and Jerry's: A New Flavor," *Business Dynamics* 31 (August/September, 1988): 1-3. Reprinted with permission.

2. Amir Levy and Uri Merry, *Organizational Transformation: Approaches, Strategies, Theories* (Westport, CT: Greenwood, 1986), 137.

3. Lawrence M. Miller, *Barbarians to Bureaucrats: Corporate Life Cycle Strategies* (New York: Clarkson N. Potter, 1989), 114-115.

# PART I

■ ORGANIZATION
THEORY FROM A
TRANSFORMATIONAL
PERSPECTIVE

# 1 Organizations and Organization Theory

*Organizations have been with mankind for a very long time, along with a great deal of practical knowledge and experience about how to structure and manage them. Yet scientific knowledge about organizations, as distinguished from practical wisdom, is almost entirely a product of the present century, and much, if not most of it, of the second half of the century.*

(Herbert Simon, "Foreword," in Gary Dessler,
*Organization and Management:
A Contingency Approach,* 1976, p. xix)

---

**SUMMARY:** This chapter begins with an answer to the question, What is an organization? The focus is then narrowed to large-scale organizations, most commonly characterized as *bureaucracies.* We look at why organizations are structured as they are. We then raise the two-part question, Why is the bureaucratic organization structure rapidly becoming dysfunctional, and what new structures are emerging?

---

For a firsthand awareness of the role organizations play in everyday life, trace your own activity today from the time you awoke. List the products and services you used just in the first hour. Mirrors, toothbrushes, appliances, food, clothing, and transportation are part of many people's daily beginnings. What organizations are connected with the products and services that you've listed?

POT - SHOTS NO. 986.

# LET'S ORGANIZE THIS THING

*Ashleigh Brilliant*

## AND TAKE ALL THE FUN OUT OF IT.

Organizations play a dominant role in our lives. They affect us in many ways, particularly those organizations in which we are members: work, leisure (health clubs, social groups), and religious or spiritual (church, synagogue). It is easy to see that organizations are omnipresent in our lives. To a degree, the antiestablishment movement in the 1960s can be seen as a reaction to the perceived intrusion of large organizations into people's lives. But what are the alternatives? Protests against organizations often evolve into organizations themselves. Even the communes popularized in the 1960s were organizations to the extent that they remained in existence. The very process of living involves daily contact, direct or indirect, with numerous organizations, many of which are large, bureaucratic entities.

## What Is an Organization?

Through the years, many people who have studied organizations have attempted to define them. Let's look at a few of these definitions, starting with that of Max Weber, the "father" of organization theory. Weber's perspective could be summarized this way:

An organization is a system of legitimate interaction patterns among organizational members as they engage in activities in the pursuit of goals.

Weber saw a business organization as a "corporate group"—as a social relationship that either was closed or limited the admission of new members by rules. Its order was enforced by a specific individual, such as a chief or head or some other member of the administrative staff.[1]

Whereas Weber concentrated on the system, Chester Barnard focused on the communication patterns among the people involved in organizations. He saw the organization as "a system of consciously coordinated activities or forces of two or more persons."[2] Here we see the importance of cooperation and agreement in organization; in order for an organization to be effective, everyone in the organization needs to be *goal oriented.*

Drawing from these traditions, Amitai Etzioni states:

Organizations are social units (or human groupings) deliberately constructed and reconstructed to seek specific goals. Corporations, armies, schools, hospitals, churches and prisons are included; tribes, classes, ethnic groups, and families [except work operations such as the family farm or family business] are excluded. Organizations are characterized by:

1. responsibilities for labor, power, and communications which are deliberately planned to enhance the realization of specific goals;
2. the presence of one or more power-centers which control and direct the concerted efforts of the organization. These power centers also continually review the organization's performance and re-pattern its structure, where necessary, to increase efficiency;
3. substitution of personnel, i.e., unsatisfactory persons can be removed and others assigned their tasks. The organization can also reorganize its personnel through transfer and promotion.[3]

Etzioni uses the concepts of *goals* and *interaction patterns,* and he brings in *politics, power,* and *reorganization.*

Richard Scott's definition introduces additional features: the notions of a *boundary, normative order,* and *incentives.*

Organizations are defined as collectives . . . that have been established for the pursuit of relatively specific objectives on a more or less continuous basis. It should be clear . . . however, that organizations have distinctive features other than goal specificity and continuity. These [features] include relatively fixed boundaries, a normative order, authority ranks, a communication system, and an incentive system which enables various types of participants to work together in the pursuit of common goals (of the organization).[4]

Richard Hall takes the process a bit further, with a more refined and succinct definition:

> An organization is a collectivity with a relatively identifiable boundary, a normative order, ranks of authority, communications systems, and member coordinating systems; this collectivity exists on a relatively continuous basis in an environment and engages in activities that are usually related to a goal or a set of goals.[5]

From these and other definitions we can derive a list of traditionally accepted characteristics common to all organizations, large and small, public and private sector, manufacturing and service. These commonalities are as follows:

- goal direction
- relatively identifiable boundary
- social interaction
- deliberately structured activity system
- culture (a broader definition for "member coordinating systems")

*Goal direction.* All organizations, from the multinational corporation to the corner grocery store, exist for a purpose. Each organization and its participants strive toward certain ends (some might be called legitimate, some otherwise). Organizations may have more than one goal, some complementary, others potentially conflicting. It is not essential for all members to endorse the organization's goals fully. However, organizational effectiveness is generally related to the extent to which organization members understand and support the attainment of organizational objectives or goals.

*Relatively identifiable boundary.* All organizations have an invisible demarcation between "us" and "them," between what is and what is not part of the organization. Membership is distinct and is regulated; there are certain "admission requirements." In a university, the admissions office regulates the organizational boundary—at least as far as students are concerned. The process of regulating an organization's boundary is one of the most important factors for the organization's long-term survival.

The organization exchanges resources with the environment, but it must maintain itself as a separate entity within its domain (according to conventional organization theory). People in the organization whose responsibility it is to bridge the gap between the organization and various aspects of its environment are called *boundary role incumbents*. Their

---

### Characteristics Common to All Organizations

- Goal Direction
- Identifiable Boundary
- Social Interaction
- Structured Activity System
- Culture

---

work provides the organization with its ability to adapt quickly to changes in the environment that affect its present and future prospects.

*Social interaction.* Individuals and groups of people constitute organizations. People interact with each other to do various organizational tasks; in fact, one of the main reasons for organizing is to increase the work output from what the same number of individuals could do independently. Although interaction patterns among people in organizations do occur in a manner not related to organizational goals, specific patterns are nevertheless predesigned. To maximize effectiveness, people must be able to communicate clearly, with minimal distortion resulting from differing expectations, assumptions, and so on—easier said than done.

*Deliberately structured activity system.* Organizations use knowledge to perform various work activities. Hence they devise systems for coordinating work flow and dividing up the work to be done. The various subdivisions of work are intended to increase work efficiency. Deliberate structure is created to coordinate and control the units in their goal-oriented work together.

*Culture.* Until fairly recently, this aspect of organizations had been considered, but not uniformly understood. Basically, an organization's culture is the "deeper level of basic assumptions and beliefs that are shared by members of an organization, that operate unconsciously, and define in a basic, 'taken-for-granted' fashion an organization's view of itself and its environment."[6]

A central theme of this book is that *the organization's culture and other shared belief, value, and attitude systems actually create and maintain its structure and its process;* these shared definitions about "how we do things around here" are powerful determinants of interpersonal behav-

© ASHLEIGH BRILLIANT 1981.  POT-SHOTS NO. 2263.

**NOW THAT WE'VE REACHED AGREEMENT,**

**ALL WE NEED IS TO GET EVERYBODY ELSE TO AGREE WITH US.**

*Ashleigh Brilliant*

ior, power relationships, what is important and what is not, and myriad other factors. The importance of culture cannot be underestimated.

## The Organization as Coalition

Another school of thought on the question of what constitutes an organization springs from the political science perspective. According to this approach, "an organization is a collection of coalitions or interest groups, held together by a common purpose, sharing common resources, and attempting to maintain legitimacy from the larger society."[7] In this view, the power and influence of the coalitions vary over time. At any given moment, there is a *dominant* coalition that controls the resources and has a high degree of influence. A number of factors determine a coalition's power: formal authority, control over resources, information (and access thereto), and the reduction of uncertainty—that is, the ability of the coalition to increase predictability and, thus, control.

In this context, it is easy to see that organization structure is clearly influenced by the needs and wishes of the dominant coalition: "The ultimate source of power is the group; and a group, in turn, is made up of people with consciousness and will, with emotion and irrationality, with intense personal interests and tenaciously held values."[8]

---

## The Assumptions
## Behind Large Organizations

---

Most people can tell at least one horror story about bureaucratic red tape. Hospitals keep us waiting; airlines lose our luggage and delay flights; automobile manufacturers produce faulty products; consumer product giants don't answer letters; and the IRS is slow with tax refunds. Employees of bureaucracies and other large organizations complain about the impersonal nature of the workplace, the autocratic managerial style, the hierarchy, the nasty, inefficient people in other departments, and so on. Are large organizations inherently just plain inefficient? Are they even suited for our day and age, or are they behemoths facing extinction?

The people who shaped today's industrial giants made a series of *assumptions* about the role of the corporation and the society in which it operated:

- Most people want the same things out of life. For most of them, economic success is the ultimate goal; therefore, the way to motivate them is through economic reward.
- The bigger the company, the better, stronger, and more profitable it will be.
- Labor, raw materials, and capital, not land, are the primary factors of production.
- The production of standardized goods and services is more efficient than one-by-one handcraft production in which each unit of output differs from the rest.
- The most efficient organization is a bureaucracy in which each suborganization has a permanent, clearly defined role in a hierarchy—in effect, an organizational machine for the production of standardized decisions.
- Technological advances help standardize production and bring "progress."
- Work, for most people, must be routine, repetitive, and standardized.[9]

This set of beliefs, attitudes, and values (and the assumptions and expectations that flowed from them) was appropriate for a society emerging into the industrial age. In the late 1800s, many workers were coming off the farm and from foreign lands, with little or no formal

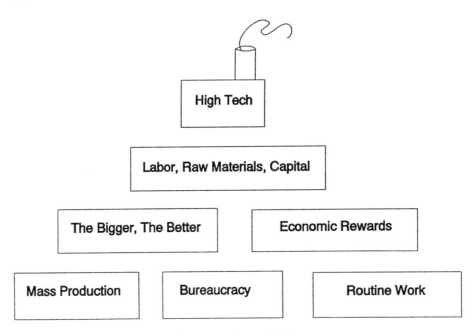

**Figure 1.1.** Building Blocks for the Industrial Giant

education and with limited expectations regarding such values as challenging work, responsibility, recognition, achievement, and advancement. The bureaucratic structure's emphasis on strict role requirements, clear lines of authority and responsibility, and copious rules, regulations, policies, and procedures was well suited to regularizing the behavior of these workers. But as we approach the twenty-first century, it is becoming increasingly obvious that this structure—and the attitudes, beliefs, values, and assumptions that support it—is, in many cases, out of step with contemporary realities.

The world that spawned the social invention of the bureaucracy has changed dramatically in the past three decades. Bureaucracy, perfected during the Industrial Revolution to organize and direct the productive activities of the firm, is "becoming less and less effective, hopelessly out of joint with contemporary reality, and new shapes, patterns, and models . . . are emerging which promise drastic changes in the conduct of the corporation and in managerial practices in general."[10]

Yet bureaucracy seems to hang on, surviving in spite of its obvious problems. Why? Also, what of these "new shapes and models"? Where are they? In the next few chapters, we will see how our paradigm is shifting, and how organizations are evolving, apparently in response to their changing external environment.

## DISCUSSION QUESTIONS

1. What are the organizations you directly interacted with today? What are the organizations you indirectly interacted with today? How is your life affected by these organizations? How would your life change if these organizations did not exist?
2. Name a boundary role incumbent in an organization of which you are a part. What is the value/function of this person?
3. What evidence do you see that our basic beliefs are under challenge?
4. Consider an organization of which you are a part. From looking at the structure of this organization, what can you say about the basic beliefs, attitudes, and values that create that structure?
5. Why is "how we do things around here" an important consideration? What role has this consideration played in your own experience of organizations?
6. What, if any, are the contexts in which there is no organization?
7. What are the conditions in which organizations have little or no impact?

## NOTES

1. Cited in Richard H. Hall, *Organizations: Structure and Process* (2nd ed.) (Englewood Cliffs, NJ: Prentice Hall, 1977), 18.

2. Chester I. Barnard, *The Functions of the Executive* (Cambridge, MA: Harvard University Press, 1938), 73.

3. Amitai Etzioni, *Modern Organizations* (Englewood Cliffs, NJ: Prentice Hall, 1964), 3.

4. W. Richard Scott, "Theory of Organizations," in *Handbook of Modern Sociology*, ed. Robert E. L. Faris (Chicago: Rand McNally, 1964), 488.

5. Richard H. Hall, *Organizations: Structure and Process* (Englewood Cliffs, NJ: Prentice Hall, 1972), 22-23.

6. Edgar H. Schein, *Organizational Culture and Leadership: A Dynamic View* (San Francisco: Jossey-Bass, 1985), 6. Used with permission from the publisher.

7. Jeffrey Pfeffer, *Organizational Design* (Arlington Heights, IL: AHM, 1978), 5; see also Richard M. Cyert and James G. March, *A Behavioral Theory of the Firm* (Englewood Cliffs, NJ: Prentice Hall, 1963).

8. Norman H. Martin and John Howard Sims, "Power Tactics," in *Harvard Business Review on Human Relations* (New York: Harper & Row, 1979), 177.

9. Alvin Toffler, *The Adaptive Organization* (New York: Bantam, 1985), 12.

10. Ibid., 3.

# 2    Of Paradigms and Paradigm Shifts

> *One of the things that a scientific community acquires with a paradigm is a criterion for choosing problems that, while the paradigm is taken for granted, can be assumed to have solutions. To a great extent, these are the only problems that the community will admit as scientific or encourage its members to undertake. Other problems, including many that had previously been standard, are rejected as metaphysical, as the concern of another discipline, or sometimes just too problematic to be worth the time. A paradigm can, for that matter, even insulate the community from those socially important problems that are not reducible to the [paradigm parameters], because they cannot be stated in terms of the conceptual and instrumental tools the paradigm provides.*
>
> (Thomas S. Kuhn, *The Structure of Scientific Revolutions*, 1970, p. 37)

**SUMMARY:** This chapter introduces the concept of paradigm, a central theme of the book. Paradigms are fixed mental sets or metaphors that purport to describe what is possible (and what isn't) with regard to a certain person, object, situation, or phenomenon. We look at how paradigms are formed and changed (paradigm shifts), and we explore the implications of all this for organizations and organizational transformation.

History demonstrates that at certain points in time, massive shifts in how people see things have occurred. One such time was when Columbus undertook his voyage based on the outrageous idea that the world was not flat, but round. Eventually, that recognition created

SOMEDAY THERE'LL BE
BOOKS EXPLAINING
WHAT'S HAPPENING NOW,

BUT BY THEN,
I MAY HAVE LOST INTEREST.

© BRILLIANT ENTERPRISES 1977.

massive changes in how people viewed reality—the scientific reality in particular. Another event was the radical view promoted by Copernicus that the earth revolves around the sun, and not the other way around. The launch of *Sputnik* in the 1950s prompted another change in beliefs, attitudes, and values that in turn altered the way people saw themselves in relation to the universe.

The set of beliefs, attitudes, expectations, assumptions, and values that determines how people construct their own personal reality is called a *paradigm*.[1] A dramatic shift in the way a collection of people constructs its personal realities is called a *paradigm shift*.

In his seminal book *The Structure of Scientific Revolutions*, Thomas Kuhn of the University of Chicago argues that every theory of science, every conception of "how things are and how they work," eventually undergoes a revolution in which the old mind-set, the old way of explaining reality—in other words, the old paradigm—is seen as increasingly dysfunctional. When the discomfort caused by holding on to the obsolete paradigm or worldview grows too great, a paradigm shift occurs. The old way of looking at things is discarded and a new "truth" is embraced.[2] This is not a smooth process. People with allegiance to the old paradigm become defensive, and conflict ensues, but eventually a new way of looking at reality gains more or less widespread acceptance.

Today, we are between paradigms. In a sense, we are "between stories," as Thomas Berry says:

> We are in trouble just now because we don't have a good story. We are in between stories. The Old Story (the account of how the world came to be and how we fit into it) is not functioning properly, and we have not learned the new story. The Old Story sustained us for a long period of time. It shaped our emotional attitudes, provided us with life purpose, energized action. It consecrated suffering, integrated knowledge, guided education.
>
> We awoke in the morning and knew where we were. We could answer the questions of our children. We could identify crime, punish criminals. Everything was taken care of because the story was there. It did not make men good, it did not take away the pain and stupidities of life, or make for unfailing warmth in human association. But it did provide for a context in which life could function in a meaningful manner.[3]

John Naisbitt, in his 1982 best-seller *Megatrends,* calls ours the "age of parentheses."[4] We are undergoing a basic and fundamental shift in the way we construct our personal reality because the old ways of constructing it *just don't work very well any more.*

## How We Construct Our Personal Reality

A collective paradigm includes shared beliefs about the nature of reality held by a specific group or nation at a point in time. According to Kuhn, what is called "normal science" is carried out under the direction of the dominant scientific paradigm, which virtually everyone accepts as reflecting the absolute truth. The basic paradigmatic assumptions are unchallenged. These subconscious "reference points" or benchmarks shape all decisions, color all perceptions, and create all the options and possibilities.

In short, the paradigm determines what one sees and, perhaps more important, what one *does not* see. Essentially, a paradigm is the basis of the way of doing, seeing, valuing, and perceiving in a given culture associated with a particular vision of reality.[5] An old paradigm is not "bad" and a new one "good"; rather, an old one often just doesn't work as well as a new one in explaining (and functioning in) the emergent reality of changing times.

The key to understanding this concept is to focus on the last part of the above definition: "associated with a particular vision of reality." We now know that we do not passively perceive a reality "out there" waiting for us to perceive it; rather, we create our own reality, using a dominant paradigm to assign meaning to what it is we think we perceive.[6] We actively, with our consciousness, create the world we perceive.

In other words, there is no meaning in the world independent of the meaning we attach to it, and the mechanism that determines the meaning we give to objects, persons, and situations is our paradigm, or model of reality. It is a collective paradigm, or shared set of beliefs and assumptions, that allows us to communicate.[7]

---

EXPERIENTIAL EXERCISE 1. Try the following experiment: On a piece of paper, write the Roman numeral for the number 9, IX. Using one un-broken line of any shape, and without erasing or changing any of the IX, *change the number 9 into the number 6*. We will provide the solution a little later.

---

A paradigm, then, is an internal mental/emotional structure of "thought forms" used to construct reality. This structure includes *beliefs* ("What I assume is real," or what we call facts), *attitudes* (judgments that proclaim "I like this and I don't like that"; statements of preferences), and *values* (judgments that proclaim "This is good and that is bad"), plus the assumptions and expectations that flow from these. Our beliefs, attitudes, and values give meaning to our world and color our percep-tions so that we can make decisions from the perspective of our personal goals and aspirations.

Research indicates that the substance of our paradigm is created from three sources:

- *Heredity:* There is some evidence that we inherit certain patterns of thoughts and feelings from our parents.
- *Social learning:* We learn, from our interactions with others, what is acceptable and what is not acceptable behavior.
- *Race memory or imprinting:* Some scientists believe that we have, embed-ded in our very DNA, memories of the history of our race on the planet.[8]

---

## How We Reinforce Our Worldview

---

Perception is not a passive process. Not only do we interpret what we see, hear, taste, smell, and touch in light of our paradigm, but the para-digm, through the power of the mind, actually creates *self-fulfilling prophecies,* such that the perceiver receives what he or she expects to receive. Self-fulfilling prophecies are thought to be created in at least two mutually reinforcing ways. First, because of what Napoleon Hill has called the "magnetic quality" of our thought forms, we tend to attract to ourselves circumstances and situations that confirm our beliefs (the mind always wants to be *right* or correct).[9] This "law of attraction" states that individuals inevitably draw to themselves people and circumstances that harmonize with their own dominant thoughts and beliefs.[10]

A second hypothesis is that our perceptual apparatus tends to allow us to "see" only what fits the parameters of the paradigm, and prevents us from seeing what does not. Psychologists call this *selective perception.* For example, a person who has just been hired may be seen as highly competent by the one who did the hiring, who sees characteristics of the hiree that will confirm the hirer's beliefs about his or her own selection skills, interview techniques, and so forth. Others who do not have such ego involvement in the hiring may see the new employee in a different light.

In other words, through a process that is only partially understood, we apparently attract to us those circumstances and situations that we either *fear* or *expect* to have happen.[11] "That which you fear will come upon you," it says somewhere in the Bible. Also, the mind, as it constructs its personal reality, perceptually distorts, or selectively removes, those aspects of the total reality that might be perceived as not in favor of agreement with the assumptions of the dominant paradigm. We see what we want or expect to see, and data that might conflict with that model of reality are selectively screened out.

Many studies in cognitive psychology have illustrated this phenomenon. An example is an experiment reported by Rosenthal and Jacobson, which involved a teacher and a classroom populated by equally gifted children. All the students had been tested on a standardized IQ instrument, and all scored the same, plus or minus two points. The teacher was then told that little Johnny and Sarah were genius-level students, and that Harry and Bernard were well below average; she was asked to keep this in mind during the semester. At the end of the semester, Johnny and Sarah were performing at a level far above the mean of their classmates, and Bernard and Harry were at a level far below that mean. What happened? Clearly, the teacher, through her expectations about all four children, communicated verbally and nonverbally that Johnny and Sarah were very bright, and they behaved to meet that expectation. The same held true with the other pair.[12]

Besides self-fulfilling prophecies and selective perception, there is a third way in which we reinforce our personal paradigms: the *self-limiting belief.*

Most people have some judgments or beliefs about who they are or what they can do or what they can become. These beliefs form a limiting self-image, a jug! The beliefs may be transparent and hard to see, or they may be as solid as a rock and insisted upon, or they may be as incomprehensible as infinite space; no matter, they limit the potential of the person.[13]

When we give ourselves permission to do something, we can overcome these self-limiting beliefs. For example, prior to Roger Bannister's 1954 record-breaking one-mile run of 3:59:4, the 4-minute "barrier," as it was then called, seemed insurmountable. Now, high school track stars run the mile in less than 4 minutes. Similarly, until a few years ago, weight lifters thought it impossible to clean and jerk 500 pounds. Then, in a preliminary heat at an event in Ontario a few years ago, the world record holder was told he was lifting 493 pounds when in fact the weight he was about to lift was 501 pounds. After he successfully lifted it, he was told the truth. Now, he can lift 500 pounds.

Let's return to Experiential Exercise 1, above. The solution is to add the letter *S* before the IX, to create the *word* SIX. Of course, the typical assumption is that one is being asked to change the Roman numeral 9 (IX) into the Roman numeral 6 (VI). Obviously, this cannot be done with one unbroken line. This exercise provides a metaphor for the dilemma of today's manager. He or she is trying to solve problems with a view of reality that limits the possibilities for solution. As the old saying goes, You can't get there from here. However, shifting one's perception of what is possible makes the answer easy. By expanding one's perception, one automatically sees possibilities that weren't contained in the former definition of reality (the former paradigmatic assumptions).

If you groaned when you saw the solution to this exercise, you're starting to understand the nature of a paradigm shift. The message is this: If you can't solve a problem with your existing assumptions, change your assumptions and the solution can come easily. Stay rigid in your worldview, and the answer will escape you. We are often trapped in our paradigmatic "boundaries."

## Language Supports Paradigms, Too

Paradigms literally determine what we perceive and what we do not; they provide the parameters of what it is possible to experience. That the framework of an individual's beliefs, attitudes, and values determines what he or she perceives is shown in the study of language.

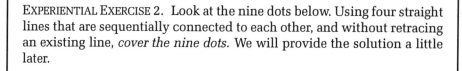

EXPERIENTIAL EXERCISE 2.  Look at the nine dots below. Using four straight lines that are sequentially connected to each other, and without retracing an existing line, *cover the nine dots.* We will provide the solution a little later.

Language provides an excellent representation of an individual's personal paradigm. As Ludwig Wittgenstein, one of this century's most influential philosophers, noted, "The limits of my language mean the limits of my world."[14]

There is an implication in this that, until a person has a name for something, that thing does not exist for that person. For example, research has shown that if someone sees a color for which he or she has no name, the individual's mind stores the color for a mere few moments and can identify it again only if it is seen again almost immediately. On the other hand, a person can identify colors for which he or she has names even after long periods of not seeing the color. The conclusion to be drawn from this is that people store colors in their minds not as colors, but as verbal labels for colors. "The colors that a speaker 'sees' depend very much upon the language he speaks," notes Peter Farb. "The human being's ability to encode experience in this way is not limited to color." Memory is strongly influenced by language.[15]

## A Paradigm Is Unexamined

A paradigm expresses a self-consistent worldview, a social construction of reality.[16] This view is widely shared and taken for granted by the members of a society, most of whom are unaware of the implicit underlying logic in what they think, feel, and decide to do. An analogy can be made here: Fish are apparently unaware of the water in which they swim. So it is with us and our paradigmatic assumptions.

We bring our largely unexamined beliefs, assumptions, and expectations with us when we construct our personal realities.[17] Without really understanding why, we just feel that this is "the way things are." We have a distinct mind-set, with certain assumptions and beliefs about the nature of reality that tend to create self-fulfilling prophecies and self-limiting beliefs that inhibit the possibilities of organization, among other things.

We filter all our experience through these contexts or paradigms. Context has no meaning in and of itself, yet it provides, in Paul Tillich's phrase, the "ground of being" from which observable content derives.

## How Paradigms Shift

A paradigm tends to become explicit only when the need for a new perspective arises through increasing dysfunction in the prevailing paradigm. When this happens, individuals sometimes distance themselves from the old paradigm and begin to search for an alternative *modus vivendi.*[18] This distancing is part of the pressure to change. If a paradigm is the glue that binds a society together and differentiates it from the external environment and other societies, then paradigm shifts are traumatic, uprooting events.

In the status quo nature of the paradigm, there is an inherent defense mechanism to protect against the trauma of change. What can penetrate that defense? One theory holds that change comes through the acquisition of information that indicates that the current approach is not working.[19]

All new information tends to be incorporated into the viewpoint of the paradigm and tends to be distorted to fit the existing assumptions and expectations. This is also true when the early signs begin to emerge that a paradigm is not working. However, when sufficient anomalies or "exceptions to the truth" build up, cynicism and depression arise around the old myths and the old paradigm.

When even those people thoroughly invested in the old paradigm can no longer deny its inapplicability, the stage is set. All that is needed then is for someone to articulate a new paradigm, a new vision, a new metaphor, and zip!—the shift occurs.

Of course, in reality it is not so easy. While the "early adopters" start lauding the new paradigm, many others still cling tenaciously, partly out of fear and partly out of determination, to the old definitions. But history tells us that, sooner or later, all paradigms do shift because they are only *partial* definitions of a complex dynamic reality and, as such, will always be superseded by what is seen as an updated version.

## North American Paradigm Shifts

Thomas Kuhn argues that a paradigm or worldview begins to break down when it simply does not work anymore to describe or operate in current reality. The period of the shift is marked by upset and discomfort, as we move from the known, which doesn't work anymore, to the unknown, which is still emerging.

A paradigm shift is a move away from the certainty of right answers to the process of transformation and a world of the unknown.[20] Naisbitt calls this "the age of parentheses"; theologians have called it "the leap into the void." Inevitably, it is a period of conflict. Table 2.1 presents a summary of the salient features of each of the three major paradigm shifts that have taken place in Western culture.

It could be said that the current paradigm shift began in the early 1960s, marked by such events as John F. Kennedy's death, the Beatles' arrival in the United States, and the early stirrings of the "counterculture."[21] This period is easily remembered as the most violent of recent times in the United States. Alvin Toffler, in his excellent book *The Third Wave*, describes the current shift in great detail.[22]

Let's return for a moment to Experiential Exercise 2. Here, as promised, is the solution:

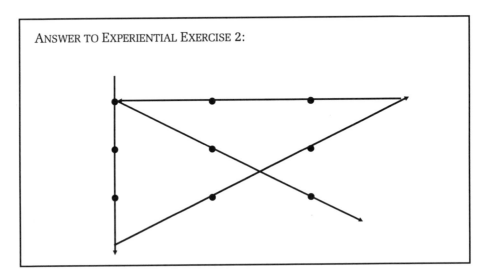

ANSWER TO EXPERIENTIAL EXERCISE 2:

If you weren't able to solve the problem, it is probably because you were *making the assumption* that you had to stay within the boundaries of the nine dots. Notice that our instructions do not say that. If your mind convinced you that you needed to, you have experienced the formation

**Table 2.1**   The Three North American Paradigm Shifts

---

Agricultural Revolution (1776-1890)
  importance of traditional religion
  family farms
  traditional values of ethics, cooperation/teamwork
  sparse population patterns
  limited education/sophistication of populace
  prominence of self-sufficiency and individualism
  survival orientation/distinctions between men's and women's roles
  folk medicine

Industrial Revolution (1890-1963)
  beginning decline of formal religion
  move to the cities (urbanization)
  harsh working conditions
  emphasis on mass production/materialism
  scientific method/"scientific management" (Frederick Taylor)
  authority/hierarchy in organization/growth of bureaucracy
  "modern" medicine (the machine model)
  still relatively great distinctions between men's and women's roles

Post-Industrial Revolution (1963-??)
  belief in spiritual values (often not affiliated with formal religion)
  importance of job satisfaction/growth of "self-actualization"
  concern for equitable distribution of power/justice
  redefinition of social responsibility of business
  growth of "technological assessment"
  rise in ecological consciousness
  beginnings of sapiential authority supplanting formal authority
  exploration of identities and roles of men and women
  alternative medicine (the holistic movement)

---

of what is called an *unchallenged assumption* or *self-limiting belief.* How many of those do you make in a day?

## Where Are We Now?

We have now fully entered a time in which the incompleteness of the mechanistic, industrial era paradigm is evident. This worldview, inaugurated by Descartes, sees life operating according to predictable, mechanical principles. The whole is seen as composed of various parts, which can be manipulated at will to suit the needs of individuals and groups.

As we will see in Chapter 4, Einstein ushered in the era of particle/quantum physics, which emphasizes our innate interconnectedness to all life. This emerging paradigm is teaching us to see the effects of individual (or corporate) self-centeredness. We are learning that acting out of self-interest inevitably produces ill effects in this intertwined whole we call Earth.

It is not just that we spew pollution into the air and water; our mechanical fixation has caused us, as Thomas Berry has suggested, to lose our love for (and enchantment with) nature itself. Losing our connection with the natural rhythms of the earth, we blindly butcher our planet in the name of industrial progress.

The paradigm shift is bringing us back into a full appreciation of our role as "cocreators," with life itself, of our earthly home. Rabbi Marc Gellman has an amusing but poignant view of this, in a *midrash* he tells about the story of creation:

> God made a man and a woman from some of the water and dust and said to them, "I am tired now. Please finish up the world for me . . . really it's almost done." But the man and woman said, "We can't finish the world alone! You have the plans and we are too little."
>
> "You are big enough," God answered them. "But I agree to this. If you keep trying to finish the world, I will be your partner."
>
> The man and the woman asked, "What's a partner?" and God answered, "A partner is someone you work with on a big thing that neither of you can do alone. If you have a partner, it means that you can never give up, because your partner is depending on you. On the days you think I am not doing enough and on the days I think you are not doing enough, even on those days we are still partners and we must not stop trying to finish the world. That's the deal." And they agreed to that deal.
>
> Then the angels asked God, "Is the world finished yet?" and God answered, "I don't know. Go ask my partners."[23]

## DISCUSSION QUESTIONS

1. What does your behavior, the way you talk, act, and do things, say about your own paradigm?

2. How does your paradigm differ, if at all, from those of your parents, teachers, friends? How is your paradigm like theirs?

3. Can you give an example of and discuss a paradigm shift that you have either experienced or noticed?

## NOTES

1. For the seminal use of this term, see Thomas S. Kuhn, *The Structure of Scientific Revolutions* (2nd ed.) (Chicago: University of Chicago Press, 1970).

2. Thomas S. Kuhn, *The Structure of Scientific Revolutions* (Chicago: University of Chicago Press, 1962); see also William E. Schneider, "The Paradigm Shift in Human Resources," *Personnel Journal* (November 1985): 14-18.

3. Thomas Berry, "Comments on the Origin, Identification and Transmission of Values," *Anima* (Winter 1978); quoted in Peter Schwartz and James Ogilvy, *The Emergent Paradigm: Changing Patterns of Thought and Belief* (report issued by the Values and Lifestyles Program, April 1979), v.

4. John Naisbitt, *Megatrends* (New York: Random House, 1982).

5. Schwartz and Ogilvy, *The Emergent Paradigm*, 31.

6. For example, see Milton Rokeach, *The Open and Closed Mind* (New York: Basic Books, 1960).

7. See any of Carlos Castañeda's books, for example, *A Separate Reality* (New York: Bantam, 1972).

8. See, for example, Richard Heinberg, *Memories and Visions of Paradise* (Los Angeles: Jeremy Tarcher, 1989); Riane Einsler, *The Chalice and the Blade* (San Francisco: Harper & Row, 1987).

9. See Napoleon Hill, *Think and Grow Rich* (New York: Fawcett, 1960), especially chaps. 1, 13.

10. For example, Brian Tracy, in "Pathways Toward Personal Progress," in *The Psychology of Achievement*, audiocassette package (Chicago: Nightingale-Conant, n.d.), calls this the law of attracting: "This law states that you are a 'living magnet' and that you inevitably attract to yourself the people and circumstances that harmonize with your dominant thoughts" (p. 3).

11. G. Michael Durst, *Management by Responsibility* (Evanston, IL: Center for the Art of Living, 1982), 37.

12. R. Rosenthal and L. Jacobson, *Pygmalion in the Classroom* (New York: Holt, Rinehart & Winston, 1968).

13. Henry Palmer, "The Unlimited Self," *Avatar Journal* 6 (Spring 1992): 5.

14. Quoted in Peter Farb, *Word Play: What Happens When People Talk* (New York: Bantam, 1973), 192. See also any of the major works of Professors George Doctors of the University of California, Berkeley, and Edward Hall of Northwestern University on *language as metaphor.*

15. Ibid., 199.

16. Peter L. Berger and Thomas Luckmann, *The Social Construction of Reality: A Treatise in the Sociology of Knowledge* (Garden City, NY: Doubleday, 1966); Karl Weick, *The Social Psychology of Organizing* (Reading, MA: Addison-Wesley, 1969). See also Ian G. Barbour, *Myths, Models, and Paradigms* (New York: Harper & Row, 1974).

17. Norman Bodek, "Werner Erhard on Transformation and Productivity: An Interview," *Revision* 7 (Winter/Spring 1985).

18. Eric L. Trist, *The Evolution of Sociotechnical Systems* (occasional paper no. 2). (Toronto: Ontario Quality of Work Life Centre, 1981).

19. J. Rounds, "Information and Ambiguity in Organizational Change" (paper presented at the Carnegie Mellon Symposium on Information Processing in Organizations, Carnegie Mellon University, Pittsburgh, PA, 1981).

20. Charles Hampden-Turner, "Is There a New Paradigm? A Tale of Two Concepts" (paper presented at a meeting of Shell International Managers, New York, January 1985).

21. Theodore Reich, *The Making of a Counterculture* (New York: Bantam, 1968).

22. Alvin Toffler, *The Third Wave* (New York: Simon & Schuster, 1982).

23. Marc Gellman and Oscar de Mejo, *Does God Have a Big Toe? Stories About Stories in the Bible* (New York: Harper & Row, 1989), 3.

# 3   The Industrial Era Paradigm

*Professionalism in management is regularly equated with
hard-headed rationality. We saw it surface at ITT with Harold
Geneen's search for the "unshakable facts." It flourished in Vietnam, where success was measured by body counts. Its wizards
were the Ford Motor Company's whiz kids, and its grand pan-
jandrum was Robert MacNamara. The numerative, rationalist
approach to management dominates the business schools. It
teaches us that well-trained professional managers can manage
anything. It seeks detached, analytical justification for all
decisions. It is right enough to be dangerously wrong, and it
has arguably led us astray.*

(Thomas J. Peters and Robert H. Waterman, Jr.,
*In Search of Excellence*, 1982, p. 29)

---

**SUMMARY:** In this chapter we examine the core beliefs, attitudes, and values that have shaped our organizations and, indeed, our ways of interacting with our world. We look at the implications of these beliefs, attitudes, and values for organization structure and process.

---

Although we are moving away from it, the industrial era paradigm has left an indelible mark on our culture and its dominant institution, the organization. Peters and Waterman identify a set of shared beliefs that came from the "rational model," or the industrial era paradigm:

1. Big is better because you always get economies of scale.
2. Low-cost producers are the only surefire winners.

3. Analyze everything.
4. Get rid of the disturbers of the peace, that is, fanatical champions (after all, we've got a plan!).
5. The manager's job is decision making. Make the right calls.
6. Control everything.
7. Get the incentives right and productivity will follow.
8. Inspect to control quality. Quality is like everything else; order it done!
9. If you can read the financial statements, you can manage anything.
10. Top executives are smarter than the market.
11. It's all over if we stop growing.[1]

A quick glance at this list reveals a number of beliefs that have dominated the industrial era, such as the following:

- "These people" need to be led/controlled.
- "They" won't take personal responsibility for their actions.
- Growth is good.
- Numbers are the key (anything worthwhile must be measured and monitored).

An example from a recent national business magazine serves to illustrate how the dominant paradigm operates. The article begins with this quote from John Brodie, president of the United Paperworkers Local 448, in Chester, Pennsylvania:

> What the company wants is for us to work like the Japanese. Everybody go out and do jumping jacks in the morning and kiss each other when they go home at night. You work as a team, rat on each other, and lose control of your destiny. That's not going to work in this country.[2]

What are the assumptions embedded in what this man is saying? First of all, he is asserting that the American *value* of individuality will not allow subversion of individual needs to group needs. He is saying that workers are united against the common "enemy," management, and therefore will not "rat" on their peers, even if their peers deserve it. He is saying that each individual has the right to his or her own destiny, independent of the group destiny (a belief). He is saying that each worker is autonomous and may or may not be liked by others in the group, and that is okay (a value). The article continues:

> Call it employee involvement (EI) or worker participation or labor-man-agement "jointness" as it is now known in the auto industry. Whatever the

term, it is clearly troubling for many Americans. At one and the same time, it promises workers autonomy over their jobs, but it also threatens their old ways of working. It gives management a powerful tool to improve productivity and quality, but could undermine their control. EI may be American industry's best hope of competing with the Japanese and Europeans, as well as low wage Third World producers. Yet, for years, timid U.S. companies have merely sloshed a thin coating of EI across an aging industrial base.

Why? Because EI goes against the core tenets of the industrial paradigm, such as that labor and management are enemies, that management makes decisions and labor does the work. But the paradigm is shifting:

> But, now, there are signs that real employee involvement is sinking into the core of Corporate America. While angry union officers such as [Brodie] still rail against participation, more and more workers and labor leaders are willing to risk EI in hopes of making their employers more competitive . . . and their jobs more secure.

There we have it. Some militant union leaders still see teamwork as a management strategy to get more work out of workers without paying them more (the age-old "speedup"), but the threat of *no* jobs causes the pressure to change. Even venerable General Motors, a classic top-down bureaucracy, has been affected. A recent article in the *Wall Street Journal* was headlined: "People power. GM woos employees by listening to them, talking of its 'team.' But skepticism about policy and turf wars still hurt this long-authoritarian firm."[3]

---

## The Major Beliefs of the Industrial Era

---

There are at least six interrelated belief systems common to people who have been socialized with the so-called industrial era paradigm:

1. adherence to the Protestant ethic
2. obedience to authority
3. attitude of separateness/self-centeredness
4. prevalence of self-centered judgment (a corollary of item 3)
5. attachment to quantifiable results
6. addiction to externals

These characteristics have implications for organization theory in a variety of areas that will be explored in greater depth later in this book.

### Adherence to the Protestant Ethic

The Protestant ethic, or a strong work ethic, is a relatively new belief structure. In ancient Greece, for example, menial work was considered onerous and left to slaves and women. In the Western world, a strong belief in the value of work essentially came from certain religious beliefs and began with the Reformation and Martin Luther.

As the industrial age emerged, the emphasis of the work ethic shifted from strictly religious (in which the path to salvation was seen as being through honest toil) to a question of self-esteem (in which the only socially legitimate route to self-esteem was seen to be through work)— hence the origin of the question popularly asked of new acquaintances, What do you do? The growth of the work ethic conveniently dovetailed with the need for many factory laborers, and the Industrial Revolution proceeded apace.

The extreme version of the Protestant ethic—that is, its dysfunctional form—is commonly called *workaholism.* In their excellent book *The Addictive Organization* (1988), Schaef and Fassel use the Alcoholics Anonymous scheme to view addictive behavior in organizations. Apparently, many "workaholics" are in fact adult children of alcoholics (ACOA). Schaef and Fassel note:

> The addiction of choice for many ACOA's is overwork. Some do it to make up for feelings of insecurity or inferiority, thereby constantly going the extra mile. Others are unable to say no to the demands of co-workers and bosses. Goldberg hypothesizes that many ACOA's are workaholics because they prefer to stick with what they know best, and ACOA's are better at work than they are at personal relationships, which they find difficult and anxiety-producing. ACOA's may well be the most dedicated workers in the company. They are rarely laggards. Most organizations love their dedication and productivity. However, while they are excelling at work, they tend to be dying emotionally.[4]

The notion that work is necessary and intimately connected to self-esteem is strong in our paradigm—so strong that losing one's work can be traumatic, as the many stories about jobless middle-aged executives attest.[5] But the Protestant ethic is in danger. Simply stated, advancing technology (e.g., computerization, robotics, automation, and cybernetics) places menial, semiskilled, and many paper-pushing middle-management jobs in jeopardy. New technologies will eliminate many more jobs than they will create, although some think that recreational/service areas and new industries—such as waste site cleanup, recycling, and safe waste disposal—will explode with growth and create new jobs to offset those lost (we are not convinced).

The wholesale elimination of these jobs has been slowed only by the existing dominant paradigm; unions have fought automation vigorously as hopes for full employment still prevail. The problem of unemployment is compounded by the fact that those displaced by mechanization—the poor, uneducated, and unskilled—are the least prepared to handle it.

**Vignette 1**

While teaching at a Canadian business school in the early 1970s, the first author had a student who worked at the local post office. One day, during a class discussion, she described her job. Basically, it consisted of sorting letter-size envelopes and larger envelopes into two separate baskets. She stated that she was "bored stiff" with the job, but was reluctant to give it up because she made (in 1973 dollars) $17,000 per year.

Here is a clear example of a job that could easily be automated. When the local union steward was asked about that, he admitted it was a routine job, but the union was fighting for its retention. The fact that the job had no challenge, no opportunity for intellectual stimulation, and no redeeming qualities (other than salary) was not considered a problem. It should be noted that this occurred in the Province of New Brunswick, Canada, which at that time had an official unemployment rate of 15% (the true rate was much higher).[6]

*Implications for Organizations*

How will the Protestant ethic weather the elimination of jobs? Implications of the erosion of the work ethic for organizations—their structures and processes—have not been fully realized. As automation and computerization continue to make inroads into the number and types of jobs available, two things might be required:

1. the development of a new ethic with a broader definition of what constitutes useful, contributive work
2. the development of a leisure ethic, so that we can see creative leisure as a viable alternative to work for self-actualization[7]

POT-SHOTS NO. 1047.

THE GREAT
WORK
MUST GO
FORWARD

Ashleigh
Brilliant

AS SOON AS
WE ALL
FIND
SOMEBODY ELSE
TO DO IT.

© BRILLIANT ENTERPRISES 1977.

There may even be, in our future, the need to *pay* for the right to work. This seemingly heretical idea was presented by Edward De Bono in his 1970 book *The Use of Lateral Thinking*.[8] Actually, since automation and computerization will eliminate what noted liberal economist John Kenneth Galbraith calls the "meanest jobs" first, most of the jobs that will likely be left in 20 years will be professional, craft, managerial, and artistic ones (with intrinsic opportunities for creativity). Of course, if our values don't shift, we may keep jobs that could be done by machines, simply because we can't cope with unemployment (an industrial era concept).

This has implications for the paragon of the industrial era: the bureaucracy. If the majority of the jobs left are complex, challenging, creative, and interesting, then forms of control such as tight job descriptions, hierarchy, rules, regulations, policies, and procedures (RRPP) will be unnecessary. Professionals have a notorious dislike for red tape (formalization).[9] These major components of the bureaucratic form (produced by the old paradigm) will be obsolete, and the pressure for a new paradigm will increase.

## Obedience to Authority

The belief in obedience to authority has been dominant in the industrial era paradigm. Obviously, ours is not the only culture that has inculcated this attitude; Japan, South Korea, Russia, China, and many others have had it for years. This "biocomputer programming" begins at a very early age; first, a child learns to obey his or her parents, then the baby-sitter, then relatives, teachers, clergy, bosses, military superiors, and so on. In fact, the typical Western socialization process could be viewed as a series of conditioning experiences designed to enhance obedience to authority.

In his classic work *Obedience to Authority,* Stanley Milgram documents his experiments concerning this learned response, in which he discovered that many people would be willing to harm other humans if told to do so by perceived legitimate authority figures.[10] We will discuss Milgram's experiments in some detail in Chapter 15; suffice it to say here that his results show that people will do almost anything legitimate authority figures tell them to do. French and Raven, in their classic work on the bases of power, have shown that persons with a strong base in reward, coercive, legitimate, expert, and/or referent power can demand and receive obedience.[11]

### Implications for Organizations

The organizational implications of the belief in obedience to authority are profound. Obedience to authority, especially formal authority, is part of the glue that holds bureaucratic organizations together; the work of the organization gets done through authority, responsibility, and accountability relationships. But it is common knowledge that obedience as described above has changed drastically over the past generation or two.

A major change in the phenomenon of obedience in organizations is the appearance of "knowledge workers," workers who know more than their bosses. Does this subvert the legitimate power base of the authority holder? Some studies indicate that it does. *Sapiential authority,* a term coined by Robert Theobald in his book *An Alternative Future for America II,* refers to authority based in what one knows (your expertise) rather than in one's formal position. It is sapiential authority that will be the glue in organizations of the future.[12]

### Attitude of Separateness/Self-Centeredness

A third broad orientation in the industrial era paradigm (and, for that matter, all other paradigms to this date) is the experience of separateness or self-centeredness. Much of what human beings say, think, and feel is based on the core assumption or belief that each person is essentially alone in a seemingly hostile universe. (This thought is developed in great detail by Joseph Chilton Pearce in his classic *Exploring the Crack in the Cosmic Egg.*)[13]

This assumption leads to a perceived need to manipulate the apparently hostile environment so that it is more pleasing (or less threatening) to the individual. Students of history will recognize this as the classic Greek notion of *hedonism.* Students of individual psychology learn that all external stimuli are seen by the self-centered observer as either threats to or potential enhancements of the self.

Individually and collectively, this manipulation is done as a matter of course. For example, in 1977 it was reported that one or more industries took advantage of a major fuel spill in Pennsylvania to dump cancer-causing industrial solvents into the Ohio River. In solving their own waste problems (enhancement of self in an organizational sense), they involved a much wider body of people, namely, the residents of six states whose drinking water was affected. This is self-centered collective behavior.

Many people have lamented the excesses of self-centered behavior. Robert Bellah and his colleagues ask the question, "Is overindulgence in individualism leading us astray?" They make the following observation:

> In many ways, individualism is a positive feature of the American character and culture. But it also has destructive potential. In the past, its dark side was constrained by society's institutions, like the small town where people knew and helped each other. But, because of the enormous social changes that have taken place in the last 100 years, there are now *fewer constraints on individualism.* In a sense, it has been allowed to run rampant.[14]

However, since the mythical event recorded as "the fall of man," allegedly from a state of oneness with the source of life (the Creator) to the state of separateness and alienation common to us now, people have operated in a self-centered manner.

To control the dysfunctional results of such behavior, society created "artificial integrators," mechanisms such as internal constraints or values (e.g., "You do not hurt others," "Do unto others . . . ") and external constraints such as regulations, laws, courts, and prisons. These mechanisms depend on obedience to authority for their effectiveness; in the days of "Do your own thing," such social constraints weaken and the full impact of self-centeredness becomes apparent. Perhaps it is not that people are more self-centered now than they were 100, 500, even 1,500 years ago, but that, because there are more people (upward of 5 billion) operating independently and the artificial integrators don't work as well as they used to, the impact is more devastating.

*Implications for Organizations*

What are the results of the separateness assumption for organizations? Individually, people organize things to suit themselves. Collectively, the organization does the same to serve itself—often at the expense of other individuals or organizations. The results are often disintegrative.

Take the example of environmental pollution. Since the dawn of the industrial age, the nation's organizations have been polluting the environment; dumping industrial solvents into the Ohio River is but one of many instances that are only now being recognized. What to do with garbage in general is now a major concern worldwide, particularly in the Western world, where a disproportionate amount of waste is generated.

We could have solved the garbage problem long before this, if we had recognized it. But our self-centered focus can obscure our ability to see a problematic trend until it blossoms into a full-blown crisis. Robert Ornstein has some interesting things to say about how our current paradigm deals with "problems":

> The world we live in is an entirely different one from the world we evolved to cope with, with the result that our minds are out of whack with our world. This has given us major problems like pollution, overpopulation, the destruction of the atmosphere, the extinction of plant and animal species, and the threat of nuclear annihilation.
>
> Our old minds are designed to look at things as they affect individuals and to respond to immediate danger—like tigers approaching us, or a sudden thunderstorm, or an earthquake. Large-scale, continuous threats are not instantaneously obvious to us, so they get ignored. For instance, one terrorist attack will cause millions of people to change their travel plans, but all the U.S. citizens ever killed by terrorists would not add up to the number who are killed every day in this country by handguns or automobile accidents.
>
> *We respond not to what is actually happening, but what we perceive to be happening.* We are programmed to respond to changes; so, for example, if the threat of nuclear weapons is slightly less than it was before, we are immensely relieved . . . instead of understanding that the threat is still probably a thousand times greater than it was at the time of Hiroshima. It's this response to change, rather than what is really out there, that is fundamental to the way we deal with the world.
>
> This is called "the boiled frog syndrome." When you put a frog in a pan of water and heat the water up slowly, it can't detect the gradual change in temperature and so will remain in the pan until it boils to death. In our case, the gradual increases in population, pollution, nuclear weapons, economic growth threaten to "boil" our civilization.[15]

From the self-centered state, our interpretation of our environment "out there" has to do with "How does this affect *me?*" With this "lens" or "filter," we look for large discontinuities or changes that might affect us, and the larger, macro changes often go unnoticed.

Another organizational implication of self-centeredness/separateness is found in the well-documented achievement motivation and "career-ism" so prevalent in our culture.[16] Individuals in organizations who experience themselves as separate and alone consequently feel a need to "do something" to get what they want. They try to manipulate their environments to produce results that will satisfy their self-centered preferences or demands.

There are two core subassumptions behind the assumption of sepa-rateness that wreak havoc for us, individually and organizationally. The first assumption is that things are wrong as they are, and that they can be "improved" through self-centered action of some kind. People are always trying to "improve things." But could the assumption that things are wrong be erroneous? A perception that things are not perfect as they are might be viewed as the direct result of myopic human judgment, made by one who is separated from an alignment with the larger whole.

The argument goes like this: Our separatist perspective, through selective perception of the self-fulfilling prophecy, allows for us to "see" only those things that are threats or enhancements to self. Everything else present to be seen in a situation is missed. So we act with inadequate data. And with inadequate data, how do we know how things should be? If things appear not to be perfect, that could be seen as the *result* of self-centered humans struggling to have things "their way," or the *cause* of the self-centered perspective, which creates the "wrongness" in the first place.

Let us look at this assumption a little more closely. How often do phrases such as the following appear in contemporary media? "Have it your way!" "Get what you want in life!" "Go for the gusto!" "Have it all!" We assume that we have to manipulate our circumstances to produce pleasing results. But self-centered human action always produces ef-fects in the world that are not pleasing. Some of these are obvious, such as a greedy person robbing a bank. Others are less obvious but just as real, such as a person hating the organizational colleague who has done him or her wrong. Through self-centered actions, thoughts, and feelings, we manifest results that increase chaos. Remember, we create our own reality. The separate human ego, feeling increasingly alienated and put upon by the results of its self-centered wanting and striving, struggles harder to "improve things." This vicious cycle only creates more chaos.

A second assumption, related to the first, is that if things are "wrong," one can discern how to make them "right," or understand what "right" would be. But all perceptions are distorted by one or some combination of three things:[17]

- *fear:* the subconscious awareness of the fragility and instability inherent in defying the design of life (to be defined in the next chapter)
- *greed:* the natural reaction to an overwhelming perception of aloneness, especially in what is perceived to be a "dog-eat-dog," competitive, even hostile world
- *shame:* the deep subconscious sadness a person feels in knowing that he or she is not all he or she was designed by life to be (John Bradshaw has referred to shame as the sadness a person feels when he or she has a basic belief that he or she is flawed.)[18]

With these powerful subconscious factors in place, self-centered humans cannot see things clearly, and therefore behave in ways they think will improve things for themselves; but, because such behavior is not aligned with the purposes of the larger whole, greater havoc results. We will explore these concepts further in Chapter 4.

## Prevalence of Self-Centered Judgment

A fourth belief, an outgrowth of the third, is that self-centered judgment is not only a right but an obligation. This form of judgment, springing from a sense of separateness from the larger whole, spawns the perception that things are not okay as they are. Who, from the narrow, self-preoccupied perspective, really knows how things should be?

People are always trying to improve things—for example, trying to eliminate world hunger and war. Hunger and war are the natural *effects* of billions of people operating self-centeredly. But where, after millennia of well-intentioned self-centered people working to improve things, is the evidence that things are in fact improving on the planet for humankind? Things may appear to improve for the short term, but then other ill effects seem to show up. For example, certain medications have been shown to have devastating long-term effects or unanticipated side effects. The acne-fighting drug Acutane and the antinausea drug Thalidomide, both developed to solve problems, also caused significant birth defects. No doubt you can think of other examples of well-intended human actions that went awry because a larger perspective was not taken.

### Implications for Organizations

Out of this enculturation has grown an organizational tendency toward self-centeredness. Organizations, as an external expression of the collective paradigm, try to maximize their self-interests. And, almost

**Vignette 2**

Perhaps there is no simpler way to convey the futility of self-centered judgment than with the fable of the wise man and the farmer.

The farmer went crying to the wise man, saying that his prize stallion had run off. The wise man said, "So who knows what is good and what is bad?" The following day, the farmer came laughing to the wise man, saying that his stallion had returned with a beautiful mare. The wise man said, "So who knows what is good and what is bad?"

The next day, the farmer came again to the wise man, this time in tears; his son had fallen off the mare and had broken his back. The wise man said, "So who knows what is good and what is bad?" The next day, yes, the farmer came again smiling, saying that the army had come through conscripting all able-bodied young men; his son was spared being pressed into service because of his broken back.

And the story goes on. In one moment things may look disastrous, and in the next they may look absolutely marvelous.

It makes more sense simply to work with the circumstances the way they are than to waste time and energy in judgment of them and then in the subsequent "blame game" that follows. Self-centered judgment is a result of a deep-seated enculturation that entails three elements:

1. the perception of "self" as a separate entity
2. the expectation of fulfillment of this separate self
3. the ongoing assessment of whether or not things, as they are, are conducive to that self-fulfillment

exclusively, organizations have defined their well-being in terms of material acquisitions; profit, growth, and market share are good examples.

Daniel Yankelovich, the noted pollster, observes that to "work hard and consume well was a patriotic duty. . . . The high value placed on acquisition and material well-being fueled the forward march of the fabled American economy."[19] But in spite of material wealth unparalleled in any modern culture, today there exists in the United States a persistent perception that "reality" has grown "dreary, flat and utilitarian."[20] Robert Johnson describes Western people as "children of inner poverty," because, in our state of separation from the reality of oneness, we desperately seek satisfaction from external forms.[21]

Yankelovich addresses this perception: "It turns out, therefore, that we all 'know' two truths about the self: one is that the self is private and

POT-SHOTS NO. 4026.

I WON'T START THINKING INDEPENDENTLY UNTIL I SEE THAT EVERYBODY ELSE IS DOING IT.

alone and wholly encased within one's body. The other is that one is a real Self only to the extent that caring and reaching beyond the self continue."[22] And "nothing has subverted self-fulfillment more thoroughly than self-indulgence."[23] To distinguish between these two "selves," we will use *self* to convey the isolated version and *Self* to convey the more expansive and connected version. Yankelovich concludes that Americans' experiments with self-centeredness have led to emptiness and despair, and that the road to self-fulfillment lies in revising the "getting/giving" contract so that there is greater emphasis on giving. This can have major implications for organizations that have believed that their raison d'être is to "get as much as we can," of profits, market share, and so on. Can this core belief be challenged?

### Attachment to Quantitative or Observable Results

A fifth belief concerns an attachment to quantitative or observable results. This stubborn underlying assumption is based in a belief that if it can't be measured, it isn't real—or, at best, it doesn't matter very much. (Refer to the quote from Peters and Waterman that appears at the beginning of this chapter.) This assumption manifests itself in a variety of ways, such as reliance on the use of statistical techniques to quantify various aspects of business, such as worker performance, cash flow, and profit. Underlying this passion for measurement is the awareness that we have no real inner security. Lacking it, we look to visible, external forms for security—things we can count and measure.

It can also be argued that the adherence to quantitative measurement is linked to our concern for predictability and control.[24] Subconsciously, we know that our habit of self-centeredness may put us at cross-purposes with our world, so we attempt to create a semblance of order and control in our lives through our adherence to measurement and hard data.

The strong concern with measurement in the industrial paradigm is closely connected to the illusion that, once the human mind understands how things work and what causes what, we will be better able to manipulate things to our advantage. So we self-centeredly seek to gain a measure of predictability and control over our world for the express purpose of "good" manipulation.

---

**Vignette 3**

The tendency to ignore the invisible, intangible aspects of life is also the tendency to ignore the latent power in organizations. One company executive is reputed to have set an efficiency consultant straight on this. The consultant recommended that the man in the corner office be fired, because every time the consultant walked by, the man had his feet up on his desk in a relaxed manner. The executive told the consultant that the previous year that same man had saved the company millions of dollars, and that his feet had been in the same position at the time.

---

*Implications for Organizations*

Quarterly financial results are the most important measure of success in the old paradigm. Managers who don't "hit their numbers" are castigated or fired. Performance appraisals seek to measure quantifiable behaviors—even if those behaviors have little relationship to success on the job. The important question here is, What are organizations missing by this bias? What behaviors and attributes vital to organizational success are overlooked?

## Addiction to Externals

The final orientation of the industrial era paradigm is the addiction to externals. This could accurately be described as a *meta-assumption*, given that many of the other assumptions discussed above are related to it. With one's personal identity firmly dependent on one's work, one needs the status and external reward provided by the job. Externals can be measured (How am I doing?), and authority figures are certainly external to the person. Self-centered people are always looking for ways to manipulate externals to their satisfaction.

The compulsion to find satisfaction outside of ourselves—in a job, a relationship, or a title—is closely connected to the previously mentioned phenomena of separateness and preoccupation with measurement and numbers. If there is no experience of meaning as being part of a larger whole, then there is a need to *create* meaning as a separate, autonomous individual through external trappings. Personal identity then becomes determined by these external factors.

If an individual believes that a job gives meaning, then his or her losing that job is devastating. And in an era of mergers and "downsizing," job loss is a distressingly common reality.[25] An epitaph on a tombstone in a Welsh churchyard reads: "Here lies the body of Thomas Jones who was born a man and died a grocer." Sad, but common: This man's identity as a "job" followed him to his grave.

By enforcing the assumption that our identity is derived from external labels, the industrial era paradigm predisposes us toward addictive patterns of behavior. Through these patterns, we are always trying to arrange our external circumstances the way we want them. Schaef and Fassel say that "since the addictive process is the norm for the society, one must assume that everyone participates addictively at some level."[26] They go on to say:

> There is a general addictive process that underlies all the various addictions. Indeed, our society itself is an addictive system and acts exactly like an individual addict in the way it functions and the processes it sets up. Thus the theory of addictive personality clouds the issue. The problem is not that there are people running around with addictive personalities; *there exists an addictive process that underlies an addictive system, and it surrounds and influences us all.*[27]

The passion with which "high achievers" pursue their material goals (and titles) shows the power of this addiction. The motion picture *Wall Street* depicts the erosion of character of a stockbroker who taps into that passion for achievement and for the things that such achievement can provide. The moment when he recognizes what he has lost through such endeavors is a pivotal point in this compelling drama. Actual events on Wall Street—the October 19, 1987, "crash"; the documented corruption within the brokerage profession; the demise of the career of "junk bond king" Michael Milken not long after the movie's release—lend an extra air of poignancy to this film.

Ask yourself a few questions:

- Am I dependent on having things the way I want them before I can be happy?
- Do external factors (job, relationship, status) determine my satisfaction in life?
- Do I find myself often wanting things to be different from the way they are?

Answers of yes to such questions may indicate that you are addicted to results that are pleasing to you, and you consequently *are* at the effect of those external things. You essentially have given your personal power over to externals; this is a definition of *addiction*.

### Implications for Organizations

Much of what occurs under the industrial era paradigm relates to addiction to the system. Political behavior, careerism, infighting, manipulation, desperately seeking organizational approval, and validation all come from this belief.[28] People display "bureaupathic behavior" (Robert Merton's term to describe acting as if rules are more important than the attainment of goals) because they are addicted to success in the eyes of organizational superiors.[29] In our organizations, we are constantly comparing ourselves with others in terms of *external* (measurable) status symbols. Our worth as human beings is constantly riding on the vagaries of external forms. It's little wonder that we feel almost constantly insecure.

---

## Personal Identity
## According to the Industrial Era Paradigm

---

The six broad cultural assumptions discussed above are interrelated, and in turn they relate to the overriding question of personal *identity*. If a person answers the question, Who am I? with "I am my work/my job role," then it is likely that individual holds the Protestant ethic as a foundational belief and gives authority to others who control this definition (the person's superiors). If the answer is, "I am my income level/my level of material wealth/my prestige," that is evidence of a concomitant addiction to external manifestations of that prestige and material success.

Unless an individual's identity is somehow part of a larger whole, his or her experience will be one of separation from everyone else. As Edward Sampson notes:

> A central theme in our culture is its underlying belief that order and coherence are achieved by means of personal control and mastery. . . . the ideal maintains that a particular structure of personal identity is required so that order and coherence rather than chaos will characterize the individual's life.[30]

The assumption of a separate personal identity runs deep. Its consequences are our continual and sometimes destructive attempts to manipulate the environment in order to gain results pleasing to this separate self.

## Some Further Thoughts

The assumptions discussed above have formed the backbone of our current industrial system of organizations. If these assumptions change, then organizations will change. Sampson proposes an alternative to what he calls the "centralized equilibrium structure":

> Developments in nonequilibrium theory in physics, deconstructionism in literary criticism, and decentralized anarchic notions of government introduce a different understanding of the means whereby order and coherence exist and thus open the possibility for a revised ideal of personhood: a decentralized, nonequilibrium ideal whose very being hinges on its continuous becoming.[31]

As Yankelovich has noted, "One is a real self only to the extent that caring and reaching beyond the self continues."[32] We are factually part of a much larger whole, whether we are conscious of it or not. It is in our best interest as a species to cooperate with the design and control inherent in that larger whole. It is as simple (and as complex) as that.

---

## The Major Values and
## Attitudes of the Industrial Era

---

Some of the dominant values and attitudes that seem to characterize the industrial paradigm include several apparent preferences: for the new over the habitual, for attention to emergency factors over long-term trends, for attending to scarce resources over abundant ones, for surface appearances over deeper qualities of character, and for close proximity over distance. These are discussed in turn below.

*Preference for the new over the habitual.* Our minds seem to be attuned to changes in the status quo; we quickly become habituated to things as they are and no longer notice them. This is an example of what Ornstein and Ehrlich call "caricatures of reality."[33] Because we cannot accept into our awareness all the stimuli we could potentially receive at one time, we are selective about what we perceive. This selection process favors sudden changes in the present situation; once a change becomes "common," we switch to a subconscious way of operating (on automatic, so to speak) and don't really notice what is present in our situation.

Thus marketers have known for years that products need to be "new and improved"—often! New fashions, new auto styles, new everything must be continually introduced. Similarly, when things are working well in organizations, what do we do? We reorganize! Because we are attuned to notice the new, we change things to signal that we are doing something to improve.

*Preference for attention to emergency factors over long-term trends.* Closely related is our mind's sensitivity to perceiving threats to our well-being. Ornstein and Ehrlich argue that this comes from our "old" mind/brain system, inherited from our ancestors, who needed to be able to react to approaching danger in the form of wild animals. So, we react emotionally to a fire, a little girl who falls down a well in Texas, a terrorist attack—while ignoring or adapting to such long-term destructive trends as acid rain, air and water pollution, and depletion of the ozone layer.

In this sense, our predicament is similar to what Ornstein and Ehrlich call the "boiled frog syndrome," in which the frog's ability to adapt to slow changes in water temperature proves to be its downfall.[34] "Habituation is built into our sensory neurons. It provides the basis for the mind's ability to ignore continuing phenomena and to seize instead upon short-term incidents."[35]

In organizations, old-paradigm managers attempt to "motivate" people by firing someone. The sudden change makes employees sensitive to a perceived threat and aware of a need to alter behavior. Other phenomena that catch employees' attention are rumors of mass firings, reorganizations, mergers, and other highly visible factors.

*Preference for attending to scarce resources over abundant ones.* The industrial era paradigm is programmed to pay attention to whatever is perceived as scarce. Apparently, "sensitivity to an immediate scarcity of resources—especially a sudden change leading to scarcity—is a default program in all animals."[36] Our minds "default" (automatically move) toward items perceived to be scarce. In a restaurant, if we are told that there is only a little fresh cod left, we want to order that. At Kmart, we rush to purchase items that are on sale for just a few minutes. Experiments have proven that items perceived to be scarce, even though they are identical to those in greater supply, are immediately given a high value.[37]

Through budgets, an organization directs its attention toward resource scarcity. We typically focus on lack, not abundance, and so resources are hoarded for a rainy day. Buffer inventory is stocked to prevent scarcity enforced by a major supplier's labor strike. Marketers use scarcity to sell us everything from hair spray to vacation condos.

*Preference for surface appearances over deeper qualities of character.* Because of our penchant for prediction and control, we try to size up situations or persons quickly, using data from our past experiences or our stereotypes. Many personnel administrators will tell you that they make hiring decisions less than a minute into an interview. According to Ornstein and Ehrlich, "Our minds are made up in the first social encounter because our attention is focused on the beginnings of events."[38] From choosing a president to dressing for success, we judge quickly. And psychologists tell us that first impressions, so formed, are difficult to change.

Thus there is an acknowledged "look" to a top corporate executive: expensive blue or dark gray suit, starched white shirt, "power" tie, expensive wingtip or French-style shoes. Except for prominent exceptions such as Steven Jobs, Ben Cohen, and Jerry Greenfield, corporate executives "dress the part" to conform to the stereotype and the value judgment therein.

*Preference for close proximity over distance.* Thanks to the self-centered emphasis of the dominant paradigm, we give our attention to factors that might immediately affect us. "For our ancestors, the focus on current and short-term, close proximity changes was certainly adaptive."[39] Television images of conflicts in other parts of the world bring war into our living rooms, but this still seems remote to most Americans—except the soldiers, medical personnel, and journalists who live through it.

At work, people are absorbed in matters close at hand: office politics, allocation of resources, hirings and firings. Rumors may waft in from distant offices, but unless these messages affect us directly, we pay little attention to them—or to other long-term trends that might affect an organization.

These dominant attitudes and values ensure that our "caricatures of reality" are predictable and consistent. We experience other people as caricatures based on the past; we are likely to convict an ugly person of a crime if we are on a jury, we are likely to believe someone is "excitable" if we are told he or she is extroverted, and so on. In our quest to keep our self-centered reality balanced and useful, we distort information, see what we want to see, and thereby miss the richness and complexity of what is right before our eyes.

As noted earlier, we create our own reality. And what determines our creation? The content of our consciousness, or our dominant paradigm. Our individual and collective paradigms act as prisms, focusing life's energy into predictable, narrow patterns. Thus, if we value scarcity over abundance, we will create a reality marked by scarcity. If we believe our identity is determined by external symbols, we will create a reality thick with them.

The recognition that we create our own reality—in other words, that we have the ability to perceive the paradigms that influence us—has distanced us from our current paradigm and brought us closer than ever to the emerging paradigm, the subject of the next chapter.

## DISCUSSION QUESTION

1. Can you think of any self-centered action that is potentially not disintegrative in some way?

## NOTES

1. Thomas J. Peters and Robert H. Waterman, Jr., *In Search of Excellence: Lessons From America's Best-Run Companies* (New York: Harper & Row, 1982), 43-44.

2. John Hoerr, "The Payoff From Teamwork," *Business Week,* July 10, 1989, 58. Used with permission.

3. Jacob M. Schlesinger and Paul Ingrassia, "GM Woos Employees by Listening to Them, Talking of Its Team," *Wall Street Journal,* January 12, 1989, A-1. Reprinted by permission of *Wall Street Journal,* © 1989 Dow Jones & Company, Inc. All rights reserved worldwide.

4. Anne W. Schaef and Diane Fassel, *The Addictive Organization: Why We Overwork, Cover Up, Pick Up the Pieces, Please the Boss, and Perpetuate Sick Organizations* (San Francisco: Harper & Row, 1988), 98.

5. See, e.g., Jolie Solomon, "Early Retirees Fall Into Career Oblivion," *Wall Street Journal,* March 24, 1989, B-1.

6. All vignettes in this volume are drawn from the personal experiences or files of the authors, unless specified otherwise in accompanying source notes.

7. Solomon, "Early Retirees." See also Bill Neikirk, "Unfortunately, We May Now Be Close to Full Employment," *Chicago Tribune*, May 1, 1983, sec. 5, p. 3; Mark Satin, "Should We Protect Jobs—or Redefine Work?" *New Options*, October 21, 1985; "The Robots Are Coming . . . and They Are Bringing a New Industrial Revolution," *Barron's*, October 1985.

8. Edward De Bono, *The Use of Lateral Thinking* (Mamaroneck, NY: International Center for Creative Thinking, 1990 [1970]).

9. Richard H. Hall, *Organizations: Structure and Process* (2nd ed.) (Englewood Cliffs, NJ: Prentice Hall, 1977).

10. Stanley Milgram, *Obedience to Authority: An Experimental View* (New York: Harper & Row, 1974); cited in Arthur Miller, *The Obedience Experiments: A Case Study of Controversy in Social Science* (New York: Praeger, 1986).

11. John R. P. French, Jr., and Bertram Raven, "The Bases of Social Power," in *Studies in Social Power*, ed. D. Cartwright (Ann Arbor: University of Michigan, Institute for Social Research, 1959); cited by Richard H. Hall, *Organizations: Structures, Processes, and Outcomes* (4th ed.) (Englewood Cliffs, NJ: Prentice Hall, 1987), chap. 5.

12. Robert Theobald, *An Alternative Future for America II* (Chicago: Swallow, 1970).

13. Joseph Chilton Pearce, *Exploring the Crack in the Cosmic Egg* (New York: Julian, 1974).

14. Robert N. Bellah, Richard Madsen, William M. Sullivan, Ann Swidler, and Steven M. Tipton, "Habits of the Heart: Is Overindulgence in Individualism Leading Us Astray?" *New Realities*, Summer 1985, 8, 10. Bellah, Madsen, Sullivan, Swidler, and Tipton are also coauthors of the best-selling book *Habits of the Heart: Individualism and Commitment in American Life* (New York: Harper & Row, 1985).

15. "We Need New Minds to Fix Old Problems," interview with Robert Ornstein, *USA Today*, January 25, 1989, 9A; emphasis added. Copyright © 1989, USA Today. Reprinted with permission.

16. David McClelland, *The Achieving Society* (New York: Random House, 1960).

17. See Richard Heinberg, *Visions and Memories of Paradise* (Loveland, CO: Foundation House, 1982); see also his more recent work, *Memories and Visions of Paradise* (Los Angeles: Jeremy Tarcher, 1989).

18. See, for example, John Bradshaw, *Healing the Shame That Binds You* (Deerfield Beach, FL: Health Communications, 1988); John Bradshaw, *Bradshaw on the Family* (television program produced by KQED-TV, San Francisco, 1992).

19. Daniel Yankelovich, *New Rules* (New York: Bantam, 1981), 223.

20. Arthur Mitzman, *The Iron Cage* (New York: Knopf, 1970); Julian Freund, *The Sociology of Max Weber* (New York: Random House, 1968).

21. Robert Johnson, *WE: The Psychology of Romantic Love* (New York: Harper & Row, 1983), 21.

22. Yankelovich, *New Rules*, 237.

23. Ibid., 243.

24. Charles Hampden-Turner, *Radical Man* (Cambridge, MA: Schenkman, 1970), chap. 1.

25. H. I. Alexander, letter to the editor, *London Times*, March 5, 1988.

26. Schaef and Fassel, *The Addictive Organization*, 6.

27. Ibid., 51; emphasis added.

28. For a gripping analysis of the consequences of workaholism, see Marguerite Michaels and James Wilwerth, "How America Has Run Out of Time," *Time*, April 24, 1989, 58-67.

29. Robert K. Merton, *Social Theory and Social Structure* (Glencoe, IL: Free Press, 1957).

30. Edward E. Sampson, "The Decentralization of Identity: Toward a Revised Concept of Personal and Social Order," *American Psychologist* 40 (November 1985): 218.

31. Ibid.

32. Yankelovich, *New Rules*, 237.

33. Robert Ornstein and Paul Ehrlich, *New World, New Mind* (New York: Simon & Schuster, 1989), 72.

34. Ibid., 74-75.

35. Ibid., 80-81.

36. Ibid., 100.

37. Ibid., 103.

38. Ibid., 104.

39. Ibid., 113.

# 4 Transformational Thinking: The Emerging Paradigm

*In the management of innovation, it is very important to create a climate, or corporate culture, in which value is placed on the ability to learn, to change, and generally to develop and promote new ideas. . . . Organizational structures and pyramidal lines of command often send subtle and not so subtle cues that people should maintain the status quo.*
(Gareth Morgan, *Riding the Waves of Change*, 1988, p. 70)

---

**SUMMARY:** In this chapter we discuss the assumptions of the emerging postindustrial era, show how transformational thought works, and then look at its implications for organizations.

---

## The Current Paradigm Shift

The world is approaching a turning point, says physicist Fritjof Capra; a massive shift in the perception of reality is under way. Thinkers in many disciplines, he notes, "are beginning to move away from the traditional, reductionistic, mechanical world view to an ecological, holistic systems paradigm."[1] Why has this happened? The primary reason has been a shift in the "scientific paradigm." The way that physicists view the world has shifted from Newtonian/Cartesian assumptions about the nature of the universe to Einsteinian/quantum mechanics assumptions. Physicists have ceased assuming that reality, at its most basic level, is composed of parts that make up a whole in a mechanistic manner, and have begun to view apparent parts as inextriably *linked to*, not separate from, the whole. This has led to a new understanding that, far from the whole being dependent on the parts, the whole *organizes* the parts. This means that any organic whole—such as the human body—actually provides a design and control function for its parts. Other assumptions inherent in the Newtonian paradigm are also under attack, as Peter Schwartz and James Ogilvy note:

> Embedded in the mechanistic view of the world are three basic assumptions. The first is that there is a most fundamental level of reality (i.e., the basic building blocks) composed of the smallest particles and the complete set of forces that govern them. Once we find that fundamental level and the laws that govern it, the world will be predictable (like a machine). Second is the assumption that the laws that govern matter and energy on the very small scale must be similar to, and hopefully identical to, those that apply on the very large scale.
>
> The governing laws thus should be universal, so that we ought to be able to build a picture of the planets moving about the sun out of an understanding of the particles of which matter is composed. Finally, there is the assumption that we, as observers, can be isolated from the experiments and the world we are studying and produce an "objective" description. All of these basic assumptions are now being challenged by theoretical and experimental findings.[2]

As Capra has pointed out, these new findings are beginning to influence thinkers in every field. And as their ideas filter into our consciousness, our paradigm is likewise beginning to show evidence of change. Many of these changes are showing up in our collective paradigm; we have chosen to call this the *transformational perspective*.

## The Origins of Transformational Thinking

The recent emergence of transformational assumptions in the field of organization theory has become apparent in the volumes of literature readily available. The origin of this modern world movement can be traced to the "T-groups" initiated in Bethel, Maine, at the National Training Laboratories in the late 1940s and 1950s. These "sensitivity groups," as they came to be called, introduced the idea of group dynamics/group norms and studied issues of trust and openness. The T-group experience proved an important point: If the *culture* of an organization (its norms and its "accepted behaviors") did not support behaviors such as openness and trust, then those behaviors quickly disappeared. This was the crude beginning of today's interest in culture as a relevant organizational dynamic.

Out of these beginnings grew what has been called the human potential movement. The U.S. Army adopted the slogan "Be all that you can be," originally coined by a commissioner of education in the state of New York and then used by a transformational consultant, Frank Burns.[3] Numerous self-help philosophies and courses proliferated, such as est, Course in Miracles, Lifestream, the Pace Seminar, Actualizations, Insight Training Seminars, Living Love workshops, DMA, and others. The steam behind the transformational movement began to build quietly.

The growth and development of these transformational technologies have been documented elsewhere; what is of interest to us here is that they are a symptom of the emergence of a larger contextual issue: the *beginning of the breakdown of the Newtonian model of reality and its assumptions.* It could be asserted that (a) these courses would not have been "invented" and (b) they would not have been as successful as they have been had not the old assumptions about the nature of reality come under question.

---

## Characteristics of the Emerging Paradigm

---

The characteristics of the emerging postindustrial paradigm can best be understood in contrast to the assumptions of the industrial era we are leaving behind. Let's look at some of them.

### Assumption 1: Everything is connected.

- *Transformational Assumption 1:* Everything (including us) is part of one large, seamless whole, and everything is connected to (and influenced by) everything else. Nothing is separate from anything else, despite appearances.
- *Industrial Era Assumption 1:* Everything is separate from everything else. Things do influence other things, but the influence can be seen, predicted, and controlled with the right (scientific) approach. The universe operates like a large machine, with each part relating to (some but not all) other parts in a predictable, mechanistic manner.

This notion of separateness is buried deep in our subconscious and is rarely challenged. All of the various fields of science have used this assumption unquestioningly. Consider psychoanalysis, for example. In her book *Necessary Losses,* Judith Viorst speaks of the "high cost of separation" when discussing the baby's separation from its mother and the trauma this apparently induces.[4] The dominant assumption is that, once out of the protective embryonic fluid of the mother's womb, the child is separate and essentially alone in a hostile universe, with only wits and survival instincts to rely on.

Life then becomes defined as a struggle to "get by," to snatch a bit of happiness along the way, but, mostly, to "make meaning out of an essentially meaningless life."[5] Joseph Chilton Pearce has argued that our "cosmic egg" (dominant paradigm) has, as its organizing principle, the assumption that life is essentially hostile.[6] As Henry David Thoreau asserts, "The mass of men lead lives of quiet desperation."

This is precisely the subconscious motivation behind an individual's investing his or her identity in a job or career; after all, without a label of importance or status, we are nothing. Given that we are assumed to be separate and alone in the cosmos, we are also assumed to have a need to create meaning for our lives; hence the need for job status or title as a confirmation of worth and meaning.

Recent discoveries of quantum mechanics tell us that the material world appears to be a complex web of relationships, with everything affecting everything else. As theoretical physicist David Bohm notes, "The notion of separate objects is an idealization that is often very useful, but has no fundamental validity. All such objects are patterns in an inseparable cosmic process, and these patterns are intrinsically dynamic."[7]

Bohm argues that the universe is a seamless, unbroken whole, and it is only our *habits of thought* that lead us to perceive ourselves as separate and isolated from the larger whole. This reductionistic thinking (seeing ourselves as separate from each other and from nature) began with René Descartes and was articulated triumphantly by Isaac Newton, who developed a consistent, mathematical formulation of the mechanistic view of nature. This approach sees entities as essentially separate from each other, behaving according to mechanistic laws of the universe. From the second half of the seventeenth century to the end of the nineteenth century, this mechanistic view dominated all scientific thought. Its assumptions affected all fields of endeavor, from medicine (humans treated as machines, with parts to be fixed or replaced) to organizations (the view of organization as machine).

The assumption that everything affects everything else is at the core of transformational thought. The notion of independence or separateness is only a product of a particular worldview or paradigm.

## *Implications for Organizations*

Organizations, if they are to adopt the transformational perspective, need to see themselves as inextricably intertwined in the larger social fabric. Everything they do affects everything else. This relates to obvious factors, such as pollution and resource waste, as well as not-so-obvious factors, such as destructive and competitive attitudes, lack of integrity, and workaholic cultures.

Ben Cohen and Jerry Greenfield are very concerned about the larger whole in which their company is embedded. They have sold common stock in their company to local Vermonters, creating a "We're all in this together" attitude. Their foundation gives 15% of its pretax profit to charity, the greatest percentage devoted to philanthropy among U.S. corporations. Finally, Ben & Jerry's corporate practices are designed to avoid pollution of rivers in the company's area.

Other organizations are also beginning to consider that a new "whole-centered" way of being, thinking, and acting is good business. For example, the president of Swissair, Otto Loepfe, a onetime car mechanic who took charge of Swissair in 1988, has ordered all managers in the company to spend at least one day each month dealing directly with customers. He wants "everyone whether they are working in finance or anywhere else to be aware that ultimately they are working on a product for a customer." He himself plans to be at a check-in or travel agency counter once a month.[8] Tom Peters, of course, has been preaching about concern for the customer and employees for some time now.[9] All of this points to an increasing awareness of the organization as an *open system*, influencing—and influenced by—its external environment.

## Assumption 2: The whole organizes the parts.

- *Transformational Assumption 2:* The whole (what we could call life) organizes the parts. This means that there is an inherent design and control present in life itself, and that everything operates in accordance with these universal principles of cause and effect. The corollary assumption is that, if there is design and control operating the cosmos, the intelligent thing for us to do is to align ourselves consciously with that design and control so as to facilitate the working of this larger purpose and design.
- *Industrial Era Assumption 2:* The parts influence the whole. If a part breaks down, the whole is dependent on fixing that part to function properly. Each part of the whole is separate from other parts, although there are certain relationships and interdependencies among the parts. The cosmos operates mechanically, according to certain mechanical laws and principles.

Bohm, in his provocative book *Wholeness and the Implicate Order*, sees a process whereby the "whole organizes the parts."[10] In other words, everything in the material world seems to fit together and move together according to some universal laws or principles (what Bohm calls the "implicate order"), and the seamless, unbroken whole spoken of earlier provides a focus for the parts, dictating their relationship to each other and to the whole. So the cosmic organizing principles, whatever they are, seem to provide design and control functions for the apparently separate parts. Bohm goes on to assert:

> The notion that all these fragments are separately existent is evidently an illusion, and this illusion cannot do other than lead to endless conflict and confusion. Indeed, the attempt to live according to the notion that the fragments are really separate is, in essence, what has led to the growing series of extremely urgent crises that is confronting us today. Thus, as is now well known, this way of life has brought about pollution, destruction of the balance of nature, over-population, world-wide economic and political disorder, and the creation of an environment that is neither physically nor mentally healthy for most of the people who have to live in it.[11]

The notion that there is an inherent design and control to life itself is becoming increasingly accepted with the popularity of "chaos theory." Considered a "new science," chaos theory "offers a way of seeing order and pattern where formerly only the random, the erratic, the unpredictable . . . in short, the chaotic . . . had been observed." In the words of Douglas Hofstadter, "it turns out that an eerie type of chaos can lurk just behind a facade of order . . . and, yet, deep inside the chaos lurks an eerier type of order."[12]

According to the transformational view, everything is in motion; patterns of invisible, vibratory phenomena create forms as we know them. Every form has behind it, you might say, a certain design in the invisible realm of vibration or the pulsating, electromagnetic implicate order, as Bohm calls it. Deepak Chopra, in his excellent book *Unconditional Life: Mastering the Forces That Shape Personal Reality*, sees everything, visible and invisible, as part of the "field" of vibrating energy patterns that is the whole.[13] Each of these subfields has an inherent design and vibrational characteristic. Solids are vibrating more slowly than liquids, and liquids more slowly than gases. Thoughts and emotions are also vibratory phenomena.

The implicate order or the inherent design of life is intimately related to the well-known concept of the *hologram*, which is based on the notion that any part of a whole contains within it the "blueprint" for the larger whole itself.[14] Apparently, there is strong evidence in the field of quantum physics that the universe is intelligent, that there are principles of design and control that can be understood and aligned with by human beings. This position is well articulated in a book called *Rhythms of Vision:*

> We are enveloped and penetrated with a tidal power which functions with total precision, from the galactic to the subatomic, and the precision is only at fault in the still-developing human consciousness. But we begin to sense, even in this darkness, that our own individual feelings are part of the musical movements of the cosmos, and *that we are one and the same breathing Leviathan of life.*[15]

## *Implications for Organizations*

What we call reality is actually made up of wholes within wholes. The national economy is contained within the world economy. A particular industry is contained within the national economy. A particular firm is contained within an industry, and so on. From the macrocosm to the microcosm, we see life organized into discrete forms of energy, each a whole unto itself. Organizations would do well to remember that the whole organizes the parts. As a part of a larger society, for example, the organization is "organized" by prevailing consumer tastes, interest rates, lending policies, competitor actions, international events, and so forth. From the transformational perspective, there is no such thing as a separate entity.

## Assumption 3: We are cocreators with life.

- *Transformational Assumption 3:* We are designed to be cocreators with life. This means that the forms we observe around us are produced in our consciousness and then made "real" externally to us by a process of creation we could call *manifestation.* We create our own worlds. To the extent that we collectively agree on "how things are" external to us, we call this *consensual reality.*[16]

- *Industrial Era Assumption 3:* Our external world is just "out there" for us to perceive. It just "happened" and our job is to try to manipulate it to our best advantage. The so-called external world is constantly impinging on us, and the best we can do is try to cope with the changes as best we can. We are essentially victims of fate and luck; we are certainly not creators of reality, but are subject to it.

Another transformational assumption is that man has a special function on the planet with regard to the aforementioned design and control principles. We have been designed with a cerebral cortex and other means so that we can consciously cooperate with the purposes of the larger whole, whatever they might be.[17] So-called lower life forms, plants, fish, insects, and so on all unconsciously cooperate with life at their level of reality; we call this *instinct,* or *genetic programming.* Likewise, many of our human functions—circulation, heart rate, organ and glandular functions—are on "automatic."

However, the transformational perspective asserts that we are also responsible for consciously allowing the integrating force of life (with its inherent design, control, and purpose) to become manifest through us, so that we might consciously cocreate with the life force. Joseph Campbell, in his best-seller *The Power of Myth,* makes this argument; in fact, George Lucas used Campbell's thesis as the basis of the "May the Force be with you!" cry in his popular *Star Wars* movies.[18]

### Implications for Organizations

We create our own reality. We use life's creative force to create various external forms by consensual agreement; organizations are but one such form. However, in a self-centered paradigm, we create forms that are not harmonious with what life *could* create through us were our thoughts not dominated by fear, greed, and shame. Richard Heinberg, in his classic *Memories and Visions of Paradise,* asserts that evidence abounds that there was a "golden age" on earth when we were consciously part of the whole and consciously cooperating with the purpose, design, and control of the whole.[19] But since the fall of man, we have created a fearful, dangerous world.

What would organizations look like if we allowed the design of life to create them? Certainly not like a machinelike bureaucracy, with its artificial integrators of RRPP, goals, and formal authority.

### Assumption 4: Harmony and integration follow alignment with life.

- *Transformational Assumption 4:* If we consciously choose to align ourselves with the immutable laws of life (the design and control principles mentioned above), then we will reap the consequences of harmony and integration; if we choose to ignore these laws in favor of our own self-preoccupied designs, we will reap the disintegration of the forms around us. Each person has meaning only as a part of the whole; each individual's purpose is to cooperate with the purposes of life.
- *Industrial Era Assumption 4:* Life is essentially hostile to human life, and our job as isolated, separate humans is to manipulate our external circumstances so as to "succeed in life," that is, to have victory over an essentially unfriendly universe. We must be self-preoccupied; after all, if I don't take

care of myself, who will? People are basically untrustworthy; everyone is out for themselves, and so I must be, too. The individual's purpose is to survive and prosper as a separate entity; meaning comes from external status symbols, money, titles, accomplishments, and so on. There is no intrinsic purpose or meaning in the larger whole.

As cocreators, we create either harmony (when in alignment with the forces of life) or disharmony (or destruction) when our self-preoccupied designs about how things *should be* (formulated from the egocentric, separated consciousness) get in the way of just cooperating with life and its larger purposes operant throughout the universe. Any paradigm, up to this point in human history, is by its very nature a human design created from the perspective of separate identity; the purpose of the paradigm is to create a reality consistent with the parameters of the self-preoccupied purposes.

If we are creators by design, and what we create is not in synchronicity with the creative force of the universe, then the results of the creation will be dissonant. If we are designed to be cocreators with life but we decide that we want things our own way, then disharmony is the only possible product. The clear energy or vibratory pattern of life is constricted and distorted to the degree that the human mind and emotional realm is absorbed in self-centered and self-protective pursuits. When they are constricted or distorted, the forms that appear in the world are not all that they could be; this is the primary reason the world seems to be so full of "lacks" and scarcity.

Always viewing and creating our world in terms of threats or enhancements to ourselves makes us ask, Who or what is out to get me? and How can this help me? Both perspectives constrict the possibilities we perceive. But approaching our world with a giving and expansive attitude—asking, How can I serve?—can create a world of abundance and potential.

## Implications for Organizations

Tom Peters and his colleagues have begun to sense the validity of this transformational assumption. The hologram demonstrates that the whole is *contained* in each part. Each organization is a microcosm of the larger economy, and is intimately connected to it. Ben Cohen and Jerry Greenfield seem to realize this, as demonstrated by their stock purchase plan for employees and fellow Vermonters, their charitable work, and their emphasis on quality and natural ingredients.

Markets have rhythms, like life itself, and these need to be respected. More and more, the phrase "Go with the flow" is beginning to replace the imperative "Make it happen!" in the corporate world. But the old paradigm dies hard. Quarterly reports, performance appraisals, and other corporate tools still largely reflect old-paradigm assumptions.

### Assumption 5: The paradigm shift is now.

- *Transformational Assumption 5:* The current paradigm shift is unprecedented in that it is calling for us to relinquish our habitual patterns of self-preoccupied function in favor of conscious alignment with the larger purposes of the whole (the implicate order). We have reached the limits of self-preoccupied human function, as evidenced by our decaying environment; escalating ethnic, racial, religious, cultural, and economic conflicts around the world; nuclear proliferation; and a host of other problems.
- *Industrial Era Assumption 5:* We are not in a paradigm shift. We do have problems, but they will be solved by bright human minds and new technologies produced by those minds. Everything is still under control, and we are heading in the right direction. Also, you can never eliminate self-centeredness from humans; it is bred into us (human nature). Therefore, the best we can hope for is relative peace and stability in a turbulent world.

The final dominant assumption of the transformational view is that we are now in a major paradigm shift on a global basis and are being challenged to examine our self-limiting beliefs, attitudes, and values *because our very survival as a species demands it.* In the past 10 years, many books have pointed to this massive shift: Robert Heilbroner's *Inquiry Into the Human Prospect,* Alvin Toffler's *The Third Wave,* and Willis Harman's *An Incomplete Guide to the Future* are but a few. The scientific literature is also replete with examples, such as David Bohm's *Wholeness and the Implicate Order,* Fritjof Capra's *Turning Point,* and Rupert Sheldrake's *The New Science of Life.*[20]

With so many voices acknowledging that we are in the midst of a major paradigm shift, so much evidence pointing out the dire consequences of old paradigm actions, and so many ecologists, such as Paul Ehrlich of Stanford, reminding us of the fragility and interconnectedness of our ecosystems, it is hard to imagine the planet surviving *without* a major shift in beliefs, attitudes, and values.

### *Implications for Organizations*

Unanticipated, a paradigm shift can put an organization—even an industry—out of business. Many paradigm "minishifts" have devastated whole industries—industries that tried hard to ignore them. The Swiss watch industry is a good example. In 1968, the Swiss controlled 65% of the world wristwatch market share and 80% of its profits. But when a Swiss craftsman invented the quartz movement, he was rebuffed by the management of top Swiss organizations. After all, it didn't look like a watch; it didn't have jewels or a mainspring! The Swiss left the innovation unprotected by patent, but displayed it at a trade show, where the Americans and Japanese saw it.

The rest is history. By 1992, the Swiss share of the global watch market was less than 10%. Thousands of workers had been laid off. Why? Because industry leadership had what Joel Barker has called "paradigm paralysis."[21] Management rejected innovation because it was unwilling to allow a shift in its beliefs, attitudes, and values.

Life *is* change; like seasons, weather patterns, and the other creative cycles of life, we must change, too. But our rigid paradigmatic parameters can keep change out of sight until it's too late—leaving us, like the Swiss watch industry, with little more than our regrets.

---

## Personal Identity
## According to the Emerging Paradigm

---

Personal identity, under the old paradigm, is defined by the world of *form*. Our meaning and identity come from external forms—our jobs, our homes, our clothes, our cars, and our friends. But defining our self-worth and identity this way is inherently unstable, because things in the external world *always* change. If a person's self-worth is tied up in his or her stock portfolio, then a market disaster like the October 1987 crash can trigger a genuine identity crisis. (In fact, psychoanalysts were very busy in the months after the crash, treating depression, fear, insomnia, and suicidal tendencies.)

In the transformational state, identity is found in the source of life itself. We *are* life; that is our identity. By identifying with life, we *are* the changes that we observe. If we are change, then change isn't terrifying; change is our nature. Fluidity and adaptability are natural by-products of people centered in their *beingness* as opposed to their *doingness*. *I am* is the clarion call of the transformational paradigm; not "I am my job" or "I am my relationship," but simply *I am*.

---

## Science and Religion:
## A Transformational View

---

The modern world is marked by a long-standing separation of science and religion; the schism is between the observable and measurable (science) and the invisible and "unprovable" (religion). It is no coincidence that the current paradigm shift is marked by a reuniting of science and, not religion per se, but spirituality (a more encompassing term) through recent discoveries in quantum mechanics.[22]

These revelations clearly point to a spiritual reality behind *all* forms. In other words, the world of form is *an effect* of an invisible *cause* (a basic transformational assumption). The one, seamless whole that organizes the parts (which Capra and Bohm, both physicists, point to) could be called the *spiritual reality* or the *true reality.*

In fact, reductionistic, separatist, self-centered thinking has produced the aforementioned schism between science and religion. Willis Harman sees no necessary conflict between the "perennial wisdom of the world's spiritual traditions and a science which has relaxed the positivistic and reductionistic assumptions that characterize much of its history." He further indicates a shift in the metaphysical assumptions underlying science and a corresponding new metaphysics, noting that "a way in which science and religion could come together . . . is for science to reconstitute itself on the basis of the third metaphysical assumption, and for religion to more and more assume the form of the 'perennial wisdom.'"[23]

## Concluding Remarks

Everywhere we look, the paradigm shift is promoting integration and wholeness: Science and religion are being seen as complementary, companies and their suppliers are regarding each other as partners instead of adversaries, international joint ventures are cropping up between former competitors. Yet, as is typical of a major shift, the die-hard holdouts of the separatist, egocentric perspective escalate their need to "be right." So we see war, racism, loneliness, mental illness, and other problems on the increase. Why the apparent paradox of integration and disintegration? The transformational perspective tells us that the world is a seamless, unbroken whole, and that the world created by the isolated ego is illusory. So the "old world" is dying—in other words, disintegrating—and the "new world" is sending a tumultuous birth announcement.

### NOTES

1. Fritjof Capra, "The Turning Point," *Futurist,* December 1982, 19.

2. Peter Schwartz and James Ogilvy, *The Emergent Paradigm: Changing Patterns of Thought and Belief* (report issued by the Values and Lifestyles Program, April 1979), 32.

3. Norman Boucher, "Transforming the Corporation," *New Age Journal,* February 1985, 36-38.

4. Judith Viorst, *Necessary Losses* (New York: Simon & Schuster, 1986).

5. For a full treatise on this viewpoint, see the work of any of the major existentialists, such as Camus or Sartre.

6. Joseph Chilton Pearce, *Exploring the Crack in the Cosmic Egg* (New York: Julian, 1974).

7. David Bohm, *Wholeness and the Implicate Order* (Boston: Ark, 1983), 21.

8. *Denver Post,* August 23, 1988, 6c.

9. Thomas J. Peters and Robert H. Waterman, Jr., *In Search of Excellence: Lessons From America's Best-Run Companies* (New York: Harper & Row, 1982); Thomas J. Peters and Nancy K. Austin, *The Passion for Excellence: The Leadership Difference* (New York: Random House, 1985).

10. Bohm, *Wholeness and the Implicate Order,* 1.

11. Ibid., 1-2.

12. These quotes come from the back cover of James Gleick, *Chaos: Making a New Science* (New York: Penguin, 1987).

13. Deepak Chopra, *Unconditional Life: Mastering the Forces That Shape Personal Reality* (New York: Bantam, 1991).

14. See Bohm, *Wholeness and the Implicate Order,* especially chap. 6.

15. Lawrence Blair, *Rhythms of Vision: Changing Patterns of Belief* (New York: Schocken, 1975), 70-71.

16. See Carlos Castañeda, *A Separate Reality* (New York: Bantam, 1972), and any other of Castañeda's books.

17. See, for example, Richard Heinberg, *Memories and Visions of Paradise* (Los Angeles: Jeremy Tarcher, 1989).

18. Joseph Campbell, *The Power of Myth* (New York: Random House, 1988).

19. Heinberg, *Memories and Visions.*

20. Robert Heilbroner, *Inquiry Into the Human Prospect, Updated and Reconsidered for the Nineteen Nineties* (New York: Norton, 1991); Alvin Toffler, *The Third Wave* (New York: Simon & Schuster, 1982); Willis Harman, *An Incomplete Guide to the Future* (San Francisco: San Francisco Book, 1976); Bohm, *Wholeness and the Implicate Order;* Fritjof Capra, *The Turning Point* (New York: Bantam, 1984); Rupert Sheldrake, *The New Science of Life: The Hypothesis of Formative Causation* (Los Angeles: Jeremy Tarcher, 1988).

21. Joel Barker, *Discovering the Future: The Business of Paradigms* (2nd ed.), videotape (Burnsville, MN: Charthouse Learning Corporation, 1991).

22. Charles Hampden-Turner, *Radical Man* (Cambridge, MA: Schenkman, 1970), especially chap. 1.

23. Willis W. Harman, "Consciousness Research and the 'Perennial Wisdom,'" *Institute of Noetic Sciences Newsletter* (Fall 1981): 5.

# 5    Creating the New-Paradigm Organization

*What's needed, in historian James MacGregor Burns' terms, is not the old style transactional leadership but a new transformational leadership. Transactional leaders were fine for the earlier era of expanding markets and nonexistent competition. In return for compliance, they issued rewards. . . . Transformational leadership is about change, innovation, and entrepreneurship. . . . We see corporate transformation as a drama that can be thought about in terms of a three-act play: Act I: Revitalization—Recognizing the Need for Change; Act II: Creating a New Vision; Act III: Institutionalizing Change.*

(Noel M. Tichy and Mary Anne Devanna,
*The Transformational Leader,* 1986, pp. viii-ix)

---

**SUMMARY:** As mentioned previously, the glue that integrates old-paradigm organizations is made up of hierarchy (formal authority), RRPP (formalization), job descriptions, and goals/objectives. What holds the new-paradigm organization together? As we shall explore in this chapter, it is a transcendent vision of the future, ownership of that vision by all employees, clear communications among employees, functional redundancy, and personal maturity.

---

## Bureaucracy:
## An Enforcer of Immaturity

---

Worker participation is a theme of both the matrix and the organic organization (Chapter 11). By its very definition, participative management requires employees to take a greater, more active role in running the company. It is logical therefore to assume that, before employees can effectively participate in the management function, they must have a sufficient level of maturity to accept the additional responsibility.

As we will discuss in Chapter 10, Douglas McGregor was the first to explore the relationship between management style and assumptions about worker maturity. Remember, if the collective agreement is that workers are lazy, irresponsible, and untrustworthy, the self-fulfilling prophecy will make it true. Organizational psychologist Eldon Mayo confirmed this when he developed his "rabble hypothesis."[1] This hypothesis is based on what Mayo believes is the underlying problem of American management—the fact that managers hold negative assumptions about their workers' human nature. Mayo found that managers view workers as being interested only in self-centered pursuits. In an earlier time, Frederick Taylor's *scientific management* assumed that workers are primarily occupied with satisfying their own physiological and safety needs.[2] Taylor saw workers as wanting to make as much money as possible with as little work as possible.

Mayo develops Taylor's assumption, saying that management organizes work on the basis of this belief. Thus work is typically organized on authoritarian, task-oriented principles. The resulting condition is one of what French sociologist Emile Durkheim calls *anomie*. Workers feel unimportant, confused, and unattached—in short, *victims* of their environment. Mayo's rabble hypothesis may be thought of as a vicious circle in which management induces what it seeks to prevent.

Influenced by Mayo, Douglas McGregor developed his "Theory X/ Theory Y" formulation. Theory X is consistent with the rabble hypothesis assumption about human nature. Managers who practice Theory X assumptions believe that workers are immature, irresponsible, and unreliable, so they respond by closely watching their employees and structuring their work with high formalization. McGregor believes that Theory X is an ineffective context from which to manage; his Theory Y reflects what he sees as more accurate assumptions about human nature. According to Theory Y, employees can be self-controlling—in other words, they can respond to internal rather than external control—if properly motivated by management with this assumption.

Organizational psychologist Chris Argyris notes that formal bureaucracies tend to treat people as children, reinforcing their feelings of insecurity and dependency.[3] He lists seven different changes individuals must go through in order to mature:

1. Infants go from a passive state to an adult active state.
2. Infants go from dependency on others to autonomy as adults.

3. Infants have a limited range of behaviors, whereas adults have a wide repertoire of behaviors for different situations.

4. Interests of infants are erratic, shallow, and casual, but those of adults are deeper and stronger.

5. An infant's time perspective is strictly the present, but an adult's perspective also includes the past and the future (we would argue that this alone is not necessarily a sign of increasing maturity).

6. Infants are subordinate to adults; adults are equal or superior to other adults.

7. Infants are unaware of the self; adults are aware of and able to control the self.[4]

Argyris notes that culture and personality seem to inhibit the development of maturity. He observes that, whereas the tendency is to become more mature with chronological age despite these restraining factors, few people ever develop to full maturity.

## Leader Behavior and Follower Maturity

Paul Hersey and Kenneth H. Blanchard's "life-cycle" theory describes the primary situational variable for effective leadership as *follower maturity*. These authors define follower maturity as an employee's being able and willing to take responsibility, having a high achievement motivation, and having task-relevant experience and education.[5] Followers must be at a sufficient level of maturity with respect to a given task; for example, a nurse might be highly mature with respect to patient care but very lax in administrative matters, showing low maturity in that area.

Hersey and Blanchard's Situational Leadership Grid provides insight into the relation between leader behavior and follower maturity. On the dimensions of task behavior and relationship behavior, the grid provides a guide as to how to adjust leader behavior in response to differing employee maturity levels. The four leadership styles are as follows:

- telling (S1)
- selling (S2)
- participating (S3)
- delegating (S4)

There are also four levels of follower maturity:

**Table 5.1**  Leadership Styles Appropriate for Differing Maturity Levels

| Maturity Level | Appropriate Style |
| --- | --- |
| M1 (low maturity): unable and unwilling or insecure | S1 (telling—directive, autocratic): high task and low relationship behavior[a] |
| M2 (low to moderate maturity): unable but willing or confident | S2 (selling—participative, directive): high task and high relationship |
| M3 (moderate to high maturity): able but unwilling or insecure | S3 (participating—participative, low on direction): high relationship and low task behavior |
| M4 (high maturity): able, competent and willing, confident | S4 (delegating—trusting the worker to get it done): low relationship and low task behavior |

a. *Task behavior* is defined as the leader focusing on the job or task completion itself in an autocratic way; *relationship behavior* is concerned with communications, self-esteem of workers, and cooperation among workers.

- low (M1)
- low to moderate (M2)
- moderate to high (M3)
- high (M4)

The relationships among leadership styles and levels of maturity are shown in Table 5.1.

The main point of this situational approach is that leader behavior can be *developmental*. The leader can play a role that helps the follower become empowered with more responsibility and, therefore, more maturity. The first author has recently developed another model that looks at a "developmental paradigm of leadership."[6] Obviously, this strikes at the core of what is needed for transformation into an organic structure. To have a flexible, responsive, adaptive structure, an organization needs workers who are self-directed, able to operate independently, and, of course, flexible and adaptive themselves.

## The Victim and Cause Perspectives

Theory X or S1 (telling) managerial attitudes produce dependent, powerless, security-oriented, and immature employees. Yet, as our world

**Figure 5.1.**  Playing Life From Effect

SOURCE: G. Michael Durst, *Napkin Notes: On the Art of Living* (Evanston, IL: Center for the Art of Living, 1982), vii. Reprinted with permission.

shrinks and global competition accelerates, a premium is now being placed on workers who are resourceful, intelligent, and proactive. Let us explore how this area relates to the concept of the paradigm.

It can be asserted that, at any time, a paradigmatic orientation is chosen between two mutually exclusive alternatives: the *victim* or *effect* perspective and the *cause* or *responsibility* perspective.[7] In the first alternative, the individual is willing to take responsibility for those outcomes that please him or her. In other words, if a person *likes* the outcome, then he or she is pleased to say, "I did it!" Getting a promotion or a raise is an outcome for which most people are happy to take responsibility. However, if an outcome is not pleasing—if the person *doesn't* like it—then the person looks for someone or some object or circumstance to blame for it.

Essentially, this means that if the outcome is judged "good," I'll take the responsibility (and the glory), but if the outcome is judged "bad," then I'll find someone to blame. This means I attribute the *cause* to myself if I like the outcome, and I attribute it to someone or something else if I don't. Convenient, eh? Obviously, the purpose of this strategy in an individual's paradigm is to prevent the person from having to *change* if ill results put in an appearance. If it is always someone else's fault, I don't have to change myself.

From the victim or effect perspective, it is never my fault; it was "the luck of the draw," "my boss (my spouse/someone) did it to me," or the like. This is a very popular orientation in the current paradigm, and is the cause of much of the "win-lose" political behavior one sees in bureaucratic settings, where "The computer department is doing it to us again!" or "Those people in sales have really screwed us now!" are common refrains.

People who proceed from a victim perspective are giving up their inherent power as creators in their circumstances. In essence, they are powerless in light of the circumstances or persons they are blaming for the results. They are "at the effect" of that circumstance. From the cause perspective, on the other hand, one assumes that one is 100% responsible for the circumstances that show up in one's world.

A key to understanding the cause perspective is an accurate definition of the word *responsibility.* In our industrial era paradigm, we equate responsibility with blame and fault ("It was your fault!"). This reflects victim thinking. The transformational definition of responsibility has three parts:

1. I am responsible for putting myself in a position to have the experience or circumstance.
2. I am responsible for my reaction to the experience or circumstance.
3. I am responsible for subconsciously or consciously attracting the circumstance to myself.[8]

This does *not* mean that I take other persons' responsibility from them. Each person in an "accident" is actually 100% responsible for creating it, but each individual can take responsibility only for him- or herself.

Let us examine each of these aspects of 100% responsibility in detail. The first supposition is fairly easy even for a victim-oriented person to accept; *Nobody but you put yourself in the position to have the experience.* Who else could have put you there? The second supposition, that you choose your reaction to a circumstance, is somewhat more difficult to accept. In other words, when you say, "She made me mad," that is not true. A more accurate statement would be, "She did [whatever] and I made myself mad because of it." Notice who caused the feeling of "mad." The third supposition is the most difficult for most people to accept; the idea that I *caused* my world to be the way it is flies in the face of everything we have been taught by our parents, teachers, and significant others. However, we have all known people whose lives are constantly in shambles; is that an "accident"? What about those people whose lives are a statement of victory—are they just "lucky"?

*Luck* and *accident* are words used within the victim or effect paradigm to deflect personal responsibility for the results produced. From the transformational perspective, we produce our worlds based on our existing values, attitudes, beliefs, assumptions, and expectations. If I operate from a core belief that "I am unlovable," I will subconsciously manipulate my circumstances to prove it (in order to be "right" about myself). A key transformational principle is this: In the egocentric state of human consciousness, the mind always strives to be "right" (which means it tries to manifest its belief systems). Werner Erhard, founder of Transformational Technologies, has noted that most people would rather be right than fully alive![9]

The cause orientation is another way of saying that one gets what one intends to have in one's world. If I take responsibility for the results I produce, I am willing to change; if it is always "someone else's fault," I will never change. After all, "they" did it to me! Personal growth and personal maturity, then, are dependent on one's willingness to accept responsibility for one's world.

Students of psychology will recognize that the cause perspective is similar (but not identical) to the concept of *internal locus of control* or *inner-directedness*, whereas the victim perspective is similar to *external locus of control* and *other-directedness*. The victim is always looking for scapegoats to blame for unpleasant circumstances!

## The Games Colleagues Play

Another group phenomenon that leads to reduced effectiveness concerns the relationship of the group members to their leader. It is the nature of such relationships (in the industrial paradigm) that members of the group have ambivalent feelings—both positive and negative—toward the authority figure. The negative feelings can be particularly disturbing, because it is hard to express such feelings directly, for fear of jeopardizing jobs or because of a sense that it is not right to attack an authority figure.

Because the hostility for the leader must be expressed, it is often transferred to another member of the group. Some other member, usually one with characteristics similar to those of the leader, will be attacked more than would realistically be expected for his or her behavior. This is called *transference*. It is also called *scapegoating*. It is not okay to attack your boss, but it is fine to go after another group member and make that person the victim. Here is the origin of political infighting in organizations.

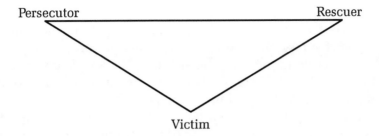

**Figure 5.2.** The Drama Triangle

SOURCE: From Muriel James, "Game Roles and the Drama Triangle," in *The OK Boss* (Menlo Park, CA: Addision-Wesley, 1976). See also James, "Psychological Games at Work," in *The Better Boss in Multicultural Organizations* (1993). Also cited in G. Michael Durst, *Napkin Notes: On the Art of Living* (Evanston, IL: Center for the Art of Living, 1982), vii.

Obviously, the victim or effect orientation is vastly more widespread in our world than is the cause orientation. Through blame, accusation, criticism, justification, and the like, we attempt to place the responsibility for our worlds outside ourselves. In fact, in the typical effect-oriented dramas we tend to play with each other, we choose one of three roles:

- victim ("They did it to me.")
- rescuer ("There, there, let me help you.")
- persecutor ("Why are you so stupid?")

Figure 5.2 depicts the "drama triangle" in operation.[10]

Based on the conceptual framework of transactional analysis, popularized by the late Eric Berne in 1964 in *Games People Play,* the following scenarios depict the triangle in operation:

When people play games, they start out in one of the three roles, and then switch to one of the other two. A subordinate playing "I'm only trying to help you!" may act as a rescuer to a boss, but, then, if help is refused, may switch to a victim and inwardly complain "I do all the work, but the boss gets all the glory." Or playing the game of "Uproar," a boss, acting as a persecutor, may bawl out an employee, then feeling victimized for exploding, may complain "whatever I try to do turns out wrong." Or a co-worker may start off in a victim position by asking for help in the "Poor Me" game, then rejecting the help that is offered by turning persecutor ("stop telling me what to do all the time.")

People who feel like victims often seek others who will act as persecutors and give them a psychological kick. They are not aware of doing this and may, in fact, complain to themselves or others "why does this always happen to me?" Or victims may seek rescuers to help them out, over and over again. After a number of instances in which the rescuer makes the victim feel good, the rescuer may begin to feel like a victim.[11]

None of these players in the drama triangle is willing to take personal responsibility for his or her role in it; the poor victim is having it done to him or her, the rescuer justifies his or her discomfort and/or projection by helping the victim, and the persecutor justifies his or her anger or projection as being "their fault." No one is being honest. The only way out of a life of drama is by taking responsibility.

Not surprisingly, the culture of a typical bureaucracy supports and sustains drama. It is easy to cite numerous examples of win-lose political games, instances of CYA, sabotage, theft, and so on, all in the name of one of these three roles. The industrial era paradigm tends to have the orientation of drama, and the structure and process of the organization reflects that.

Notice that many bureaucratic organizations have elaborate accountability systems designed to fix blame when things go wrong. Notice the incidence of conflict over *jurisdictional ambiguity* in bureaucratic structures; this is an example of structural conflict. Notice how important rules and regulations are for trying to fix blame. Notice how political reprisals and other counterproductive organizational processes are the result of drama orientations.

## Cycles of Maturity: The Transformational Perspective

The transformational perspective holds that there are *cycles of maturity* that a person can choose to pass through.[12] Holistic health practitioner Bill Bahan states:

> The most wonderful part about experiencing maturity is that it is something that already is. Human beings are in fact mature. Unfortunately, they have been identified with that which is immature. Now, in order to experience this maturity . . . we need to initially recognize that we are in a very sad, sad state of immaturity. Actually, the greatest need in the world today is for men and women that are mature.[13]

How can we be, as Bahan says, already mature and also in a sad, sad state of immaturity? The key to understanding this statement is Bahan's assertion that "we have been identified with that which is immature." The transformational assumption is that our true identity is with life, the whole, the creator (however you want to phrase it). Life is mature; it knows exactly what it is doing. Life never is a "victim." However, human beings, in all the previous paradigms, have assumed that our identity was with the separate, isolated ego-self. In other words, we have assumed that we were small, helpless, self-centered victims. But that is not who we really are! So the key to maturity is to identify with that which is already mature. The proper orientation in life or the whole brings automatic maturity.

Now, in the course of human growth, we naturally move from a state of dependency (the effect state) to a state of maturity or true adulthood. This is the way it *should* go. However, somewhere on the way from physical childhood to adolescence, we begin to adopt the prevailing view of reality, which holds that we are subject to being manipulated by the external world. Our parents and our peers all assume that life is hard, that one must struggle in a self-centered posture to get what one needs, and so on. We come to believe that we must arrange our external circumstances in order to get satisfaction. So we become misaligned. The further we go along this path of egocentrism, the more we become convinced of the validity of the effect view. Hence the cycles of maturity become aborted and we end up with a narrow, limited identity full of insecurities and fears.

The transformational view, then, is to identify with the whole, with life. Try Exercise 1.

---

EXERCISE 1. Imagine that you are part of a great baseball team, a pennant-winning team. You probably feel pretty powerful. Now see yourself as separate from your teammates—separate, isolated, and alone. Where did the feeling of power go? Now, take this to the other end of the spectrum. Imagine the galaxies, the stars, and beyond. Imagine that you are connected to the power that moves the galaxies. Can you feel small and insecure with such an orientation? Now, imagine that you are separate from all that is. You are alone in a seemingly hostile universe with only your mind and body and emotions to help you survive. Doesn't that make you feel helpless? From that identity, "luck" and "accidents" seem to play a large role.

Who, in reality, are you? What is the nature of your true or core identity? Personal responsibility and maturity are natural attributes of the true identity. You don't have to try to be mature from that perspective; life is mature. Practice adopting the true identity. See how often you slip back into self-limiting assumptions about yourself. Notice how well you have been convinced that your ego identity was your true identity.

We have all been told that we have to "be something" when we grow up. The not-so-subtle implication is that we are nothing without an education, job, or status. Most of us buy into that belief. But is it true?

---
## Transformational Leadership Skills
---

To succeed in organic forms, management needs a "new state of mind" or a shift in the *way* it thinks, as contrasted to *what* it thinks, says Perry Pascarella, a transformational consultant.[14] He advocates "contextual management," a breaking through of personal and organizational limits (the idea being that limits are self-created). Contextual management views the organization from the outside, examining the whole context into which the organization fits. In other words, the transformational approach is to see the organization as part of a larger, organic whole, with a specific role to play in that whole. In contrast, the traditional view sees the organization from the inside as a separate entity being "boxed in" by external constraints.

In this new mind-set, the role of the manager is to provide *a clear intention* so that a *shared vision* might be created for the organization. A vision of the whole (in this case, the whole organization) provides the organizing principle for the parts (the departments, groups, teams, and so on). The manager also must engender purpose, empowerment, and spirit.

### Vision and Intention

A clearly communicated vision can be much more powerful than a sophisticated, detailed strategic plan.[15] President Ronald Reagan did this with his conservative vision for the United States. Organizational consultants James Collins and Jerry Porras state: "A true visionary is someone who recognizes a need or opportunity and, regardless of conventional wisdom and skeptics, does something about it. Vision isn't forecasting the future; it is creating the future by taking actions in the present."[16] When he founded Apple Computer, Steve Jobs had a vision:

> We designed our first computer because we couldn't afford to buy one. We didn't have the whole idea about building a computer company until we built our first computer, and saw how neat it was for us and our friends. As the people it was neat for expanded, we got more excited. We didn't sit in a chair one day and think, "My God, ten years from now everyone is going to be using personal computers!" It didn't happen that way. It was more of a gradual process.[17]

A vision is an evolving image of possibility; as it becomes clearer to the visionary, that person invests more and more of his or her *intention* to manifest the vision. Then, using the law of attraction mentioned earlier (we tend to attract to ourselves that which is consistent with our dominant beliefs and assumptions), the vision comes into form.

Ideally, this vision comes from an accurate understanding of and alignment with the movement and change of the larger whole. As cocreators, if we are aligned about what it is we are to create collectively, it stands to reason that the collective creation will be stronger than would manifest from an attitude of "every man for himself."

Ben Cohen and Jerry Greenfield of Ben & Jerry's Homemade Inc. have clearly articulated a vision: producing a wholesome product, providing enriching and empowering work for their workers, and adding something to the larger context through their charitable endeavors. Their original 5:1 rule (that no manager could earn more than five times the pay of the lowest-level worker) supported this vision, and produced a flat structure with minimal status differential. In recent years the ratio of management pay to lowest-level worker pay has undergone some adjustment, but the structure of Ben & Jerry's is still a reflection of its founders' vision.

## Purpose

An organization's purpose answers the question, Why is the company in business? Purpose, it is found, needs to inspire the employees; "15% return on investment" just doesn't do it. Apple Computer's original vision ("to create a personal computer that will transform the world") was a bold, inspiring, even transcendent purpose.

Purpose itself is not a goal; it is a context for goals. It is a broad framework within which goals can be reached. It is a direction or context; one does not *achieve* purpose. Collins and Porras state:

> A guiding overall aim, when clear and shared, is so powerful that it can even form the backbone of motivation for an entire country. Writing about Israel in 1967, Barbara Tuchman remarked: "With all its problems, Israel has one commanding advantage, a sense of purpose . . . to survive. Israelis may not have affluence or television, or enough water, or the quiet life. But they have what affluence tends to smother; a motive."[18]

They add:

> Leaders are most effective when they translate a broad and enduring purpose into a specific, gut-grabbing mission (or set of goals) that people can sink their teeth into. A focal point of effort will help keep people moving in the same direction without losing sight of where they are headed. Producing the Macintosh is another example of purpose translated into mission.[19]

Purpose also needs to fit into the larger picture. If the purpose of the organization doesn't blend with the needs of the larger whole (in this case, the society), the organization might go out of business. A transcendent purpose is the integrator, the glue that can bind the efforts of a divergent group of essentially self-preoccupied people into a coherent whole.

The purpose of Ben & Jerry's is to demonstrate the viability of new-paradigm thought in an organizational context. The organization communicates this with company picnics, softball games, teamwork, caring management, and other inclusive management techniques.

## Empowerment

Empowerment is the art of giving employees an opportunity to commit to something (a transcendent purpose) that provides an opportunity for personal growth. The key is the release of potential; a manager in this context is seen as a facilitator, a developer of people (rather than a controller or dictator, as in the industrial paradigm).[20] Richard Walton observes:

> Only lately have [managers] begun to see that workers respond best—and most creatively—not when they are tightly controlled by management, placed in narrowly defined jobs, and treated like an unwelcome necessity, but, instead, when they are given broader responsibilities, encouraged to contribute, and helped to take satisfaction in their work.[21]

General Mills in Lodi, California, stresses the empowerment of its employees through self-directed work teams. These teams carry out many of the traditional management functions, such as hiring, firing, training, and evaluating each other.

## Spirit

The last, but, in some ways, most critical component of transformational leadership is the acknowledgment and use of spirit. Harrison Owen writes:

> In 1988, Shell Canada took out a full page ad in the Winter Olympics program which was headlined "Sustaining the Spirit." It went on to say "Our business is finding and developing the oil and gas. But the wealth of a community is made up of other resources as well. Amongst the greatest of these is the vitality of the human spirit." Shortly before, a Drexel Burnham ad, appearing in the *Wall Street Journal*, sought to explain the value of their "junk bonds" in terms of providing capital for new, growing

firms. The ad said, "But often a growing company has something a top-rated company doesn't. The kind of energy and spirit that can move mountains." Strange words in strange places.[22]

The word *spirit* has a number of meanings in our language. It can refer to the sense of connection to the universe that a young child feels; to affiliation with a group, as in "school spirit"; to the type of feeling peace demonstrators in the 1960s felt when they marched in protest against the Vietnam War; to the purpose one feels in one's work; to a religious concept, as of a universal spirit; and so on. However, there is a practical way to look at spirit:

> What is common among all of the connotations of *spirit* is the sense of being a part of and being connected to something larger than oneself, i.e., a high school basketball team's victory or a political cause; doing work that is meaningful, that makes a contribution to the larger whole; experiencing the "divine" (however any of us understand that). It is in this sense of the term; the connection to something larger than self, e.g., to group or organization, to customers or suppliers, to local or world community, wherein lies an important pathway to transformation. Spirit is the connection and experiencing the connection.[23]

For our purposes in this volume, we define spirit as *the invisible essence that animates any form, the energy of the universal design and control as it comes to focus in any living form.* According to this definition, there is one spirit; it is animating everything, all the time. We, as humans, are unique differentiations of that one spirit, and our connection to that larger whole is through spirit. When we use the term *spirit,* we use it in this expansive way, not specifically to mean school spirit, company spirit, or the like, even though those uses have validity.

## Organizational Structure Will Mature— When We Do

We can conclude that, in order for matrix or even pure "organic" organizations to operate effectively, they need managers and workers of high maturity. Managers will have to empower their workers to discover their inherent maturity. In fact, it has been suggested that the appropriate role for new-paradigm managers is "manager as developer."[24] This, of course, is consistent with the life-cycle theory of leadership effectiveness, which argues for developing the maturity of subordinates through various leadership style changes.[25] Managers *should* develop employee

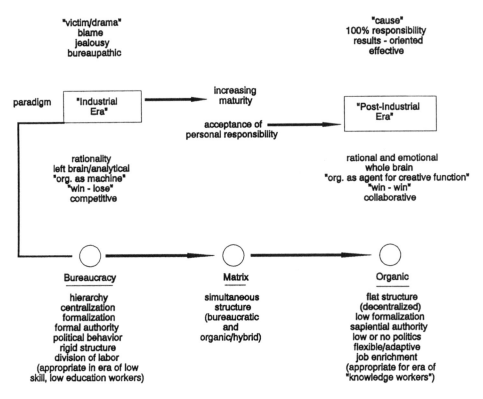

**Figure 5.3.**   The Changing Paradigm of Organization

maturity, not reinforce dependency and submissiveness. Also, new-paradigm leaders or managers will have to articulate a compelling vision or purpose for the organization that provides the glue to bind the work effort together.[26] This vision is provided in bureaucratic organizations through formal authority relationships, formalization, goals, and organizational objectives.

Let us summarize the development of organization structure (and its causes) with the aid of Figure 5.3. Notice, on the left side of the figure, the industrial era paradigm and its product, the formalized, centralized bureaucracy. The paradigmatic orientation is primarily "victim/drama" and the style of thinking is linear/sequential, emphasizing logic, rational thought, and analysis. The notion is that the organization is a well-oiled machine in which, ideally, people compete in a win-lose fashion to rise up the hierarchy—an organizational form suitable in an era of low-skill, uneducated workers and for production methods that emphasized large quantities of mass-produced items for consumption.

As the paradigm shift begins to gain momentum, one would expect new organizational forms to emerge. The first of these is the simultaneous structure called the *matrix*. With increasingly mature workers, such a flexible form can work, but, initially, with a predominance of security-oriented, "hygiene-seeking" bureaucratic workers, there will be resistance to the change.

As workers begin to be comfortable with increasing responsibility and the hierarchy begins to flatten as a result, some organic attributes will begin to put in an appearance. In fully organic organizations, everything will be the opposite of the bureaucratic form. Workers will be responsible, managers will be developers, win-win solutions will be sought for conflict resolution, and a collaborative atmosphere will prevail, maintained by a compelling vision or corporate purpose. Results, not excuses or justifications, will be the focus. The organization will serve to empower workers to reach their creative potential. All will be encouraged to develop their whole-brain capabilities.

Lest this sound like nirvana, we hasten to reiterate the primary requirement: personal maturity, the willingness to operate from cause rather than effect. Without mature managers and workers, the shift will not occur. A natural consequence of worker maturity is clear, consistent sharing of relevant information with others (good communications).

A second element must also be present for the organic form to work: There must be a shift from self-centeredness to whole-centeredness. This is no small order. Since the dawn of recorded human history, people have been self-centered, seeing themselves as separate from the whole and trying to manipulate circumstances to maximize their benefit. It seems impossible for people to be otherwise. Yet we seem to have run up against the limits of self-centered behavior. It is hard to imagine the human race surviving for another 50 years ruled by greed, fear, and "every man for himself."

What do we mean by *whole-centeredness?* We mean the conscious recognition that we are part of a larger whole (as Bohm, Senge, and others have stated) and that our actions have an impact on the whole. People operating from a context of separateness (self-centeredness) will not see themselves as connected to the larger whole and, therefore, to others. Taken in an organizational context, the organic form will work only if people see the mission of the larger whole (in this case, the organization) as being *their* mission. Another dimension of whole-centeredness is what Gareth Morgan calls "functional redundancy."[27] This means that, instead of the functional specialization so common in machinelike bureaucracies, each person is able to do *several* jobs, thereby increasing organizational flexibility.

This is what is meant by *psychological ownership* of purpose or vision. From the transformational perspective, the organization is part of a larger whole (the environment), and the individuals in it are part of the organizational whole. Acting out of a concern for the whole produces effectiveness; acting out of self-centered desires produces chaos. This is the fundamental shift that must take place if we are to move into organic forms in any large way.

---

## Challenges Along the Way
## to the Organic Form

---

The history of organic organizations to date is that they work well when they are small. As such organizations grow, they get to the point where they must hire people who are not committed to the larger mission and are there just for the paycheck. When this happens, the bureaucracy is just a step away.

Ben & Jerry's is going through such times right now. As mentioned earlier, the company originally had a policy that no one could make more than five times the salary of the lowest-paid worker. As the company grew, this policy was questioned by some of the managers. At least one flatly rejected it, saying, "I, for one, am materialistic. I'm also a career person. I'm an expert at what I do. I've been trained for years and years. I don't think a five to one ratio recognizes that."

Where is this man's identity? Who does he see himself as being? Clearly, from the industrial paradigm perspective, this transformational concept of quasi-parity is totally incomprehensible! Managers in the company feel that the company must grow to survive and fulfill its obligations. But Ben and Jerry are committed to maintaining the value system that was the core of their company's original culture.

Communication within the company is becoming another problem. In the early days, everyone was in on all decisions. Now, more and more people are feeling left out. The board has agreed to handle this by developing its internal organization so that participation can be maintained.[28] The board is striving to keep all workers abreast of what the company is doing, to allow them to keep participating in decisions that affect them.

Apple Computer is another example of a company that has shed its organic form. When it was small and had people committed to its mission, it was flexible, innovative, and effective. However, as it grew, it had to hire people who did not share the vision, and in that growth lay the seeds of bureaucracy.

How can a company grow and still maintain an organic form? Apparently, we have not progressed far enough in the paradigm shift to be able to produce a large organic organization. What will it take? Clearly, the key ingredient is a nucleus of truly mature, cause-oriented individuals aligned with a purpose greater than themselves. With self-centeredness pushed to the background and a perspective of transcendent purpose (one of service to the whole), the organization can theoretically remain organic in form, and its effectiveness, flexibility, and resilience can continue unabated.

## NOTES

1. Eldon Mayo, *The Human Problems of Industrial Civilization* (New York: Macmillan, 1933).

2. Frederick Taylor, *The Principles of Scientific Management* (New York: Harper & Brothers, 1911).

3. Chris Argyris, *Integrating the Individual and the Organization* (New York: John Wiley, 1964), 34.

4. See Chris Argyris, *Interpersonal Competence and Organizational Effectiveness* (Homewood, IL: Irwin, 1962); Argyris, *Integrating the Individual*, 37.

5. Paul Hersey and Kenneth H. Blanchard, *Management of Organizational Behavior* (2nd ed.) (Englewood Cliffs, NJ: Prentice Hall, 1972), 134.

6. David K. Banner and John W. Blasingame, "Towards a Developmental Paradigm of Leadership," *Leadership and Organizational Development Journal* 9, no. 4 (1988).

7. G. Michael Durst, *Management by Responsibility* (Evanston, IL: Center for the Art of the Living, 1982).

8. Ibid.

9. Norman Bodek, "Werner Erhard on Transformation and Productivity: An Interview," *Revision* 7 (Winter/Spring, 1985).

10. Muriel James, *The OK Boss* (Menlo Park, CA: Addison-Wesley, 1976).

11. G. Michael Durst, *Napkin Notes: On the Art of Living* (Evanston, IL: Center for the Art of Living, 1982); see also Eric Berne, *Games People Play* (New York: Ballantine, 1985 [1964]).

12. William Bahan, "Cycles of Maturity," in *Spirit of Sunrise*, ed. Emissaries of Divine Light (Loveland, CO: Emissary Foundation International, 1978), 178-192.

13. Ibid., 178.

14. Perry Pascarella, "Can Management Break Out of Its Box?" *Industry Week*, June 13, 1983.

15. Warren Bennis, "The Four Traits of Leadership," *Educational Network News* 3, no. 3 (1984): 1-3. This article was subsequently published in book form: Warren Bennis and Burt Nanus, *Leaders: The Strategies of Taking Charge* (New York: HarperCollins, 1985).

16. James C. Collins and Jerry I. Porras, "Making Impossible Dreams Come True," *Stanford Business School Magazine*, July 1989, 17.

17. Ibid., 16.

18. Ibid., 14.

19. Ibid.

20. Stanley M. Davis, "The Curious Case of the Missing Management Model," *The Review*, January/February 1982.

21. Richard E. Walton, "From Control to Commitment in the Workplace," *Harvard Business Review* (March/April 1985), 77.

22. Harrison Owen, "Spirit at Work," *OD Practitioner* 21 (June 1989): 1.

23. Mary V. Gelinas, "Spirit and Transformation: What Do We Mean Really?" *OD Practitioner* 21 (June 1989): 6.

24. David L. Bradford and Allan R. Cohen, *Managing for Excellence* (New York: John Wiley, 1984).

25. Hersey and Blanchard, *Management of Organizational Behavior.*

26. John D. Adams, ed., *Transforming Leadership: From Vision to Results* (Alexandria, VA: Miles River, 1986).

27. Gareth Morgan, *Images of Organization* (Beverly Hills, CA: Sage, 1986), 99.

28. Erik Larson, "Forever Young," *Inc.*, July 1988, 50-62.

# 6  Systems Thinking
# in Organization Theory

*Systems thinking is a discipline for seeing wholes. It is a framework for seeing interrelationships rather than things, for seeing pattern of change rather than static "snapshots." It is a set of general principles—distilled over the course of the twentieth century, spanning fields as diverse as the physical and social sciences, engineering and management. It is also a specific set of tools and techniques. . . . during the last thirty years, these tools have been applied to understand a wide range of corporate, urban, regional, economic, political, ecological, and even physiological systems. And systems thinking is a sensibility for the subtle interconnectedness that gives living systems their unique character.*
(Peter M. Senge, *The Fifth Discipline*, 1990, pp. 68-69)

---

**SUMMARY:** In this chapter, we see how the organization can be seen as an open system, affecting (and affected by) its external environment. We then move to what has been called "postcontingency" (or transformational) theory and investigate its startling implications for the organization-environment interface.

---

**W**e are now going to look at how transformational ideas have been permeating organizational theory. A good place to start is with systems theory. Taken from engineering and the "hard" sciences, systems theory asserts that the parts of a whole interact with each other *and* with the larger world external to the whole.

## The Organization as an Open System

The core transformational assumption that the universe is a seamless, unbroken whole and everything is related to everything else has not gone unnoticed even in the industrial era paradigm. In organization theory, much work has been done in the field of systems theory, especially as it concerns the organization's relation to its external environment.

What is an organizational system? Organizations essentially take a set of inputs—people, money, raw materials, plant and equipment—and, through a series of processes internal to the organization, transform these inputs into various outputs—finished goods, job satisfaction for the workers (one hopes), profits, and so on. In simple terms, this describes a *closed system*. A more technical definition follows:

> All social systems, including organizations, consist of the patterned activities of a number of individuals. Moreover, these patterned activities are complementary or interdependent with respect to some common output; they are repeated, relatively enduring, and bounded in space and time. If the activity pattern occurs only once or at unpredictable intervals, we could not speak of an organization. The stability or recurrence of activities can be examined in relation to the *energic input* into the system, the *transformation of energies within the system,* and the *resulting product or energic output.*[1]

Putting it another way, closed systems are complete unto themselves; they take inputs and, through some conversion process, convert them into outputs. The conversion process itself is usually composed of the interaction of parts or subsystems, which are themselves subsystems within larger systems (there can be several levels of subsystems). From an organizational perspective, this would all take place within the organization's *boundary.*

However, it is easy to see that organizations are affected by a variety of structures and organizations external to themselves, such as the government, consumer groups, unions, and the legal environment. A truly closed system receives no energy or influence from any outside source and releases no energy into its surroundings. A thermostat is a good example: It activates and deactivates air temperature controls based on the room temperature, without exchanging any energy with an outside environment except for the energy to power the thermostat.

Obviously, the closed system model does not accurately explain organizational reality. Organizations are affected by their environments,

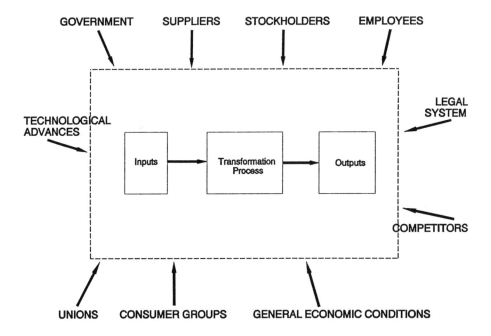

**Figure 6.1.**   The Nature of an Open System

and, in turn, affect their environments. The *open system* model reflects the dynamic interaction of the organizational system with various aspects or systems in the external environment.

## Influence of the External Environment

Organizations generally obtain their raw materials and human resources from the external environment. They also depend on clients or customers from the external environment to absorb their output. Most organizations want to make good impressions on certain aspects of their external environments (public relations) and to influence certain other organizations (sales and purchasing). Some organizations even have professional "flak catchers" whose job it is to take the "heat" from other organizations. These are vital *boundary roles* related to the adaptation of the organization in a rapidly changing world.

Many companies seem to operate as if they were closed systems in an open systems reality. This can lead to their premature demise. For example, at one time it appeared as if General Motors assumed that

# IF EVERYTHING
# IS PART OF A WHOLE,

## WHAT IS
## THE WHOLE
## PART OF ?

Ashleigh
Brilliant

people would buy whatever GM produced. And for many years that was true. But the effects of changing consumer tastes, militant stockholders, and government regulations, and the dramatic impact of foreign competition, have changed all that.

In fact, GM has always been an open system; it brought in capital and raw materials from an external environment, made cars, and sold them to consumers in the environment. During that time, it employed market researchers, advertising agencies, a sales force, and auditors, all to better deal with the external environment. Still, 1973 and the Arab oil embargo seemed to catch it off guard. GM is now more responsive to and interactive with its external environment. Even so, in early 1992, GM announced massive layoffs as sales languished.[2]

IBM, despite its vaunted customer-service orientation, has followed a similar course. The recent huge successes of foreign-made "clones" of IBM personal computers have awakened the manufacturer to the reality of an intensely competitive environment. IBM has finally begun to take aggressive steps to reverse its slide from industry dominance, but the company's recent economic performance, like that of GM, shows that it still has a way to go before it is fully responsive to its environment.

Monitoring the external environment for threats and opportunities has become a necessity for large corporations, as changes in technology, competition, and consumer tastes have become very rapid in recent years. The turbulent markets in which these corporations operate are characterized by high rates of change and high levels of instability, a combination that makes for uncertain forecasting and planning activities.

---

**Vignette 1**

Prior to 1973, Winnebago, a company known for recreational vehicles, was very successful, benefiting from increased middle-class disposable income and rising interest in outdoor recreation. Then the Arab oil embargo hit the United States and, within six months, Winnebago was near bankruptcy; sales lots were full of gas-hungry vehicles that suddenly couldn't be sold.

During the height of the first video game craze, the video game company Atari was flying high, increasing inventories and planning for a bright future. Suddenly, the craze was over and Atari found itself in serious financial difficulty, with warehouses full of unsold game cartridges.

---

Organizations depend on a wide range of external systems and structures for support and sustenance. The *systems approach* builds on the principle that organizations are open to their environments and must achieve appropriate relationships with those environments in order to survive. This is called the *institutional/adaptive* function of the organization, and it is performed primarily by boundary role incumbents such as forecasters, salespeople, and public relations experts.

The organization must develop a creative and mutually rewarding relationship with elements in its *task environment,* such as customers, suppliers, competitors, labor unions, and government regulators, as well as the broader *contextual* or *general environment.* All this has important implications for organizational practice, stressing the importance of the following:

- the ability to scan and sense changes in task and general environments
- the ability to bridge and manage critical boundaries and areas of interdependence
- the ability to develop appropriate strategic responses

Much of the widespread interest in corporate strategy is a product of this realization that organizations must be sensitive to what is occurring in the world beyond.[3]

---

## Elements of the Contingency
## (or Systems) Perspective

---

The open systems perspective has been fully developed by Katz and Kahn, among others. They suggest several common characteristics shared by all open systems:

- energy
- throughput
- output
- homeostasis
- entropy/negative entropy
- requisite variety
- equifinality
- system evolution

Let's look at each of these.

*Energy.* New supplies of energy, called *inputs,* are brought into the system by organizations in the general environment; this energy is in the form of new people and materials.

*Throughput.* This is the work that is done in the system and its subsystems; the inputs are altered in some way as the materials are processed and/or clients receive services (also called the conversion process).

*Output.* Whatever emerges from the processes of throughput is used or consumed by elements in the environment.

*Homeostasis.* This concept refers to the ability of systems to be self-regulating and stable. Homeostatic processes that perform this function are called *negative feedback.* Action is then taken to correct any deviation from what is considered desirable.

*Entropy/negative entropy.* Closed systems suffer from entropy, or the natural tendency for systems to run down. Open systems, on the other hand, maintain themselves by importing energy from their external environments to try to offset entropic effects. This is negative entropy.

*Requisite variety.* This principle states that the internal regulatory mechanisms of a system must be at least as diverse and complex as the environment in which it operates. Lawrence and Lorsch's concept of *differentiation* (the increased complexity of an organization in terms of specialization of function) is related to requisite variety. When an organization begins to grow, it must differentiate and add specialists to its workforce (e.g., market researchers, lawyers, public relations people) to deal with problems and opportunities presented by an increasingly complex environmental context. Any system that fails to increase its complexity as the complexity of the environment increases tends to atrophy and fail.

*Equifinality.* This principle implies that there are many different paths to the same end (as the saying goes, There's more than one way to skin a cat!). This is true for open systems but not for closed systems. In closed systems, system relations are fixed in terms of structure to produce specific cause-effect chains. For example, in an open system one can market a product effectively using a mix of strategies such as direct marketing, retail, and multilevel marketing.

*System evolution.* The capacity of a system to evolve, that is, to change and adapt to new circumstances, depends on its ability to move to new levels of differentiation and integration. This evolutionary process enables the system to meet the challenges posed by an increasingly complex and turbulent environment.[4]

Because all organizations are open systems, much of their nature can be captured by this theoretical perspective. The increasing popularity of this view of organizations is reflected by the increasing orientation of chief executive officers of companies to their external environments. It has been estimated that a CEO must spend up to 90% of his or her time on matters relating to the external environment in order to be considered effective.[5] This activity is doubly important in high-change, turbulent environments such as the computer and microelectronics fields. The timely adaptation of organizations to the ever-evolving opportunities and constraints in the environment will separate the organizations that succeed from the ones that don't.

This necessity for vigilance has ushered in a new perspective in organizational analysis: the *contingency* or *systems approach*. Under this theory, management must be concerned with achieving a "good fit" between the organization and its environment. Stated differently, there is no one "best" way of organizing; the appropriate organizational form depends on the nature and characteristics of the environment in which it is embedded.

Systems theory has brought organizational analysis a long way. Many CEOs and organizational consultants now routinely see organizations as embedded in the larger economic, political, and cultural context. This has brought an increased awareness of interconnectedness, inherent in the transformational perspective. However, as powerful as systems theory has been for organizational analysts, some are beginning to see its limitations.

---

## Postcontingency Theory

---

*Postcontingency theory* (another term for transformational thinking) has complemented contingency theory. As systems thinkers began to apply their skills to organizations, they became aware of the infinite complexity of the myriad interconnections among organizational subsystems and of the relationship of those subsystems to the external environment. Peter Senge, the director of MIT's Center for Organizational Learning, notes that this theoretical "messiness" has become a major issue in the field of organization theory:

> This messiness is probably the greatest single trap workers in systems dynamics fall into. If you look deeply into any system and the relationships between the members, you will find infinite complexity. There are *no boundaries,* which is one of the pitfalls of the systems approach. You don't run into it in other disciplines, because you define the boundaries *a priori.* Economics, sociology, ecology are strictly defined disciplines, although this is increasingly becoming a drawback as the world becomes more interrelated.
>
> The economist untrained in ecology may know nothing about natural resource problems. Yet, resource constraints can have a substantial impact on economic performance, as we have learned in recent years. You open up a Pandora's box when you say the world is an interconnected economic, sociological, cultural, ecological, spiritual system, and there are no inherent bounds.[6]

He goes on:

> To resolve this question of the unbounded quest (and the concomitant "messiness") in a systems approach to a problem, you have to start off by realizing that *there is no inherent end to a system.* Systems are inherently infinitely complex. . . . This is a problem that exists in all sciences—there is no such thing as a complete theory.[7]

Senge further indicates that businesspeople find it difficult to accept this complexity because of the industrial age bias that we should "know all" and our trust that the mind is capable of grasping all we need to know. Many businesspeople think they need to be in control at all times; they have been trained that way. The concept that everything is interconnected and that we are never going to grasp with our minds the complexities inherent in that interconnectedness is often frightening to such individuals. This preoccupation with prediction and control is one of the most dominant characteristics of the industrial era paradigm, and one of the hardest to shake.

Senge identifies an essential step in "debunking the hierarchical mentalities" that exist in most organizations: debunking the belief that managers need to know about and control all of which they are in charge. Despite evidence to the contrary, most people are deeply convinced that people "above" them know what is going on, thanks to years of conditioning by parents, bosses, teachers, and other authority figures. But a growing emphasis on *sapiential authority*—authority based in knowledge and expertise, rather than in formal position or roles—is beginning to change that.[8]

So systems or contingency theory has taken us to the edge of a new awareness—an awareness that everything is one big system with infinite, interconnected, interdependent subsystems. What we are now discovering is that managers need to *understand* systems theory, but they should resist the rational mind's instinctive desire to use it to predict and control organizational events. Organizational reality will not conform to any logical, systemic thought pattern. Deepak Chopra, Peter Senge, Fritjof Capra, and others are telling us that organizations are *patterns of energy,* operating within the pattern of the whole.

## Some Current Transformational Themes

As Newtonian assumptions have proven increasingly untenable, a window of opportunity has opened for transformational consultants to present to an increasingly receptive audience a new model of organizations and how they change.[9] The decline of many heavy industries in the Northeast and Midwest have led executives to examine their companies' adaptability and competitiveness in the marketplace.

Transformational or postcontingency theory is providing a new perspective on old problems, and this approach is being more widely entertained as the old paradigm continues to fail. Instead of being fixated on *forms* (e.g., hierarchy, centralization, formalization, com-

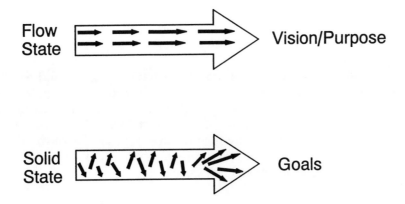

**Figure 6.2.** The Flow State and the Solid State

plexity), we begin to see an organization as a potentially fluid, creative entity that could encourage (or bring forth) the innate creativity of all its participants.

## The Organization as Energy Field

Linda Ackerman's approach derives from quantum mechanics and Eastern philosophy.[10] Ackerman views the organization as an "energy field." In this view, the organization's *purpose* is seen as the thing that directs the energy created by the "polarities" or competing forces within it. Ackerman has coined the term "flow-state manager" to describe the person who can orchestrate the competing forces into a coherent, synergistic whole. This person makes sure the energy does not become blocked and that everyone within the organization remains "charged" with purpose (see Figure 6.2).

Their less-flexible counterparts, with Newtonian-type assumptions, are called "solid-state managers"; they try to control through policies, procedures, formal structure, and authority. So the job of the flow-state manager is to articulate the vision/purpose of the organization and assist others in aligning with that vision; the solid-state counterpart attempts to control workers with rules, regulations, policies, and procedures. Martin Goldberg, another transformational consultant, echoes Ackerman's approach:

> My own sense is that the way energy functions in an organization results in what, for the most part, we call a system's culture. Chronically blocked systems, in which the spirit or driving energy remains trapped and cannot be effectively expressed, results in ineffective organizational functioning. I have come to understand my own practice as essentially a reversing of

this process by dissolving the blockages at the places where the system gets stuck and thereby allowing the work energy or spirit of the system to flow out freely.

Practically speaking, this means that I have sought to address the immediate concerns of clients in a way that also frees up their underlying *emotional energy dynamics* (the invisible level). In working sequentially from the surface to the depths of an intervention over time, I have consistently been impressed by how much energy is unleashed and by how this has moved clients to make lasting, systemic and aligned shifts in their functioning, structure and beliefs.[11]

## The Metanoic Organization

Peter Senge uses the term "metanoic," a word used by the early Christians to describe a "reawakening of intuition and personal responsibility" (Senge's words), to articulate a fundamentally new organizational model with five traits in common:

1. a clear vision or sense of purpose
2. "alignment" of employees around that purpose
3. a corporate culture that values individual growth ("empowering people")
4. decision-making and financial responsibility at the lowest level possible (structural integrity)
5. a balance of reason and intuition[12]

Practitioners of the transformational approach envision that getting organizations to work this way

> creates a whole new way of thinking, a new consciousness about influence, information, planning, decision-making and resource sharing. It breaks down divisional/departmental barriers as well as the barriers between an organization and the world outside it. The culture of the organization therefore becomes refreshed by the culture of the rest of the world.[13]

## Spirit

Science and spirituality are blending as the paradigm shifts; so are spirituality and organization. The Latin definition of *spiritus*, the root of *spirit*, is "breath." In the organizational context, spirituality breathes life into the organization. Harrison Owen, in his article "Leadership by Indirection," argues that, if we were to get "back to basics," we would see our organizations as "spirit and flow" and that leadership would be seen as the capacity to "focus spirit and enhance its power."[14] This perspective, of course, directly challenges the Newtonian assumptions behind traditional departmentalization and hierarchy.

Stan Davis, a UCLA-based management consultant, sees organizations as "potential energy, not static matter," and notes that a "manager who manages context doesn't have to tell people what to do, but creates the environment for people to manage themselves, and to be all they can be."[15] *Context* is defined as "the unquestioned assumptions through which all experience is filtered, the ground of being from which we derive the content of our reality, and that which determines the way we put things together in our minds."[16] How do managers manage the context? By articulating an inspiring vision, by "enrolling" others in it, and by being "cheerleaders" who urge people on to their fullest potential.

## Challenging Self-Limiting Beliefs

Perry Pascarella, a writer on leading-edge management topics, states that managers need to learn to break through self-imposed limits to their thinking.[17] The only way to break through these limits, according to this view, is to create a new level of awareness, a new perspective, "just as Roger Bannister did for himself and others when he broke the four minute mile barrier, which previously was seen as an unsurpassable human limit."[18] This is another way of saying that we can transcend the limits of self-limiting beliefs or self-fulfilling prophecies.

How does a leader help with this process? By challenging his or her own assumptions openly, by encouraging others to do the same, by allowing (even encouraging) experimentation and risk. In order to discover a new way, people must have the courage to break with the familiar and challenge the status quo; *they must be able to challenge their assumptions about how things are done.* Being able to surface and challenge existing assumptions and beliefs about reality is fast becoming an essential management tool.[19]

Having fully explored the basic transformational assumptions and theories, we now move our attention to the theoretical underpinning of and a full articulation of the metamodel.

## NOTES

1. Daniel Katz and Robert L. Kahn, "Organizations and the Systems Concept," in *Perspectives on Behavior in Organizations*, ed. J. R. Hackman, E. Lawler, and L. W. Porter (New York: McGraw-Hill, 1983), 98-99.

2. Alex Taylor III, "Can GM Remodel Itself?" *Fortune*, January 13, 1992, 26-34.

3. Gareth Morgan, *Images of Organization* (Beverly Hills, CA: Sage, 1986), 45.

4. Katz and Kahn, "Organizations and the Systems Concept," 98-99.

5. R. Alec Mackenzie, *The Time Trap* (New York: AMACOM, 1972), 130.

6. Quoted in Rachel Gaffney, "Systems Thinking in Business: Philosophy and Practice, an Interview With Peter Senge," *Revision* 7 (Winter/Spring 1985), 56-57; emphasis added.

7. Quoted in ibid., 57.

8. Robert Theobald, *An Alternative Future for America II* (Chicago: Swallow, 1970).

9. Norman Boucher, "Transforming the Corporation," *New Age Journal*, February 1985, 39.

10. Linda S. Ackerman, "The Flow State: A New View of Organizations and Managing," in *Transforming Work*, ed. John D. Adams (Alexandria, VA: Miles River, 1984), 114-137.

11. Martin Goldberg, "Hidden Within the Spirit," *OD Practitioner* 21 (June 1989): 8.

12. Charles F. Kiefer and Peter M. Senge, "Metanoic Organizations," in *Transforming Work*, ed. John Adams (Alexandria, VA: Miles River, 1984).

13. Boucher, "Transforming the Corporation," 43.

14. Harrison Owen, "Leadership by Indirection," in *Transforming Work*, ed. John Adams (Alexandria, VA: Miles River, 1984), 3; see also Owen's book, *Spirit: Transformation and Development in Organizations* (Potomac, MD: Abbott, 1987).

15. Stanley M. Davis, "The Curious Case of the Missing Management Model," *The Review*, January/February 1982, 11.

16. Ibid., 6.

17. Perry Pascarella, "Can Management Break Out of Its Box?" *Industry Week*, June 13, 1983.

18. Ibid., 1.

19. See, for example, Chris Argyris, *Overcoming Organizational Defenses* (Boston: Allyn & Bacon, 1990); Peter M. Senge, *The Fifth Discipline: The Art and Practice of the Learning Organization* (Garden City, NY: Doubleday, 1990).

# 7 The Metamodel of Organization

*The dominant reality directs relations within the firm by specifying the values, expectations, assumptions that people who make up the organization are supposed to hold. It also directs relations with people outside the firm by specifying the basic premises that under-lie the conduct of the organization's business.*

*It provides the guidelines for representing the organization's products and services, for identifying target customers and clients, for characterizing the organization's position in the marketplace and for deciding how products and services are to be marketed and promoted. . . . In short, the dominant reality provides order in what otherwise would be a highly idiosyncratic interplay of individual beliefs and actions and it provides the grounds for people to hold each other accountable.*

(Samuel A. Culbert and John J. McDonough,
*Radical Management*, 1985, p. 91)

**SUMMARY:** We now come to the core model of this book. The metamodel of organization is a model of organizational reality based on transformational assumptions. Many of the concepts we have presented up to this point are incorporated into the model, including the notions of cause and effect, personal responsibility (maturity), change first as an individual (and then a collective) process, and the mind (using paradigmatic assumptions and beliefs) as "shaper" of form.

The metamodel of the creation, maintenance, and change of organizations is a way to understand how any collective paradigm creates

89

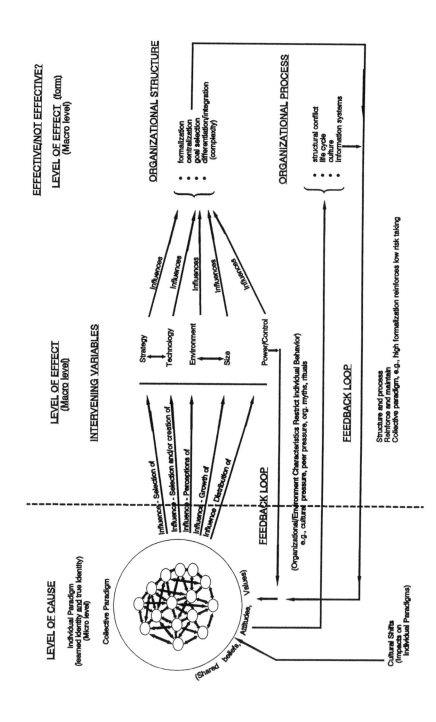

Figure 7.1. The Metamodel of Creating, Maintaining, and Changing Organizations

90

organizational reality. It is an open system. Data or input from sources outside the organization continually impinge on the primary causal variable (the collective paradigm). *All* types of organizations (from centralized bureaucratic to organic) are created as the model describes.

---

## The Metamodel:
## A Transformational Model of Organization

---

The model starts with an individual and his or her personal paradigm—beliefs, attitudes, and values concerning work, the organization, and role expectations/requirements. As individuals are grouped together in common purpose, their collection of personal paradigms serves to influence one another, depending on the power (personal and positional) of the persons involved and the readiness (maturity) of those who would be influenced. The result is the *collective paradigm,* a subset of which is called *corporate culture.*

What is present as shared beliefs, attitudes, and values leads to some basic assumptions and expectations about what should happen in the organization. From the standpoint of the organizational designer (typically, the leadership of the company), this shared paradigm leads to certain structural and process outcomes.[1] Table 7.1 lists some of the dominant beliefs that have led to the structural manifestations we call the centralized, formalized bureaucracy. These manifestations are the result of a certain mind-set or way of looking at reality. Professor Edgar Schein notes:

> The accomplishment of the organization's goals, even though they are directed towards the outside, requires the creation of a structure inside the group that makes that accomplishment possible. The kind of internal structure that evolves, the way in which roles, resources, and tasks are allocated, will ultimately reflect both the externally oriented intentions of the founders and the internal dynamics of the members.[2]

Thus the shared set of internal mental/emotional constructs is the primary causal variable in the creation and maintenance of structure. By *structure,* we mean several things:

- *formalization:* the degree to which rules, regulations, policies, and procedures (RRPP) constrain worker behavior
- *centralization:* the degree to which decision-making power is concentrated at the top of the organization

**Table 7.1**  Typical Bureaucratic Beliefs and Their Structural Effects

| Belief | Structural Manifestation |
| --- | --- |
| People need to be controlled so they can be "effective." | centralization; close supervision; formalization |
| People need a leader to tell them what to do. | centralization; hierarchy of authority |
| People are lazy/unmotivated. | close supervision; "carrot/stick" reward systems |
| People don't like change/they like security. | job definitions; procedures manuals; standardization; organization charts |
| People are motivated only by money. | "carrot/stick" systems of reward and punishment |
| People are stupid and slow to learn. | division of labor; job descriptions; standardizations |
| People can't be trusted to do the right thing organizationally. | formalization; close supervision; centralization |
| People are interchangeable. | machine bureaucracy |
| People are motivated to "get ahead." | hierarchy; meritocracy |
| Conflicts are "bad." | formal authority; formalization; appeals procedures |

- *complexity or differentiation:* the degree of horizontal, vertical, and spatial complexity in the organization, plus other structural attributes such as division of labor, job descriptions, organization charts, and spans of control
- *goals:* the ways in which the organization focuses on producing specific outcomes
- *integration:* the ways in which the organization seeks to coordinate and control the activities of its members

In addition, the collective paradigm creates and maintains the *process* elements of the organization, such as power/politics, conflict, culture, effectiveness, organization learning, and organizational life cycle. It also provides a context in which technology is selected, size is determined, and environmental factors are dealt with.

There is a feedback loop in the model. The organization structure itself will reinforce the existing dominant paradigmatic orientation. For example, if a person has been in a Theory X-created structure for some 20 years, that person may have given up hope (if he or she ever had any) of being included in decisions of personal importance. So, in effect, the existing structural configuration reinforces and maintains the collective paradigm that created it. The 20-year Theory X "veteran" may have become a fearful, non-risk taker concerned only with the paycheck. The structure and process thus create and help maintain this mind-set.

**Vignette 1**

The director of a health care clinic with 14 staff members wanted to institute innovation and hired a consultant to assist. The innovative approach included the freedom for staff to create policy and make decisions relative to their jobs/roles. Although this was generally accepted with enthusiasm, one staff member wanted nothing to do with "the whole picture," that is, the purpose of the clinic, or with having to make decisions. Her attitude was, "Just tell me what to do and I'll do it from 9 a.m. to 5 p.m." Because the dominant paradigm has supported this kind of attitude for so long, it is not surprising to find it in workers.

This concept manifests in organizations in a number of ways. If a dominant belief among corporate managers is that "my employees are basically stupid and/or unimaginative," then that organization will manifest a highly formalized structure characterized by many rules, policies, strict job descriptions, and regulations. Similarly, a collective core belief that "my employees are lazy and they will try to get out of work if they can" will be structurally expressed through close supervision, strict accountability procedures, and high centralization. As the leadership of the organization sets the culture, so the dominant beliefs of the "ruling elite" will create the initial design of the structure.[3]

In *The Neurotic Organization*, Manfred Kets de Vries and Danny Miller posit that,

much as [the president] sets the tone for his administration, the government and the country, the person or people in control of an organization have a considerable effect on both its structure and strategies—including the goals, focus and any marketing and manufacturing processes. If these top guys (most firms are run by men) are irrational or pathological, so—to a greater or lesser extent—is the company.[4]

As we have seen, employees who sense the beliefs and values held by their authority figures may act to fulfill these expectations, thereby letting the leaders be "right" about their employees and allowing the employees to complain about their lot without having to take personal responsibility for initiative, risk taking, and creativity. Thus the hierarchy itself is created by the belief "Leaders lead and followers follow," and the roles are mutually exclusive.

## The Metamodel and Organizational Change

Typical structural change processes engender resistance. By working at the level of *effect* (the structure of the organization) rather than the only substantial source of change, the level of *cause* (the shared paradigm), the change agents create a tension between the internal belief systems and the structures that naturally evolve from those systems. This tension will be resolved in one of two ways: Either members of the organization will resist the new change and keep old beliefs and attitudes or they will change their beliefs and attitudes so that they are congruent with the new structures.

In the past, the first approach has been the more common one. A recent study has shown that structural change strategies, such as change in reporting relationships, departmental arrangements, and "reorganization" in general, are considered the least effective strategies by organization development change agents.[5] This approach to change is like trying to change a reflection in a mirror without addressing what is *causing* that reflection.

Trying to create an "ideal" environment by manipulating the external form of things reflects old-paradigm assumptions and is in stark contrast to an appreciation of the power for change that lies at the invisible, intangible level of thought and attitude. Such an awareness is exemplified in an article by Martin Glass titled "Money Versus People":

The power that transforms our lives into money is lethal. The whale and redwoods, for example, were gone before the harpoon struck or the ax fell, from the moment they became money. The same with all the fur, plumes, hides, shells, flesh and fibre, the hardwoods and habitats. The same with ideas, memories, history, child care, healing, silence, and peace of mind.[6]

**Vignette 2**

In *The Goal,* a novel designed to change American business practices, the main character, Alex, tells his friend Eric about a revolutionary idea that Alex's plant has initiated. Eric immediately wants to bring the same change to his plant:

Alex shook his head. "First of all, remember that you are advocating new ideas here!"

"You mean I'm going to get resistance?" said Eric.

"That's right . . . resistance," said Alex. "As soon as people sense you are about to suggest something new, even if it might be better, they tend to focus on why it won't work."

"Well, you are probably right," admitted Eric. "But why? Why do people do that?"

"Whether it is better or not, improvement is still change. And change, for whatever reason, means uncertainty. We venture from what is safe and known into what is unknown. This is a move most people are afraid to make," said Alex.

"So, when you suggest improvement, it translates into fear . . . is that it?" said Eric.

"Change is the hardest thing for an organization to do," said Alex. "Did you ever stop to think that much of what we do as managers is actually directed against change? Management strives for control, predictability, and certainty in the midst of all the factors. And it isn't just management who is against change . . . it's everybody!"

SOURCE: Eliyahu M. Goldratt and Jeff Cox, *The Goal* (rev. ed.) (Croton-on-Hudson, NY: North River, 1986).

With these thought-provoking words, Glass acknowledges that the first step of change occurs at an invisible level: Change begins with thought. Implied in this passage is that the desire for or love of money (and perhaps what can be bought with money) initiated a process that eventually took several forms, such as the harpooning of whales and the cutting of redwoods. It might be seen that it is not the desire to cut trees but the desire for more and more for its own sake that would be the point of initiation of the actual action. Behind the inordinate desire for money, then, might be a belief or value system in which money is understood to bestow importance (personal identity).

Despite these points, some transformational thinkers see structural change as the way to create attitudinal change, and they are backed up

**Vignette 3**

A community development project outlined in 1988 was based on the notion that changing the structure can change the experience. The $100-trillion price tag indicated the degree of belief in this possibility: the developer (the Maharishi Mahesh Yogi, of transcendental meditation fame) asked Canadians to help him finance and build a "heaven on earth . . . a string of lavish cities around the world where people can live in 'heavenly bliss.' " These cities "would be walled off to keep out noise, crime, pollution and drugs. . . . the residents would be able to buy $500,000 mansions." People have been dreaming of designing utopias for years, but, unfortunately, such "utopias" have included self-centered, immature people.

SOURCE: Canadian Press, *Times Colonist*, April 11, 1988.

by a number of psychologists who have argued that changed attitudes follow changed behavior. Essentially, the argument is that if you can get people to behave differently, they will change their attitudes so as to create congruence with the new behavior. We have no problem with this observation; we merely note that the *collective paradigm* is what creates structure, not the other way around (although the feedback loop is acknowledged).

Peter Block, in his excellent book *The Empowered Manager*, argues that empowerment can come from structural changes. He mentions turning the organizational pyramid upside down (showing people at the lowest levels on the top, as the president of SAS airline has done), changing the ground rules about when a supervisor supervises, introducing self-managing teams, revising the performance appraisal process, and so on.[7] He also notes:

> There is a quiet revolution taking place in many organizations. The source of the revolution is the growing realization that tighter controls, greater pressure, more clearly defined jobs, and tighter supervision have, in the last fifty years, run their course in their ability to give us the productivity gains we require to compete effectively in the world marketplace. Attention is shifting *to the need for employees to personally take responsibility for the success of our businesses if we hope to survive and prosper.*[8]

Herein lies the crux of the metamodel. We create and maintain organizational forms consistent with our level of collective maturity and our shared identity. If we see ourselves as separate, fearful, shame-ridden people whose best hope for happiness is to manipulate our external circumstances so that they please us, we get the bureaucratic form. If we are willing to accept personal responsibility for expressing transcendent values, for living in true, spiritual identity, we will create flexible, nonhierarchical, politics-free organizations. *We create our own reality.* We produce what is consistent with our inner structures of consciousness.

One of the most important transformational principles is the notion that there is a design and control operating in the universe and that one spirit is animating everything, everywhere. We could call this the vibratory rhythm of life itself. If everything is vibrational substance, as quantum physicists suggest, there is an underlying rhythm to the universal pulse of change. This rhythm is the tone, or the dance, of life:

> How fluid and flexible are we to move in the directions that life indicates? Clearly [in the musical presentation just made], if the dancers and the musicians had not paid attention to the music, the result would have been chaotic. It is no different with respect to the whole range of life experience. There is a precise rhythm to the dance, a precise rhythm to the music. Can we hear it? And, if we hear it, are we willing to coordinate exactly with it (the Dance of Life)? Or do we have other things going on in our minds and hearts?
>
> For those whose attention has been occupied with the external factors in their lives, it often seems as though the less audible music of the dance is very distant, if indeed it exists for them at all. . . . Nonetheless, all of us are affected by the rhythm of the cosmic music. This is not just a matter of playing with words. There is what we might call the music of the spheres, cosmic music, a rhythm which guides everything. *Whether we are conscious of it or not, we are affected by it.* In these days there seems to be an increasing intensity in our world. This manifests in ten thousand different ways. For many, this intensity comes out as feelings of friction and anxiety, perhaps even anger. *These feelings are then often directed towards circumstances or the people around, when what is really being sensed has to do with the rhythm of the music.*[9]

Here is an invitation to operate beyond one's paradigm, one's set of fixed structures of idea, belief, concept, preference, and to let the design and control of life itself animate our thoughts and our feelings, instead of the human addiction to reaction to external circumstance. Only then will we create organizations that really work.

## Summary and Implications

The metamodel of organization involves the individuals who comprise the organization and their respective levels of maturity. The key influences in determining the organization culture generally are the chief decision makers; the organization will tend to reflect their beliefs and values. The culture and resulting structures of the organization then will tend to perpetuate the status quo. Change is generally resisted.

According to the old paradigm, change effectively begins at the level of external form; according to the metamodel, change occurs at the level of individual identity and maturity. Once change has occurred at the individual level, the combined identities of the individuals who constitute an organization may permit change at the corporate identity level. We attempt a complete summary of the transformational approach below.

*Wholeness already exists.* Everything is related to everything else. The only problem is with the human mind, which has developed the habit of thought that each of us is separate from everything else and therefore must struggle to manipulate external circumstances to get what we as separate, autonomous beings want. Because the whole (the design and control principles inherent in life itself) organizes the parts, everything is being moved by life's design, but we as humans are largely unconscious of that fact. We charge around like bulls in a china shop, trying to maximize our self-interest, while life is quietly working according to its ancient and immutable principles. We are designed to be cocreators of life's design, but because of our distorted, self-preoccupied orientation, what we create is not congruent with what would naturally emerge into form if we allowed it to.

*We create our own reality with the parameters of our paradigm, that is, the beliefs, attitudes, values, expectations, and assumptions that we implicitly hold in our conscious and subconscious minds.* These inner structures provide the template with which the outer reality is drawn. The beliefs, attitudes, and values that we have developed to help us cope in the self-centered, illusory worlds of our own creation would be totally unnecessary if we were humble and would admit that our minds don't know it all. If we were willing to yield to life's design and relinquish our human designs, harmony and balance would result. But, instead, we keep thrashing around, trying to solve those problems "out there" and, in so doing, we create more havoc.

Our ego-driven minds and emotions think they know what is good and what is bad, so we set goals and manipulate our external worlds to get what we want. But all this creation is done from the limited, self-preoccupied view and, as such, fails to take into account all the factors in a situation. Hence we unwittingly create havoc by our striving and goal-oriented actions, because they do not respect the workings of the creative process of life.

*David Bohm's implicate order (what we have called the design and control parameters inherent in the vibratory pulsations of life) cannot move from the invisible levels of cause (being) to the visible levels of form (achievement) without the proper, clear, uncluttered emotional and thought channels of human beings (humans free of fear, greed, and shame patterns out of the past).* Our consciousness is rightly the channel through which the design of life can be made manifest in the world of form here and now. Again, the channels through which these vibratory patterns emerge are our mental and emotional capacities. Spirit is perceived through the emotional realm first; the "still, small voice" referred to in many spiritual texts cannot be heard over the din of the fearful, demanding, ego-driven emotional capacity. Similarly, our mental capacity was designed to be used to sense what needs to come forth in any situation that would *complement the needs of the greater whole.* Obviously, in the separate, ego-driven state, the mind is used to produce results pleasing to the individual, without regard for the ramifications of those results for the larger whole.

*Organizations are created by an agreement of the collective mind.* The thoughts and emotional forms we share in consciousness determine the structure and process of our organizations. They also determine the constraints and possibilities of those organizations. Hence ego-driven, fearful, effect-oriented people will naturally create centralized, formalized, bureaucratic organizations, using people as commodities to produce goods and services. As people develop greater maturity and willingness to relinquish at least some of their ego demands, the path becomes open for more decentralized, empowering organizations. Organic, flexible organizations require mature, responsible people to maintain them and operate them effectively.

One can speculate about the ultimate form and process of the organization created by whole-centered, fully responsible people. Life's design would be given a clear opportunity to come forth into form, and this would no doubt result in flexible organizations that adapt to the needs of the moment. Life would create organizations that would complement the purposes of life. Without further speculation, it seems likely that flexible, adaptive, fluid organizational forms will emerge increasingly as we proceed with this paradigm shift.

## DISCUSSION QUESTIONS

1. What major changes have you personally experienced and how have you handled them?
2. What effects have the changes you discussed in your answer to question 1 had on organizations to which you belonged at the time?
3. How would you describe your own "spirit"? How would others describe it?
4. How does your spirit affect others around you? How would others describe that effect?
5. How have you been affected/influenced by the culture or spirit of an organization in which you were a part?
6. What are some external factors that affect you?
7. What are some external factors that have affected an organization in which you were a part?

## NOTES

1. Actually, others have come to this conclusion. For example, see John W. Meyer and Brian Rowath, "Institutionalized Organizations: Formal Structure as Myth and Ceremony," *American Journal of Sociology* 83, no. 2 (1977): 340-363.

2. Edgar H. Schein, *Organizational Culture and Leadership: A Dynamic View* (San Francisco: Jossey-Bass, 1985), 57. Used with permission from the publisher.

3. Ibid.

4. Manfred F. Kets de Vries and Danny Miller, *The Neurotic Organization: Diagnosing and Changing Counterproductive Styles of Management* (San Francisco: Jossey-Bass, 1984); cited in ibid.

5. See the lead article in the fall 1984 issue of *OD Practitioner.*

6. Martin Glass, "Money Versus People," *Sun* (Chapel Hill, NC), June 1987, 31.

7. Peter Block, *The Empowered Manager: Positive Political Skills at Work* (San Francisco: Jossey-Bass, 1987), 67-70.

8. Ibid., xiii; emphasis added.

9. Michael Exeter, "Dance to the Universal Music" (address presented at the Sunrise Ranch, Loveland, CO, August 20, 1989), 1-2.

# 8 Transformation and Organizational Effectiveness

*A quick scan of the literature on organizations reveals little agreement on what the concept of organizational effectiveness really means. . . . This confusion in the literature is more than semantic. Variations in the definitions of organizational effectiveness are an impediment to the development of knowledge about complex organizations. Differences in the criteria used to measure effectiveness make it impossible to compare the results of one study with another. In the absence of comparative analysis, the development of models of organization design and development suffers.*

(Robert H. Miles,
*Macro Organizational Behavior,*
1980, pp. 355-356)

*It makes sense to me to try to create business organizations so they use all the talent there is, because clearly that is what is necessary to be effective. . . . If economic efficiency were the point, we should have never ended slavery.*

(W. Matthew Juechter,
"Bringing Spirit Back Into the Workplace,"
*Training and Development Journal,* September 1988, p. 35)

---

**SUMMARY:** Everyone wants to have an effective organization, but no one can agree on what that would be. At the egocentric level of human functioning, there is no agreement about what constitutes effectiveness; it all depends on one's opinion (a concept at the level of the mind). At the level of spirit, the unifying level, the level of oneness, there is a definition that makes sense; we explore that in this chapter.

---

**N**owhere in the applied social sciences is there a topic with as little universal agreement as *organizational effectiveness* (OE). Everyone agrees that we should try to make organizations "effective," but no one agrees on what effectiveness is, or how to go about measuring it. Nor is anyone quite sure how much organization design contributes to effectiveness.

In this chapter, we will look at the major schools of thought concerning organizational effectiveness, examining the strengths and weaknesses of each. We will also examine the role of goals in the effectiveness issue, in part through a transformational view of goals. Finally, we will explore the influence of culture on organizational effectiveness, and examine it from the transformational perspective.

## What Is an "Effective" Organization?

A cursory look at the available literature on organizations reveals very little agreement as to what constitutes "good performance" or effectiveness.[1] Not only is there little agreement on just what OE is, there is also poor agreement about how to go about measuring it. Just a partial list of ways to measure OE include the following:

| | |
|---|---|
| productivity | readiness |
| flexibility/adaptation | motivation |
| efficiency | utilization by environment |
| goal consensus | morale |
| profit | evaluations by external constituencies |
| role and norm congruence | |
| quality | control |
| managerial skills | stability |
| growth | conflict/cohesion |
| information management and communications | value of human resources |
| job satisfaction | participation and shared influence[2] |

An early, deceptively simple approach defined organizational effectiveness as the degree to which an organization achieves its goals.[3] Soon it was noticed that this definition was not as useful as it looked. Other questions had to be asked, such as the following:

- *Whose* goals were important (the employee's, the owner's, the customer's)?
- *Which* goals were important (the official goals of the organization or its *real* or operative goals)?
- *For what time frame* were the goals designed (short-term goals versus long-term goals)?

Immediately, the complexity of the effectiveness question increased.

Let us begin by looking at some definitions of OE that have been offered to date.

Organizational consultant Jeffrey Pfeffer sees effective organizations as those that (a) accurately see patterns of resource interdependence, (b) correctly perceive demands, and then (c) respond to those demands made by the groups that control the most critical interdependencies.[4] Pennings and Goodman say that effective organizations are the ones that can satisfy relevant constraints and produce results that satisfy a set of referents for multiple goals.[5] A completely different perspective is offered by Larry Cummings, who sees effective organizations as "ones in which the greatest percentage of people perceive themselves as free to use the organization and its subsystems as instruments for their own ends."[6] Yuchtman and Seashore argue that the effectiveness of an organization is defined by its bargaining position, as reflected in its ability to exploit its environment in the acquisition of scarce and valuable resources.[7] Finally, Georgopoulos and Tannenbaum view effectiveness as the extent to which the organization, with given resources and means, fulfills its objectives without incapacitating its resources and placing undue strain on its members.[8]

## The Peters and Waterman Definition

Contemporary definitions of OE are perhaps best reflected by Peters and Waterman in their best-seller *In Search of Excellence*.[9] These authors see effective organizations as follows:

- Effective organizations are able to manage ambiguity and paradox.
- Effective organizations have a bias for action.
- Effective organizations strive to stay close to the customer.
- Effective organizations value autonomy and entrepreneurship.
- Effective organizations build productivity through people.
- Effective organizations are hands-on and value driven.
- Effective organizations "stick to their knitting."
- Effective organizations maintain simple form and lean staffs.
- Effective organizations balance simultaneously loose and tight structure.

We look at each of these elements in turn below.

*Managing ambiguity and paradox.* Noticing that we live in a world of ambiguity and paradox, Peters and Waterman see the old, traditional, "cookbook" approaches to managing as hopelessly out of date. Effective organizations are those that can change to reflect changing situations, what Gareth Morgan calls "riding the waves of change."[10]

*A bias for action.* Peters and Waterman see that the old, left-brain-dominant paradigm wants to analyze, analyze, analyze—when what is needed is to *do something.* There is nothing inherently wrong with planning, but in a turbulent, competitive environment, often a company just needs to move. This experimental spirit can really pay a premium in effectiveness.

*Staying close to the customer.* This one seems pretty obvious, but industrial paradigm managers hold a very arrogant and elitist posture when it comes to their customers. These are the managers who say, without bothering to ask, "We know what the customers want!" Effective organizations stay in close and constant touch with their customers, continually asking, "What do you want?"

*Autonomy and entrepreneurship.* A hallmark of new-paradigm leadership is the recognition that mature people want to lead themselves. The growth of "intrapreneuring"—creating small, entrepreneurial ventures to test new products or enter new markets—in companies such as General Electric and Singer Sewing Machine is a symptom of this attitude. Effective companies find ways to give people autonomy and independence, and to encourage risk taking, experimentation, and creativity.

*Productivity through people.* Industrial paradigm structures and processes encourage low risk taking, defensive strategies, and timid rule following—tactics that will not work in the new world of rapid change, complexity, and ambiguity. In the new paradigm, the phrase "People are our most important resource" is not just a homily—it's a fact! Effective organizations empower people to release their inherent creativity and resourcefulness in the workplace.

*Being hands-on, value driven.* This is a tacit recognition that people work for managers who are involved in what is happening, not shielded in a corporate ivory tower. Also, we see that effectiveness is created by commitment to values, not just profits. An organization has to stand for something. Effective organizations have core values

© BRILLIANT ENTERPRISES 1972

POT-SHOTS NO.312

IF YOU DON'T DO IT,

YOU'LL NEVER KNOW

WHAT WOULD HAVE HAPPENED

IF YOU HAD DONE IT.

Ashleigh
Brilliant

that inspire the participants and managers who stay "close to the shop floor."

*Sticking to the knitting.* The conglomerates of the 1960s and 1970s are becoming dinosaurs. Effective organizations know their business and expand in ways that enhance rather than dilute that business.

*Maintaining simple form, lean staff.* New-paradigm managers recognize that large, cumbersome staffs are a drag on effectiveness. Thus the trend toward downsizing staffs, which began in the "recession" of 1980-1981 and continues to this day. Peters and Waterman also point to the "three pillars of the structure" that will be important in the coming decade:

1. *stability:* simple, basic underlying form with dominant values and simplified interfaces
2. *entrepreneurship:* small, flexible units, task forces, project teams
3. *breaking old habits:* shifting attention by regular reorganization to prevent stagnation; experimental units[11]

*Simultaneous loose and tight properties.* This is the coexistence of firm central direction, driven by the core values of the organization,

> "Change can be exciting and it can be fearsome, but I'm convinced that the price of doing nothing is the suspension of one's existence."
>
> —Robert E. Lee, chairman, First Interstate Bank of Denver, quoted in the *Denver Post*, August 2, 1988, p. 3.

with loose, entrepreneurial motivation and individual autonomy.[12] Effective organizations give people autonomy (loose), but provide control and direction through values and vision (tight).

**Vignette 1**

A "bias for action" is important, but it doesn't always work. A 1988 article in *Forbes* featured Mr. Bildner of J. Bildner and Sons, Inc., an upscale Boston grocery store that offered personalized services such as phone orders, credit card payment, and free delivery. By 1987, Bildner controlled a public company with 21 stores, more than 2,000 employees, and about $49 million in sales.

J. Bildner, however, is a classic example of "ready-fire-aim." The company didn't do enough homework as it rapidly expanded. "They were going around getting leases before they even tested the markets," said a representative of a consulting firm hired by Bildner. Other costly errors could be attributed to the company's bias for action, such as underestimating construction costs for new stores by 30%, overlooking the influence of a union that affected expenses and delayed the opening of at least one store, and being unprepared for competition in new territories. A bias for action needs to be predicated on *some* homework; otherwise, it's nothing more than shooting from the hip.

SOURCES: Claire Poole, "Too Much Too Fast," *Forbes*, October 31, 1988; Buck Brown, "James Bildner's Spectacular Rise and Fall: Rapid Growth Causes Downfall of Entrepreneur," *Wall Street Journal*, October 24, 1988, 31.

From the varied criteria of organizational effectiveness cited above, we can see that the older ones represent the "best" of old-paradigm thinking, whereas Peters and Waterman's approach is an example of new- and old-paradigm assumptions blended together. Remember, it is not that one is "bad" and one is "good"; the issue is *what works*. In today's world, the assumptions and beliefs that are characteristic of the emerging paradigm seem to be more effective than those of the industrial era.

## Structure and Effectiveness

Although researchers differ as to what they consider to be effectiveness, they agree to some extent on structural qualities that seem to be valid and applicable in effective organizations across a wide spectrum (see Table 8.1). Charles Perrow has argued that these "prescriptions and proscriptions" for the "correct structure" depend on the environment, technology, the organization's most critical function, and the stage of its development.[13]

*Environment.* The correct structure depends on the environmental context in which the firm operates. In a stable, static environment, the bureaucratic structure seems more effective, whereas in a dynamic, turbulent environment the organic, flexible structure seems more appropriate.

*Technology.* The correct structure also seems to depend on the type of technology a firm uses to do its work. If the work is predictable and routine in nature, a bureaucratic structure should be most effective. If, on the other hand, a firm is doing nonroutine, complex, and potentially ambiguous work, a matrix or organic structure would be appropriate.

*Critical function and stage of development.* Correct structure seems to depend on the most critical function of an organization as well as its stage of development. For instance, a production-centered organization would use a bureaucratic structure, whereas a marketing-oriented or development-oriented organization would more effectively utilize an organic form. Also, in its earlier stages, the company will be more organic (e.g., Apple Computer as it began in Steven Jobs's garage); in later stages, the structure will change to reflect increased routinization and standardization.[14] This "size" argument is similar to one made by Stephen Robbins, who correctly notes that when organizations reach a certain size, they begin to bureaucratize—inevitably, in his estimation.[15] According to the metamodel of organization, this is because the collective paradigm creates the structure. In other words, we will not see large, organic organizations

**Table 8.1**   Structural Qualities That Relate to Effectiveness

|  | *Bureaucratic Structure* | *Organic Structure* |
| --- | --- | --- |
| Environment | stable; static | dynamic; turbulent |
| Technology | predictable; routine | nonroutine; complex; ambiguous |
| Critical function | production centered | marketing centered; development oriented |
| Stage of development | late (mature) | early (entrepreneurial) |

until we have sufficient numbers of mature, responsible people to put in them.

### Child's Requirements for Effectiveness

John Child summarizes three "universals" in his "requirements for effectiveness"; these combine Peters and Waterman's work and the work of Abernathy, Clark, and Kantrow in their excellent book *Industrial Renaissance:*[16]

1. *An emphasis on methods to communicate key values and objectives and to ensure that action is directed toward these.* Some studies suggest that managers in higher-performing companies select a few key objectives and then concentrate resources single-mindedly on fulfilling them.
2. *The delegation of identifiable areas of responsibility to relatively small units, including work groups.* These units are encouraged to carry out their responsibilities with considerable autonomy and scope for initiative, but they are subject to performance assessments that manifest a preservation of tight, central control.
3. *Use of a simple, lean structure of management that is intended to avoid the rigidities of bureaucracy, the complexities of matrix, and the overheads of both.*[17]

These three universals are a mix of new-paradigm and old-paradigm assumptions. The emphasis on tight, central control is clearly an old-paradigm form, appropriate when workers are immature and/or unwilling to take personal responsibility, and/or when goals, objectives, and procedures are ambiguous and hard to follow for the worker.

Here is an area where the Japanese companies seemingly have a more effective approach than our old-paradigm model. By using "implicit control," through the articulation of corporate values and philosophy to the workers, Japanese companies obviate the need for tight, central control. If everyone has "bought into" the same guiding principles, there is much less need for central supervision.[18]

---

## The Major Schools
## of Organizational Effectiveness

---

Most of the research and writing on organizational effectiveness can be categorized into five schools of thought:

- the goals school
- the systems school
- the strategic constituencies school
- the competing values school
- the contradiction school

The strengths and weaknesses of each approach are examined below.

### The Goals School

By far the most popular school of thought on effectiveness is the goal school. This approach focuses on the organizational *ends*—that is, the result of effectiveness. It is concerned with whether or not an organization achieves its goals. Some commonly understood goal-attainment criteria include profit maximization, winning the NBA title, and having the highest-rated accounting firm in the country. The goals school of thought is most explicit in the popular technique/philosophy known as *management by objectives* (MBO).

Under MBO, an organization and its members are assessed by how well they achieve specific goals that several levels of management have jointly set. Measurable, time-oriented, realistic goals are set, starting at the top of the organization, and each lower level sets goals based on the next higher level. Actual performance is then measured and compared with the goal. Because an organization and its members either accomplish their goals or fail to, this approach seems very objective and satisfying.

A certain set of assumptions is inherent in this approach. First, organizations are viewed as rational sets of arrangements between people and resources that are instrumental in achieving certain agreed-on ends or goals. In other words, organizations are seen as deliberately

© ASHLEIGH BRILLIANT 1985

POT-SHOTS NO. 3432.

Ashleigh Brilliant

I'M SURE MY EFFORTS DESERVE MY GOALS, BUT SOMETIMES WONDER IF MY GOALS ARE WORTH MY EFFORTS.

rational, goal-seeking entities. From this perspective, effectiveness is measured in terms of goal attainment. Were goals attained or were they not? The appeal is to a quantitative, yes/no type of evaluation.

However, these assumptions lead invariably to other assumptions that call the validity of the approach into question. First, in order to measure effectiveness according to the goals school, organizations must have valid goals. These must be identified and well-enough defined to be widely understood by all participants. There must be general agreement on these goals in the organization, and, finally, the goals must be measurable.

Serious problems arise when it comes to identifying goals. The public goals of an organization, called the *official goals*, are widely printed in annual reports, corporate philosophy pronouncements, and the like. They tend to be quite abstract and "motherhood/apple pie" oriented in tone. Often, they bear little resemblance to the goals the organization is actually pursuing, called the *operative goals*. Operative goals are the standard against which performance is measured and toward which organization members are supposed to direct their efforts. In general, we can say that operative goals are official goals as modified by people, politics, and the external environment.

*People*. People modify goals because whenever new leaders or managers come into an organization, they usually bring their own agendas with them. In a business school, for example, a new dean can change the goals from a teaching emphasis to a research/publishing emphasis in a short period of time, and shift the reward criteria to reflect this.

*Politics.* Shifts in internal power arrangements can bring about goal shifts. When the marketplace cries out for accountants, for example, you would expect the accounting department of a school of business to be most powerful. The goal set of the business school, then, would necessarily reflect the priorities of the accounting department. If the marketplace changes and marketers become preeminent, expect a change to marketing-tinged goals.

The influences of people and politics converge when a person or a group with particular notoriety becomes involved. The boss's son, an award winner, a local government figure, or a group that generates venture capital, secures grant monies, or gets big contracts for the company can have strong influence on official goals.

*The external environment.* Changes in the external environment bring about changes in goals. For example, prior to 1975, the goal of the Public Broadcasting System was to produce "high-quality programming." With the rousing success of the British series *Upstairs, Downstairs*, however, the goal set shifted perceptibly to "high-quality

POT-SHOTS NO. 2315.

THE GREATEST OBSTACLE TO ACHIEVING MY GOALS

IS THAT I DON'T KNOW WHAT MY GOALS ARE.

Ashleigh Brilliant

© ASHLEIGH BRILLIANT 1981.

---

EXERCISE 1. A large realty company has managers, a sales force, and support staff. The sales force is ostensibly the "ticket" to productivity and OE, and therefore, in any case involving a conflict between a salesperson and any support staff (and sometimes even managers), the salesperson inevitably has the cards stacked in his or her favor. The support staff therefore lives in fear of any such conflicts and goes to great lengths to see that they don't happen. This produces a climate of less-than-honest interaction. What is the predominant factor at work here—people, politics, or environment?

---

commercial programming." In other words, the operative *assumption* was that commercial success and quality programming were incompatible outcomes until a high-quality offering became commercially successful.

Operative goals are often linked to official goals. Also, operative goals may develop that have no relationship to official goals. Speaking to this phenomenon, Charles Perrow argues:

> Unofficial operative goals, on the other hand, are tied more directly to group interests, and while they may support, be irrelevant to, or subvert official goals, they bear no necessary connection with them. An interest in a major supplier may dictate the policies of a corporate executive. The prestige that attaches to utilizing elaborate high-speed computers may dictate the reorganization of inventory and accounting departments.
> Racial prejudice may influence the selection procedures of an employment agency. The personal ambition of a hospital administrator may lead to community alliances and activities which bind the organization without enhancing its goal achievement. On the other hand, while the use of interns and residents as "cheap labor" may subvert the official goals of medical education, it may substantially further the official goal of providing a high quality of health care.[19]

Operative goals, then, are often derived from official goals, but not always. We notice that *goals change over time, influenced by people changes, political changes, and environmental contingencies.* Organizational goal setting is affected by competitive, co-optative bargaining and coalitional factors related to the environment. Organizations change goals in the face of competitive pressures. They also respond to *co-optation,* the "process of absorbing new elements into the leadership or policy-determining structure of the organization as a means of averting threats to its stability and existence."[20] (For example, General Motors elected the Reverend Leon Sullivan, a prominent black activist, to its board of directors in the 1970s, apparently in response to civil rights pressures.) Co-optation changes goals as a result of trade-offs agreed to with suppliers, customers, and other organizations. Coalition, the actual combining of two or more organizations, can also result in a new goal set, as was illustrated countless times during the "merger mania" of the 1980s.

It is often difficult to identify just what an organization's real or operative goals are. A good rule of thumb is to look at where the resources are directed. A second problem is that goals may be differentiated throughout the organization, with members of major subunits pursuing different, often conflicting goals. Often, organizational goals serve as a "front," legitimating the goals of powerful coalitions within the organization. Add in the reality of goals imposed by powerful external constituencies, and we begin to see why the relatively straightforward approach the goal attainment model offers is replete with difficulties. The situation can be put thus:

> To define organizational effectiveness in terms of goal attainment adds to the complexity because goals are one of the most confusing and controversial topics in the literature of organization. Yet . . . organizational effectiveness is inextricably linked to the concept of goals, and . . . an explicit specification of goals cannot be avoided if one is to identify and operationalize the effectiveness of an organization. Thus, an assessment of organizational effectiveness requires a confrontation and resolution to the problem of goals.[21]

There is also the related yet separate problem of *whose goals are most important*. The dominant coalition of the organization? The employees? The middle-management group? The board? Key external constituencies? Whose goals shall govern? How can relative importance be allocated to goals that may be incompatible and that represent diverse interests?

A final problem is that, for many organizations, goals do not direct activities.[22] It is commonly assumed that goals must be consensual prior to action, but, in reality, goal consensus is impossible unless there is something around which to "rally the troops." This something may be a goal that has already been accomplished. In some cases, official goals may be rationalizations to explain past actions rather than real goals intended to guide future ones. Organizations may act first, then magically "create" goals to justify what they did.

Researcher Petro Georgiou has offered a "counterparadigm" to the goal school. He argues that the commitment to a "goal paradigm" has actually retarded organizational analysis by "requiring the disassociation of the conceptual scheme from incompatible findings on organizations."[23] By this he means that all researchers and students of organization alike assume that the dominating presence of a goal marks off an organization from other kinds of systems. He continues:

> Yet almost invariably, studies demonstrate the fruitlessness of understanding organizations as goal-attaining devices. The paradigm retains its primacy not because of the insights it yields, but because it is embedded so deeply in our consciousness that it is a reality rather than a theoretical construct to be discarded when it ceases to enlighten. Intellectually exhausted, the goal paradigm has become a procrustean bed into which all findings are forced and even incipient counter paradigms absorbed, regardless of their promise of greater insight.[24]

Georgiou sees Chester Barnard's incentive system analysis as providing the basis for a counterparadigm, and he makes suggestions for its development along the lines of the statement, "The individual is the basic strategic factor in the organization." He summarizes his case by saying that "organizations are not viewed as analytically distinctive social units given meaning by their goals, but as arbitrary focuses of interest, marketplaces whose structures and processes are the outcomes of complex accommodations made by actors exchanging a variety of incentives and pursuing a diversity of goals."[25] One example of tunnel vision with respect to goal attainment is presented in Vignette 2.

© BRILLIANT ENTERPRISES, 1974

POT-SHOTS NO. 572

*Ashleigh Brilliant*

## TO BE SURE OF HITTING THE TARGET,

## SHOOT FIRST

## AND, WHATEVER YOU HIT, CALL IT THE TARGET.

© BRILLIANT ENTERPRISES 1975

# I HOPE I GET WHAT I WANT

Ashleigh Brilliant

## Before I stop wanting it.

**Vignette 2**

Ed, a luggage manufacturer who at one time made excellent profits with a West Coast Sears account, has one goal: to give Sears, his only customer, a good product at a low price. By focusing on that goal, however, he neglected to notice changes in his marketplace and to acknowledge the dangers of putting all his eggs in one basket. His criterion for organizational effectiveness was the achievement of his goal.

As it turned out, luggage styles changed, and Ed found himself stocked too heavily with obsolete styles. Sears refused to buy the old stock, and it took Ed six months to retool for the new models. Ed went into bankruptcy and lost the business.

SOURCE: Buck Brown, "James Bildern's Spectacular Rise and Fall: Rapid Growth Causes Downfall of Entrepreneur," *Wall Street Journal*, October 24, 1988, B1. Reprinted by permission of *Wall Street Journal*, © 1988 Dow Jones & Company, Inc. All rights reserved worldwide.

The goal school has the obvious strength of *measurability* and its congruence with the Western paradigm of competition and winning. Yet its shortcomings have provided the impetus for the development of other approaches.

## The Systems School

Born of the systems approach to the study of organizations, the systems school evolved largely as a reaction to the deficiencies of the goal school of organizational effectiveness, which it compensates for. Rather than focusing on organizational ends, the systems school looks at *means.* Instead of looking at results of operations, it looks at how the ends are achieved, emphasizing the interdependencies among important functions in the organization. Its major emphasis is the long-term survivability and health of the organization.

The systems analyst would look at such things as the following:

- How well are people in the organization communicating with each other?
- How cooperative are people in the organization with one another?
- How much slack (excess resources) does the organization have to withstand a harsh turn of economic events?
- How much reinvestment (human and capital) does the organization do in revitalizing itself?

This approach assumes that the organization is an open system, composed of interrelated parts that interface with an external environment. Subsystems that perform poorly will affect the whole.

To be effective according to the systems school, the organization must maintain productive relations with all aspects of its environment, including suppliers, customers, unions, government agencies, and other constituencies. It must also read and react to changes in consumer tastes, economics, technology, societal values, and the like. In other words, the organization must maintain its legitimacy in the eyes of its various external constituencies.

A systems evaluator would look at the organization's overall *health* (as measured by lack of absenteeism, turnover of employees, and good morale and cohesion), its *ability to acquire resources* needed to compete effectively in the marketplace, its *flexibility/adaptability* in responding to environmental changes and demands, its efforts at *employee development and self-potential enhancement,* and its efforts to *allocate internal resources adroitly* to meet changes as required. Researchers at the University of Michigan who studied the performance of 75 organizations using the systems school picked 10 effectiveness dimensions:

1. *business volume:* dollar amount of sales relative to size of organization
2. *production cost:* cost per unit of sales volume
3. *new-member productivity:* how much people with less than five years service are contributing
4. *youthfulness of members:* productivity of members under 35 years of age

5. *business mix:* ability of the organization to pursue several different strategies successfully

6. *workforce growth:* relative and absolute changes in workforce levels

7. *devotion to management:* sales commissions earned by agency managers

8. *maintenance cost:* cost to maintain new business

9. *member productivity:* average new business volume per employee

10. *market penetration:* proportion of potential market being exploited[26]

This approach also has its problems. It is just a question of semantics whether one considers "business volume" to be one form of resource acquisition or a goal. Either way, resource acquisition does not just happen; it is the result of goal striving. It would appear that attempts to separate process issues from end results (goals) artificially are contrived, and not valid.

Also, Richard Hall notes that the systems model

> makes the assumption that if an organization is of any size at all, the demands placed on it are so dynamic and complex that it is not possible to define a finite number of organizational goals in any meaningful way. Rather, the organization adopts the overall goal of maintaining its vitality or existence through time without depleting its environment or otherwise fouling its nest.[27]

According to this perspective, to assess organizational effectiveness one should "try to find out whether an organization is internally consistent, whether its resources are being judiciously distributed over a wide variety of coping mechanisms, whether it is using up its resources faster than it should, etc."[28] Goal school proponents do not disagree with this, but argue that it is incomplete, because focusing on the *means* for effectiveness while ignoring the *ends* for which these means are applied skirts a central issue. Instead of measurable, specific ends, the systems school focuses on the vague, idealistic goal of organizational *survivability.*

Not only is this concept hard to operationalize, but the actual processes themselves—flexibility/adaptability, organizational health, and the like—have proven hard to nail down. Moreover, the systems school has not provided linkages between the processes and the "end," survivability. We all know of mature and obviously ineffective organizations that simply do not die, whereas others that effectively achieve their mission may go out of business.

The choice between the goals school and the systems school comes down to this: *Is how you play the game important, or is the result of the game all that matters?* If ends are achieved, are means important?

**Vignette 3**

One large corporation has a procedure for establishing departments that takes approximately a year to complete. This process includes a proposal, board consideration, studies, more board consideration, discussion, and, finally, implementation. A new department was formed to handle a function that became obsolete when a new law banned the product for which the department was responsible. However, the department was maintained for several years with no function to perform, just in case the law was repealed, because it would take so long to reinstate the department that it was seen to be worthwhile to retain it even with no purpose.

## The Strategic Constituencies School

A relatively recent perspective on OE holds that an effective organization will strive to satisfy the demands made on it by "strategic constituencies"—various external and internal groups on which the organization depends for its continued existence.[29] This is similar to the systems view, except the organization is concerned only with those aspects of its environment that are strategic to its survival, rather than its entire environment.

A constituency is said to be strategic if it satisfies one or more of the following requirements:

1. It can create a large amount of uncertainty for the organization.
2. The organization is unable to replace the constituency or avoid depending on it in some way.
3. It can disrupt the operations and/or plans of the organization by direct action.[30]

Unlike the goal school, which views organizations as rational, goal-seeking groupings, the strategic constituencies school views organizations as political entities where vested interests compete for control over resources. In such a context, effectiveness becomes the ability of the organization to minimally satisfy the demands (sometimes competing) of various constituencies central to its survival and development. The operative word here is *minimally*, because each of an organization's constituencies has different goals and value orientations that are unlikely to be satisfied completely.

**Vignette 4**

One of the authors was involved some years ago in an entrepreneurial venture wherein the founders designed, marketed, and manufactured a hand tool called the CLINCHER. This company, called the ToolWorks, Inc., had to make the tool through a series of "job shops" because no major tool manufacturer would take a chance on investing in an untried product. So the founders hired a forge, a heat-treating operation, a company to stamp out some steel bars (part of the tool), a chrome plating operation, and so on. They also contacted a Chicago-based venture capital firm for funds for market research, product development, and setup of a distribution network.

After giving the company founders a letter of intent to invest $100,000 for 11% equity ownership in the ToolWorks (which allowed the founders to raise an additional $500,000 in guaranteed bank debt), the venture capital firm—obviously one of the ToolWorks's strategic constituencies—backed out. The founders then borrowed some money on their personal signatures to keep the project afloat.

Next, unforeseen manufacturing problems developed with another strategic constituency: the forging operation. The problems took so much time to work out that the founders ultimately had to tell their customers that they could not deliver. They could not replace the forge because the forge owned the dies to make the tool, and there was no money left with which to buy them from the forge. The forge created uncertainty for the ToolWorks, disrupted operations, and, ultimately, could not be replaced. The company was stuck with the forge, and it proved fatal for the business.

To apply this approach in a practical way, one first of all has to identify relevant strategic constituencies. In the example given in Vignette 4, these would certainly include the venture capital firm and the forging operation, as well as the bank, customers, suppliers, and the founders themselves (and their spouses!), as well as others. The next step would be to determine what each of the constituencies expected (or demanded) from the organization, and then determine the relative importance of each constituency to the ToolWorks.

One would then have to look at the goals of the organization (and its means to satisfy them) and see if they are compatible with the expectations of the most important strategic constituencies. A preference ordering of the constituencies and their expectations would be compared with the operative goals of the organization for compatibility. The organization's effectiveness would then be its ability to satisfy these imposed (by some constituency) goals at a minimal level.

This approach, too, has its problems. Because the environment changes rapidly, what is strategic today might not be so tomorrow. Also, what separates the strategic from the marginally strategic? Furthermore, because each person in the organization views the environment through a different paradigm, there will be genuine differences of opinion as to which constituencies are most important to the company.

The strategic constituencies perspective is an ongoing process, not a one-shot deal. The mix of imposed goals will shift as the constituencies shift and/or as the constituencies themselves undergo strategic changes. Instead of thinking of effectiveness as a static concept, it is institutionalized within the organization as it attempts to find a market niche that is congruent with that organization's capabilities and limitations.

## The Competing Values School

This approach recognizes the fact that effectiveness is in the eye and the values of the beholder. The criteria an individual uses to assess effectiveness depend on who that person is. Stockholder groups, employees, suppliers, unions, and customers all rate effectiveness differently—which indicates that ratings often tell us more about the values of the rater than about the effectiveness of what is being rated.

This approach assumes that there is no one best set of criteria for measuring OE. However, competing values go beyond just acknowledging that people make decisions from different value assumptions. It assumes that these diverse preferences can be consolidated and organized. This approach, developed by Quinn and Rohrbaugh, attempts to integrate the diverse set of indicators used by managers to gauge effectiveness.[31] These researchers had a panel of experts rate the similarity of items on a comprehensive list of performance indicators; this produced underlying dimensions of effectiveness that represent competing values.

The common themes that emerged from Quinn and Rohrbaugh's research boil down to three basic sets of competing values:

1. *Flexibility versus control:* These are essentially two incompatible features of an organization's structure. Flexibility favors innovation, creativity, and adaptation, whereas control favors predictability, order, and stability. It is recognized that one is not "better" than the other.
2. *Organizational emphasis—people versus organization:* This is similar to the concern for production/concern for people dichotomy so common in the literature on leadership.
3. *Means versus ends concern:* The former stresses concern with internal dynamics (the systems school), whereas the latter looks at final outcomes (the goal school).

These three dimensions can be combined into eight cells or sets of effectiveness criteria, which can be illustrated as in Figure 8.1.

The competing values of an internal/external focus are illustrated on the horizontal axis of the figure, and flexibility/control on the vertical axis, with people concern and productivity concern on one diagonal axis and means/ends on the other. Research based on this model has revealed that, although it is theoretically possible for an organization to have high values on each of the dimensions, the more likely result is for an organization that is effective in terms of control to be less effective in terms of flexibility.[32]

The eight cells can be divided into four basic models. The PFM (people-flexibility-means) and PFE (people-flexibility-ends) cells are both subsumed under the *human relations model,* which emphasizes flexibility. This model would define OE in terms of a cohesive (as means) and skilled (as ends) workforce. The *open systems model* includes the OFM (organization-flexibility-means) and OFE (organization-flexibility-ends) cells. Effectiveness in this model is defined in terms of flexibility (as means) and the ability to acquire resources (as ends).

The third model, the *rational goal model,* includes the OCM (organization-control-means) cell and the OCE (organization-control-ends) cell. An organization that has specific plans and goals (as means) and high productivity and efficiency (as ends) is an effective organization under this model. The fourth model, the *internal process model,* contains the PCM (people-control-means) cell and the PCE (people-control-ends) cell. It emphasizes people and control and stresses adequate information flow (as means) and order (as ends) in the assessment of effectiveness.

Each of the models represents a particular set of value preferences and has a polar opposite with a contrasting emphasis. In transformational terms, these are paradigmatic orientations, and each has its structural counterpart. To summarize:

> The human relations model with its effectiveness criteria reflecting people and flexibility stands in stark contrast to the rational goal model's value-based stress on organization and stability. The open system model, defined by values of organization and flexibility, runs counter to the internal process model, the effectiveness criteria of which reflects a focus on people and stable structures.[33]

How would one use this approach? As with the strategic constituencies approach, one first needs to identify the relevant constituencies. Next, one would need to infer the relative importance each of the constituencies places on the eight value orientations. There are questionnaires available to assist in this process. Then, just as in the strategic

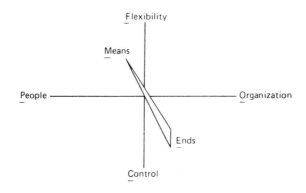

| THE EIGHT CELLS | DEFINITIONS OF THE EIGHT CRITERIA |
|---|---|
| OEC | *Productivity/efficiency.* Volume of output, the ratio of output over input. |
| OCM | *Planning and goal setting.* The amount of emphasis on the planning, objective setting, and evaluation process. |
| OFE | *Resource acquisition.* The capacity to capture assets and develop external support. |
| OFM | *Flexibility/readiness.* The ability to adapt to shifts in external conditions and demands. |
| PCE | *Stability/control.* Smoothness of internal conditions, continuity, equilibrium. |
| PCM | *Information management/communication.* Sufficiency of information flows, adequacy of internal orchestration. |
| PFE | *Value of human resources training.* The enhancement and maintenance of overall staff capacity. |
| PFM | *Cohesion/morale.* The level of communality and commitment among the staff members. |

**Figure 8.1.** A Three-Dimensional Model of Organizational Effectiveness

SOURCE: Robert E. Quinn and Kim Cameron, *Organizational Life Cycles and the Criteria of Effectiveness* (working paper) (Albany: SUNY, 1979). Also reprinted on p. 70 in Stephen P. Robbins, *Organization Theory: Structure, Design, and Applications* (3rd ed.) (Englewood Cliffs, NJ: Prentice Hall, 1990). Reprinted by permission of Prentice-Hall, Englewood Cliffs, New Jersey.

constituencies approach, one would calculate how well the organization is satisfying the demands of the various constituencies in terms of their value preferences.

This approach, of course, suffers from the same problems inherent in the strategic constituencies approach. It is better at assessing how a constituency thinks an organization is doing in terms of the value criteria than in actually clarifying which criteria the constituency is using.[34]

## The Contradiction School

This approach attempts to skirt some of the problems inherent in the other approaches by claiming that it is folly to try to conceptualize organizations as effective or ineffective.[35] In fact, several authors have urged that effectiveness not be used as a scientific concept.[36] Despite this disclaimer, it is recognized that there are issues and findings relative to effectiveness that are useful. This seeming contradiction can be resolved, according to Richard Hall, by using his *contradiction model.* His approach is described as follows:

> Simply put, a contradiction model of effectiveness will consider organizations to be more or less effective in regard to the variety of goals which they pursue; the variety of resources which they attempt to acquire; the variety of constituencies inside and outside the organization; whether or not they are part of the decision-making process; and the variety of time frames in which effectiveness is judged. The idea of variety in goals, resources, and so on is key here, since it suggests that *an organization can be effective in some areas of its operations and less so in others.*[37]

The model itself is summarized as follows:

1. *Organizations face multiple and conflicting environmental constraints.* A company can have constraints placed on it by government regulatory agencies (such as the Environmental Protection Agency), the vagaries of its suppliers, the demands of its customers, the price strategies of its competitors, and so on; many of these can be conflicting. As a general rule, the larger and more complex an organization, the greater the variety and range of organizational constraints it faces.

2. *Organizations have multiple and conflicting goals.* An organization may have many goals, such as profit maximization, return on shareholder investment, growth, effective use of resources, innovation, and stability, many of which may be conflicting. As Pfeffer and Salancik have shown, decisions on budgetary allocations are the result of power coalitions, which have certain value preferences for some goals over others. The potential for conflict here is high.

3. *Organizations have multiple and conflicting external and internal constituencies.* Just by looking at the goals of unions, customers, suppliers, the government, shareholders, and executive committees, one can see the potential for conflict. Add to this welfare rights groups, environmentalists, consumer protection groups, anti-nuclear power activists, and civil rights advocates, and the complexity is obvious.

4. *Organizations have multiple and conflicting time frames.* The classic case of time frame differentials is the cause for conflict between production and sales. Salespeople, to get orders, promise delivery "tomorrow"; production people, on the other hand, want more time so that they can ensure quality. Also, environmental constraints tend to vary over time. Finally, the stage in the organizational life cycle (from entrepreneurial to mature) plays a role here.

Using this model, an analyst would look at the constraints on the organization, its goals, constituents, and relevant time frames, then examine the compromises made in each area. According to Hall, only by looking at the contradictions inherent in organizational function can we come to grips with effectiveness in a meaningful way.

## A Transformational Perspective

Each of the approaches examined here offers valid perspectives on effectiveness. The transformational perspective would go beyond any of these by considering one primary factor: How does the organization operate as part of a larger, seamless organic whole? Let us take a look at how this transformational perspective might be operationalized.

As in the systems approach, from the transformational perspective the organization is seen as part of a larger whole. However, the systems approach sees the organization as separate from the environment, marked off by a distinct boundary. From the transformational perspective there is no separation between the organization and its environment, although the organization has a role to play in the whole.

Maturana and Varela have an interesting theory about all this. They postulate that all living systems are functionally closed, autonomous systems that factually make reference only to themselves.[38] That organizations *seem* to adapt to their external environments is only an explanation from the old-paradigm perspective; factually, organizations, through the processes of circularity, self-reference, and autonomy, tend to self-create and self-renew. Here we find an acknowledgment of the power of the collective paradigm factually to *create* or *enact* an environment "out there" (which is essentially a projection of what is contained in the collective paradigm) and then react to it as if it were separate. Organizations tend to enact their environments in such a way as to facilitate their self-production and survival.

The degree to which the organization senses an appropriate role for it to play (in a dynamic manner) in its so-called external environment would be an indicator of its effectiveness. As discussed previously, an organization's environment is enacted by the organization members themselves; we select what to pay attention to and what not to pay attention to. So a truly effective organization would transcend a self-centered "What's in it for us?" perspective in this "fit" process. The goal of effectiveness would not be the old-paradigm approach—How can we, as a separate entity, manipulate or "manage" the environment to get what we want? It would be, How can we be of service in complementing the purpose of the greater whole? These are radically different perspectives.

Also, the organization would have to be *flexible and adaptive* in order to be effective. From the transformational perspective, this does not necessarily mean it would have an organic structure. There could be parts of the organization required to perform routine, repetitive tasks, and the organization might choose to formalize those tasks. Other areas might have low formalization; the operative concept here is to organize to get the job done, whatever it is defined to be, out of a primary concern for fitting into the larger whole.

Also, from the transformational perspective, the organization would have to create an internal environment in which people are encouraged to express their true nature (or their true identity). By this, we mean to transcend their role identity and begin to see themselves as powerful creators, unfettered by limiting belief systems and fears. This atmosphere would nourish and promote a high level of *mature function* among managers and employees alike. People would be supported in taking personal responsibility for their worlds, and "victim" behavior would not be reinforced. In the transformational organization, status differences would be minimized and sapiential authority would reign supreme; leadership would shift as needed to get the job done. Mutual respect and helping attitudes would be widely observable. The structure would most likely be mostly organic in nature, with the possible exceptions listed above.

## Culture and Effectiveness

Structure, as we have said, is an *effect* of culture (or, more specifically, the collective paradigm of the organization). To change a structure without changing the paradigm that supports it, according to Schein, "will not lead to successful change. The organization will simply revert to its prior way of operating. If a group has had enough of a history to develop a culture, that culture will pervade everything."[39] In order for an organization to be effective, it must have a culture or collective paradigm that supports effective function.

What kind of culture would that be? One that encourages risk taking and exploration. One that values the personal maturity of its employees. One that changes structure and strategy as required by the changing environmental contingencies. One that has no sacred cows or habits of function that are there just because of historical precedent. One in which all employees "own" the purpose of the company and operate in a flexible role posture to get the job done. One in which CYA attitudes are not reinforced and in which everyone takes personal responsibility for producing results. One in which everyone is encouraged to have a balanced work/play schedule to minimize potential stress.

---

EXERCISE 2. Form a work group with three other people and generate a two-minute presentation of three characteristics, other than those listed above, of a culture that supports effective function. Share your work with the larger group.

---

## A Recapitulation

Organizations and the environments in which they operate have become increasingly complex and turbulent. This fact alone has made the measurement of effectiveness more problematic. *Any successful attempt to measure organizational effectiveness must be multifaceted.* As we have seen from the various models presented in this chapter, there are aspects of each that are valid. Each model reflects a different view of the nature of organizations.

Managers often have choices about the nature of the evaluations of their organizations' effectiveness. In such cases, it is critical for managers to understand the nature of the evaluation, its implicit and explicit value assumptions, the definition of effectiveness being used, and the assessment criteria. It is not that one school is better than another—all are simply models and, as such, incomplete. The important thing to remember is that what is "discovered" in an assessment of organizational effectiveness depends on the questions asked and the point of view of the asker, as well as the answers given and the point of view of the person responding.

# NOTES

1. See, for example, Robert H. Miles, *Macro Organizational Behavior* (Glenview, IL: Scott, Foresman, 1980), 355; John Child, *Organization: A Guide to Problems and Practice* (2nd ed.) (London: Harper & Row, 1984), 208; Richard H. Hall, *Organizations: Structures, Processes, and Outcomes (4th ed.) (Englewood Cliffs, NJ: Prentice Hall, 1987)*, 261; Stephen P. Robbins, *Organization Theory: Structure, Design, and Applications* (2nd ed.) (Englewood Cliffs, NJ: Prentice Hall, 1987), 26.

2. This list is adapted from John P. Campbell, "On the Nature of Organizational Effectiveness," in *New Perspectives on Organizational Effectiveness*, ed. Paul S. Goodman and Johannes M. Pennings (San Francisco: Jossey-Bass, 1977), 36-41.

3. Amitai Etzioni, *Modern Organizations* (Englewood Cliffs, NJ: Prentice Hall, 1964), 8.

4. Jeffrey Pfeffer, "Power and Resource Allocation in Organizations," in *New Directions in Organizational Behavior*, ed. Barry M. Staw and Gerald Salancik (Chicago: St. Clair, 1977).

5. Johannes M. Pennings and Paul S. Goodman, "Toward a Workable Framework," in *New Perspectives on Organizational Effectiveness*, ed. Paul S. Goodman and Johannes M. Pennings (San Francisco: Jossey-Bass, 1977).

6. Larry L. Cummings, "The Emergence of the Instrumental Organization," in *New Perspectives on Organizational Effectiveness*, ed. Paul S. Goodman and Johannes M. Pennings (San Francisco: Jossey-Bass, 1977), 57.

7. Ephraim Yuchtman and Stanley E. Seashore, "A System Resource Approach to Organizational Effectiveness," *Administrative Science Quarterly* 11 (1967): 380.

8. Basil Georgopoulos and Arnold S. Tannenbaum, "A Study of Organizational Effectiveness," *American Sociological Review* 22 (1957): 535.

9. Thomas J. Peters and Robert H. Waterman, Jr., *In Search of Excellence: Lessons From America's Best-Run Companies* (New York: Harper & Row, 1982).

10. Gareth Morgan, *Riding the Waves of Change* (San Francisco: Jossey-Bass, 1988).

11. Peters and Waterman, *In Search of Excellence*, 316.

12. Ibid.

13. Charles Perrow, "The Short and Glorious History of Organizational Theory," *Organizational Dynamics* 2 (Summer 1973): 12.

14. Ibid., 12-13.

15. Robbins, *Organization Theory*, especially chap. 5.

16. William J. Abernathy, Kim B. Clark, and Alan M. Kantrow, *Industrial Renaissance: Producing a Competitive Future for America* (New York: Basic Books, 1983).

17. Child, *Organization*, 213.

18. William G. Ouchi and Richard L. Price, "Hierarchies, Clans and Theory Z," *Organizational Dynamics* 7 (Autumn 1978).

19. Charles Perrow, "The Analysis of Goals in Complex Organizations," *American Sociological Review* 26 (1961): 856.

20. James D. Thompson and William McEwen, "Organizational Goals and Environment: Goal-setting as an Interaction Process," *American Sociological Review* 23 (1958): 27.

21. Andrew H. Van de Ven, "A Process for Organizational Assessment" (working paper, The Wharton School, 1977), 3-4.

22. Karl Weick, *The Social Psychology of Organizing* (Reading, MA: Addison-Wesley, 1969), 8.

23. Petro Georgiou, "The Goal Paradigm and Notes Toward a Counter Paradigm," *Administrative Science Quarterly* 14 (1970): 291.

24. Ibid., 292.

25. Ibid.

26. Stanley E. Seashore and Ephraim Yuchtman, "Factorial Analysis of Organizational Peformance," *Administrative Science Quarterly* 11 (December 1967): 377-395.

27. Hall, *Organizations*, 269.

28. Campbell, "On the Nature," 20.

29. Jeffrey Pfeffer and Gerald Salancik, *The External Control of Organizations* (New York: Harper & Row, 1978).

30. Miles, *Macro Organizational Behavior*, 375.

31. Robert E. Quinn and John Rohrbaugh, "A Spatial Model of Effectiveness Criteria: Towards a Competing Values Approach to Organizational Analysis," *Management Science* 29, no. 3 (1983).

32. John Rohrbaugh, "The Competing Values Approach: Innovation and Effectiveness in the Job Service," in *Organizational Theory and Public Policy*, ed. Richard H. Hall and Robert E. Quinn (Beverly Hills, CA: Sage, 1983).

33. Quinn and Rohrbaugh, "A Spatial Model," 138.

34. Robbins, *Organization Theory*, 49.

35. Campbell, "On the Nature."

36. See, for example, Michael T. Hannen and John H. Freeman, "Obstacles to Comparative Studies," and Robert L. Kahn, "Organizational Effectiveness: An Overview," both in *New Perspectives on Organizational Effectiveness*, ed. Paul S. Goodman and Johannes M. Pennings (San Francisco: Jossey-Bass, 1977).

37. Hall, *Organizations*, 264; emphasis added.

38. Humberto Maturana and Francisco Varela, *Autopoesis and Cognition: The Realization of the Living* (London: Reidl, 1980).

39. Edgar H. Schein, *Organizational Culture and Leadership: A Dynamic View* (San Francisco: Jossey-Bass, 1985), 33. Used with permission from the publisher.

# PART II

## ■ THE STRUCTURE
## OF ORGANIZATIONS

# 9 Macro Structural Variables

*Boy, do I hate bureaucracy!!!*
                              (Anonymous)

---

**SUMMARY:** In this chapter, we take a look at the major structural variables in organizations (complexity, formalization, and centralization). We explore the impacts of these structural aspects on the people in organizations and, conversely, and more important, how the collective paradigm determines these impacts. We examine structural variables from both traditional and transformational perspectives, with an eye toward synthesizing the two views.

---

Organization structure may be at least partially understood through the use of an analogy: The structure of an organization may be compared with the skeletal structure of the human body. However, this analogy is imperfect, because organization structure evolves as a result of changes in the collective paradigm and/or to changes in technology, power, strategy, environment, and size (depending literally on how one looks at it). An organization's structure provides a framework within which the following things take place:

- Jobs are divided up among people (called *differentiation* or *complexity*; the terms are essentially synonymous).
- Guidelines are specified in rules, regulations, policies, and procedures (*formalization*).
- Authority relationships are delineated (*centralization*).
- The entire organization is linked together by various coordinating mechanisms (*integration*).

131

Structure can also be likened to a form of private government.[1] This private government controls the behavior, to a degree, of all the people in the organization at a particular point in time. As we move from one organization to another, we move into the domains of essentially different governments.

**Vignette 1**

At a well-known computer software firm in Dallas, Texas, one of the conditions of employment was that employees were not to drink to excess in public places. If one wished to work for this firm, one had to obey this rule. One employee knew of several people who had been fired for violating this "governmental decree."

Here is an illustration of organizational structural components to which most readers can relate. The typical American university has a high level of differentiation or complexity; it encompasses a number of colleges (e.g., law, engineering, business, liberal arts) as well as subspecialties within each of these areas (e.g., within business, there are finance, accounting, management, policy, marketing, economics, production). Further, within each subspecialty there are further sub-subspecialties; for example, in management there are organization theory, organizational behavior, organization development, and management, as well as personnel management/human resource development. This is an illustration of what is meant by *high horizontal differentiation*.

The university also has a number of hierarchical levels—instructor, assistant professor, associate professor, professor, associate dean, dean, vice president, president, regent. This is *vertical differentiation*. The university might have satellite campuses at other geographic locations; this is *spatial dispersion*. Horizontal differentiation, vertical differentiation, and spatial dispersion all combine to make up an organization's *complexity*.

All of this differentiation or complexity requires coordination and control, hence the need for *integration*. One of the ways an organization integrates is through *formalization*, the establishment of specific rules, regulations, policies, and procedures to regularize behavior. Also, the university uses *centralization*, the locus of decision-making control at the top of the organization, to achieve integration; memos and directives are used to integrate the functions of the university. Goals and objectives serve as integrators, too, as their purpose is to get everyone moving "in the same direction." For specialized areas needing coordination—for example, the development of a course in business ethics might require an economist, an organizational behavior professor, a professor from religious studies, and a philosophy professor—the university might use a task force. This is an example of a *nonconventional integrator.*

For many years organization theorists have concerned themselves mainly with the prescribed, formal, and relatively enduring features of structure. However, it is increasingly recognized that many so-called informal features of organization (e.g., group norms, patterns of communication, myths, and rituals) play an important part in the creation, maintenance, and change of structural configurations. Ignored in formal organization charts are the informal power structures and political arrangements that influence organizational behavior (and formal structural arrangements). Also, theorists have learned that structure is not homogeneous within an organization; that is, in one organization different departments and groupings can have radically different structural configurations.

---

## Organizational Complexity

---

Two commonly mentioned aspects of differentiation are specialization and division of labor. *Specialization* refers to role-specific behavior that focuses on certain duties and activities for which one needs training/competence (this is also called *social specialization*). Basically, this means giving highly trained specialists a comprehensive range of activities to perform. *Division of labor, or functional specialization,* on the other hand, usually refers to the practice of taking a large job and breaking it up into smaller, less complex, and more routinized tasks, such as assembly-line work. This is the process of minutely subdividing the task so that any nonspecialist can perform it.

Both specialization and division of labor are associated with differentiation and complexity, or the state of segmentation in an organization that divides it into specific groupings. In general, the more different occupations and skills an organization requires, the more complex it is. So, for example, at a McDonald's restaurant, one will find a manager, maintenance people, cooks, servers, cleanup people, and purchasing people.

There are three basic forms of differentiation: horizontal, vertical, and spatial dispersion. These are discussed in turn on the following pages.

## Horizontal Differentiation

*Horizontal* differentiation refers to the degree of difference between units at the same level of organization. This degree of difference can be measured in terms of time orientation, goal orientation, the language(s) the people use, status differences, the nature of the tasks they perform, their education/training levels, and the like.

How does horizontal differentiation occur? When organizations are small, they have low horizontal differentiation. The boss does everything, because he or she can't afford to pay for help. However, as the organization begins to be successful and to grow, there is a need to hire specialists, such as market research employees, new product development people, salespeople, a public relations person, a lawyer, a computer person, and so on. In fact, the more a company grows, the more it needs specialized help. In the short run, the growing organization can get by with outside consultants, but, eventually, the roles need to be formalized. In general, the more complex the organization's external environment (the greater the number of environmental components important for the survival and prosperity of the firm), the more differentiated the structure should be.[2]

The more horizontally differentiated a firm becomes, the more the potential for conflict grows, because all of the people at the different units speak different languages and have different time horizons, goals, training, status, and so on. The greater the differences among people, the more the potential for misunderstanding and disagreement. For example, the production unit and the sales unit of an organization may be at the same hierarchical level organizationally, but their orientations are quite different. Sales staff want the organization to be flexible and adaptive in meeting environmental contingencies, so they can offer the product *now* and please the customer. But employees in production want the organization to be stable and predictable, so they can have the time they need to assure product quality and safety. Different organizational units pay attention to different goals, and sometimes even speak different languages. Computer people talk about "bits" and "bytes," whereas marketing speaks of "target markets" and "segmentation."

The potential for conflict is high in a company with high horizontal differentiation, where differences exist within given organizational levels. Resolving these conflicts and integrating these areas is a major challenge for bureaucratic structures—perhaps their central management problem.

## Vertical Differentiation

*Vertical* differentiation has its own built-in integrator; if there is a conflict between levels, the person with more formal authority wins.

POT-SHOTS
NO. 2174.

OPINIONS ARE DIVIDED
AS TO WHETHER OR NOT THERE IS
REAL UNANIMITY
IN OUR ORGANIZATION.

Vertical, or hierarchical, differentiation is a less complicated matter than horizontal differentiation. Basically, it consists of the number of levels in the organization's hierarchy. There are three ways to measure an organization's vertical dimension:

1. Examine the proliferation of supervisory levels.[3]
2. Count the number of job positions between the chief executive officer and the employees working on the output.[4]
3. Count the number of levels in the deepest single division and the mean number of levels in the organization as a whole.[5]

**Vignette 2**

Although Ben & Jerry's Homemade Inc. is still classified as a small business, it has definitely been experiencing growing pains. As of 1990, the original purposes and values of the cofounders were being questioned, the communication network was failing, and the company was looking for ways to grow and still keep the original vision intact.

## Vignette 3

In the mid-1980s, Nike's Air Jordan basketball shoes took the company to the top. Then people began buying Reebok athletic shoes, and Nike began to lose market share. But things have begun to turn around for Nike; profits have tripled and the stock price has increased in recent years. At the same time, Reebok has announced that earnings have dropped.

Nike's rebound is owed in part to consumers' switch to performance-oriented shoes, and in part to the fact that the company was able to take advantage of the trend. That is because Nike was able to take care of some management problems that dated back to the early 1980s, when Nike was an "entrepreneurial firm run by former jocks."[6] Then, top management changed every six to eight months; this fluid management team had difficulty coordinating design, marketing, and production functions. "We had the belief that, if we built the best shoe, the consumer had to buy it," said CEO Philip H. Knight.[7] Now, Nike knows that, with growth, integration becomes more and more critical. Nike's entrepreneurial days are over.

The paradigmatic assumption operating here is that the higher the level in the organization, the greater the formal authority of the person in the job title. But the organizational investigator needs to make sure that a nominal level really operates as a level in the organization. This may not be so in the case of "dual career tracks" used to motivate professionals who do not want to take the managerial track in an organization. For example, Mobil Oil Company research labs offers a dual career track for scientists to accommodate both those who do not want managerial authority/responsibility and those who do.

A relatively deep hierarchy generally concentrates power at the top (centralization). Below the top, each supervisor has a "span of control"—the number of subordinates a supervisor can effectively direct. If the span is wide, the manager will have a large number of subordinates reporting to him or her. If it is small, the manager will have few subordinates. The smaller the span, in general, the taller the organization, and vice versa. As Harold Koontz notes, "Simple arithmetic will show that the difference between an average management span of, say, four, and one of eight in a company of four thousand managerial employees can make a difference of two entire levels of management and of nearly eight hundred managers."[8]

Opinion is divided about the relationship between horizontal and vertical differentiation. One major study has found that the two do not vary together, whereas another indicates that they do.[9] Common sense would dictate that they do not necessarily have to vary together; some organizations are "tall and narrow," others "short and wide."

## Spatial Dispersion

The final element in the complexity picture is *spatial* dispersion, a form of horizontal differentiation. Activities can be dispersed geographically according to either vertical or horizontal functions. An example of horizontal spatial dispersion is the home office that retains central power while the field office performs essentially the same tasks. A California bank may have branches in many cities that do the same business that one Illinois bank does in one location.

An example of vertical spatial dispersion would be a manufacturing plant with satellite plants, each specialized by technology or product. Senior executives may reside in one city, middle managers in several other cities, and lower-level employees toil in offices around the world. Universities use spatial dispersion to offer courses and degree programs over a wide geographic area. Obviously, as geographic dispersion increases, so do problems of communication, coordination, and control.

Do the three elements of complexity vary with each other at all? Apparently not. Some organizations are low in all three (e.g., the corner grocery store), some are high in all three (e.g., IBM), some are low in vertical and spatial but high in horizontal differentiation (e.g., some small colleges), some are high in vertical and low in horizontal and spatial (e.g., an army chemical battalion), and so on.

If complexity causes problems, why is it necessary? Organizations in complex environments must increase their complexity to cope with the demands/expectations of various external strategic constituencies. As competitive pressures increase, experts in a variety of disciplines are needed for a variety of geographic areas, such as market researchers, public relations staff, legal experts, patent attorneys, and communications staff. But the economies and efficiency that differentiation gives an organization are offset by the increased burden of keeping the organization together (control, coordination, and conflict resolution).

The reader should be aware that all of the foregoing is a *direct result of how we think*. That is, we think in mechanical ways and therefore we create mechanical organization structures, which we proceed to integrate in mechanical ways, too.

There does not seem to be a way for an organization to grow big in a turbulent, complex environment without also becoming more complex and bureaucratic. Big organizations seem to need committees, cross-functional teams, management information systems, rules, goals, and hierarchy to integrate their efforts.

## A Transformational View of Complexity

Complexity is the natural result of the industrial era paradigm and its emphasis on our separateness. Each separate person, then, develops a specialty that is "marketable" in the world of business, but that must then be integrated if there is to be coherent movement toward goals.

Complexity also stems from our addiction to externals. Because we tend to define our meaning and our importance by external symbols of success, a high position in a bureaucratic hierarchy is prized. Herein lies the paradigmatic justification for vertical differentiation. Status differences evolve as we create a structure where leaders lead and followers follow. This clear separation by rank allows for a status hierarchy, with differential rewards and levels of authority and responsibility.

Spatial dispersion results again from our propensity to separate things and then try to bring them back together in a unified whole. We break off, in a mechanistic manner, entities that purport to reproduce the functions of the larger organization in a specific geographic area, such as sales offices in cities other than the headquarters city.

## The Process of Integration

In large bureaucratic organizations that lack coordination and control, the right hand often does not know what the left hand is doing, and vice versa. This is cause for much consternation and blame placing among organization participants, and is seen by Peter Drucker, among others, as the key management problem of the 1990s and beyond. An example pointed out by John Child illustrates the potential severity of this problem in a story of needless human suffering:

> The American Agency for International Development (AID) and the United Nations Food and Agriculture Organization (FAO) are the two agencies in question. The aid donated by countries was generous in itself. . . . up to October, 1973, over twenty countries had provided some 60 million pounds (British). Yet sickness and malnutrition continued at an alarming level, considerably worse than that recorded at the time in Bangladesh, which was suffering a similar crisis.
>
> The Carnegie Endowment Report identifies inadequate bureaucratic organization as the culprit, with several instances of poor integration. Warning telegrams from the drought-stricken areas were not adequately collated or acted upon . . . instead they were tucked away in filing cabinets scattered around the world. Even when the rescue operation got underway, plans proved to be un-coordinated. Grain piled up in Dakar, Senegal, because there was insufficient transportation to move it inland.
>
> The report alleges that these failures were due in part to a lack of cooperation between different groups. It states that the entire program, in spite of the dedication of many officials at many levels, was a failure. . . . There was the shadow of bureaucratic factors in the US or UN which bore hardly any relation to the human suffering in Africa . . . programs continued or initiatives neglected out of institutional inertia, rivalries between offices and agencies, and unwillingness to acknowledge failures to the public.[10]

Large organizations seem inevitably to break down into smaller groups or cliques, often with competing attitudes. Communication links become tenuous as people stick to talking to "their own kind." The natural differences in time horizons, goals, styles, and cultures seem to lead to the forming of stereotypes; for example, people in sales begin to see the production people as natural enemies. A strong identity with a given field seems to make integration more difficult. Pugh has developed a list of "warning signs" of poor integration:

1.  persistent conflict between departments
2.  fudging integration issues through a series of committees
3.  overloading top management (to settle disputes)
4.  the ritual of red tape
5.  empire building by coordinators
6.  complaints by customers, clients, and other external parties[11]


Lawrence and Lorsch's classic studies in organizational integration, begun in 1967 and continued until 1974, sought to answer the age-old question, What makes organizations effective? More specifically, Lawrence and Lorsch sought to determine the effects of various environmental contingencies on organization structural effectiveness. Their results were published in many places, but the classic source is their 1969 book, *Organization and Environment*.[12]

In all the studies, the common goal was to determine the influence of the organization's environment on the effectiveness of various structural arrangements. Lawrence and Lorsch collected data on organizational performance (to reflect effectiveness), structural characteristics, and characteristics of the environment. For the purposes of their study, they defined *integration* as the "quality of the state of collaboration that exists among departments that are required to achieve unity of effort by the demands of the environment."[13]

They chose a sample of six high- and low-performing firms in each of three industries for their studies. The first industry, *plastics,* was characterized by a very high level of innovation, technological change, and competition (in other words, a highly complex environment). The second industry, *food,* had a moderate level of complexity, and this was reflected by moderate organizational differentiation. The third industry, *containers,* was, at that time in history, a rather stable industry, with low competition and low levels of technological innovation, so firms in this industry tended to have low levels of differentiation.

When Lawrence and Lorsch searched for features common to the excellent companies in each industry, they found that all excellent companies were well integrated. Each had sufficient mechanisms of control and coordination in place to facilitate unity of action. However, firms in different industries had to do different things to become integrated. In the plastics industry, excellent firms had to use nontraditional integrators, such as cross-functional teams and an integration department, in addition to standard bureaucratic integrators (such as hierarchy, rules, memos, directives) to achieve an adequate level of integration. In the less-differentiated food industry companies, the excellent ones used an integration person (usually an assistant to the president or the like) and temporary cross-functional teams as needed, plus the bureaucratic integrators. When used correctly, their standard bureaucratic integrators were adequate to achieve high levels of integration.

Stated differently, Lawrence and Lorsch found that, in environments of low change and complexity, one can get along quite nicely with the standard bureaucratic integrators. A well-run bureaucracy will do just fine, thank you. However, when the organization is in a moderate or highly dynamic environment, bureaucracy, no matter how well run, is not sufficient to handle the differentiation and integration demands placed on it. In order to survive in such an environment, the organization must differentiate to a high degree and therefore must use extraordinary measures (nontraditional integrators) to achieve unity of effort.

There are several messages here. The first is that there is no one ideal organizational model. Different environmental contingencies require different structural modifications to achieve differentiation and integration. Second, the price for increased differentiation is more energy spent on achieving integration. This energy comes in the form of nontraditional integrators, that is, cross-functional teams and integration specialists. Obviously, these are costly to implement and should be used only when they are required. Third, companies should move to more organic models of organization only when, all other things being equal, they are forced to by increasing environmental complexity. Organic structures are hard to implement without sufficiently mature, responsible people to maintain them, and it is costly to train people to take personal responsibility as well as to be proficient in their jobs. Because the paradigm has not completely shifted, people who are comfortable with a bureaucratic structure that corresponds to their paradigmatic beliefs and assumptions will have difficulty getting used to organic structures.

To orient its employees to its matrix structure, Dow Corning, Inc., in Midland, Michigan, takes new employees who have come out of bureaucratic structures directly to an orientation program of several weeks' duration, the object of which is to change the paradigms of the workers. The workers are trained in team building, communication skills, corporate purpose and strategy, conflict resolution skills, and the like. With this foundation, "fitting in" to their new jobs is much easier for them.

## A Transformational View of Integration

The process of integration was devised to get the parts of an organization working together in a mechanistic manner. Basically, integration is conflict resolution. It is assumed that the separate parts will necessarily come into conflict over scarce resources and differences in goals, status, time orientation, and so on, so some mechanisms must be in place to ensure unity of effort. When the separate parts do not work together as a coherent whole, waste, conflict, and low output result; this is called *suboptimization.* Vignette 4 presents a metaphor to help illustrate the transformational perspective concerning effectiveness, integration, and agreement.

**Vignette 4**

The conductor of a symphony orchestra makes no sound when conducting— the orchestra produces the music. If the sound the orchestra produces is to be music (rather than noise), the orchestra members must have tuned instruments and must follow a score. The score is the design, if you will, for the production.

There is a score, or a design, inherent in life. How willing are we to allow this design to integrate our activities into a harmonious whole? Would we rather play our own instruments according to our self-centered designs, oblivious to the design of the larger whole? True integration, from the transformational perspective, comes from being attuned to the design and control inherent in the life force or energy of the cosmos.

When we choose self-centered designs over the design of the whole, we need "artificial integrators": traditional bureaucratic integrators include RRPP, memos and directives from on high, close supervision, and management by objectives. These are appropriate in a bureaucratic organization in which it is assumed that the goals of the workers and the goals of the organization are not congruent, and that workers must be forced or directed to work toward organizational goals (Theory X assumptions). But, in an organic organization, the assumption is that the worker psychologically "owns" the corporate purpose, that a sufficiently compelling vision has been articulated by top management to instill in the worker loyalty and motivation, that the worker's personal goals may be easily met through the accomplishment of the organization's purposes, and that all workers take 100% personal responsibility for results.

As the paradigm continues to shift, we can conclude that traditional ways of integrating will become increasingly inadequate for the task of bringing together a diverse group of people with different preferences, personal goals, likes and dislikes, and so on. The presence of a compelling, inspiring vision will become essential in "enrolling" workers psychologically in the pursuit of the organization's purposes.[14]

## Formalization

Another dimension of organization structure is formalization, which can be described as the extent to which work behavior is constrained by rules, regulations, policies, and procedures. Generally, when individual discretion as to job performance is low, formalization is high. The clearer, more detailed, and more unequivocal the specifications, the greater the intolerance for deviations, the higher the formalization. Some organizations may be required by higher authorities to develop extensive RRPP, but do not enforce them; this is de facto low formalization. High formalization requires both high expectation specificity and high compliance enforcement.[15] The familiar McDonald's restaurant is run with high formalization.

One of the early definitions of formalization holds that it "denotes the extent to which rules, procedures, instructions, and communications are written."[16] The paradigmatic implications of formalization should be clear. The degree to which an organization is formalized is an indication of how top decision makers view their subordinates; if members are assumed to be capable and willing of exercising self-judgment and self-control (all other things being equal), there will be low formalization. If, on the other hand, workers are viewed from the typical Theory X perspective, formalization will be high. Workers viewed as being incapable of or unwilling to make good decisions will be directed from above via formalization. Formalization, then, is essentially the amount of organizational control over the individual.[17]

Formalization (or RRPP) is used to give direction on how to handle contingencies that might arise, how to make routine decisions, how to deal with customer complaints, and other functions. The extreme case of formalization has come to be called *standardization*, which is "any procedure that occurs regularly, is legitimized by the organization, has rules that cover circumstances, and apply invariably."[18]

### Measures of Formalization

It doesn't much matter whether the rules are written or unwritten; if they serve to limit worker discretion on the job, they are for all practical purposes elements of formalization. However, most definitions of formalization emphasize written systems. Jerald Hage notes:

Organizations learn from past experiences and employ rules as a repository of that experience. Some organizations carefully codify each job, describing specific details, and then ensure conformity to the job description. Other organizations have loosely defined jobs and do not carefully control work behavior. Formalization, or standardization, is measured by the proportion of codified jobs and the range of variation that is tolerated within the rules defining the jobs. The higher the proportion of codified jobs and the less the range of variation allowed, the more formalized the organization.[19]

A similar definition is as follows:

> Formalization represents the use of rules in an organization. Job codification is a measure of how many rules define what the occupants of positions are to do, while rule observation is a measure of whether or not the rules are employed. In other words, the variable of job codification represents the degree to which the job descriptions are specified, and the variable, rule observation, refers to the degree to which job occupants are supervised in conforming to the standards established by job codification. Job codification represents the degree of work standardization while rule observation is a measure of the latitude of behavior that is tolerated from standards.[20]

A somewhat humorous example of the kind of thing that can result from rigid standardization is presented in Vignette 5.

---

**Vignette 5**

The following appeared in the *Denver Post* in 1988: "The wife of American hostage Alann Steen said Sunday the U.S. Internal Revenue Service has demanded that her husband, held captive for more than 24 months, pay back taxes or face prosecution. Virginia Rose Steen said she received the computer printout from the IRS two weeks ago requesting payment of his 1984 taxes within 30 days."

SOURCE: *Denver Post*, November 14, 1988, 1.

---

## Formalization and Other Aspects of Organization

Formalization does seem to have a relationship with a number of other organizational properties. It seems to be weakly associated with centralization. At first glance, this would seem to be in line with the paradigmatic model; if top managers do not trust workers to do things right, they would establish a lot of RRPP. They would also, the logic goes, tend to want to tell employees what to do. In general, this is true. Several studies have shown that organizations with few decision makers at the top tend to rely on RRPP and close supervision as a way of ensuring correct performance by the workers.[21] However, this type of organization typically has less well trained and professional staff; when there does exist a professional staff to whom top management can delegate (thereby creating decentralization), formalization tends to decrease. One author states:

> Rigidity in some respects may breed flexibility in others. Not all aspects of bureaucracy are concomitant. The bureaucratic elaboration of formalized personnel procedures and rigid conformity with these personnel standards do not necessarily occur together, and neither aspect of bureaucratization of procedures gives rise to a more rigid authority structure, at least not in employment security agencies. Indeed, both strict conformity with civil service standards and the elaboration of these formalized standards have the opposite effect of fostering decentralization, which permits greater flexibility.[22]

In other words, having strict merit rules in one area may tend to breed people with a greater ability to act autonomously, thereby permitting more decentralization. Especially in professional organizations, this tends to be true. Setting standard rules for handling certain problems allows for more decentralization by letting lower-level employees handle these situations without having to consult higher authority. A high-tech company in Seattle that sells expensive medical equipment used to require extensive paperwork and top management approval for replacement of faulty equipment; now, through delegation and decentralization, field personnel can authorize replacement. Employee morale and customer satisfaction have improved markedly since this change.

Professionals inherently dislike high formalization, because their professional training itself provides rules or guidelines for their behavior in certain situations, and they tend to resent the organization's telling them what to do. Their internal rules are often in conflict with the external rules of the organization. By selecting highly qualified and well-indoctrinated individuals to perform organization roles, the organization lessens the need for high formalization.[23]

Additional research has shown that technology tends to be associated with formalization, in a predictable way: "Organizations with routine work are more likely to have greater formalization of organizational roles."[24] By *routine*, we mean that the technology tends to have very few exceptions coming up (exceptions being problems that differ from the norm) and there is relatively little difficulty in solving those few problems that do arise (low coping difficulty).

From the paradigmatic perspective, this would follow: A simple, routine job would lend itself easily to high formalization. Take the making of french fries at McDonald's restaurants, for instance. McDonald's is actually selling *consistency* of product, so it wants all McDonald's french fries to taste exactly the same in every restaurant, all around the world. Hence management resorts to high formalization to ensure that uniformity.

For nonroutine jobs, one would expect low levels of formalization, and that is exactly what research shows. For example, if a company is formulating an original ad campaign for one of its new products, the formalization associated with this endeavor is likely to be low.

Formalization also seems to be related to the cultural development of the organization. If the tradition of the organization, as articulated by early chief executives, is toward lots of RRPP, then that tradition seems to be upheld even in light of evidence that it is no longer needed. As a mechanism for control over individuals, formalization can grow in power as a symbol of management control even beyond its "objective" standards.[25] For example, a particular commercial kitchen had a rule that forbade women to wear long pants to work. The owners kept this rule in effect until the 1980s, because "we've always done it this way!" Those who questioned the rule were seen as rebellious or unable to accept authority.

## Dysfunctional Consequences of High Formalization

Robert Merton draws attention to the dysfunctional aspects of bureaucratic life in his seminal work on the "bureaucratic personality." He suggests that these arise as a consequence of the system itself:

> The bureaucrat's official life is planned for him in terms of a graded career, through the organization's devices of promotion by seniority, pensions, incremental salaries, etc., all of which are designed to provide incentives for disciplined action and conformity to the official regulations. The official is tacitly expected to and largely does adapt his thoughts, feelings and actions to the prospect of this career. But these very devices which increase the probability of conformance also lead to an over-concern with strict adherence to regulations which induces timidity, conservatism and technicism. Displacement of sentiments from goals onto means is fostered by the tremendous symbolic significance of the means (rules).[26]

This leads us to the primary dysfunctional forms of behavior found among bureaucratic personalities: bureaupathic behavior and bureautic behavior.[27] *Bureaupathic* behavior results when a person values the rules themselves more than the goals of the organization. This personality type is overly concerned with covering his or her own ass, always writing memos to protect him- or herself, and eager to report infractions of the rules. This person has learned that, to succeed in the organization, he or she must follow the rules, avoid making waves, and, above all, eschew innovation and creativity. The bureaupathic individual has developed a cynical survival strategy, and, given the realities of bureaucratic life, who is to say that is wrong?

**Vignette 6**

A classic story about rules becoming more important than goals is that of the airline flight attendant who was "only adhering to the rules" when she closed the door on a woman in a wheelchair who was waiting for assistance. The flight attendant explained that the door had to be closed at a certain time.

On the other hand, there is the story of the British bus driver who drove right past potential passengers waiting at the proper stops. When asked why he did this, he replied that if he stopped for all those people he would never get to where he was supposed to go on time!

In *bureautic behavior*, a person alienated by being treated as a child rebels by manifesting antisocial behavior, such as worker sabotage on an assembly line, chronic absenteeism, tardiness, or, in extreme cases, physical violence. Bureautic behavior involves personalizing every encounter with a rule, personally striking out at the ubiquitous "system," and interpreting every rule as being designed for one's own frustration. Victor Thompson suggests that these behaviors result from the employee's feelings of insecurity. He writes that the most significant source of insecurity in modern organizations is:

> the growing gap between the rights of authority (to review, to veto, to affirm) and the specialized ability or skill required to solve most organizational problems. The intellectual, problem-solving component of executive offices is being increasingly diverted to specialists, leaving hierarchical rights (and duties) as principal components of executive posts. Persons in hierarchical positions are therefore increasingly dependent upon subordinate and non-subordinate specialists for the achievement of organizational (or unit) goals.
>
> The supervisor tends to be caught between the two horns of a dilemma. He must satisfy the non-explicit and non-operational demands of a supe-

rior through the agency of specialized subordinates and non-subordinates whose skills he only dimly understands. And, yet, to be counted a success, he must accept this dilemma and live with its increasing viciousness throughout his life. He must live with increasing insecurity and anxiety.[28]

These pressures tend to produce more and more RRPP to protect officeholders in traditional bureaucratic organizations. But in organic organizations, where sapiential authority is replacing authority of position, authority based in knowledge will obviate the need for high formalization, as leadership in a work project shifts from one person to the next as particular expertise is needed.[29]

In summary, formalization can be seen as central to a bureaucratic strategy of control. Its use is clearly more suitable in times of relative stability, with routine technologies, and with relatively less-educated workers who have low expectation levels regarding job enrichment. But even with these factors in place, it can still be argued that treating people as children by telling them what to do and when to do it leads to increasing levels of immaturity, dependency, and demotivation. Of course, when product or service uniformity is crucial to one's marketing approach, as is true of McDonald's, then one might be willing to accept these dysfunctional elements to attain that uniformity. Formalization—and its extreme, standardization—will lead to uniformity unless the presence of bureaupathic and bureautic behaviors erodes the desired outcome.

---

## Centralization

---

Centralization can be said to be the degree to which decision making is concentrated at a "single point" in the organization. Usually, this implies that decision making is at the top of the organization, in a chief executive officer or an executive group. High concentration of decision-making power means *high centralization* and low concentration of (or diffuse) power implies *decentralization*.

Until recently, the Ford Motor Company was a classic example of centralization. For years, it was run by a member of the Ford family or by a representative of the family; all decisions of any importance were made by the Ford in charge. In contrast, Alfred Sloan initiated the profit-center, decentralized model at General Motors, and that company has become a model of decentralized management. In effect, each of the divisions of General Motors—Chevrolet, Oldsmobile, Cadillac, Buick—

is a separate company, and each division CEO reports to the president (but has a wide leeway in decision-making authority).

Basically, *centralization* refers to the amount of dispersion of authority to make decisions in the organization. The issue is simply this: Where are the decisions made in the organization? Are they made only at the top, or are they made by the decision makers closest to the action?

Research indicates that as organizations grow, so do the pressures for decentralization. As noted earlier, greater formalization in a large organization like General Motors permits the decentralization of routine decisions because rules tend to define the decision-making parameters, so that decisions can be made at lower levels without loss of control. Thus it would appear that one key to successful decentralization is to have some mechanism in place to ensure conformity with organizational norms, rules, and values in the decision-making process. This conclusion tends to be supported by the work of William Ouchi in his classic *Theory Z*.[30] Ouchi discusses the use of *informal, implicit controls* in Japanese businesses. These controls are cultural, in that the Japanese manager is indoctrinated with the company philosophy and value system on a daily basis so that his decisions are always informed by that point of view. Ouchi contrasts this style with the American reliance on *formal, explicit controls*—rules, policies, quarterly statements, and so on.

Stephen Robbins points to a series of problems associated with the common definition of centralization:

1. *Do we look only at formal authority?* Obviously, centralization of decision making takes in all those with legitimate or formal authority, but what about those with informal authority? What about the boss's son who is now a menial clerk, but who everyone knows is the heir apparent?

2. *Can policies override decentralization?* A number of organizations have pushed decisions down in the organization, but existing RRPP hamper and delimit effective decision-making discretion. So, is it really decentralized or does it just look that way?

3. *What does "concentration at a single point" mean?* Does a single point mean a person, a group of people, a committee, a level in the organization? And if the operating people are not allowed to participate in decisions that affect them, does it really matter if the decisions are made at the top or two levels above them?

4. *Does an information-processing system that closely monitors decentralized decisions maintain centralized control?* Modern computer technology allows for effective decentralization, but how decentralized is it really if the boss can see what you are deciding and reverse the decisions in an instant?

5. *Does the control of information by lower-level members result in the decentralization of what appears to be centralized decisions?* Lower-level participants routinely decide what to send up the line and what not to

send, thereby effectively screening the information on which top decision makers base their decisions. This filtering process brings into question the validity of so-called centralized decisions.[31]

These caveats demonstrate that the concept of centralization is not as easy to grasp as first contact would indicate. A more specific definition may help. According to Robbins, "Centralization can be described more specifically as the degree to which the formal authority to make discretionary choices is concentrated in an individual, unit, or level (usually high in the organization), thus permitting employees (usually low in the organization) minimal input into their work."[32]

Formal authority and the notion of the hierarchy are intimately related, and one could not survive without the other. The hierarchy is held together by the belief that "leaders lead and followers follow." Leaders are given formal authority through the formal organization sanction that permits them to make decisions and direct the work efforts of subordinates. Our collective paradigm acknowledges that bosses have the right to tell subordinates what to do and when to do it.

As we mentioned previously, one of the symptoms of the industrial paradigm breakdown is the increasing incidence of bosses who know demonstrably less about their subordinates' work than do the subordinates themselves. This undermines the mythology of superior dominance and will certainly continue as a trend in our information-oriented society.

## NOTES

1. Corrine L. Gilb, "Public or Private Governments," in *Handbook of Organizational Design* (2nd ed.), ed. Paul C. Nystrom and William H. Starbuck (New York: Oxford University Press, 1981).

2. Robert H. Miles, *Macro Organizational Behavior* (Glenview, IL: Scott, Foresman, 1980), 20.

3. Marshall W. Meyer, "Two Authority Structures of Bureaucratic Organization," *Administrative Science Quarterly* 13 (September 1968).

4. James D. Thompson, *Organizations in Action* (New York: McGraw-Hill, 1967), 78.

5. Richard H. Hall, J. Eugene Haas, and Norman Johnson, "An Examination of the Blau-Scott and Etzioni Typologies," *Administrative Science Quarterly* 12 (June 1967): 126.

6. Barbara Bueld, "Nike Catches Up With the Trendy Frontrunner," *Business Week*, October 24, 1988, 88.

7. Ibid., 88.

8. Harold Koontz, "Making Theory Operational: The Span of Management," *Journal of Management Studies* 20 (October 1966): 229.

9. Compare Peter M. Blau and Richard A. Schoenherr, *The Structure of Organizations* (New York: Basic Books, 1971), with Dennis S. Mileti, David S. Gillespie, and J. Eugene Haas, "Size and Structure in Complex Organizations," *Social Forces* 56 (September 1977).

10. John Child, *Organization: A Guide to Problems and Practice* (2nd ed.) (London: Harper & Row, 1984), 111.

11. Donald Pugh, "Effective Coordination in Organizations," *Advanced Management Journal* (Winter 1979).

12. Paul R. Lawrence and Jay W. Lorsch, *Organization and Environment* (Homewood, IL: Irwin, 1969).

13. Ibid., 11.

14. See especially Charles F. Kiefer and Peter M. Senge, "Metanoic Organizations"; Roger Harrison, "Leadership and Strategy for a New Age"; and David Nicoll, "Grace Beyond the Rules"; all in *Transforming Work*, ed. John D. Adams (Alexandria, VA: Miles River, 1984).

15. William G. Ouchi and Reuben T. Harris, "Structure, Technology and Environment," in *Organizational Behavior: Research and Issues*, ed. George Strauss, Raymond E. Miles, and Charles C. Snow (Madison, WI: Industrial Relations Research Association, 1974).

16. D. S. Pugh, D. J. Hickson, C. R. Hinings, and C. Turner, "Dimensions of Organization Structure," *Administrative Science Quarterly* 13 (June 1968): 65-105.

17. Stewart Clegg and David Dunkerly, *Organization, Class and Control* (London: Routledge & Kegan Paul, 1980).

18. Child, *Organization*, 92.

19. Jerald Hage, "An Axiomatic Theory of Organizations," *Administrative Science Quarterly* 10 (December 1965): 295.

20. Jerald Hage and Michael Aiken, "The Relationship of Centralization to Other Structural Properties," *Administrative Science Quarterly* 12 (June 1967): 79.

21. See, for example, Peter M. Blau, "Decentralization in Bureaucracies," in *Power in Organizations*, ed. Mayer N. Zald (Nashville, TN: Vanderbilt University Press, 1970); Hage and Aiken, "The Relationship of Centralization."

22. Blau, "Decentralization in Bureaucracies," 160.

23. Blau and Schoenherr, *The Structure of Organizations*, 347-367.

24. Jerald Hage and Michael Aiken, "Routine Technology, Social Structure and Organizational Goals," *Administrative Science Quarterly* 14 (September 1969): 371.

25. Clegg and Dunkerly, *Organization, Class and Control*.

26. Robert K. Merton, *Social Theory and Social Structure* (Glencoe, IL: Free Press, 1957), 200-201.

27. Victor Thompson, *Modern Organizations* (New York: Knopf, 1961).

28. Ibid., 156-157.

29. Robert Theobald, *An Alternative Future for America II* (Chicago: Swallow, 1970).

30. William G. Ouchi, *Theory Z: How American Business Can Meet the Japanese Challenge* (Reading, MA: Addison-Wesley, 1981).

31. Stephen P. Robbins, *Organization Theory: Structure, Design, and Applications* (2nd ed.) (Englewood Cliffs, NJ: Prentice Hall, 1987), 73-75.

32. Ibid., 75.

# 10   The Creation and Evolution of Organization Structure

> *It is horrible to think that the world could one day be filled with nothing but those little cogs, little men clinging to little jobs and striving towards bigger ones. . . . this passion for bureaucracy . . . is enough to drive one to despair. It is as if in politics . . . we were deliberately to become men who need order and nothing but order, who become nervous and cowardly if for one moment this order wavers, and helpless if they are torn away from their total incorporation in it. . . . the great question is therefore not how we can promote and hasten it, but what can we oppose to this machinery in order to keep a portion of mankind free from this parcelling out of the soul from this supreme mastery of the bureaucratic way of life.*
>
> (Reinhold Bendix,
> *Max Weber: An Intellectual Portrait*, 1960, pp. 455-456)

---

**SUMMARY:** In this chapter we address the creation of the organization under the dominant collective paradigm. We examine both Newtonian and Einsteinian assumptions, and then discuss the evolution or change of organization structure over time, focusing on the mechanistic or bureaucratic form.

---

**W**e have now seen how the collective paradigm creates the world of our experience. We literally create our own reality, using the "software" of our beliefs, attitudes, and values and the "techniques" of the self-fulfilling prophecy, self-limiting beliefs, and selective perception. Organizations, too, are shaped by the collective paradigms of their members and are influenced by dominant societal beliefs, attitudes, and values.

Slowly but surely, organizations are changing their *structures* and *processes* as a result of the shifting paradigm. The old "top-down," command-and-control bureaucratic structure is becoming increasingly obsolete, especially in turbulent environments. Replacing or augmenting it are a vast array of team structures, "network" organizations, peripheral "broker" arrangements, and the like. The emphasis in these emerging structures is on flexibility and adaptability. However, new- and old-paradigm organizations have this in common:

> An organization is a "world" with a particular view that colors what its members see and let in from the outside world. An organizational world consists of people practicing their technologies, organized by their tasks, and structured into relationships kept dynamic by the way they are measured and controlled. Inevitably, these people are, to some degree, self-selected, inadvertently or deliberately, and share values and attitudes. All this is directed toward some end—sometimes explicit, sometimes implicit.[1]

## Two Views of the Organization: Newtonian and Einsteinian

The shift from Cartesian/Newtonian assumptions about the nature of the universe to Einsteinian/quantum mechanics assumptions is beginning to transform the way we look at organizations. Instead of conceiving of organizations as machines that are separate, and that can be "fixed" as one would fix a car, the new paradigm sees the organization as an organic whole, embedded in, influencing, and being influenced by the larger whole of society in general. Any "fixing" must therefore take this larger whole into account.

Under the transformational perspective or paradigm, the notion of organizational boundaries is also taking on new meaning. The term *boundary* makes sense only within the context of the Newtonian paradigm. If reality is an unbroken, seamless whole with only relative permanence, as Bohm asserts, then what becomes of boundaries between organizations and their so-called external environments? Figure 10.1 illustrates the difference between the industrial paradigm view of organizations and the Einsteinian view.

Organizations from the
Cartesian/Newtonian viewpoint

Organizations from the transformational
perspective

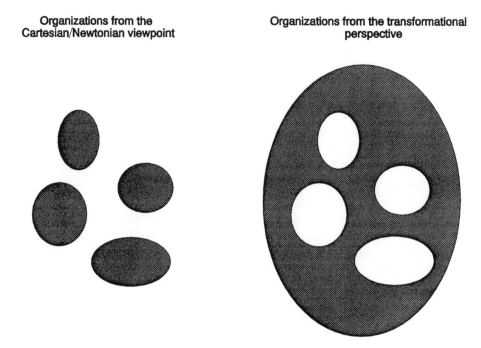

**Figure 10.1.** Model of Cartesian/Newtonian Paradigm Versus Einsteinian/
Quantum Mechanics Paradigm

Under Cartesian or Newtonian assumptions, we concentrate on the
*form* of things. In the case of organizations and organization theory, we
have tended to describe the structures and processes of organizations
and have attempted to explain the manifestation of these organizational
forms by attributing them to external causes such as technology, environment, and size or to internal causes such as politics/power and strategy.
According to this view, a routine assembly-line technology "causes" a
bureaucracy; that is, the structure is the result of the technology.

The transformational perspective is radically different: The forms
perceivable to our five senses are merely *effects* of an invisible cause that
operates at the level of the mind, or, in the case of organizations, the
collective mind of the organization.

## Implications of the
## Paradigm Concept for Organizations

The concept of paradigm is essential for an understanding of how new
institutions are created and old ones are maintained and changed. The

structures of an organization flow naturally from the dynamics of the members' interrelationships and assumptions about reality and their place in the organization. Social rules and norms can be inferred from various human behaviors.

---

A *collective paradigm* is an implicit and collectively shared view of "how things are" that determines the structural form of an organization. A paradigm is challenged only when increasing dysfunction appears.

---

But what determines those rules, norms, and other observable phenomena in organizations? People interact in organizations on the basis of an overall framework (paradigm) of shared beliefs, attitudes, and values: "What is so about this place"; "We like this and we don't like that"; "We think this is good and we think this is bad."[2] These invisible patterns of mental and emotional structures are the *cause* behind whatever observable structures and behaviors we might notice. They also influence the outcomes of events. The same event will have different consequences depending on beliefs *about* that event. For example:

*EVENT:* A person in the workplace has been diagnosed with AIDS.

—*Belief 1:* Any person with AIDS will contaminate those around him or her.

*CONSEQUENCES:* Fear, protests, resignations.

—*Belief 2:* It is possible to work with a person with AIDS and not be harmed.

*CONSEQUENCES:* Ongoing and successful work relationship.

Paradigms are the logics or mental/emotional models that underlie the social architecture of institutions: the mission, system of governance, and organizational culture and structure (including sociotechnical systems). Paradigms provide the medium in which the members of the organization exist, determine the modes of managing change, and influence the manner of creating and resolving disputes between different organizational entities. Competing paradigms can also lead to standoffs between parties. No doubt there are countless examples of such standoffs, such as the case described in Vignette 1.

**Vignette 1**

A small professional firm employed four staff members. One year at Christmastime, the partners were discussing bonuses for the staff. One partner had a conventional attitude about money: "Give the employees as little as possible." The other partner was concerned more with ways to spread the profits of the company out among those who helped to earn it. The first partner was responsible for determining the bonuses, however, and issued checks for sums that turned out to be embarrassing to the second partner. This event created tension between the partners that eventually required intervention by a third party.

SOURCE: Files of Renaissance Business Associates, Inc.[3]

The point of this vignette is that decisions on all matters are based on individuals' personal paradigms, which include professional attitudes or values; one person's decisions may be in sharp contrast to those another would make, because of differences in the basic paradigms of the two people.

---

## How Paradigms Structure Organizations

---

Traditional explanations for organizational structure have all assumed that structure is the result of the influence of some *external* factor, such as strategy, size, technology, power relationships, or environment. But according to the transformational approach, structure has an *invisible* internal cause.

It has been well recognized that organizational structure influences the behavior of the people involved and this, in turn, affects the performance of organizations. What is not so widely recognized, however, is that structure is the *result* of the collective agreement in the organization regarding basic beliefs, attitudes, and values. This agreement leads to certain assumptions and expectations concerning people in the organization, the nature of the environment, the technology employed, and other factors. The primary influence on an organization is the nature of the collective agreement among key decision makers, which determines the pervasive atmosphere of the company and the organization's structural configuration. However, for a structure to remain relatively permanent, *all* organizational members (not just the decision makers) must accept it. Not only must they accept it, but they must operate as though it were a given.

The importance of the notion that beliefs shape behavior and process in organizations was originally recognized by Douglas McGregor in his now-famous Theory X and Theory Y formulations. The Theory X model makes the following assumptions about human beings:

1. The average person has an inherent dislike for work and will avoid it if he or she can.
2. Because of this human characteristic of dislike of work, most people must be coerced, controlled, directed, or threatened with punishment to get them to put forth adequate effort toward the achievement of organizational objectives.
3. The average human being prefers to be directed, wishes to avoid responsibility, has relatively little ambition, and wants security above all.

The Theory Y model, in contrast, makes these assumptions:

1. The expenditure of physical and mental effort in work is as natural as play or rest.
2. External control and the threat of punishment are not the only means for bringing about effort toward organizational objectives. People will exercise self-direction and self-control in the service of objectives to which they are committed.
3. Commitment to objectives is a function of the rewards associated with their achievement.
4. The average human being learns, under proper conditions, not only to accept but to seek responsibility.[4]

McGregor recognizes that beliefs tend to stimulate self-fulfilling prophecies. In other words, if managers think that workers are lazy, stupid, and so on (Theory X), they will treat them that way, and the workers will act in ways that will verify the beliefs of the managers.

Leon Festinger, and others who subscribe to his *cognitive dissonance* view, has extended this notion. Festinger asserts that it is obvious that thought forms—such as beliefs, attitudes, and values—not only "color" what is perceived in an individual's personal reality, but actually *determine* what the person perceives and does not perceive.[5] He has shown that when individuals are exposed to stimuli that are totally alien to their expectations or paradigms, cognitive dissonance—confusion, stress, or anxiety related to the inability to reconcile the perception with known reality—results. A person who is experiencing cognitive dissonance feels a need to resolve the situation somehow, either by denying what he or she has seen or by adjusting his or her beliefs to include the new reality. Out of this research came the concept of *selective perception*.

As research on the phenomenon of selective perception has been extended, it has confirmed that thought forms (beliefs, attitudes, values), rather than being passive filters through which personal reality is perceived, in fact serve to direct a person to his or her expected outcomes. They also seem to influence the individual so that he or she attracts circumstances that will fulfill the prophecy.

If these thought forms or collective agreements about beliefs, attitudes, and values actually create and sustain the structures and processes in organizations, then changing organizations requires working at the less visible level of cause (collective patterns of beliefs, attitudes, and values) rather than at the more easily seen level of effect (structure). Trying to change the structures of organizations to improve their effectiveness is a bit like looking in a mirror, not liking what you see, and trying to change the reflection in the mirror to improve the looks of your face— that is, it amounts to trying to change the effect, rather than the cause.

If this hypothesis about the importance of causal factors is true, it offers an explanation of the widely documented "resistance to change" phenomenon that occurs as organizations are restructured or reorganized. Essentially, this structural change approach creates an incongruence between the "new" structure and the collective paradigm that designed, legitimated, and maintained the "old" one.

In summary, then, the transformational view holds that structure is *caused* by the consensual agreement among all organizational members about the appropriate nature of power and authority relationships, norms of conduct, value systems, beliefs about people in general and organizational members in particular, and so forth. If you change the external form (the structure), you are essentially tampering with the collective creation of the members *without asking their permission;* no wonder they resist change!

But organizations have changed and are changing as the dominant paradigm shifts. Let's look at the different incarnations of organizations as they have changed in relationship to changes in the dominant paradigm.

## The Evolution of Organizational Structure

As a consequence of the shifting paradigm, organizational structure is beginning to evolve beyond the highly structured machine bureaucracy—in short, away from *mechanistic* structures and toward more *organic* structures. In a now-classic study, Tom Burns and G. M. Stalker looked at 20 English and Scottish firms to determine how their organizational structures might be influenced by environmental conditions.[6] After interviewing a number of managers and observing the natures of the organizational environments, they found that a certain type of structure, which they call "mechanistic," seemed to work best in stable or static environments and that another type ("organic") seemed to work best in rapidly changing or dynamic environments.

The mechanistic structures they found were characterized by the following:

- high complexity (both horizontal and vertical differentiation among jobs, levels, and so on)
- high formalization (many rules and regulations)
- high centralization (power concentrated at the top)

People in these structures performed routine tasks, relied heavily on programmed behaviors, and were relatively slow in responding to the unexpected.

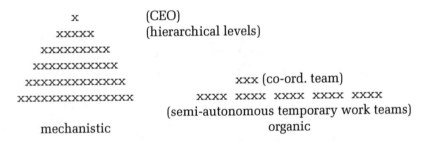

**Figure 10.2.** Mechanistic and Organic Structures
NOTE: The organic structure is essentially one level, with people constantly flowing in and out of various teams.

On the other hand, the organic structures were relatively flexible and adaptive. They emphasized the following:

- lateral rather than vertical communications
- influence based on expertise (i.e., sapiential authority) rather than formal authority of position
- loosely defined responsibilities rather than rigid job descriptions
- emphasis on exchanging information rather than giving orders

Burns and Stalker assert that the environment is the determining factor in which structure is adopted. In other words, a mechanistic design is suitable in a stable, certain environment, whereas an organic structure will work better in a turbulent environment. One design is not better than the other—it is just more suitable vis-à-vis particular environmental conditions. Also, few organizations are purely mechanistic or organic; these ideal types are the opposing ends of a continuum.

---

## Organization as Machine

---

The great German sociologist Max Weber did the foundational work on the development of the mechanistic industrial organization form, the bureaucracy. Weber, who observed the parallels between the mechanization of industry and the proliferation of machinelike bureaucratic forms of organization, noted that the bureaucratic form routinizes the process of administration exactly as the machine routinizes production.[7] This was a logical outgrowth of the thinking of the time; an industrial revolution, with mechanized productive apparatus (one form), would naturally inspire a mechanized organization (another form) to complement it.

In Weber's work we find the first comprehensive description of the bureaucratic form as one that emphasizes speed, efficiency, clarity, regularity, reliability, and precision. Obviously, as the Industrial Revolution got under way in the United States (with a workforce made up largely of uneducated workers straight off the farm or from overseas), this form was ideally suited to the situational constraints of the era.

According to Weber, a bureaucratic organization has the following fundamental features:

1. division of labor based on functional specialization
2. a well-defined hierarchy of authority
3. a system of rules covering the rights and duties of employees
4. systematic procedures for dealing with work situations
5. impersonality of work relations (to deal with the problem of capricious worker treatment)
6. promotion and tenure based on technical competence[8]

When viewed from the perspective of the dominant cultural paradigm, it is no accident that the bureaucracy became so popular. Remember, *engineers* provided the impetus for the revolution itself. Given that the revolution was machine-based, it was natural to design "organizations as machines." Many of the early "classical management" writers at the turn of the century were, in fact, engineers by training or inclination, such as Henri Fayol, F. W. Mooney, Lyndall Urwick, and, most popular of them all, Frederick Taylor. The basic thrust of their thinking was the notion that management is a process of planning, staffing, directing, organizing, and controlling the work effort. To design an organization, you simply define the authority relationships, specialize the jobs (so that almost anyone can do them with a modicum of training), provide plenty of RRPP to guide the effort, separate the line from the staff jobs, provide for accountability, have reasonable spans of control (the number of people one person can effectively supervise), and get started.

In other words, organizations were designed so that people could be "plugged in" like any other component. Taylor did deal with the problem of motivation, but from the assumption that people are motivated only by money (hence the piece-rate system). Much of modern management theory has flowed out of this basic set of assumptions, including management by objectives; planning, programming, and budgeting systems; and other methods stressing rational planning and control.

## Machine Versus Professional Bureaucracies

There have come to be two ways to describe the bureaucratic form: the machine bureaucracy and the professional bureaucracy.[9] The *machine bureaucracy*, designed by Weber and popularized by Taylor and the classicists, uses the elements of the bureaucratic structure to create an organization for the manufacture of some good or goods using a routine technology (such as an assembly line). The backbone of the industrial era, it continues to be widely used in the manufacture of goods both here and abroad. The U.S. Postal Service, airlines, prisons, and manufacturing companies share the characteristics of standardized work; large, stable environments; and control by some external body.

The *professional bureaucracy* is of more recent vintage. Since the mid-1950s, white-collar workers have outnumbered so-called blue-collar workers in the United States, paralleling the rise of service industries in our economy. Universities, law firms, medical centers, and local social service agencies are all examples of professional bureaucracies. What all of these organizations have in common is reliance on trained, professional workers; in fact, work is standardized through professional or craft training.

The key factor in these organizations consists of the skills and knowledge of the operating workers. Instead of differentiating jobs through division of labor, the professional bureaucracy relies on specialization, another word for professionalism. Workers receive specialized training so that they can perform complex jobs with a minimum of supervision.

A classic study by Richard Hall reveals several characteristics concerning the uneasy relationship between professionals and the bureaucratic form.[10] For one thing, professionals are often uneasy in a bureaucratic framework. They cite such reasons as stifled creativity, unreasonable bosses, and lack of understanding for "the demands of the craft/profession." From a paradigmatic perspective, however, the problem is much simpler; people object to having rules and regulations imposed on them that conflict with the internalized "rules and regulations" of their professional training.

In other words, their individual paradigms have been "programmed" with a set of acceptable and unacceptable behaviors, attitudes, beliefs, and so on, and the formalized organization is seen as an unwelcome imposition (unenlightened, at best) on their way of doing things. Hall found that, the stronger the professional attitude, the more people "didn't like bureaucracy." Actually, what they didn't like was formalization and centralization. He also found that there is no *inherent* conflict between professionalism and bureaucracy; rather, conflict often comes about as a result of high formalization.

## Some Common Bureaucratic Departmentalization Schemes

Bureaucratic organizations generally choose to group their activities and work together in departments, providing a pattern for interaction and organizational goal accomplishment. The pattern of structure tends to assume one of four forms: functional, divisional, hybrid, or matrix.

### Functional Departmentalization

In a functional organization, the guiding principle is that all people contributing to the same functional area need to be located together physically. Therefore, in a manufacturing organization, all people concerned with the marketing of the product—the people in direct sales, the market researchers, the product development specialists, the media experts, the trade-show people—are located together. Similarly, all those concerned with manufacturing problems tend to be together, all personnel people together, and so on. A simplified organization chart of a functional organization is shown in Figure 10.3.

This most popular form of departmentalization found in bureaucratic organizations provides a number of advantages:

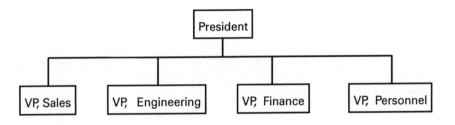

**Figure 10.3.** A Functional Organization

1. organizationwide access to specialized personnel
2. good morale (people seem to like working with "their own kind")
3. ease of supervision
4. adherence to the principle of occupational specialization
5. maintenance of the power and prestige of major functions
6. simplification of training
7. economy and efficiency in operations
8. establishment of a means of tight control at the top

Let us look at this last advantage from a paradigmatic point of view. A centralized organization is very compatible with a functional departmentalization scheme because the CEO can give direction to the leaders of the functional areas, who then translate those directions into the languages and contexts of the different areas. This allows for tight control at the top and accountability upward. However, the functional form does have its problems:

1. responsibility for profits at the top only
2. overspecialization and narrowing of the viewpoints of key personnel
3. difficulty for the economic growth of the company as a system
4. reduction of coordination among functions
5. limitation of the development of general managers

These are potentially very serious weaknesses. When responsibility is concentrated at the top only, the rest of the organization is not motivated to "own" the goals and purposes of the organization. Overspecialization tends to lead to myopia; a general manager needs to see how all of the functions interrelate to form the big picture of the organizational system. The company cannot really grow to its optimal size because the functional approach tends to produce poor coordination among functional areas, and, potentially, a lot of conflict. In fact, as Pradip Khandwalla summarizes:

The more extensive the functional departmentalization in an organization, the greater is the possibility of conflict among the personnel of interfacing departments.

The greater the interface between functionally organized departments, the greater is the need for coordinative mechanisms such as planning, standard operating procedures, committees, a common boss, and communications/human relations training.[11]

## Divisionalization

Divisionalized companies aggregate specialists to produce a given product or service. To do so, they may organize around products, geographic regions, or customer groups. For example, if a firm markets three distinct products, it may choose to set up three self-contained divisional profit centers to handle these products. This form of divisionalization, called *product departmentalization,* was popularized by General Motors under Alfred Sloan. GM contains a Chevrolet Division, a Buick Division, a Pontiac Division, a Cadillac Division, and an Oldsmobile Division. Basically, a product divisionalized organization can be represented as shown in Figure 10.4. Geographic divisionalization is similar; see Figure 10.5. The third variant, customer divisionalization, is shown in Figure 10.6.

These forms all have certain advantages and disadvantages. The main advantages seem to be that divisionalization does the following:

1. places attention and effort on a particular product line (or geographic area or customer group)
2. places responsibility for profits at the divisional level, for better delegation and use of human resources
3. facilitates improved coordination of functional activities
4. furnishes a training ground for general (top) managers
5. permits organizational growth of products, services, and so on
6. gives the division head a high degree of autonomy, which makes planning and coordination easier and allows for much faster adaptation to market changes

The disadvantages of divisionalization include the following:

1. requires more persons with general management experience
2. tends to make maintenance of economical central services difficult
3. presents an increased problem of top management control
4. often results in duplication of staff and facilities
5. can foment sometimes destructive competition within the larger organization

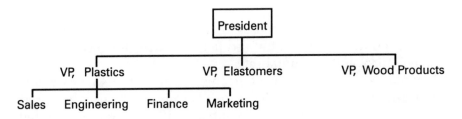

**Figure 10.4.** A Product Organization

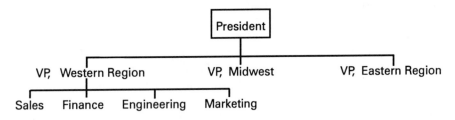

**Figure 10.5.** A Geographic Organization

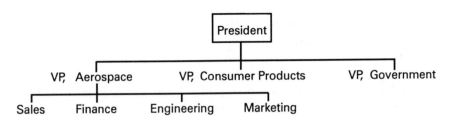

**Figure 10.6.** A Customer Organization

To summarize, Khandwalla points out:

> The more divisionalized the organization, the more centralized the staff functions commonly used by all the divisions.
> The more divisionalized the organization, the better the intradivisional co-ordination but the more intense the interdivisional rivalry.[12]

Many companies apply the divisionalized model because, as companies grow in size and scope, decentralization becomes necessary. One person cannot know enough or be in enough places to maintain executive control in a centralized manner. Alfred Sloan's profit center concept has been adopted by many companies to address the problem of decentralized management for purposes of motivation and performance, keeping certain functions centralized (e.g., finance and accounting) to maintain control and accountability.

Self-contained divisions permit organizations to grow to a very large size and still maintain control. They are also advantageous when products, locations, and clients are substantially different from each other. Let us look at the location issue for an example. In most multinational organizations, autonomous divisions can more easily adapt than can centralized organizations to the different political and cultural factors in particular countries. The failure of centralized advertising is humorously illustrated by Stanley Davis:

> In one classical gaffe, for example, advertisement for a major U.S. based banking firm used a picture of a squirrel hoarding nuts. The idea was to convey an image of thrift, preparedness, and security. When the same advertisement appeared in Caracas, however, it brought a derisive reaction, since Venezuela has neither winters nor squirrels as we know them. Instead, the image evoked a thieving and destructive rat.[13]

## The Hybrid Structure

In reality, many organizational structures in the "real world" do not exist in the pure functional or divisionalized form. One important variant is the *hybrid* form, which combines features of both functional and divisionalized forms. When an organization starts to get very large, it is typically organized into some self-contained units. Functions that seem to be important to each product or market are decentralized to the units; however, some functions are centralized at headquarters. Typically, the centralized functions are relatively stable and yield economies of scale or desired control over divisional autonomy. Most often, financial and accounting functions are centralized for these reasons. By combining the features of the functional and divisional structures, organization designers hope to minimize the weaknesses and emphasize the strengths of each.

Figure 10.7 is a representation of a hybrid structure. The functional part of the organization is reflected in the departments centralized at the corporate level. However, each of the product divisions has specialists in functional areas to assist with problems and opportunities that arise in the local markets. This structure enables the organization to pursue an adaptive strategy within the product divisions while at the same time achieving efficiency in the functional departments. It also provides alignment between corporate goals and the product divisions. The prod-

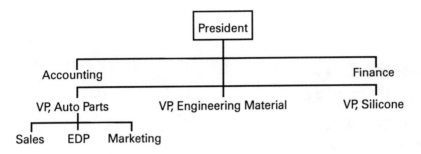

**Figure 10.7.** A Hybrid Organization

uct groupings provide effective coordination within divisions, and the central functional departments provide coordination across divisions.

A major weakness of this form is administrative overhead. Some organizations require a buildup of corporate staffs to oversee divisions. There is often duplication of effort. Division managers may resent what they see as headquarters "meddling in their affairs" and the headquarters staffs may resent divisions' desires to "do their own thing."

## The Sector Structure

Some very large organizations have moved to a variant of the divisionalized structure called the sector structure (see Figure 10.8). Essentially, this provides an additional layer of management between the corporate staff and the divisions, called *sectors;* a sector will control $1-$4 billion in sales annually and allows for the grouping of similar businesses together for the sake of control. The obvious purpose of this structure is to provide some control beyond that exercised by a divisional executive; when a corporation begins to have some 15 to 20 businesses, all in related fields, it makes some sense to group them together for administrative purposes.

The largest proponent of this structure, General Electric, stopped using it in the late 1980s, as most major corporations began the down-

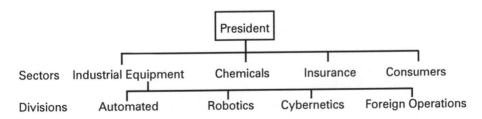

**Figure 10.8.** The Sector Organization

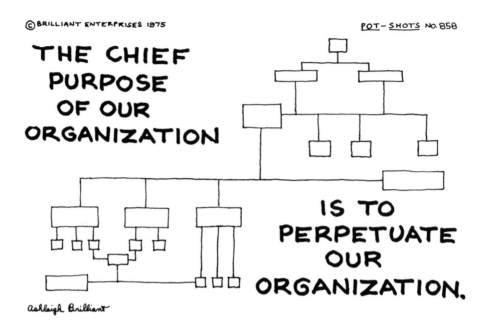

sizing trend that continues today. Whenever a company eliminates a level of hierarchy, it saves money.

## The Problem With Bureaucracy

It should be recognized that, for the time in which it was initially designed, bureaucracy worked well. Considering what it replaced (a system of paternalistic autocracy with widespread worker oppression and maltreatment, capricious treatment of women and children, and so on), bureaucracy was a blessing. It was also the perfect organizational form to facilitate mass-production technology and the standardized production of consumer goods, using skilled and semiskilled workers doing mainly routine tasks.

Since the inception of bureaucracy, however, our world has changed dramatically. In these days of increasing foreign and domestic competition, rapidly changing technologies, shifting consumer tastes, and workers seeking higher-level need satisfaction, the slow-moving bureaucratic form seems more out of date than ever. By the time a major decision inches up the hierarchy for review and implementation, a company can miss an opportunity to respond to a major environmental change.

But turbulent organizational environments and/or complex, highly interdependent technologies are not the only factors besieging bureaucracy. It has also suffered from its apparent inability to foster personal growth and development. Boxed in by excessive rules, regulations, policies, and procedures, many bureaucratic workers complain of being treated "like children."[14] In fact, researchers have cited a number of "bureaucratic pathologies," some of which are listed in Table 10.1.

These problems have not gone unnoticed in the organization development field. Many "interventions"—such as team building, job enrichment, quality circles, management by objectives, survey feedback, organizational mirroring, and participative management—have been designed with one or more of these "pathologies" in mind. These are sure signs that the bureaucratic paradigm is beginning to crack. Remember, when the existing paradigm comes under increasing stress because it no longer "fits reality," adherents of that dominant paradigm will go to great lengths to prop up the failing structures built by the paradigm. Hence these well-intentioned efforts to make bureaucracy functional *without changing the core beliefs, values, and assumptions that create it.* But each of these new "approaches" to increasing organizational effectiveness will ultimately fail unless it is accompanied by a concomitant change in the dominant paradigm.[15]

POT-SHOTS NO. 17

## FOR GOD'S SAKE
## TELL ME WHAT TO THINK!

Ashleigh
Brilliant

**Table 10.1**   Bureaupathic Pathologies

*Bureaupathic behavior:* Robert Merton's term for the tendency of employees to become more interested in the rules (and their enforcement) than in the purposes and goals of the organization.

*Bureautic behavior:* An adaptive response seen in large bureaucracies whereby frustrated workers, bottled up by high formalization, resort to sabotage, absenteeism, and the like to express their alienation and powerlessness.

*Groupthink:* Coined by Irving Janis, this term refers to the tendency in groups or organizations for people to go along with the suggestions or directives of a dominant elite, even if they have doubts about them.[a]

*Lack of personal growth:* Argyris, among others, has pointed to the tendency for large organizations to treat people like children, thereby stifling their opportunities for personal growth and maturity.

*Failure to acknowledge the informal organization:* The bureaucracy does not officially acknowledge the influence of the informal power system, the "coffee klatch" or gossip mill.

*Outdated systems of control and authority:* Formal authority is obsolete in relation to "knowledge workers," who may know more about how to do a job than their bosses.

*Poor conflict resolution technology:* "Win-lose" strategies are the order of the day in bureaucracies; this often leads to dysfunction.

*Distorted communications:* Many studies have shown how upward, downward, and horizontal communications are distorted to achieve certain goals important to the senders.[b]

*Mistrust, fear of reprisals, CYA rampant:* This is common wherever people are preoccupied with self-safety strategies and staying within their job descriptions.

*Poor management of technology:* Often private sector companies have few or no inherent safeguards for the management of new technologies—such as cloned viruses and other genetically manipulated materials.

*Organization man syndrome:* Introduced by William Foote Whyte, this refers to the tendency to marry the organization, getting one's personal rewards there and becoming dependent on the bureaucracy and the rewards it dispenses.[c]

*Poor reaction to change in the external environment:* This is perhaps the biggest weakness of bureaucracy, exacerbated by current turbulent environments characterized by foreign competition, technological innovation, and changing consumer tastes.

SOURCE: Adapted from Warren Bennis, *Beyond Bureaucracy* (New York: McGraw-Hill, 1966), 6.

a. Irving Janis, *Groupthink: Psychological Studies of Policy Decision* (2nd ed.) (Boston: Houghton Mifflin, 1982).

b. Robert C. Ford, Barry R. Armani, and Cherril P. Heaton, *Organization Theory: An Integrative Approach* (New York: Harper & Row, 1988), 329-330.

c. William Foote Whyte, *Organization Man* (New York: Simon & Schuster, 1972).

# IF YOU'RE CAREFUL ENOUGH, NOTHING BAD OR GOOD WILL EVER HAPPEN TO YOU.

Actually, from a transformational perspective, there is a larger view to acknowledge:

If we see the way things actually work, then we do not need some sort of a bureaucracy to administrate the working. Obviously, anything that human beings do in human ways has seemingly necessitated bureaucracies of all kinds, whether from the standpoint of government or business or anything else. These unwieldy creatures expand in size and scope unceasingly. We consequently are somewhat frustrated, with everybody else, because of all the red tape that ensues, so much of this that it is difficult apparently in the human world to move at all.

We're all tied up, and this is what is used as a reason for not being able to do this or that: "I'm all tied up!" It's true! Everybody gets more and more tied up. Administration along these lines is very inefficient and leads to increasing immobility. . . . However, becoming aware of this fact, we may shift our focus a little, recognizing that control rightly extends out of [spirit]. It is an invisible control which is nevertheless perceptible and comprehensible to those whose expression of living is based in spirit.

This involves a larger perspective. . . . This seems like a large order to the minuscule vision of self-centered humans. Yet, until there begins to be an association with this larger extent of the operation of the creative process (of life), we can't possibly understand what is happening next to us. . . . But our attunement is rightly with spirit.[16]

**Vignette 2**

The first author uses a macro organizational simulation (written by Bob Miles and Alan Randolph) in his undergraduate and graduate classes. He has run the game for more than 11 terms/semesters, and the students do the same things every time, with startling regularity. For example, in the first session, when chaos reigns and ambiguity is high, everyone is looking for a leader (someone to tell them what to do). As the game progresses, people tend to adopt bureaupathic behaviors (the rules are more important than the goals). There is a high emphasis on conformist, "don't rock the boat" behaviors. People tend to give a lot of credence to those who sound like they know what they are talking about (expert power).

The list goes on and on. The point is that their behavior is predictable because they share a common paradigm that causes them to make the same decisions at the same times, go through the same processes, create the same structures, and so on. At the beginning of a session, it is possible to predict with awesome accuracy how a group will respond to environmental conditions, changes in technology, and the like—of course, the author doesn't tell the students this until the end of the game, because they would be offended, but it illustrates a key point.

---

## The Staying Power
## of the Bureaucratic Form

---

In 1966, Warren Bennis pronounced bureaucracy a dead duck. His famous declaration was as follows:

> This form of organization [bureaucracy] is becoming less and less effective, is hopelessly out of date with contemporary realities, and new shapes and models—currently recessive—are emerging that promise drastic changes in the conduct of the corporation and in managerial practices in general.[17]

Bennis predicted that, in the next 25 to 50 years, we would see the end of bureaucracy in North America. But bureaucracy persists. Bennis underestimated some of the aspects of the bureaucratic paradigm that help perpetuate the form:

- *Human fallibility:* Our beliefs in the limits and fallibility of the human potential cause us to create organizations that keep us small and limited, thereby creating the illusion that this is all we can be.
- *Bureaupaths and hygiene seekers:* People in bureaucracies tend to become what Robert Merton calls "bureaupathic"—that is, they tend to value rules more than the goals of the organization. They also become "hygiene seekers"—in other words, they look for improvements only in their own job situations, not in the quality and challenge of the work itself.[18] Hygiene seekers tend to resist any threat to the security and predictability of their jobs, even if the promised changes will bring more stimulating and rewarding work. The literature on resistance to change is replete with examples of bureaucratic people resisting any change in the status quo. So, although the bureaucracy might not be personally satisfying, at least it is a known quantity, and the people in it understand their role expectations.
- *Addiction to externals:* In a bureaucracy, people become dependent on external sanctions for motivation/status rewards and external authority for direction (it may also be that a bureaucratic structure attracts people with that propensity).[19] This is the *addiction to externals* phenomenon mentioned earlier. Bureaucratically conditioned people feel very uncomfortable without a clear leader with the power to impose sanctions in a group, and only mature groups can effectively utilize shared leadership.
- *Competitive atmosphere:* The bureaucratic form, with its emphasis on individualism and meritocracy, does not promote collaboration and teamwork. This isolation, in a "dog-eat-dog" competitive atmosphere called careerism, alienates persons from one another and makes them even more dependent on the bureaucratic reward and status system.

- *Reluctance to lead:* In bureaucracies, the leaders lead and the followers follow, and the followers rarely assume responsibility for the success or failure of a project. Roles are strictly defined. This is why it is often difficult to get hardened bureaucratic employees to accept delegation; they know that the risks (personal and professional) of failure far outweigh the potential rewards of success. Hence the bywords are "Keep your nose clean"; "Stay within your job description and do your job—no more"; and the ever-popular "CYA," or "Cover your ass."
- *Unwillingness to share power:* Finally, in a bureaucracy, people who have competed and climbed up the ladder to grab power and status are not generally willing to share power and decision-making privileges, as many of the organic organizational forms require. In other words, few high-ranking bureaucratic employees will give up their hard-won power easily.

Bureaucracy endures because we tend to maintain it with our present collective paradigm. But as the paradigm shifts, so are new organizational forms emerging as the *effect* of this changing *cause*.

## NOTES

1. Alan Sheldon, "Organizational Paradigms: A Theory of Organizational Change," *Organizational Dynamics* (Winter 1980): 61.

2. See, for example, Martin Fishbein and Icek Ajzen, *Belief, Attitude, Intention, and Behavior: An Introduction to Theory and Research* (Reading, MA: Addison-Wesley, 1975).

3. Renaissance Business Associates, Inc., an international organization in which we have participated since we were among the founding members in 1983, has as its purpose to "demonstrate the power and effectiveness of integrity in business." The organization now has some 300 members in the United States, Europe, South Africa, Australia, New Zealand, and Canada; it publishes a newsletter, and members participate in extensive networking activities as well as an annual membership gathering. T. Elaine Gagné is currently president of RBA; David Banner is a former board member and was a founding member in 1983 along with Gagné.

4. Douglas McGregor, *The Human Side of Enterprise* (New York: McGraw-Hill, 1960), 33-34, 47-48.

5. Leon Festinger, *A Theory of Cognitive Dissonance* (New York: John Wiley, 1959).

6. Tom Burns and G. M. Stalker, *The Management Innovation* (London: Tavistock, 1961).

7. Gareth Morgan, *Images of Organization* (Beverly Hills, CA: Sage, 1986), 24.

8. See Warren Bennis, *Changing Organizations* (New York: McGraw-Hill, 1966), 5.

9. See the classic in this area: Henry Mintzberg, *The Structuring of Organizations* (Englewood Cliffs, NJ: Prentice Hall, 1979).

10. Richard H. Hall, "Professionalization and Bureaucratization," *American Sociological Review* 33 (1968): 92-104.

11. Pradip N. Khandwalla, *The Design of Organizations* (New York: Harcourt Brace Jovanovich, 1977), 491.

12. Ibid., 494-495.

13. Stanley M. Davis, "Trends in the Organization of Multinational Corporations," *Columbia Journal of World Business* 11 (1976): 61.

14. Chris Argyris, *Personality and Organization* (New York: John Wiley, 1962).

15. See, for example, the classic article by Richard Walton, "From Control to Commitment in the Workplace," *Harvard Business Review* (March/April 1985): 77-84.

16. Martin Exeter, "The Passing of the Bureaucratic Rule" (extemporaneous talk given in Corona, CA, March 23, 1986), 2.

17. Warren Bennis, *Beyond Bureaucracy* (New York: McGraw-Hill, 1966), 4.

18. Frederick Herzberg, *Work and the Nature of Man* (New York: New American Library, 1973).

19. Lawrence M. Miller, *American Spirit: Visions of a New Corporate Culture* (New York: Warner, 1984).

# 11 Emerging Organizational Designs

*Organizational design is currently a major topic in both the descriptive literature on formal organizations and the literature dealing with how to manage such organizations. The structural approach, if not replacing the emphasis on psychological concepts, has certainly gained importance in the literature of management and organizational behavior. It is well recognized that* structures affect and constrain behavior, and affect performance, coordination and the activities that go on in organizations.

(Jeffrey Pfeffer, *Organizational Design*, 1978, p. xiii; emphasis added)

**SUMMARY:** In this chapter we examine some relatively new organizational forms, including the matrix, arguably the first external manifestation of the shifting paradigm, along with Miles and Snow's dynamic network form, Austrom and Lad's hybrid transorganizational systems, intrapreneurship, the virtual organization, and, finally, the organic form, which may prove to be a dominant structural form of the postindustrial age. What all of these designs have in common are decentralization, worker empowerment (emphasis on personal responsibility), flexibility, adaptability, and authority based on knowledge.

**A**s the paradigm shifts, new organization forms, radically different from the traditional bureaucracy, are putting in an appearance. Arguably, the first such structure is the matrix.

# The Matrix:
# A Simultaneous Structure

The matrix was born in the aerospace industry, as engineers saw the utility of grouping teams of specialists to facilitate the completion of projects. The matrix is referred to as a *simultaneous structure*, because it combines elements of the bureaucratic structure with elements of the organic. The perfect transitional structure, it shows the influence of new patterns of thought while retaining the older habits of thought that have characterized the industrial era. The structure is depicted in Figure 11.1

The matrix actually is two simultaneous structures, bureaucratic and organic, side by side. There are several possible variants of the matrix, but, for the purposes of this discussion, let us examine a relatively common type. The bureaucratic "half" of the organization is a typical functional departmentalization, with marketing, finance, production, engineering, and personnel divisions. This half acts as a talent pool for the other half, the organic component.

When the company decides to develop a new product, a project team leader is appointed, and this team leader negotiates with functional area managers for the use of specialists to work on bringing the new product from the idea stage to production status. A leader may be in charge of several projects at various stages of completion at any given time.

The team leader is, in many ways, an entrepreneur securing money from "backers" to complete a bid project within a given time frame to certain specifications and price. He or she literally signs performance contracts with functional managers. These agreements specify the time estimated for the completion of the project, and the specialists are lent to the team leader for that time. A typical project team might include the following members:

1. a marketing specialist to help design the product, conduct market research, and decide on pricing, packaging, promotion, and distribution
2. an engineering specialist to work on materials, design specifications, tolerances, and the like
3. a lawyer to develop patent rights and foresee legal implications of the product
4. a cost accountant to cost out the manufacture of the product
5. a personnel specialist to ascertain the hiring and training implications of the new product
6. a public relations person to begin to develop press releases and other promotional materials

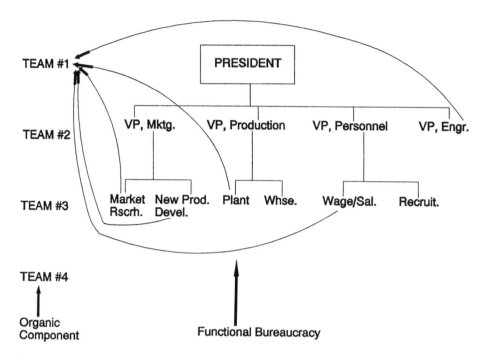

**Figure 11.1.** The Matrix Organization

7. a finance specialist to compute the capital required for the tooling, human resources, plant expansions, and so on

These specialists come together, do their work, and then, when the project is completed, return to their functional "homes" in the bureaucracy. These *temporary project teams* are the hallmark of the matrix structure, and they represent the organic "half" of the structure. In a typical matrix structure, it is not uncommon to have several matrix teams working simultaneously on different projects while the bureaucracy is doing the routine, administrative work of the organization.

In many ways, the organic part of the matrix is the exact opposite of the bureaucratic half. Whereas the bureaucratic side is *hierarchical* in nature, the organic half is decentralized (a flat structure with everyone essentially at the same level). The bureaucracy is typically *formalized*, whereas the organic side depends on flexibility and low formalization. The bureaucracy runs on *formal authority*, or authority by position, whereas the organic teams use *sapiential authority*, authority based on knowledge. This feature is quintessentially organic; when the team is working at the point in the developmental cycle of the product that requires marketing expertise, the marketing specialist becomes the leader. Likewise, for a production question, the production specialist becomes the leader. This shifting leadership pattern is typical of an organic structure.

Whereas bureaucracies are characterized by intense political behavior of the "win-lose" variety, the mature organic structure has lower internal politics, given that the purpose of the team tends to override selfish concerns. But the mature organic structure requires mature workers. Without mature people, the matrix flounders; in practice, this has happened frequently.

The bureaucracy is characterized by a *rigid* structure, whereas organic teams are *fluid and flexible,* with constantly shifting roles, responsibilities, and leadership patterns. Finally, the bureaucracy is typically differentiated with *division of labor,* whereas the organic team uses *job enrichment* (complete jobs with personal accountability). Thus the bureaucratic form is well suited for routine work using relatively unskilled, uneducated workers, and the organic form is better suited for creative tasks with some ambiguity, using "knowledge workers."

Another critical factor in the matrix structure is the nature of the relationships among the project team leaders, the project director (who supervises the team leaders and doles out the financial resources for completing the projects), and the functional area managers. These relationships must be characterized by clear communications, respect for one another's roles, and clear commitment to the organization's overall purpose.

Here is a description of the departmental interdependence required to develop a new product using the bureaucratic approach:

> Information from the sales department about customer needs and from production about processing limits has to be passed on to the research unit so that this information can be assimilated with the scientific feasibility of developing or modifying a new product. . . . [T]he research units are then required to come up with a new development. If they succeed, it is then necessary to transfer information back to the sales department . . . and to the production department. . . . With this information, sales should be in a position to make and implement market plans, and production should have the data for planning and executing its task of manufacturing the product.[1]

Can you see how long this work would take and how fraught with red tape it would be? Project teams attempt to manage this process at a level low enough in the organization so that bureaucratic approval is not required every step of the way. Obviously, this saves a lot of time. Higher-level executives lack the specialized knowledge required to make such judgments, but cross-functional teams are excellent at deciding these matters.

Companies who have used the matrix structure for some time will tell you that it hasn't been easy. Rarely is such a radical departure from the standard bureaucratic form adopted with ease and comfort. This difficulty, of course, is predictable. When a structure (level of effect) is changed, people are naturally upset, because the structure is the external manifestation of their collective agreement on beliefs, attitudes, and values.

## Dow Corning's Matrix Structure

In 1967, Dow Corning reorganized from a conventional divisionalized organization to a matrix.[2] The original concept was two-dimensional; businesses were organized along product lines—for example, fluids and lubricants, resins and chemicals, elastomers, medical semiconductors, and new ventures—and cost centers were set up according to functional areas—marketing, manufacturing, technical services, legal and administrative, and so forth. Dow Corning eventually expanded the structure into two more dimensions: geographical areas (to encompass the increasingly international nature of its markets), and space and time ("fluidity and movement through time"). Discussing the keys to effectiveness of this complex structure, William C. Goggin writes:

> In a multidimensional organization like the one we developed, decision making tends to be flattened out or spread across the organization. No longer is the chief executive or the president required to pass judgement on every important issue. Most of the decisions are made at the middle management level, but not unilaterally; the intent is to push the decision making responsibility as far down in the organization as possible and encourage group consensus.
> What are the requirements of making such a system work? The first requirement is that the communications within the corporation be thorough and complete. Timely and relevant data must go to all who have a need to know. . . . The second requirement is that those in charge of projects be able to understand and use the available data.[3]

Dow Corning's matrix has recently undergone another significant mutation. The primary product of the company is silicone, a plastics derivative. Because Dow has held many of the important patents to this process, it has been a technology-driven company with little competition. But now that all the patents have run out, Dow is facing stiff competition domestically from General Electric and overseas from the West Germans and the Japanese. To compete, it must become a more marketing- and customer-driven company. Hence its new matrix configuration has substituted a customer dimension for the product dimension.

## Advantages of the Matrix

Obviously, the matrix structure has a lot of advantages over other structures. Some of these might include the following:

1. *Creative solutions to problems:* Getting input from a variety of functional specialists results in decision synergy.
2. *Enhanced risk taking:* Group decision making encourages much more risk taking than does individual decision making, because the responsibility is diffuse.
3. *Greater utilization of resources:* Matrix teams use people well, and their expertise is fully tapped.
4. *Faster response to market:* This is a key advantage; when a company needs flexibility and adaptability, this form can be very useful.
5. *Faster rollout of new products:* This is similar to the preceding advantage; the elapsed time from prototype to production run of a product is significantly shortened with this structure.
6. *Better planning:* Especially at the developmental stages, this form gives more input and better, more realistic plans.
7. *Enhanced communications and information transfer:* Done properly, this form greatly increases the amount and quality of information flow.
8. *Enhanced managerial growth:* Managerial maturity is a natural outgrowth of this model.
9. *Dual boss benefits:* Sometimes seen as a disadvantage, this feature of the matrix (having at least two bosses, the functional boss and the team leader) can actually be a source of professional growth and enrichment.

Davis and Lawrence summarize the advantages of the matrix this way: "The matrix's most basic advantage over the functional or product structure is that it facilitates a rapid management response to changing market and technical requirements. Further, it helps middle managers make trade-off decisions from a general management perspective."[4]

## Disadvantages of the Matrix

It would be naive to assume that this form comes without potential "costs." Some of these are as follows:

1. *Tendencies toward anarchy:* Anarchy here is defined as a formless state of confusion where people do not recognize a "boss" to whom they feel responsible.[5] Because the matrix is inherently ambiguous, a worker un-

familiar with the structure and its inherent expectations on worker behavior will possibly panic and fear the worst: anarchy. This tendency is
worsened with a latent or informal matrix; relationships between matrix
teams and their functional counterparts need to be spelled out in no
uncertain terms.

2. *Power struggles:* "Managers jockey for power in many organizations, but
the matrix design almost encourages them to do so. The essence of a
matrix is dual command. For such a form to survive, there needs to be a
balance of power, where its locus shifts constantly, each party always
jockeying to gain an advantage."[6] Political behavior, of course, is a direct
result of a self-centered paradigm; because we learn to compete for
extrinsic rewards as "proof" of our worth, bumping heads becomes second
nature. A compelling, involving organizational vision or purpose can help
minimize this problem.

3. *Severe groupitis:* Managers should expect difficulties if they believe group
decision making to be the essence of matrix behavior. Sapiential authority
will dictate that select individuals will be called on to make individual
decisions rather frequently. The use of too many group meetings wastes
time and contributes to lowered morale. Successful matrix organizations
realize that not everything needs to be decided by a group.

4. *Collapse during economic crunch:* When business declines, the matrix
structure may become the scapegoat for poor management and may be
unceremoniously discarded. Thanks to our industrial age paradigm, we
tend to allow decentralization, group decision making, and other participative techniques when things are going well, but start centralizing and
making decisions individually when the crunch hits.

5. *Excessive overhead:* On the face of it, matrix structure will cost more
because of the double management costs inherent in the dual chain of
command. Also, the training costs associated with getting everyone up to
speed on matrix expectations is initially high. The research on matrix
overhead shows that, although costs are indeed higher in the initial phase,
as the matrix matures these extra costs disappear and are offset by
production gains.[7]

6. *Sinking to lower levels:* The matrix seems to have some difficulty in
surviving at high levels in a corporation. It tends to sink to group or
division levels, where it succeeds well. This is often because senior
managers don't really understand the matrix form, or are unwilling to give
up any functional control to allow it to work. Sinking is not necessarily
bad, however; the matrix structure does seem to work better with full
support from the managers involved.

7. *Uncontrolled layering:* Matrices that lie within matrices that lie within
matrices result from the dynamics of power rather than from the logic of
design. Layering is a problem only if it begins to metastasize, to use an
analogy from medical science. This means that some layering (when one
dimension of a matrix, e.g., one product, forms a functional expertise
distinct from the functional units at the next level up) might be just fine,

but uncontrolled layering and unnecessarily complex relationships will be problematic.

8. *Navel gazing:* Managers in a matrix structure can become so preoccupied with internal matters of politics and coordination that they lose touch with the "outside world." This tendency, of course, is a direct result of the self-centered aspect of the paradigm; coming from that perspective, it is difficult to see the bigger picture.

9. *Decision strangulation:* The matrix structure can promote a climate in which everyone wants to vote on everything, consider everything to the *n*th degree, and so on, and never decide anything. Everything has to be cleared with the functional boss as well as the product manager; this can be time-consuming as well as frustrating. This often arises as a failure of delegation, not of the matrix. The purpose of a matrix is quick action, responsiveness to changing market demands.

## Managing the Matrix: Some Issues

All of the "pathologies" listed above are really caused by lack of experience on the learning curve with the matrix structure, and/or by immature behavior on the part of the incumbents. However, the form has had great successes and its advantages are increasingly seen as outweighing potential problems. A few guidelines, however, are worth mentioning.

The matrix structure should be employed only when there is a need for high differentiation and integration, when specific outcomes are uncertain or not easily subject to planning, and when a high degree of flexibility and creativity is desired. If an organization is in a static environment with a simple technology, a matrix is probably not useful. This structure succeeds only with a careful culture-building effort to support the norms of cooperation, trust, openness, interpersonal responsibility, lack of politics, power and influence based on expertise rather than position, and the relative unimportance of status. Accessibility to all personnel throughout the organization, egalitarian management style, a culture that values temporary relationships and flexibility, and personal maturity are a few of the necessary ingredients.

---

## The Dynamic Network Structure

---

The matrix structure is only the tip of the iceberg of a host of new organizational forms. The dynamic network is another emerging form.[8] Raymond E. Miles and Charles C. Snow argue that two major outcomes of the contemporary search for new competitive forms are already apparent:

> First, the search is producing a new organizational form, a unique combination of strategy, structure, and management processes that we refer to as the *dynamic network*. The new form is both a cause and a result of today's competitive environment: The same "competitive beast" that some companies do not understand has been the solution to other companies' competitive difficulties.
>
> Second, as is always the case, the new organizational form is forcing the development of new concepts and language to explain its features and functions, and, in the process, is providing new insights into the workings of existing strategies and structures. In the future, many organizations will be designed using concepts such as vertical disaggregation, internal and external brokering, full-disclosure information systems, and market substitutes for administrative mechanisms.[9]

A dynamic network is composed of a group of businesses, partnerships, or individuals who subcontract their services to the "broker" core, which provides coordination, supervision, and control of a given project or contract (see Figure 11.2). In this way, the network organization keeps human resources and overhead very low while increasing its flexibility and responsiveness to customers.

Dynamic networks have been emerging as joint ventures, subcontracting and licensing agreements across borders, and intrapreneurship. Miles and Snow categorize four major design features of these new forms: vertical disaggregation, brokers, market mechanisms, and full-disclosure information systems.

*Vertical disaggregation.* Business functions such as finance, marketing, and product design are performed by independent organizations tied together in a network. In his classic book *Megatrends*, John Naisbitt heralds the advent of networking as a replacement of the hierarchy in conventional bureaucracies. Naisbitt sees networks as offering what "bureaucracies can never deliver—the horizontal link."[10] He also points out that "the 'old boy network' is elitist, but the new network is egalitarian."[11] These statements are consistent with the paradigm shift we are experiencing as a culture.

*Brokers.* The separate functions are brought together by brokers who play a lead role by subcontracting for needed services. In other cases, linkages among equal partners are facilitated by various brokers specializing in particular services or functions. Sometimes, one network element will use a broker to locate one or more other functions.

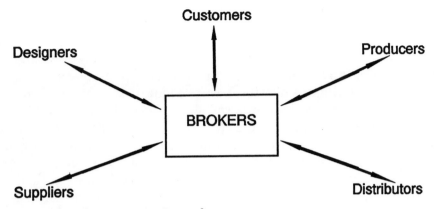

**Figure 11.2.**   The Dynamic Network

*Market mechanisms.* The major functions are bonded together by market forces rather than by formalized structures and plans. Contracts and payments are based on performance, and close supervision is not the norm.

*Full-disclosure information systems.* Participants in the network are linked together by elaborate information systems so that individual contributions (value added) can be mutually and instantaneously verified.

### Advantages and Paradigmatic Implications of the Dynamic Network

This new form offers a number of advantages. The individual participant gets to pursue a distinctive competence. "A properly constructed network can display the technical specialization of the functional structure, the market responsiveness of the divisionalized structure, and the balanced orientation characteristic of the matrix."[12] Because each part of the network is a complementary part of the whole, there is a synergistic relationship among the parts (the whole is greater than the sum of the parts). This complementarity allows for the creation of elaborate networks to handle complex, transnational projects. Because continued participation is based on results produced (accountability is strict and a broker can fire a firm for noncompliance), everyone is encouraged to participate responsibly. And, using what Miles and Snow call *industry synergy*, each firm plays a role of implicit interdependence with other firms in the network.

There are several paradigmatic implications of all this. First, we are beginning to see that the boundaries of organizations are artificial constructs, and might not apply as rigorously in the changing world as they did in the past. Second, we are beginning to see the organization as a transnational citizen. Toffler (in *The Third Wave*)[13] and others have long spoken about the nature of the multinational corporation, but here we are seeing organizations that have as their parts pieces of many organizations. With this new form, we can more easily see the shrinking nature of our world and our increasing interdependence.

Miles and Snow argue that the greatest barriers to success of network organizations in today's world are outmoded views of what an organization must look like and how it must be managed. Future forms will feature some of the properties of the dynamic network form, particularly heavy reliance on self-managed work groups and a greater willingness to view organizational boundaries and membership as highly flexible.[14]

In future forms, it is likely that key business units will be assembled and disassembled as needed to meet increasingly complex business challenges. The principle here is the same as the one behind the matrix, except we are talking about business units instead of people; the emphasis is on flexibility and adaptability, and the key to success again is personal (and organizational) responsibility.

## Hybrid Transorganizational Systems

Austrom and Lad, in a similar vein, discuss hybrid transorganizational systems. They argue that "these collaborative organizational ventures reflect a much larger transformation in contemporary society, a transformation that encompasses but extends well beyond the technological revolution to address the implicit assumptions, ideologies, and values on which our society is based."[15] As Lodge argues, it may be that our present premises are inadequate:

> What is happening is that the old ideas and assumptions, which once made our great institutions legitimate, authoritative, and confident, are fast slipping away in the face of a changing reality and are being replaced by different ideas and different assumptions, which are as yet ill-formed, contradictory and shocking. The transition is neither good nor bad; there is the possibility of plenty of both. The point is that it is taking place.[16]

Austrom and Lad articulate the new logics of the emerging paradigm as manifest in these transorganizational systems:

1. an ecological perspective (instead of mechanistic logic)
2. context set by collaboration (rather than competition)
3. recognition of interdependence (rather than a focus on differences)

4. ideology both Lockean and communitarian (rather than the traditional
   Lockean ideology of self-contained individualism)

A recent version of this structure is the "virtual organization," a type of
geographical matrix in which different departments are pulled together
from different companies in different locations to make a temporary
organization.[17]

## Bureaucratic/Organic Variants

Schermerhorn, Hunt, and Osborn describe two other variants that have
appeared recently. The first is the *mechanistic core within an organic
shell*. This occurs when an organization produces only a few standardized products with a long-linked or modal technology, but faces an
uncertain or turbulent environment. Functions that can be mechanized
(finance, production, personnel, and so on) are structured that way,
whereas those that deal with the external environment (customer affairs,
sales, purchasing, and the like) are structured in an organic format.

The other variant is the *organic core with a mechanistic shell*. In this
type of organization, the modal technology is typically intensive in
nature, requiring an organic structure to maximize effectiveness. Research and development is often an intensive technology, and, if the
company is research driven, this should be organic. However, the staff
or support units for this research effort (personnel, finance, marketing,
and so on) can be mechanistically structured, especially if the external
environment is not turbulent. These two variants combine the best
features of both structural types to good advantage.[18]

## Intrapreneurship:
## Enhancing Creativity and Flexibility

Popularized by Gifford Pinchot in his best-selling book of the same
name, *intrapreneuring* has caught on in a big way with several large
multinationals as a way of enhancing innovation and creativity while
keeping a measure of corporate control.[19] Essentially, the scenario goes
like this: A large corporation wants a new product or market developed
and top management realizes that the bureaucratic way is too slow and
cumbersome, so a new company (a "spin-off") is created, staffed by some
corporate "best and brightest," and charged with the job of developing a

new product or whatever. The new company has the advantage of the financial backing of the large corporation, yet it has the freedom and the flexibility to pursue whatever means seem justified to produce the desired results. General Electric has been a pioneer in this field, with admittedly mixed results.

---

**Vignette 1**

A middle-level sales engineer for the silicone products division of GE was asked to join an "intrapreneurial company" to be formed that would find markets for a new product, silicon carbide (a substance with unusual heat-resistant properties). Initially, the product seemed ideally suited for the oil-field industry, and the fledgling company began to develop contacts.

Six months into the new venture, the oil industry began its long slide, and Hughes Tool (a potential customer) cut back on its orders. Unable to find new markets quickly enough, the intrapreneurial venture folded, and the people associated with it were offered jobs within the GE hierarchy.

---

Stimulating innovation in large corporations has been a hot topic of late. Rosabeth Moss Kanter, in her excellent book *The Change Masters*, has called the modern bureaucracy in its most rigid incarnation a "segmentalist" organization; by this, she means the bureaucracy offers an antichange, compartmentalized perspective on corporate problems. Her prescription is the development of participative management skills and cultures to encourage innovation at the lowest possible levels.[20] Peters and Waterman, in their best-seller *In Search of Excellence*, talk about "skunk works," set-aside areas where people can bypass corporate rigidity and rules to create and innovate.[21] However, Pinchot has had the greatest influence in this area, and his prescription for resurgent corporate health is being bought by many companies. Another article has some glowing predictions:

> Allan Kennedy, co-author of *Corporate Cultures*, ex-McKinsey and Co. partner, and now president of Boston-based Selkirk and Associates, is probably the most enthusiastic of the "small is beautiful" advocates.
>
> "If I had to go out on a limb," Kennedy said in an April 1984 interview in *Inc.* magazine, "I would say that large corporations as we have known them will not exist in 30 years' time.
>
> "They won't be able to sustain their position. They won't be able to hold onto their people; everyone will know too many other people who have

gone out on their own and made a fair amount of money. So all the good people will be spinning off." Kennedy contends that the large corporation of tomorrow will be essentially a holding company that simply makes money available to people with ideas and in return owns large blocks of small subsidiaries of around 100 employees each. Why 100 employees? According to Kennedy, "the evidence seems to point to between 50 and 100 people as the most efficient work unit."[22]

Not everyone is so sanguine about intrapreneurship. For one thing, it is doubtful whether real entrepreneurial risk taking is encouraged when the purse strings are still controlled at corporate headquarters. For another, why would someone with the pride of authorship typical of a real entrepreneur create a new company when it is understood that, if successful, that company will eventually be folded back into the corporate hierarchy? Further, in practice, there are political problems and realities that go with intrapreneurship. Although large companies expect things to develop slowly at first, fiscal pressures do build, especially in a down economic cycle, where budget cutting is the norm. Despite these problems, intrapreneurship can be seen for what it is: a symptom of the shift toward a paradigm in which flexibility, creativity, and innovation are valued.

## The Organic Structure: A Product of the Postindustrial Paradigm

Discussing the completely organic structure is discussing the future—a difficult task, as it requires us to articulate the results of a changed paradigm while we are still lodged in a transitional paradigm. However, there does seem to be consensus about certain features of this evolving form; these are discussed below.

### Characteristics of the Organic Form

The organic organization will no doubt be found primarily in the information/service/knowledge arena, because mass-production technology demands a more structured approach. It will be very decentralized, with many autonomous work groups, probably of a temporary matrix character. These configurations will come together and disband as needed in the accomplishment of the organization's purposes. The key feature of this structure will be flexibility and adaptability.

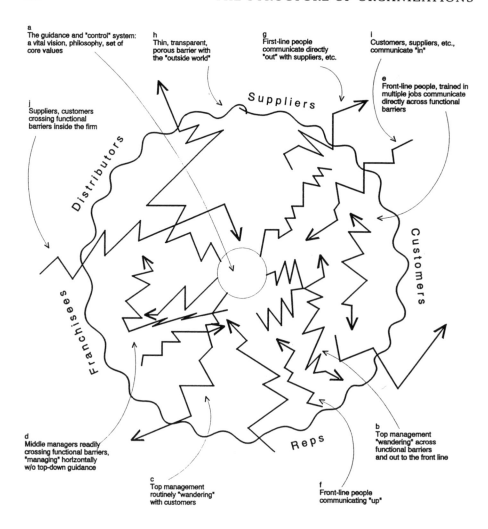

**Figure 11.3.** The Organic Structure (Tom Peters's version)

SOURCE: Thomas J. Peters, "Restoring American Competitiveness: Looking for New Models of Organizations," *Academy of Management Executive* 2, no. 2 (1988): 106. Used with permission.
NOTE: In the original, the caption for this figure reads as follows: "The flexible, porous, adaptive, fleet of foot organization of the future: Every person is paid to be obstreperous, a disrespecter of formal boundaries, to hustle and to be fully engaged with engendering swift action, constantly improving everything."

Where the bureaucratic structure is held together or integrated by rules, regulations, policies, procedures, and finite goals, the organic organization will use *vision or purpose* as organizational glue. A compelling, transcendent purpose will be essential to galvanize effort and commitment. The members of the organization will need to "own" this vision so that their efforts are naturally aligned with it.

The organic organization will, by definition, be staffed by mature, responsible people. Anything less, and the organization will fail, or at best be suboptimal in its functioning. These people, working primarily in small, face-to-face groups, will constantly be attuned to the "big picture" through meetings, briefings, teleconferencing, and the like. There will be no need for the punitive or coercive strategies used to "motivate" workers so common to bureaucratic organizations. Intrinsic motivation will be the order of the day. Compensation, time off, and other human resource functions will be handled by the people themselves in a mature manner, taking the needs of the whole into account.

Sapiential authority will prevail. When a particular expertise is in focus, the person who has that expertise will be the "leader." Formal authority, as we have come to know it, will cease to exist. Emphasis will be on "win-win," collaborative strategies. The joy will come from self-actualized workers giving of themselves in a collective effort to create something that manifests a vision. Jobs will be whole, rather than fragmented in the division-of-labor format so common to today's bureaucracies. Because workers will not be addicted to externals, status and politics as we have known them will diminish in importance.

Although the form will be decentralized in the extreme, it would be a serious error to assume that it will have no leaders. In addition to the aforementioned floating leadership function manifest by sapiential authority, there will be a person or group responsible for articulating and maintaining the focus on the vision. This focus of leadership might rotate (as it does in the Israeli kibbutz), but there will need to be a point of focus for the efforts of the organization. In other words, there will be a design, but, rather than being based on formal authority as in the bureaucratic form, it will be based on personal maturity and the needs of the whole.

## Simulating the Organic Form

In the past few years, a number of businesses have tried to take some of the characteristics of the organic form and put them into their structures. But because the collective paradigm creates the form or structure, such efforts are doomed to failure in the long term in the absence of mature, responsible people.

A case in point is People's Express, an airline started by Donald Burr in the early 1980s. This company's innovative management practices received a lot of media attention. For example, all employees were required to own 100 shares of stock in the company (to encourage psychological ownership), to work at all different jobs in the company before settling into a specific job (to encourage a sense of the big picture, functional redundancy, and the interrelatedness of the parts), and to forgo such common perks as secretaries and special parking privileges for managers (to deemphasize status and hierarchy). Unfortunately, overpurchases of new aircraft and a heavy debt burden played a large role in the company's demise, so we really don't know how well these structural changes might have worked in the long term.

Another case in point is W. L. Gore and Associates. Bill Gore created this company around a unique product, Gore-Tex, which is a synthetic fiber made from Teflon. His company's management philosophy and structure are also unique. Gore believes that "groups respond to recognized authority or to individual commitment. If you are going to have a lot of change in an organization, you better get a commitment. In the process, natural leaders will evolve."[23] There are only three officers in the company, and no middle-management executives; the officers are Gore, his son (president), and his wife (secretary-treasurer). Everyone else is an "associate." The company's 4,000 employees are divided up into groups of no more than 200, thereby avoiding the problem of bureaucratization. Gore's associates are carefully chosen; new employees are recruited by "sponsors" within the company, thereby ensuring a level of personal responsibility and commitment to the corporate culture. Thus far, the formula has worked. The company has shown an annual growth rate of 30%-40%.

## Personal Responsibility and the Organic Form

Successful matrix and organic organizations will come about only when there is a critical mass of people who agree with this structural arrangement at the paradigm level. However, the industrial era paradigm preoccupation with the *form* of things will no doubt continue to cause us grief in this area, as we try to make companies more flexible and adaptable. Flexible and adaptable companies can come only from flexible and adaptable—in other words, mature and responsible—people. As Alvin Toffler has noted:

> The adhocracies of tomorrow will require a totally different set of human characteristics. They will require men and women capable of rapid learning (in order to comprehend novel circumstances and problems) and imagination (in order to invent new solutions). In short, to cope with first-time or one-time problems, the corporate man of tomorrow will not function "by the book." Instead, he must be capable of exercising judgments and making complex value decisions rather than mechanically executing orders sent down from above. He must be willing to navigate through a diversity of assignments and organizational settings, and learn to work with an ever-changing group of colleagues.[24]

The single most crucial independent variable for the success of this form is *personal maturity*. As the bureaucratic form depends on adherence to external rules and sanctions for integration and effectiveness, so must the organic form depend on *vision* and *responsibility.* People must be willing to own the vision and, more important, the success of the organization. Victim attitudes (e.g., "It's not in my job description!") have no place in the organic form.

This is all easier said than done. One of the strongest human habits is to blame others when things go wrong and to deny personal responsibility for any result that is not favorable to oneself. Here is where a compelling, transcendent vision can play its biggest role: in assisting self-centered humans to transcend their petty, egocentric concerns and focus on a larger whole. As we have noted, the new paradigm focuses on the interrelatedness of things and the fact that everything is part of a larger whole.

Through the use of a vision, the transformational leader can get people to focus on the needs of the whole.[25] However, this transformation will be short-lived unless the people in the organization are truly mature, because as soon as someone wants to "do better" than someone else, the competitiveness of the old paradigm will come shining through. Also, as the organization grows and begins hiring people who do not share the vision but just want their paychecks, there is a danger that bureaucracy will set in again.

In summary, personal maturity, or living with 100% personal responsibility, is so important that Peter Senge calls it one of the core disciplines needed for the building of the learning organization.[26] As we have seen in this chapter, newer forms are emerging, just as our metamodel would predict. In other words, form follows collective paradigm; when the paradigm shifts, new forms naturally emerge.

## NOTES

1. Jay W. Lorsch and Paul R. Lawrence, "Organizing for Product Innovation," *Harvard Business Review* 43 (1965): 110-111.

2. William C. Goggin, "How the Multidimensional Structure Works at Dow Corning," *Harvard Business Review* 52 (January/February 1974).

3. Ibid., 58-59.

4. Stanley B. Davis and Paul R. Lawrence, "Problems of Matrix Organizations," *Harvard Business Review* 56 (May/June 1978): 132.

5. Ibid. This and all the problems in this list are drawn from Davis and Lawrence's article.

6. Ibid., 134.

7. C. J. Middleton, "How to Set Up a Project Organization," *Harvard Business Review* 45 (March/April 1967): 24.

8. Raymond E. Miles and Charles C. Snow, "Organizations: New Concepts for New Forms," *California Management Review* 28 (Spring 1986).

9. Ibid., 62.

10. John Naisbitt, *Megatrends* (New York: Random House, 1982), 196.

11. Ibid., 197.

12. Ibid., 65.

13. Alvin Toffler, *The Third Wave* (New York: Simon & Schuster, 1982).

14. Miles and Snow, "Organizations," 73.

15. Douglas Austrom and Lawrence Lad, "Collaborative Approaches to Social Issues Management: The New Logics of Hybrid Transorganizational Systems" (paper presented at annual meeting of the Academy of Management, Social Issues in Management Division, New Orleans, 1987), 2.

16. George Lodge, *The American Ideology* (New York: Knopf, 1975).

17. John A. Byrne, "The Virtual Corporation," *BusinessWeek*, February 8, 1993, 37-41.

18. John R. Schermerhorn, James G. Hunt, and Richard N. Osborn, *Managing Organizational Behavior* (New York: John Wiley, 1988), 358-359.

19. Gifford Pinchot, *Intrapreneuring: Why You Don't Have to Leave the Corporation to Become an Entrepreneur* (New York: HarperCollins, 1986).

20. Rosabeth Moss Kanter, *The Change Masters: Innovation for Productivity in the American Corporation* (New York: Simon & Schuster, 1983).

21. Thomas J. Peters and Robert H. Waterman, Jr., *In Search of Excellence: Lessons From America's Best-Run Companies* (New York: Harper & Row, 1982).

22. Edgar H. Schein, "What You Need to Know About Organizational Culture," *Training and Development Journal* (January 1986): 32. All quotes by Schein from this article are reprinted from *Training and Development Journal*. Copyright © January 1986, the American Society for Training and Development. Reprinted with permission. All rights reserved.

23. Quoted in David J. Rachman and Michael H. Mescon, "A Structureless Organization?" in *Business Today* (5th ed.) (New York: Random House, 1987), 135.

24. Alvin Toffler, *The Adaptive Corporation* (New York: Bantam, 1985), 70-71.

25. Noel M. Tichy and Mary Anne Devanna, *The Transformational Leader* (New York: John Wiley, 1986).

26. Peter M. Senge, *The Fifth Discipline: The Art and Practice of the Learning Organization* (Garden City, NY: Doubleday, 1990), especially chap. 9.

# PART III

■ THE CONTEXT

OF ORGANIZATIONS

# 12   The Environment of Organizations

*Large companies are discovering that, to compete in a changing marketplace, they must adopt many of the values of small business. . . . Many large companies watched small businesses get the jump on them in the marketplace. IBM, one of the best managed companies in the world, watched Digital Equipment Corporation take the lead in minicomputers and Apple in personal computers. Clearly, the strategies that once worked so well are out of date in a new marketplace and an economic environment that seems to favor small businesses and individuals that can move fast.*

(John Naisbitt and Patricia Aburdene,
*Re-inventing the Corporation*, 1985, pp. 71-72)

**SUMMARY:** In this chapter, we look at the organization's relationship to its so-called external environment, or everything outside the boundary of the organization—suppliers, competitors, customers, the legal framework, regulatory framework, economic factors, technology changes, unions, and such. We will review the traditional literature in this field and then explore the transformational perspective on organizations and their environment.

## The Organization in Its Environment: The Traditional View

In the heady early days of classical organization theory, most theorists viewed the bureaucratic organization as a closed system. Management's major goal was to achieve and maintain optimal internal efficiency.

Because organizations existed in stable environments, little attention was given to how an organization should adapt to its environment.

Today, open systems theory has helped us see organizations as open systems—yet the organizational environment is still seen by many as existing *separate from* and *outside of* the organization's system. "Managing" an environment has become an important managerial goal—especially because the environments in which many of our largest multinationals operate are characterized by increasing turbulence, or rapid change coupled with increasing uncertainty. Unless an organization can adapt quickly to changes in its environment, it can be out of business in short order.

The external environment, from the traditional point of view, is the source of opportunities and threats, of constraints and possibilities for the organization. Managing the interface between the organization and the environment can clearly mean survival (not to mention prosperity) for the organization.

Here is a contemporary example of how organizations traditionally try to manage their environments to reduce uncertainty. Recently, a large airplane manufacturer in the southern United States signed a contract with a components supplier for a six-month fixed price on a crucial part, hired a former Pentagon official to head its new product development effort, made a contribution to a political lobbyist looking after the interests of this industry, and made an offer to purchase a supplier of electronic components. With each of these actions, the focal organization (the organization being affected by its environment) attempted to manage its environment. By buying a supplier, the company became *vertically integrated*, controlling more of the raw material supplies it needs to produce its products. The contribution to the lobbyist was made in an effort to influence legislation and regulation that might effect the organization's operations. The hiring of the former Pentagon official gave the organization access to his numerous contacts in the military, a large buyer of jet aircraft. The fixed-price contract protected the focal organization from inflationary (or other) price increases.

## A Newer Perspective on
## Organization-Environment Relations

As the paradigm begins to shift, so are the traditional organizational approaches to managing the environment. Here is a contemporary example of one of the new ways in which organizations are dealing with turbulence and competition:

> Some business owners he's tried to talk to are skeptical, even suspicious, of Harry Brown. It's not that he is proposing anything obviously illegal, and the things he wants to talk about—shop floor procedures and capabilities—aren't really secret. But still, they are no one else's business, and they surely are no business of a company owner who might, conceivably, be a competitor someday.
>
> To understand what Brown is proposing, try to keep an open mind. Clear your head of all the assumptions you have about the kinds of relationships that should exist among independent companies doing business, then listen to Brown as he explains how a different relationship might work.[1]

Harry Brown is interested in establishing "flexible manufacturing networks," a system in which potential competitors share information and help each other out. These dynamic networks "all grow out of the idea that a large number of small companies acting in partial concert with one another can achieve more than a single company of similar aggregate size."[2] Cooperation with one's competitors—a symptom of a changing paradigm?

Strategies for dealing with the environment perceived under the industrial paradigm will be radically different from those formulated under the new paradigm. Specifically, the old-paradigm approach seeks, through prediction and control, to manipulate those factors that are seen as "influenceable" and to monitor those that are not. The new-paradigm approach will be to sense the needs of the larger whole (the society or the international environment, for instance) and seek to provide what is required to play a significant part in that whole in a proactive (not reactive) way.[3] One transformational author has noted:

> What great executives will do in the 1990's is to create different paradigms that are appropriate to the commitments in various parts of the organization. They will be able to shape organization-wide paradigms that are appropriate to the moving sands, changing markets, changing competition, and introduction of new technologies. As fast on its feet as an organization is today in changing its focus, that's how fast it will have to be to be able to change the paradigms in which the focuses are developed.[4]

Paradigm flexibility will be required so that the environment can be viewed with different "lenses." In this way, the company can discern what is *really* happening "out there" and seek to make appropriate proactive responses. But before we fully contrast the two approaches,

© BRILLIANT ENTERPRISES 1972                    POT-SHOTS NO. 330

# THE WORLD NEEDS
# MORE PEOPLE LIKE US
# AND FEWER LIKE THEM.

*Ashleigh Brilliant*

let us examine the impact of an organization's environment on its design and function from the old-paradigm perspective.

---

## Organizational Interdependencies
## With the Environment

---

How an organization is structured can depend on how interdependent and interrelated it is with its environment. Emery and Trist, who conducted a classic study at the Tavistock Institute in England, have argued that in order to understand the organization's structure and process, one needs to ascertain the various types of linkages within the environment in which the organization finds itself.[5] These authors identify three interdependencies: internal, transactional, and environmental.

In each example presented below, *L* refers to some connection (presumably lawful), *1* refers to the focal organization, and *2* refers to some aspect of the focal organization's environment. Thus L12 means the link between the focal organization and some aspect (in this case, output) of its environment.

*Internal interdependencies (L11).* These are linkages between units in the focal organization, such as those between production and sales.

*Transactional interdependencies (L12 and L21).* There are two kinds of transactional interdependencies: *Input transactional interdependencies* (L21) are direct linkages between the focal organization and the input environment, such as relationships between the organization and the union (supplier of people), raw materials supplier, and so forth; *output transactional interdependencies* (L12) are direct linkages between the focal organization and the output elements in its environment, such as the relationship between the sales department and a major customer.

*Environmental interdependencies (L22).* These are linkages through which aspects of the external environment of the focal organization become related to one another. Examples include a relationship between two suppliers to the focal organization and a relationship between a governmental regulating agency and a supplier to the focal organization.

In Figure 12.1, L11 linkages represent the internal interdependencies within the focal organization itself, such as the relationships between departments that must work together or divisions that are geographically separated. Typically, these relationships seem somewhat manageable and pose little threat to the organization's survival. When conflicts or misinterpretations occur, they can usually be resolved with an integrating mechanism such as an arbitrator.

The transactional interdependencies (L12 and L21) relate to the organization's need to acquire resources for its particular transformation process (L21) and the need to dispose of the products of this process (L12). These relationships obviously can create uncertainty. A supplier can have a strike, or a customer can experience a business downturn and stop ordering from the focal organization. These linkages involve mutual dependency and, as such, need to be managed carefully (from the traditional perspective). Mutual problem solving is the road to typical solutions in these linkages.

The L22 linkages (environmental interdependencies)—what Emery and Trist called the "causal texture" of the organization's environment—can determine the ultimate survival of the firm. They arise indirectly to the organization as interdependencies belonging to the environment itself. Changes in these relationships tend to be detected much later by the organization than those of the L12 and L21 variety; hence organizational reactions to these changes can lag seriously.

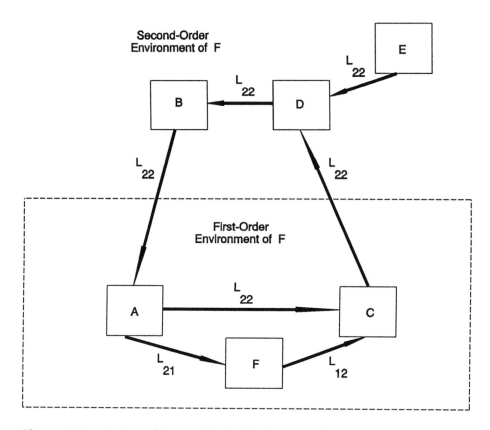

**Figure 12.1.**  First- and Second-Order Environments

SOURCE: Robert H. Miles, *Macro Organizational Behavior* (Glenview, IL: Scott, Foresman, 1980), 202. Reprinted with permission from the author.

Obviously, the first-order or *specific* environment refers to elements in the environment that most directly impinge on the focal organization. The second-order or *general* environment is composed of those elements that do not directly affect the organization, but the actions of which can impinge indirectly—the government, regulators, legal changes, and the like. These L22 linkages are not under the direct control of the organization, but contribute a great deal to the uncertainty faced by decision makers in the focal organization. Monitoring and forecasting these linkages and their changes is seen as a key to survival for many organizations. An organization's *boundary role* personnel track such linkages continually.

## Emery and Trist's Typology of Environments

Emery and Trist have developed a simple typology of environments based on the nature of their causal textures (see Table 12.1). Organiza-

**Table 12.1**  The Four-Environment Model

| Environmental Types | Causal Texture | | Appropriate Coping Techniques |
| :---: | :---: | :---: | :---: |
| | Movement | Connectedness | |
| I | placid | random | tactics |
| II | placid | clustered | strategies |
| III | disturbed | reactive | operations |
| IV | turbulent | mutual-causal[a] | multilateral agreements |

SOURCE: Robert H. Miles, *Macro Organizational Behavior* (Glenview, IL: Scott, Foresman, 1980), 204. Reprinted with permission from the author.

a. A conceptualization suggested by J. Stacy Adams, "The Structure and Dynamics of Organization Boundary Roles," in *The Handbook of Industrial and Organizational Psychology*, ed. Martin D. Dunnette (Chicago: Rand McNally, 1966), 1175-1199.

tional environments are arranged on a continuum from low to high causal texture based on two variables: strength of interconnectedness between the elements and rate of movement among the elements.

*Interconnectedness* refers to the extent to which changes in one element in the environment affect another. High interconnectedness leads to greater uncertainty, because a ripple effect of changes can occur. *Movement* refers to the extent to which environmental elements experience change. The higher the rate of change (especially unexpected change), the greater the decision-making uncertainty. The four types are placid-randomized, placid-clustered, disturbed-reactive, and turbulent (see Table 12.1).

*Type I: Placid-randomized.* The simplest of environments in which to operate is characterized by a low level of movement or change among the environmental elements and a low degree of interconnectedness among the elements. In other words, the environment is stable and the parts are disconnected. This type of causal texture is the least threatening to the focal organization. Planning can be rational and can extrapolate on prior trends. Tactics are the predominant coping technique in this environment. As the focal organization learns how to deal with each element in the environment through trial and error, what works is continued and what doesn't is dropped. An example of such an environment is the packaging industry of the 1950s. The technology was relatively static, the competition was predictable, and the general economic environment was stable.

*Type II: Placid-clustered.* In this rather simple environment, the level of change is low, but the degree of interconnectedness is higher. Clusters of L22 linkages can be found here. Although they have a predictable pattern of interaction with the focal organization, the fact that coalitions can form has implications for strategic planning and decision making. Unilateral tactics, which work well in the Type I environment, can fail miserably here because the elements are closely interconnected. Tactics need to be supplanted by *strategies,* which take these interdependencies into account. An example of this type of industry is the auto industry in the United States prior to the Arab oil embargo. Auto companies are linked to their suppliers, dealerships, and customers.

*Type III: Disturbed-reactive.* Much more complex than the first two types, this environment is one in which many companies find themselves. Unpredictable movement and change coupled with close interconnectedness (mutual dependency) is a recipe for complexity. The environment is full of mutually interdependent companies whose fates are mutually codetermined. The method of coping is operations, "a campaign involving a series of planned tactical initiatives, calculated reactions by others, and counteractions."[6] Operations can, and often do, include various proactive and reactive coping strategies through which the focal organization attempts to reduce its risk. More organizational energy is spent collecting and analyzing data about environmental changes that can potentially affect the focal organization. The auto industry environment of today is an example of the disturbed-reactive environment.

*Type IV: Turbulent.* The disturbed-reactive environment demands that large amounts of organizational resources be spent on acquiring and analyzing data from the field. Characterized by rapid movement, high interconnectedness, and high levels of uncertainty, the turbulent field is a challenge for most companies. The focal organization cannot adapt quickly enough or with enough certainty by just examining what individual elements of its environment are doing. Changes affecting the focal organization arise not out of the separate actions of individual firms in the environment, but out of a field or synergistic effect from the interrelated actions of many players in the environment. "The accelerating rate and complexity of interactive effects exceeds the component system's capacities for prediction, and, hence, control of the compounding consequences of their action."[7] In a turbulent environment, the focal organization's fate is largely determined by forces outside its direct control; therefore, any unilateral action on the part of the organization is likely to fail because of the close interconnectedness of the L22 elements. A good example of this type of environment is that of personal computer manufacturers in the late-1980s and early 1990s.

Thus organizations vary in the complexity of the environments they operate in, and in their interdependence in those environments. The worst case for an organization is to deal with a lot of external complexity and turbulence coupled with high levels of interdependency on elements of the environment. It gets even trickier if L22 linkages are high.

As noted above, bureaucracies can manage well in simple, static environments, but as an environment becomes more complex, interdependent, and turbulent, a more sophisticated organizational structure is required, such as matrix or organic structure, or something even more flexible.

---

## Strategic Responses to Environmental Uncertainty

---

Resource dependency and uncertainty are two of the critical factors that influence strategic thinking. Obviously, the more dependent a focal organization is on a particular supplier of a resource, the more disruptive an interruption in that resource will be. Coupled with the uncertainty dimension, this makes contingency planning rather difficult. But companies do develop strategies—affected, of course, by the collective paradigm.

### How Organizations Adapt: The Use of Boundary Roles

Organizations, especially those in turbulent environments, tend to rely on people or subunits to scan their environments, monitor potentially important events, interpret their perceptions, and report them to the appropriate organizational decision makers. These organizational *boundary roles* differ greatly from the more traditional, "internal" roles that most organizational members occupy.

Under the industrial era paradigm, an organization has a boundary or demarcation between that which is part of the organization and that which is not. The organization is said to "manage its boundary" by regulating who gets in and for how long. Thus the boundary is a de facto

**Figure 12.2.**   Organizations and Their Boundary Roles

statement of organizational identity. Regulating it, under the old paradigm, is a major organizational function.

*Boundary-spanning activities*, then, are those activities that serve to assist the organization in effectively adapting to the changing demands and opportunities of the environment. These activities serve to regulate the flow of inputs (raw materials, money, people, and so on) and outputs (products, services, dividends to shareholders, and the like), and to keep the organization apprised of environmental changes that could affect the functioning of the organization.

People operating in the boundary roles of the organization are crucial to its survival, especially in rapidly changing and uncertain environments (see Figure 12.2). This is why this function is termed *institutionally adaptive.* The perceptions of these role incumbents determine

strategic options and organizational futures. Here again is a practical application of the metamodel: The paradigm determines what these individuals see and what they *don't* see as well. Certain assumptions made by boundary role incumbents will color what they "scan."

Boundary role incumbents tend to have some common features. These people link up units with different (and possibly conflicting) goals and attempt to forge a "fit" between the organization and its environment. Boundary role incumbents are typically viewed with distrust and suspicion by their internal counterparts because they operate at the fringes of the organization, sometimes winging it, with little formal authority and a lot of moxie.

Boundary role incumbents are often the targets of influence attempts, for example, the purchasing agent who is plied with fancy meals and favors by vendors. They also are the sources of such attempts, such as the salesman who promises the moon to get the order from the customer. These people are typically extroverted, very verbally proficient, and high risk takers. They are very visible and, when they succeed, they are rewarded handsomely; however, the downside is equally true—a mistake can be very costly to a career. To do their work, they need a great deal of autonomy, yet the organization wants to have some means of regulating their behavior.

## Boundary Role Functions

Boundary role incumbents perform a number of essential functions:

- *representing the organization* to external constituencies, as public relations professionals who act as the "face" of the organization[8]
- *scanning and monitoring* environmental events relevant to the organization—searching for major discontinuities in the environment that create opportunities or problems for the firm, and tracking environmentally strategic variables, such as the price of oil
- *protecting the organization* from threats originating in the environment, as in preventing public relations crises, buffering a company against "stock-outs" by increasing inventories of a crucial part, designing pricing strategies to smooth demand over 12 months, or implementing rationing plans of inputs when demands exceed capacity
- *information processing and gatekeeping*, through observing trends in their particular settings and reporting those that seem to be important to organizational decision makers in a timely fashion
- *transacting with other organizations*, for example, acquiring inputs (purchasing) or disposing of outputs (sales)
- *linking and coordinating activities* between organizations or parts of the same organization[9]

## Boundary Roles and the Metamodel

Uncertainty is a matter of perception (see Figure 12.3). As Weick argues, we enact our environments out of our past experiences, value systems, belief structures, attitudes, and assumptions (see the appendix to this volume). All managers see what they "see" through their own personal "filters." Perceptions are limited by the fact that any person sees only part of the larger whole. Personal prejudices, ideas about "how things really are," the influence of significant other "opinion leaders," and other factors also play a role in determining what an individual "sees." As a result, information about what is really occurring in the environment may not be getting to the decision makers. People may significantly misread what is happening (and the implied demands of that on the organization), leading to reduced effectiveness.[10]

Therefore, it becomes crucial for the organization to use multiple measures of "what is going on out there" to reduce the probability of error in perception. Also, the skill of paradigm flexibility, mentioned earlier, can be helpful here. As the metamodel notes, the paradigm creates strategic choices. The limiting effect of the paradigm, which determines what we can and cannot see, determines the data that can be analyzed. The strategic action taken is a direct result of the paradigm of the decision makers.

**Figure 12.3.** Perception of Environmental Uncertainty

* "Enacted" by collective agreement in consciousness (one view of the larger whole, limited by paradigmatic blinders).

Thus the boundary role functions are critical to seeing beyond a given paradigm and obtaining information needed for strategic decisions. These functions enable the organization to adapt its structure and strategy accurately to changes in the external environment. As an organization grows in size, the need for boundary role incumbents becomes more apparent, but small organizations need such people as well. The intense internal focus that occurs as a new organization gets off the ground can cause its members to overlook significant changes until it is too late for them to respond effectively.

In general, as environmental turbulence increases, so does the need for quality boundary role functioning. As Lawrence and Lorsch discovered, environmental complexity seems to demand organizational complexity (one aspect of which is the position of boundary role incumbent).

Autonomous, flexible boundary role incumbents would seem to be a must for effective adaptation.

---

## Institutional Adaptation:
## More Research

---

How an institution adapts to its environment is obviously a function of what it perceives in its environment. Miles calls this the "readaptive strategy." He defines an organization as being in a state of readaptation when its performance is simultaneously efficient and effective.[11] This process can also be called the *institutional adaptive function*. Especially in turbulent environments, the boundary role functions of monitoring and forecasting become even more crucial. There are a number of implications to this process of managing the environment.

Organizations rely on a number of industrial paradigm strategies to minimize risk and uncertainty in their environments. One large study that examined the ability of companies in the record industry and pharmaceutical industry to manage their environments found that the relative effectiveness of the two industries is caused by the differential control over the environment of each.[12] In general, the pharmaceutical industry employs much more successful strategies to counteract external dependence and uncertainty than does the recording industry. Effectiveness, in this case, can be seen as the organization's ability to manipulate the external environment so as to reduce uncertainty/unpredictability.

Robert Miles and Charles Snow have identified four particular strategies for adaptation that illustrate the interactions between strategy and structure; they call the companies that employ these strategies defenders, prospectors, analyzers, and reactors.[13] The first three strategies are considered effective when used in appropriate applications; the fourth is considered an ineffective adaptation strategy.

- *Defenders:* These companies have very small market niches (product market domains) and are highly expert in their constricted areas of operation. They tend not to search for new areas of operation, but, rather, stay with the tried and true. As a consequence of their narrow focus, they do not often change their technologies, structures, or processes; instead, they attempt to increase their efficiency by cost-cutting and by streamlining their operations. Examples of the kinds of companies falling into this category are some specialty clothing companies and boutique food producers.

- *Prospectors:* These innovative companies are always on the lookout for new market opportunities. They are constantly experimenting with potential responses to emerging trends. Because of their concern for market innovation, these firms often create problems of uncertainty for their competitors and tend not to be very efficient. Examples in this category are computer services companies and electronics firms.

- *Analyzers:* These firms typically operate in two types of environments, changing and stable. In stable domains, these organizations tend to be very bureaucratically structured, with high levels of formalization. In more turbulent domains, management tends to watch competitors for new ideas and to copy them very quickly. These types of companies, then, tend to have a bureaucratic component (for the stable environment) and an organic component (for the turbulent). Examples are some electronics companies and some hospitals.

- *Reactors:* These companies tend to respond very slowly, if at all, to environmental changes. They lack a coherent strategy-structure relationship and will fail unless found in a very stable environment (where resource dependence and uncertainty are low). Reactors will not change until forced to by environmental contingencies. Examples are some types of food processors and some publishers.

All of these strategies represent attempts to manage the environment and to monitor the unmanageable parts. All are based on the separatist, industrial era perspective. There is no trust in the inherent intelligence of the design of life to organize the external world successfully; separated human consciousness seeks to manipulate to its own perceived advantage.

## Further Structural Implications

In a classic study of organizations and their environments, William R. Dill found contrasts between two companies in Norway.[14] "Alpha" was a company with a stable, homogeneous, and predictable environment, whereas "Beta had a task environment that was highly differentiated and unstable. Dill found that the complex environment of Beta required high managerial autonomy and flexible structural arrangements, whereas the stable environment of Alpha allowed for close controls based on rules, procedures, and restricted autonomy. Dill concludes that the structural differences between the firms was caused by differences in their task environments.

Beta's environment seemed to call for more flexible structure and more managerial autonomy; the more organic structure permitted the quick response time and adaptability required in uncertain environments. Alpha's more predictable and more homogeneous environment allowed for the use of more traditional bureaucratic controls, such as hierarchy and rules, regulations, policies, and procedures (with concomitant restricted managerial autonomy).

Dill also examined the information-processing demands of the organization. He concludes that complex, uncertain environments require that more energy and emphasis be placed on information processing: "It is not the supplier or the customer himself that counts, but the information that he makes accessible to the organization being studied about his goals, the conditions under which he will enter into a contract, or other aspects of his behavior."[15]

Another study that relates organization structure to environmental complexity is the classic Lawrence and Lorsch research discussed in Chapter 9.[16] Although the authors define *differentiation* and *integration* as two major structural variables, the main thrust of their work is to show how organizations become more complex in response to increasing environmental complexity. According to Lawrence and Lorsch, increasing environmental complexity requires increasing organizational complexity (or differentiation) to cope effectively with environmental demands. However, increasing differentiation brings about increased problems of integration, and they found that highly differentiated organizations need to make extra efforts to integrate. Hence there is a need for more organic forms to deal with problems of integration in highly differentiated firms.

Lawrence and Lorsch postulated that the complexity of the environment determines the complexity of a successful organization's structure. A dynamic environment seems to have more influence on structure than does a static one.[17] A turbulent environment can be a more important factor than the imperative of large size and/or routine technology. Organizations with departments that are very dependent on aspects of the environment tend to be less hierarchical.[18]

Stable environments tend to lead to high formalization, because there is minimal need for rapid response and there are efficiencies to be gained through programmed, standardized activities. Conversely, dynamic environments seem to lead to lower levels of formalization, but not necessarily throughout the organization. There appears to be some evidence that dynamic environments force the boundary-spanning activities or subunits to be less formalized, but may not affect the rest of the organization.[19]

Finally, the more complex the environment, the more decentralized the structure, all things being equal.[20] Obviously, the more complex the environment, the less possible it is for one person or group to know everything needed to make timely, accurate decisions.

## Can Organizations Adapt?
## The Population Ecology Perspective

The goal of much organizational research is to discover how organizations adapt to change, but one school of thought has as its hypothesis that organizations *cannot* adapt very much, but are "selected." This is the *population ecology model*.[21]

All ecological perspectives attribute patterns in nature to the action of *selection* processes, whereas the bulk of the literature on organization-environment relations focuses on the *adaptation* perspective. According to the adaptation perspective, subunits of the organization, usually managers or dominant coalitions, scan the relevant environment for opportunities or threats, formulate strategic responses, and adjust organizational structure accordingly.[22] In this view, effective managers are able either to buffer the organization from environmental turbulence or to arrange smooth adaptations that require minimal disruption of organization structure.

The natural selection perspective acknowledges that organizations adapt, but argues that it is presumptuous to assume that the great structural variability among organizations reflects only (or even primarily) adaptive response. First of all, there are limits on how much an organization can actually adapt; most organizations of any size have a certain amount of bureaucratic inertia that prevents strategic adaptation. These inertial pressures include *internal contraints* such as plant and equipment investments that are not easily transferable, political constraints caused by redistributing resources across subunits, and historical constraints such as company rules and procedures and conventional wisdom. *Environmental constraints* also can be strong. External pressures toward inertia can include legal and fiscal barriers to entry and exit in markets, constraints on the availability of (and validity of) information, especially in turbulent environments, and limitations on legitimacy (in other words, can the organization adapt the way it needs to and still keep the support of its constituencies?).

The crux of the natural selection view of population ecology is that the environment selects particular types of organizations to survive and others to fail based on their "fit" between structural characteristics and environmental characteristics. Population ecologists argue that a given organization must fit an environmental niche or fail. Because constraints or inertia makes it difficult for organizations to adapt their structures to a given set of environmental conditions, an organization must find a niche where its particular structural strengths are useful.

Obviously, this is the Darwinian perspective brought to organizations. According to this doctrine of the survival of the fittest, the environment naturally selects some organizations as "okay" and others as "not okay." Furthermore, population ecologists argue that those selected as okay typically have more structural dimensions and resources to use in fitting in.

## The Underlying Assumptions of Population Ecology

This particular theory is based on a number of assumptions concerning the organization-environment interface. First of all, it represents an extremist, determinist view. The environment is considered to be the sole relevant variable in the determination of organizational effectiveness; if the organization does not fit the environment, there is little that management can do, given all the aforementioned constraints. Survival (and effectiveness) are totally determined by how well the organization fits its niche.

Second, this theory tries to explain why organizations operating in similar environments end up with similar structures. The argument goes like this: At first, there are many variations in structures operating in a given environment, but as the environment rewards certain structural characteristics over others, firms with the "correct" characteristics survive, whereas the others slowly but surely stumble.

Finally, the organizations themselves seek to retain those characteristics that have come to be known as relevant to success, ensuring their relative permanency. In the long run, however, even the positively selected characteristics tend to be "selected out" because the environment itself changes and different structural variations are favored.

Another assumption of this theory is that any environment has a saturation point beyond which it cannot support more organizations of a given type, such as mental health clinics. This sets up a competitive mechanism whereby some organizations fail and others succeed. Still another assumption is that it is valuable to focus on groups or populations of organizations rather than single organizations. For example, this theory would tend to explain the success of large chain discount drugstores over the service-oriented "corner drugstore" as being caused by the chain's better fit with environmental contingencies such as customer habits and price consciousness. Airlines and afternoon daily newspapers are two other examples of industries whose environments changed, thanks to deregulation in the first case and the rise of television news in the second.

Obviously, to argue that the sole (or even major) variable affecting organizational survival is the environment is to ignore the managerial variable and the apparent ability to "manage" the environment. It would seem that this theory has greatest applicability to small and relatively powerless organizations with limited ability to adapt to environmental contingencies.

Despite population ecology theory's apparent validity and support in the organization theory field, it is unlikely to receive widespread support because of the prevailing paradigm. A basic premise of the industrial paradigm is the manipulation of external circumstances to produce results pleasing to the individual (or the organization). An argument that luck or happenstance (being at the right place at the right time) is the major factor in determining organizational survival will not be accepted by those who are wedded to the view that managerial decisions, strategic and tactical, control a firm's destiny.

## The Nature of Environment: A Transformational View

Most definitions of an organization's environment see it as being outside the boundary of the organization. One old-paradigm definition argues that the environment is composed of those institutions or forces that affect the performance of the organization but over which the organization has little or no control.[23] This emphasis on *control* is logical, given that one of the key tenets of the old paradigm is attempted control over uncertainty and unpredictability in one's world.

In the mechanistic, Newtonian paradigm, this is a fairly simple definitional matter. However, in the new paradigm, where everything flows into everything else in a seamless whole, such a neat definition becomes problematic. What is "outside the organization" in the transformational view, if everything is interconnected and interdependent? And, in fact, if everything is really a seamless whole, each separate firm trying to "manage" its environment without any sense of how it (the firm) is connected to everything else will most likely produce turbulent effects in that environment. There is consensus today that environments are becoming more turbulent, yet very few people recognize that acting on the belief that it is possible to manipulate (manage) one's environment actually causes turbulence.

### Turbulence: Where Does It Come From?

The transformational perspective recognizes that we create our own reality, basing it on the dominant belief systems, attitudes, values, and assumptions that are shared by a critical mass of people. So if everyone shares in the creation of reality, and the dominant paradigm sees the individual and the organization as separate entities both needing to plan and manipulate to get what they want, then it does not require a great leap in logic to see how turbulence in the environment is merely a mirror, a reflection, of the collective inner state.[24]

The spirit of life (or the vibratory patterns of design and control, the "implicate order" described in Chapter 4) moves through the mental and emotional capacities of human beings to create reality (using the existing paradigmatic assumptions); if self-centered assumptions are present, then trust in life's ability to organize the whole will be lacking. So people will be struggling to "make things happen" without any regard for (or sensitivity to) how their actions affect the larger whole or just what life's larger purposes might be. Since it is a fearful state to be separated from our source (the spirit of life), our fear and anxiety get projected onto the so-called outer environment. Inner emotional turbulence (what Jung called the "shadow") is translated into environmental turbulence, which is then reacted to by "effect-oriented" people, as the cycle intensifies.

Alvin Toffler, in *Future Shock*, speaks of the "premature arrival of the future," the increasing rate of change that threatens to overwhelm us, and the "death of permanence."[25] In the years since that book appeared, we have seen the development of genetic engineering, babies born through in vitro fertilization and other medical advances that have raised serious ethical questions, increasing population pressures, rapidly increasing technological change, environmental pollution—the list seems endless. All of this turbulence has created a veritable nightmare for corporate decision makers. The National Industrial Conference Board has identified a set of problems emerging as a result of this increasing turbulence, problems decision makers must tackle:

1. the rate of change, which is shrinking research and planning horizons
2. outdated criteria used to examine new problems and opportunities
3. micro and piecemeal ways of dealing with problems at the macro level
4. public insistence on "instant" solutions and leader impatience with problems that demand attention over long periods of time
5. pushing and pulling on the part of those who, because of fear or selfish interests, resist change and those who want to lead it and accelerate it
6. inexperience in bringing out large-scale collaboration on the part of leaders in and between the private and public sectors
7. competing demands for scarce talents and resources, and the increasingly frequent absence of needed skills
8. uncertainty on the part of decision makers and institutions as to the nature of their new roles and responsibilities in a changing society

POT-SHOTS NO. 420

## MY PICTURE OF THE WORLD KEEPS CHANGING BEFORE I CAN GET IT INTO FOCUS.

Ashleigh
Brilliant

9. the temporary inability of our system of checks and balances, of regulations and controls, to function correctly during the transition between paradigms
10. the question of how to regularize the irregular[26]

Even business schools, long the bulwark of the traditional way of doing things, find it is "time to think in global terms." Helping students to understand the relationships among the political, social, and biological environments is increasingly seen as the "key to effective management in the future."[27] Students are now finding courses with names such as "Systems Thinking in Business," "Business and Society," and "Political Economics" to be increasingly common fare. Here is at least tacit admission that we are part of a larger context.

---

## The Transformational Perspective on Organization/Environment

---

The environments in which organizations operate have become steadily more turbulent. If the collective paradigm (cause) produces organization structure and process (effect), then the collective paradigm is also producing the environment itself—in fact, it produces the entire world of form. What we see and experience as the world "out there" is nothing more or less than a reflection of what is contained (and agreed on) in consciousness. If we see a scary world, this is an indication that we are scared inside. If we see a turbulent world, we have turbulent thoughts and feelings inside.

As more and more people, all operating self-centeredly without any concern for or awareness of their impact on the larger whole, create more and more dissonance, they will react with fear and step up their efforts to control their environment. The result will only be more chaos. Similarly, organizations that operate self-centeredly—that is, with regard only for their own success—will produce effects that will have impacts on others in their sphere of influence. This is rather easy to see as it relates to competitive strategy, but more obscure (but nonetheless just as valid) when it comes to more subtle effects. The point is this: When an individual or an organization operates in a mutually interdependent system (which is operated by the forces of life itself), any action taken that is not consonant with (or complementary to) the rhythms of life operating at that moment will necessarily produce dissonant results.

© BRILLIANT ENTERPRISES 1976.

POT-SHOTS NO. 909.

I HOPE
THE LIFE-INSPECTOR
DOESN'T
COME AROUND
WHILE
I HAVE
MY LIFE
IN SUCH A MESS.

Ashleigh Brilliant

## Where Are We Heading?

Many analysts agree that the rate of external change is accelerating.[28] The consensual agreement is that we are entering a new era, variously called the "information age," the "communications age," or the "post-industrial age," depending on whom you are reading. We have left behind an economy dominated by cheap raw materials and wages and an industrial/mechanical technology in favor of a knowledge-based economy dominated by cheap—primarily electronic—information. This knowledge-based economy will certainly have implications for the shape and structure of organizations.[29] Robey tells us:

> In this more service oriented economy, information rather than physical materials becomes the raw material for most people's work. Because it has no physical substance, information can be duplicated, transmitted, combined, and renewed quite independent of location or time. Working with information does not require large plants or offices, but it does require the ability to react quickly to frequent changes in information. The information age means that more and more organizations will need to prepare for almost constant change in their environments because of the ease with which information itself changes.[30]

Most writers agree that in addition to constant change, the environment of the future will be characterized by interdependence, uncertainty, and resource scarcity.

### Interdependence

Today, events that occur in China, the European market, and Africa have almost immediate impact on the United States. This "butterfly effect of chaos" theory, which says that the beating of a butterfly's wings affects everything in the whole world, is just one sign of the interdependence of our "global village."[31] The world is being brought together into a state of wholeness by the power of life's design. From the transformational view, life is the "natural integrator"; inherent in the design and purpose of life is *wholeness.*

Various environmental crises are increasing our awareness of the interconnectedness of all life: ozone layer depletion, polluted oceans and groundwater, disappearing rain forests, vanishing species and decreasing biological diversity, nuclear waste, toxic dumps, and more. And it is finally beginning to dawn on us that this planet is, in one sense, a closed system; merely moving a polluting factory to Taiwan does not rid the biosphere of the contaminants it creates.

The Earth is a web of life kept in perfect homeostasis by the design of life, but our self-centered paradigms have been distorting the design so that ill effects and imbalance have been showing up. It is becoming obvious even to self-centered humans that attempts to manipulate the environment for our own gain have torn at the delicate fabric of life. Strip mining, industrial pollution, the dumping of toxic wastes, and oil spills are all reminders that there is a high cost to self-centered activity.

**Vignette 1**

When the 1988 *Exxon Valdez* accident triggered a massive oil spill off the shores of Alaska, people immediately began to search for someone to blame. First the apparently drunk captain of the ship was blamed, then the company itself. But nowhere did we read about the central cause of the spill: our consumption-oriented Western culture, which demands oil for transportation, heating, manufacturing, and more. That demand caused the pipeline to be built, the tankers to be loaded, and the events that caused the spill to begin.

*We* were responsible for the oil spill. Because none of us wants to acknowledge it, we looked for a scapegoat. If we were actually to take personal responsibility for the spill, we would have to examine our habits of profligate and wasteful consumption. Under our present paradigm, we don't want to, and we don't have to. Sadly, this is all too symptomatic of our current malaise.

## Uncertainty

According to the transformational view, patterns of emotional upset and reaction are causal elements in the increasing rate of change—and the resulting uncertainty—on our planet. Because the environment is a product of our collective agreement in consciousness, it is only logical that as greater numbers of self-centered humans try to "get satisfaction," they create conflict and react to that conflict, and their turbulent emotions and thoughts in turn create increasingly turbulent environmental effects. As these attitudes of reaction, blame, and criticism cause more apparent external disturbance, self-centered humans (mired in fear and shame) try harder to "get" peace, and find it more and more elusive.

Uncertainty is the result of fear patterns and a lack of trust in the creative processes of life. Fear-based projections into the world of form create objects of fear, which are then reacted to, creating more uncertainty. Because of a lack of connection with the invisible source or spirit, people try to get their security from external forms, which are always in flux, guaranteeing rampant insecurity.

If the transformational view is accurate, we can expect more turbulence and uncertainty as more and more corporations and nations, beset by increasing "problems," attempt to manipulate their external environments with policies and strategies. These self-centered strivings, implemented with little or no concern for their impact on the larger whole, will predictably produce effects that will be disruptive, because the strategies are not in alignment with life's greater purposes. Then other groupings, not liking those effects, will attempt to manipulate their circumstances to get what they want, and the cycle will escalate.

## Resource Scarcity

Buckminster Fuller, designer of the geodesic dome, once claimed that we have enough technology and resources to feed and clothe every man, woman, and child on the planet at a very high standard of living *now*. Why don't we, then? Because our fear- and effect-oriented paradigm needs inequality so we can each strive to get better, richer, stronger than others. Meaning in our world comes from externals, so the best manipulators seem to be rewarded for their efforts. The class system and the meritocracy are the result. Resources are in fact finite, but, with a paradigm shift toward oneness and interconnectedness, we will be able to do much more with less. Many so-called mainstream Americans now see the rampant, materialistic values so prominent in the 1980s as essentially obsolete today.

## Creating Environmental Strategy
## From the Transformational Perspective

The transformational perspective reveals the ultimate futility of the traditional "manage your environment" approach. It might appear to produce favorable short-term results, but, because the organization is part of a much larger, interdependent whole, its actions produce effects that reverberate throughout the whole. Fortunately, the new paradigm holds a few concrete suggestions for whole-centered strategies that can effectively replace the old self-centered ones.

*Seek to play one's part in the whole.* Peters and Waterman tell the story of Stewart Leonard's grocery in Westport, Connecticut. This

© ASHLEIGH BRILLIANT 1980                    POT-SHOTS NO. 1701.

Life is not a problem ~

Life is the closest
God has yet come
        to a solution.

*Ashleigh Brilliant*

grocery store does a weekly volume of some $1.5 million, whereas local competitors average $200,000-$300,000 per week. The secret to Leonard's success is so simple it sounds ludicrous: *Listen to the customer.*[32] Unfortunately, many organizations fail to listen or serve their customers, acting instead out of an arrogance inherent in the industrial paradigm: We know what they want (or what is best for them).

*Stay flexible.* Like the seasons of the year, most living entities seem to progress through cycles of growth (expansion) and decline (contraction). The competitive company will sense these changes—in products, and in their organization—by staying open to them, listening for them, and adjusting accordingly.

*Focus on moving with the cycles rather than trying to "manage" them.* Just because self-centered action wreaks havoc doesn't mean one should be paralyzed into inaction. There is always something creative one can do. The issue is the attitude with which it is done. Is the company trying to "capture a market" (note the militaristic connotation of the words themselves), or is it seeking to blend with the larger whole by playing a particular role in that environment? It is a question of making the right move at the right time. Morgan notes

POT-SHOTS NO. 3229.

CREATION
ALWAYS
REQUIRES
DESTRUCTION:

BUT
WHAT'S BEING
CREATED
ISN'T ALWAYS
WORTH
WHAT'S BEING
DESTROYED.

©ASHLEIGH BRILLIANT 1985

that "if the timing is incorrect or the 'windows of opportunity' are different from those anticipated, the best laid plans can flounder."[33] With product life cycles as short as 18 months, a product can be obsolete before it gets to the market, especially if it takes years to develop. Timing is crucial.

*Seek to establish collaborative, win-win relationships with elements of the external environment.* Much of the collaboration in business today is between parties that have traditionally not collaborated with each other (or, in some cases, have been adversaries). The dawning awareness of mutual interdependence is encouraging these collaborative approaches, which emerge as a result of problems or issues that affect all the parties. Some examples are regional economic survival, neighborhood crime watches, and dramatic turnarounds such as the Ford casting plant in Windsor and GM in Lordstown.[34] Although still essentially self-centered in motivation (i.e., survival oriented), these efforts do signal the beginning of a shift into the transformational paradigm. Metcalfe has argued:

> Organizations generally are not designed to accommodate easily to changes in the problems they have to solve. Poor results are more likely to lead to redoubled efforts in preestablished directions than to systematic diagnosis and redefinition of problems. The relations between organizations and

their environments are an area of organizational life where problem-solving-capabilities are conspicuously underdeveloped and increasingly necessary.[35]

In response to what Capra calls the "crisis of adaptability," many organizations have been using a variety of collaborative methods and organizational forms to address these complex issues.[36] Actually,

> collaborative approaches to problem-solving can be found at all levels of the organization and across virtually all functional areas; for example production (Just-in-Time manufacturing), human resources management (employee involvement, quality circles, participative management), organizational design (matrix structures, ad hoc task forces), marketing (co-op advertising and cause-related marketing), strategy (joint ventures) and business-government relations (industry self-regulation, trade associations, and public-private partnerships).[37]

All of these can be viewed as symptoms of the ongoing shift toward whole-centeredness from self-centeredness.

---

**Vignette 2**

The just-in-time (JIT) system is an excellent example of collaborative partnership. The idea is for a manufacturer to keep in close contact with suppliers, and the suppliers agree to supply items at short notice. The manufacturer therefore saves on inventory costs by keeping stock levels low—new supplies, theoretically at least, arrive just in time for manufacture.

However, if suppliers sense that a manufacturer is "using" suppliers to pick up the tab for inventory, they will not cooperate. Carefully nurtured relationships between manufacturers and suppliers can sour if suppliers sense they are being manipulated. Mutual trust and a win-win climate are required to make this work.

SOURCE: Dexter Hutchins, "Having a Hard Time With Just-in-Time," *Fortune*, June 9, 1986, 64-66. © 1986 Time Inc. All rights reserved. Used with permission.

---

The spirit of this shift in paradigm is captured in a *Fortune* magazine article about Donald Petersen of Ford Motor Company:

> Petersen transformed Ford by radically reshaping one of the most autocratic and politicized corporate cultures in the U.S. Picture the opposite

of Henry Ford II, Lee Iacocca, and a host of other egotistical managers who once starred at Ford, and you get the man who could be Detroit's first Japanese-style chief executive. He lives and breathes participative management, taking to heart suggestions from vice presidents and assembly workers. Most remarkably, *he subordinates his ego to the needs of the company.*[38]

*Look for "fracture lines" in the environment.* Gareth Morgan has observed:

> Outside-in management keeps an organization in close contact with its evolving environment and enhances its capacity to rise to challenges and opportunities in an ongoing way. This outside-in philosophy contrasts with the "inside-out" philosophy so common today, where managers relate to the environment in terms of what they and their colleagues want to do, rather than what is necessary to meet the challenge of new technologies and the evolving demands of external stakeholders.[39]

Morgan defines "fracture lines" as dramatic events that signal significant shifts in environmental contingencies that have implications for many firms. Examples include the Chernobyl nuclear accident, the Bhopal tragedy in India, any dramatic rise or fall in the price of oil, a key breakthrough in some aspect of research or technology, radical demographic shifts (e.g., move to the Sun Belt), and free trade legislation.[40]

*Develop a proactive mind-set.* Morgan recommends cultivating the ability to get out of the "react mode" so that one is in the driver's seat, seeking opportunities in an entrepreneurial way. Managers must develop the skill to understand trends and potential fracture lines and translate their implications into action plans before the effects take the organization by surprise.

---

"*Competition* comes from the Latin *competere,* which means 'to come together,' 'to agree,' 'to be suitable,' 'to seek together.' Putting these images into the business world, we could say that competition is individual companies inspired by one another, seeking new ways to improve the quality of their services, resulting in an upliftment of the industry as a whole."

—Marianne S. Weidlein and Stephanie F. Roth, *Visions and Business* (Boulder, CO: Megabooks, 1987), 17.

POT- SHOTS NO. 84

**CHANGE** 👉

IT'S TIME FOR US
TO MAKE SOME BIG CHANGES —

WHY DON'T YOU CHANGE FIRST?

Ashleigh
Brilliant

© BRILLIANT ENTERPRISES 1968

All of the strategic changes discussed above are practical steps any organization can take to move consciously from a manipulative, "let's get all we can" approach to a more holistic direction. The first step in this process is for organizational leaders to see themselves and their organizations as part of an interdependent web of organizations and institutions. It is a fact that no man—or organization—is an island.

## NOTES

1. Tom Richman, "Make Love Not War," *Inc.*, August 1988, 56. Reprinted with permission of *Inc.* Magazine © August 1988 Goldhirsch Group, Inc.

2. Ibid., 57.

3. Gareth Morgan, *Riding the Waves of Change* (San Francisco: Jossey-Bass, 1988).

4. Werner Erhard, "Breaking Out of the Box," *The Review*, January 1990, 6.

5. Fred E. Emery and Eric L. Trist, "The Causal Texture of Organizational Environments," *Human Relations* 18 (1965): 21-32; also, much of this discussion was adapted from Robert H. Miles, *Macro Organizational Behavior* (Glenview, IL: Scott, Foresman, 1980), chap. 7.

6. Miles, *Macro Organizational Behavior*, 207.

7. Shirley Terreberry, "The Evolution of Organizational Environments," *Administrative Science Quarterly* 12 (1968): 593.

8. See, for example, Stuart M. Klein and R. Richard Ritti, *Understanding Organizational Behavior* (2nd ed.) (Boston: Kent, 1984), chap. 7.

9. Much of this list is derived from Miles, *Macro Organizational Behavior*, chap. 11.

10. Anthony M. Tinker, "A Note on Environmental Uncertainty and a Suggestion for Our Editorial Function," *Administrative Science Quarterly* 21 (1976).

11. Miles, *Macro Organizational Behavior*, 316-350.

12. Paul M. Hirsch, "Organizational Effectiveness and the Institutional Environment," *Administrative Science Quarterly* 20 (1975): 327-344.

13. Raymond E. Miles and Charles C. Snow, *Organizational Strategy, Structure, and Process* (New York: McGraw-Hill, 1978).

14. William R. Dill, "Environment as an Influence on Managerial Autonomy," *Administrative Science Quarterly* 2 (1958): 409-443.

15. William R. Dill, "The Impact of Environment on Organizational Development," in *Concepts and Issues in Administrative Behavior,* ed. S. Maillick and E. Van Ness (Englewood Cliffs, NJ: Prentice Hall, 1962), 96.

16. Paul R. Lawrence and Jay W. Lorsch, *Organization and Environment: Managing Differentiation and Integration* (Boston: Harvard Business School, Division of Research, 1967).

17. David Jacobs, "Dependency and Vulnerability: An Exchange Approach to the Control of Organizations," *Administrative Science Quarterly* 19 (March 1974): 45-59.

18. Anant R. Negandhi and Bernard C. Reimann, "Task Environment, Decentralization and Organizational Effectiveness," *Human Relations* (April 1973): 203-224.

19. Stephen P. Robbins, *Organization Theory: Structure, Design, and Applications* (2nd ed.) (Englewood Cliffs, NJ: Prentice Hall, 1987), 171.

20. Henry Mintzberg, *The Structuring of Organizations* (Englewood Cliffs, NJ: Prentice Hall, 1979), 273-276.

21. Michael T. Hannan and John Freeman, "The Population Ecology of Organizations," *American Journal of Sociology* 82 (March 1977): 929-964.

22. Ibid., 930.

23. C. W. Churchman, *The Systems Approach* (New York: Dell, 1968), 36.

24. See Brian Tracy, "Pathways Toward Personal Progress," in *The Psychology of Achievement,* audiocassette package (Chicago: Nightingale-Conant, n.d.). Tracy calls this the "law of correspondence": "According to this law, your outer life is a mirror of your inner life; your external world reflects your internal world" (p. 4).

25. Alvin Toffler, *Future Shock* (New York: Random House, 1970).

26. National Industrial Conference Board, *Perspectives for the 1970's and 1980's: Tomorrow's Problems Confronting Today's Managers* (New York: National Industrial Conference Board, 1970).

27. Ibid.

28. See, for example, Alvin Toffler, *The Third Wave* (New York: Simon & Schuster, 1982); Willis Harman, *An Incomplete Guide to the Future* (San Francisco: San Francisco Book, 1976); Peter Vaill, *Managing as a Performing Art: New Ideas for a World of Chaotic Change* (San Francisco: Jossey-Bass, 1989); Morgan, *Riding the Waves of Change.*

29. Alan Raymond, *Management in the Third Wave* (Glenview, IL: Scott, Foresman, 1986), 9; Toffler, *The Third Wave.*

30. Daniel Robey, *Designing Organizations* (2nd ed.) (Homewood, IL: Irwin, 1986), 543.

31. James Gleick, *Chaos: Making a New Science* (New York: Penguin, 1987).

32. Thomas J. Peters and Robert H. Waterman, Jr., *In Search of Excellence: Lessons From America's Best-Run Companies* (New York: Harper & Row, 1982).

33. Morgan, *Riding the Waves of Change,* 45. Used with permission from the publisher.

34. Douglas Austrom and Lawrence Lad, "Strategic Management in a Turbulent Era: The Significance of Collaboration" (paper presented at the ASAC Conference, University of Toronto, Ontario), 6.

35. Larry Metcalfe, "Designing Precarious Partnerships," in *Handbook of Organizational Design,* ed. Paul C. Nystrom and William H. Starbuck (London: Oxford University Press, 1981), 503.

36. Fritjof Capra, *The Turning Point* (New York: Simon & Schuster, 1982).

37. Austrom and Lad, "Strategic Management," 1.

38. Donald Petersen, "A Humble Hero Drives Ford to the Top," *Fortune,* January 4, 1988, 23; emphasis added. © 1988 Time Inc. All rights reserved. Used with permission.

39. Morgan, *Riding the Waves of Change,* 5. Used with permission from the publisher.

40. Ibid., 20.

# 13  Organizational Technology and Structure

*Technology has a profound impact on organizations. Manufacturing firms, retail establishments, hospitals, universities, and other organizations are uniquely affected by the technologies they adopt. Although the search for technology began with the use of fire and primitive tools, it was not until the Industrial Revolution of the late eighteenth century that organizations began to develop and exploit the technology of machine manufacture.*

(Billy Joe Hodge and William P. Anthony,
*Organization Theory,* 1988, p. 426)

---

**SUMMARY:** In this chapter we explore one of the so-called causal factors of structure: organizational technology. We review many studies that purport to show the connection between the modal (or dominant) technology employed and the structural configuration of the organization. We close the chapter with a transformational perspective on technology and its relationship to the organization.

---

One variable widely thought to be a primary influence on organization structure is technology. The term *technology* actually refers to a method or process of doing something. Hodge and Anthony define it as the "art and science employed in the production and distribution of goods and services."[1] In practice, the term is also used to describe techniques for processing information (computers) and transmitting sensory information (telecommunications). It is also used to describe

229

work flow, or the process of work. In this chapter we will consider the term *technology of work* to mean work flow. As will become clear below, this distinction is important. For ease and simplicity, in this book, when we speak of technology, we are referring to the technology of work.

---

## Defining Technology

---

*Technology of work* refers to the process by which an organization converts inputs to outputs, or, more precisely, the knowledge, skills, techniques, and actions used to transform inputs into outputs.[2] Figure 13.1 summarizes the relationship. Basically, the technology of work is the process of exactly *how* inputs are transformed into outputs. All organizations begin with certain raw materials, act on them with human labor (usually), and convert the inputs to some outputs. However, the ways in which they perform this conversion process differ widely. One organization processes insurance forms, another handles tax accounting; one manufactures automobiles, and still another designs blueprints for the construction of skyscrapers. A university takes in students as raw materials, processes them in various ways, and then graduates them as "finished product." The technology in schools usually involves grouping students together in classrooms where they receive auditory, visual, and written information from teachers. The choice of technology affects the design of the organization in certain ways, as we shall see.

Some other definitions are perhaps in order. *Work flow* is a term used to describe the way in which programs, activities, and events are sequenced in the input-transformation-output cycle of the organization. The work done in an organization influences the type of equipment chosen to facilitate that work, and the kind of equipment used powerfully influences the work flow.

*Operations technology* refers to the role of mechanical aids in transforming inputs into outputs. *Informational technology* is the name for the role that mechanical/electronic aids play in transforming informational inputs into informational outputs. However, for our purposes, we will simply refer to technology as the transformation process of inputs to outputs.

Certain goals and/or strategic decisions can affect work flow. For example, a primary goal of efficiency can lead to one work-flow design, and the goal of high employee satisfaction can lead to another. In automobile manufacturing, for example, the classic way to organize work for efficiency is the mass-production, assembly-line format, in

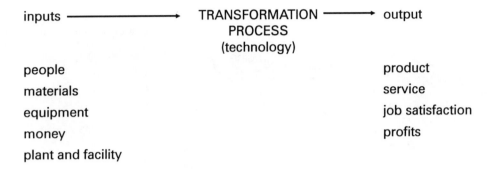

**Figure 13.1.** The Role of Organization Technology

which each activity on the line precedes the next activity in a certain order. However, various studies of job design have shown that this approach can lead to bored and unmotivated workers.[3] Hence, to increase worker job satisfaction, Swedish automobile manufacturers Volvo and Saab have instituted a work flow that includes a series of semiautonomous teams, each performing a complete subassembly of the automobile (see Figure 13.2).[4] This kind of work flow, which is intended to stimulate employee satisfaction, encourages teamwork, participation, "job enrichment" (Frederick Herzberg's term for complete, challenging jobs rather than small, routine tasks), and job rotation.

Work flow can also be affected by pressure from the environment and by demographic changes; environmental turbulence may cause a firm to standardize its operations to cope with worker turnover. Service organizations can have substantially different work flows than manufacturing operations.

## Technology and the Industrial Paradigm

Under the industrial era paradigm, what has been consistently rewarded in American industry is analytic, logical, rational thought.[5] The best managers are thought to be cool, unemotional people who look at all the factors in a linear, sequential manner, pick the best alternatives from the available options, and make the best decisions. These managers view the organization as a machine, with interchangeable parts that can be manipulated to produce certain "desirable" ends. Competition has been encouraged, and we have valued, and continue to value, material success and the acquisition of material rewards/comforts.

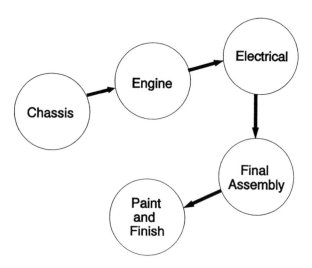

**Figure 13.2.**   Volvo's Work Flow

It has been argued that this left-brain dominant, rational, analytic pattern of thought is a predominantly male pattern of thinking. Some current thinkers in the behavioral sciences have argued that success in business has required this kind of thinking, and that this has placed women at a disadvantage, because women's "typical" style of thinking is more right-brain dominant.[6] In any event, the pattern of thinking associated with success in the industrial era has emphasized rational, linear/sequential thought, negation of emotion and intuition (until very recently), and dependence on analytic proof and quantitative measurement.

According to the metamodel of organization, the collective paradigm (the shared values, attitudes, and belief systems of the people in the organization) actually creates the structure. Taking it a step further, we posit that the collective paradigm also creates and sustains the technology of the organization. It then appears obvious that if technology dictates (or at least influences) structure and the paradigm creates the structure, then technology might be an intervening variable in this process, as Figure 13.3 shows.

A linear/sequential, rational thought process will naturally produce a technology that reflects these characteristics: the assembly line, a linear/sequential process of manufacturing. It is no accident that the assembly line has been the dominant manufacturing process of the industrial age. And, so, the long-linked technology seems to dictate a bureaucratic structure, the "machine model," which reflects the preferences of industrial era thinkers.

Even our process for discovering new technologies is subject to the paradigmatic assumptions of the industrial era. Our use of the suppos-

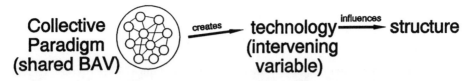

**Figure 13.3.** The Paradigm, Technology, and Organization Structure

edly value-free "scientific method" has, intrinsic to the method itself, mechanistic, Newtonian assumptions about the nature of reality.[7] As the paradigm shifts, we begin to hear cries for a move away from empiricist, quantitative research models to holistic, qualitative ones.[8]

If the metamodel is correct, we would expect new organizational forms and new technologies to be appearing as the dominant paradigm shifts from left brain to whole brain, from separateness to unity, from competitiveness to collaboration, from win-lose to win-win. As the matrix, hybrid transorganizational forms and other organization designs have begun to put in an appearance, so have new technologies.

## Does Technology Determine Structure?

Among organization theorists there is little agreement on whether or not the technology chosen by an organization actually dictates its structure. The notion that technology dictates structure is commonly called the *technological imperative*. This school of thought argues that the technology chosen to perform the transformation process (from input to output) is a primary determinant of the organization's structure and processes. The other widely held view is that, for all but the smallest organizations, technology plays a role in structural determination, but not a central one. Let us look at these studies with an eye toward resolving these different views.

### The Technological Imperative: The Woodward Studies

The origin of the concept of the technological imperative is found in the work of Joan Woodward, conducted in the 1950s. Her work was (and, in some quarters, still is) very influential in the development of the notion that technology dictates structure. Woodward and a team of researchers in England gathered information on the following variables from firms with more than 100 employees that were using a wide range of production methods:

1. the success of the firm, based on such factors as share of the market, fiscal data, and the considered judgment of industry executives
2. the technology of the firm (the type of manufacturing process involved)
3. the extent to which the tasks were formalized and relationships were specified (the style of management used)
4. the form and shape of the organization structure, such as spans of control, administrative component, and number of levels[9]

Woodward and her group examined their data to determine what caused success or lack of success among these firms. They looked at different organizational patterns and concluded that there was no relationship between business success and organizational practice. But when they looked at technology, they seemed to be onto something. Woodward identified three major categories of production processes that varied on a scale of technical complexity:

1. *unit or small-batch production:* a custom house or "job shop," where one-of-a-kind items are produced
2. *mass or large-batch production:* basic assembly-line technology (large quantities of production)
3. *process production:* long, continuous runs through standardized, repetitive procedures (as in chemical manufacturing)

Technical complexity seemed to increase as one moved from the unit or small batch to the continuous technologies. More capital investment was needed, and the procedures became far more standardized. As technical complexity increased, structure changed. Spans of control became wider, additional levels of hierarchy were created, and administrative ratios (ratios of administrative staff to workers) increased. Unit and process technologies seemed to work better with smaller spans and organic structure, whereas the mass-production technology seemed to flourish with wider spans and bureaucratic structure.

Many people have attempted to replicate Woodward's findings. One of the first was Edward Harvey, who argued, "It is not only important to take into account the form of technology, as Woodward has done, but also to consider the amount of change within a given form."[10] His results supported Woodward's findings; as technical diffuseness (his term for product change over time) decreased, there was an increase in structural variables such as the number of specialized subunits, the ratio of management to total personnel, the extent of formalization (RRPP), and the number of levels of vertical hierarchy.

These and subsequent studies by Zwerman, who repeated the Woodward study in the Minneapolis area with 55 firms, and by both Perrow and Thompson, who developed models to explain how technology affects organizational structure, point to the same conclusion.[11] They seem to indicate that, when the technology of production is not matched correctly to a suitable structure, additional costs are incurred by the firm, leading to less-than-optimal success.

All of the researchers discussed above emphasize that technology is an important variable in the design of organizational structure. But whether technology actually dictates structure is another question. There seems to be ample evidence that it does not.

## Technology—Important, But Not Causal: The Aston Studies

The Aston Group was a team of researchers who also looked at the relationship between technology and structure.[12] Conducted in Birmingham, England, their study focused on organizations with a minimum of 250 employees. The central technology variable used was *work-flow integration,* the degree of automated, continuous fixed-sequence operations in the technology.

The Aston Group examined how work-flow integration varied with respect to structural variables, that is, the structuring of activities, the concentration of authority (centralization), the line control of the work flow, and the supportive component. Technology was found to be moderately related to these variables, but the researchers found other factors that could explain more of the variation in structure.[13] This study concluded that organization *size* was more important than technology as a determinant of structure.

More specifically, the Aston researchers distinguished between *modal technology* and *unit technology,* the former being the technology most characteristic of the whole organization, and the latter being the technology of the major subunit of the organization. For example, an automobile manufacturer such as General Motors will have a modal technology of assembly line (or "large batch," in Woodward's terms), but individual departments of the company (such as research and development) might employ a craft (one-of-a-kind) unit technology.

The Aston researchers found that, in firms of small size, the technological imperative seemed to be proven; the dominant technology did seem to dictate structure. However, in larger organizations, size became the predictor of structural configuration. Also, modal technology seemed more important for units directly impinged on by the work flow. The overall conclusion was that unit technologies are more important as a determinant of structure in larger organizations, and modal technology in smaller ones. Thus for a small manufacturer, with annual revenues of $5 million or less, the modal technology would be expected to have a large impact on the structure of the total company. However, for General Motors, unit technologies will affect structure in each of the separate units.

### Technology Does Determine Structure: The Work of Howard Aldrich

In criticizing the Aston Group's research, Howard Aldrich argued that its theoretical implications were weak and did not exhaust other explanations for the technology/size/structure results.[14] Aldrich's own model of the relationship proposed a developmental sequence in organizations that seems to uphold the Woodward thesis of the technological imperative. Work-flow integration or technology, in his model, plays a central role in determining structure. Size is then seen as resulting from technology, "operating variability," and structure. In brief, Aldrich's argument is that, if technology precedes size, and size follows structure, only technology can logically cause structure. Detractors argue that, if both structure and technology precede size, then you cannot necessarily say that technology causes structure.[15]

To summarize, it is clear that technology alone probably does not dictate structure, as Woodward and others would have us believe. However, it is nonetheless important. It may be a moderator variable; that is, it may alter the relationship between other variables and structure. Also, many studies have used different measures of technology or work-flow integration, and this alone could account for some of the discrepancies in the findings.

---

## Types of Technologies: The Work of Thompson and Perrow

---

Although not advocates of the technological imperative view, James Thompson and Charles Perrow saw technology as an important determinant of organization structure. Thompson categorized types of technology on the basis of *task interdependence,* identifying low, medium, and high levels of interdependence needed to perform tasks.[16] He also

**Table 13.1** Thompson's Classification of Organizations by Task Interdependence

| Technology Type | Dominant Form of Task Interdependence | MANAGEMENT AND DESIGN REQUIREMENTS | | | Organizational Example |
|---|---|---|---|---|---|
| | | Demands Placed on Decision Making and Communications | Extent of Organizational Complexity | Types of Coordination Required | |
| Mediating | Pooled<br>X Y Z (O) | Low | Low | Standardization and Categorization | Commercial bank |
| Long-linked | Sequential<br>X→Y→Z | Medium | Medium | Plan | Assembly Line Automobile |
| Intensive | Reciprocal<br>X⇄Y⇄Z | High | High | Mutual adjustment | General hospital |

SOURCE: Adapted by Miles from James D. Thompson, *Organizations in Action*, in Robert H. Miles, *Macro Organizational Behavior* (Glenview, IL: Scott, Foresman, 1980), 66. Reprinted with permission from the author.

argued for structural and managerial specifications for each type of interdependency: mediating technologies, long-linked technologies, and intensive technologies. His work is summarized in Table 13.1.

*Mediating technologies.* This type of technology is low interdependence, which is to say that the different parts of the whole organization are relatively independent of each other. Few demands are placed on coordination of the parts, cooperative decision making, and the like. This *pooled interdependence* can be illustrated by a bank or a savings and loan company, which has a checking department, loan department, international department, and other departments that deal directly with external clients or customers and have little to do with each other. This type of technology is best suited to a bureaucratic structure, with high standardization as the dominant integrator.

*Long-linked technologies.* Characterized by moderate interdependence, technologies with *sequential interdependence* are typified by auto assembly plants or school cafeterias. Step 1 must be done before Step 2, Step 2 before Step 3, and so on. Because these technologies demand coordination among the parts, management needs to plan ahead—for raw materials, for labor, for machine utilization and maintenance, and so on. Hence a bureaucratic structure with planning as an integrator is best suited for this technology.

*Intensive technologies.* Thompson's third type of technology, *reciprocal interdependency*, has the greatest amount of task interdependency. It makes the greatest demands on managerial decision making and communication/coordination. The potential for conflict is high. Complex coordinating mechanisms (relying on mutual adjustment in response to the object being changed from input to outputs) are essential.

An intensive technology uses a variety of techniques, but what distinguishes it from the other two is that "the selection, combination, and order of their application are determined by feedback from the object itself (being changed into an output state)."[17] Examples of organizations using this type of technology include construction firms, mental health clinics, and hospitals. In the hospital setting, the patient and his or her progress determine the next step in the healing process. This technology needs an organic structure (or matrix structure, at least) to facilitate mutual collaboration.

The implications of Thompson's work are clear. If the best structure for a hospital is organic because of hospital work's intensive technology, then perhaps part of the blame for ineffective hospital administration and patient care can be laid at the doorstep of the commonly used bureaucratic structure. Also, one can see intuitively that a bank would not be well served by organic organizational structure (low levels of formalization and centralization). Thompson's thesis, then, can be said to have intuitive validity.

Charles Perrow's contribution is equally seminal. Like Thompson, Perrow classified different aspects of technology and prescribed the type of structure best suited for each. His core dimension was the degree of nonroutineness of the task performed.[18] Perrow looked at knowledge technology rather than production technology in coming up with two dimensions of a technology's routineness or nonroutineness. The first of these is *task variety* or *task variability,* the number of exceptions (or problem areas) that come up as one does one's work. There will be few exceptions if a task is routine, such as cooking hamburgers at McDonald's, and many exceptions with a nonroutine task, such as research and development.

The second dimension, *task coping difficulty* or *problem analyzability,* concerns the search for solutions necessary when an exception is discovered. If a problem is easily solved, then the search is well defined. For example, when a problem comes up on an assembly line, a manual usually has a quick answer. But ill-defined problems, such as those associated with the nonroutine technologies found in an R&D lab, require a great deal of search and effort to solve. Perrow put together a two-by-two matrix to describe these dimensions; it is depicted in Figure 13.4.

In cell 1 of this matrix are those types of work involving technologies with easy-to-solve problems and very few exceptions. Examples would

Task Variability

|  | Few Exceptions | Many Exceptions |
|---|---|---|
| High<br>Task Coping<br>Difficulty | Craft<br>Work<br>(2) | Nonroutine<br>Work<br>(3) |
| Low | Routine<br>Engineering<br>(1) | Engineering<br>Technology<br>(4) |

**Figure 13.4.** Perrow's Classification Scheme

SOURCE: Charles Perrow, *Organizational Analysis: A Sociological View* (Belmont, CA: Wadsworth, 1970), 83. Copyright © 1970 by Wadsworth, Inc. Reprinted by permission of Brooks/Cole Publishing.

be a McDonald's cook, a bank teller, and an assembly line worker. Routine technologies can be facilitated best through the use of standardized coordination and control. Nonroutine technologies (cell 3) demand very flexible structures; these would be decentralized, would use sapiential authority, and would have high levels of interaction among the participants and minimum formalization. Craft technologies (cell 2) require that problem solving be accomplished by those with specific professional training; this implies decentralization. Finally, engineering technology (cell 4), with many exceptions but relatively easy analyzability, should be centralized but with low formalization.

Withey, Daft, and Cooper have developed a scale to measure task variability and task coping difficulty as described by Perrow. The scale has five questions for each of the two dimensions. To measure task variability, Withey et al. ask:

1. How many of these tasks are the same from day to day?
2. To what extent would you say that your work is routine?
3. Do people in this unit do the same job in the same way most of the time?
4. Do unit members perform repetitive duties in doing their jobs?
5. How repetitious are your duties?

To measure task coping difficulty, they ask:

1. To what extent is there a clearly known way to do the major types of work you normally encounter?
2. To what extent is there a clearly defined body of subject matter which can guide you in doing your work?
3. To what extent is there an understandable sequence of steps that can be followed in doing your work?

4. To do your work, to what extent can you actually rely on established procedures and practices?

5. When you come across a problem in your work, how long does it usually take to solve it?[19]

Perrow also argued that the two variables are positively correlated. It would be hard to find circumstances where tasks had few exceptions and the problems were clearly unanalyzable. Conversely, tasks with many exceptions typically are not associated with an easy search process. When a chemist in a research lab runs across a problem that has never come up before, the problem's solution is usually the result of a prolonged search.

From Perrow's research, it would appear that the bureaucratic structure is most suitable for routine technologies (low variability and low coping difficulty) and low to moderate task interdependency (mediating and long-linked technologies). In other words, the more routine the technology, the more structured (formalized and centralized) the organization should be. On the other hand, the organic structure is best suited for technologies with high task variability, high coping difficulty (non-routine), and high task interdependency (intensive technologies).

Bureaucracies, we have pointed out elsewhere in this book, are not necessarily bad. For routine, low-interdependence technologies, the bureaucratic structure, even with its associated problems, is still best. Only in high-tech companies with turbulent environments is the organic form really necessary.

## Technology Zones

Defined by Robert Miles, *technology zones* are specific organizational regions (they could be several departments or units) that share the same technology.[20] Miles uses the example of an automobile manufacturer to illustrate this concept. This manufacturer has four organizational levels:

1. the operating level (where the work is done)
2. the unit level (first-line supervisors)
3. the department level (where logistics, production control, production, and controller reside)
4. plant management level

The five technology zones for this manufacturer are depicted in Figure 13.5.

Technology Zone A is the area where the traditional assembly-line or long-linked technology exists. The sequential interdependence is designed in a carefully preprogrammed work flow. Here the mechanistic

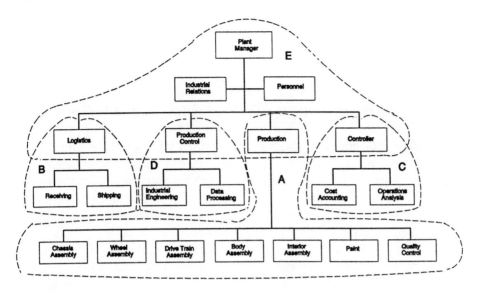

**Figure 13.5.** Technology Zones in an Automotive Assembly Plant

SOURCE: Robert H. Miles, *Macro Organizational Behavior* (Glenview, IL: Scott, Foresman, 1980), 79. Reprinted with permission of the author.

bureaucracy really works well; formalization is high, with extensive planning and resource allocation.

Technology Zone B represents the shipping and receiving functions of the organization. These functions deal with different aspects of the transformation process, and therefore they need to have little to do with each other. Their interdependence is pooled (mediating technology) and the work is routine (relatively low variability and little difficulty with search for solutions when exceptions do occur). A structure with high formalization (bureaucratic) is therefore appropriate.

Technology Zone C consists of the cost accounting function grouped with operations analysis. Here is a mix of unit technologies. The cost accounting unit, with its emphasis on figures, figures, figures, is staffed by clerks handling various aspects of the function, typically with little interaction; hence this is pooled interdependence. Right across the hall is the operations analysis group, a small, informal group of MBAs whose work is mainly nonroutine and reciprocal in task interdependence. These people interact with many other subgroups of the organization, solving problems and assisting in the smooth flow of work. They sometimes encounter a fair amount of problems (exceptions) that often need quite a bit of search for solutions.

The two groups have very little interaction with each other, so their relationship is pooled interdependence. Because the work they do is so different, it is common to have such groups physically separated. The structure for the cost accounting group is bureaucratic, whereas that for the operations group is organic. Obviously, the two groups need to be supervised differently. The accountants are required to follow the rules and guidelines in place for their function, whereas the operations MBAs often proceed without a "road map."

Technology Zone D contains the production control function, with industrial engineering and data processing. Here is an example of "high task interdependence and high task nonroutineness within and across both units."[21] Production control engineers typically encounter problems that require creative solutions not found in procedures manuals. These people work with the plant manager, the systems people, other engineers, and so on to solve problems that could shut the plant down. The data-processing people (systems workers and programmers) also find themselves involved in frequent exceptions that require search and collaboration to solve. Lateral relations are common, heightened interaction is the norm, and an organic structure is clearly appropriate for the structure of both units as well as the coordinating mechanism between them. This is a good example of reciprocal interdependence (intensive technology).

Technology Zone E is the plant management team. When looking down into the organization, the plant manager sees many subsystems that need to be managed differently. The relationships among the various departments tend to be reciprocal. However, many of the tasks are highly routine (cost accounting) and many are nonroutine (operations analysis); also, routineness varies within a department during a given period (e.g., model year changeover). During periods of nonroutineness (many exceptions and high coping difficulty), frequent face-to-face meetings are required and an organic structure is appropriate. When things calm down and a routine pace of work is reestablished, a bureaucratic structure is reintroduced.

When viewed as a whole, the organization in this case seems to be most influenced by the long-linked technology of the assembly line, the modal technology. Thus, according to the theory presented thus far, the overall structure of the company should be bureaucratic—and it is.

Miles also introduces the concept of *technological impingement.*[22] According to this concept, units that are closely connected in function to the core or modal technology tend to be influenced by that technology and its resultant structure. If the shipping and receiving units do not perform their jobs in a timely fashion, the flow of materials for the core production line will be interrupted. However, other areas, such as operations analysis, perform relatively independently from the core technology and are therefore not as affected by its design and structure. Unit coordination mechanisms must fit the unit technologies involved. It would seem that the smaller the organization, the more influence the modal technology has; as companies get larger, size seems to become a more dominant independent variable.

---

## Technology and Structure: Some Implications

---

Evidence suggests that the concept of a technological imperative is a bit overstated; technology does seem to be a determinant of structure, but perhaps not the main one (or even a major one). The key dimensions on which differing technologies rest are *routineness* and *interdependence.*

Routine technologies do seem to be associated with low complexity.[23] The greater the routineness, the less training is required by incumbents and the fewer professional groups are needed. Also, formalization seems to be highly correlated with routineness, but this relationship tends to disappear when organization size is controlled for.[24] Therefore, smaller organizations with routine technology need high formalization at the technology's core.

Common sense would dictate that high centralization goes with routineness.[25] Nonroutine technologies would seem to go with decentralized structures, although the research on this is inconclusive.[26] Some studies seem to indicate that routine technology goes with centralization *if* formalization is low; otherwise, with high formalization and routine technology, you could easily have a decentralized structure.

---

## A Transitional Theory: Sociotechnical Systems

---

When the term *sociotechnical systems* was introduced by Eric Trist and the Tavistock group in the 1950s, it represented a major breakthrough in the way people thought about the design of work and the design of organizations. For the first time, sociotechnical systems advocates argued for the inevitable interaction between the technical and social subsystems of an organization, and for the need to incorporate *both* in the design of organizations.[27] This seems rather obvious to us now, but earlier thinking was exclusively oriented to the technical requirements of the work. Henry Ford was alleged to have said:

Machines alone do not give us mass production. Mass production is achieved by both men and machines. And while we have gone a long way toward perfecting our mechanical operations, we have not successfully written into our equations whatever complex factors represent Man, the human element.[28]

Now we know that technology constrains the social system by shaping the very behaviors required to operate it. This is what some people mean when they speak of the technological imperative (a different meaning from that discussed above): the behavior-shaping capacity of a given technology. This definitional ambiguity can be confusing to readers of technology/structure literature.

The designers of tasks within an organizational context need to take into account the interface between the technology concerned and the people who are to implement that technology. If job designers ignore the attitudes, skills, preferences, habits, and physical capacities of the workers, their interaction patterns, and their social skills, then the very best technical system will certainly be underutilized.

Let us look at a few of the basic tenets of sociotechnical systems.[29] In the traditional technical approach, the technology dictates human performance; in sociotechnical terms, we talk of *joint optimization*. The traditional view is that people are extensions of machines; the sociotechnical view is that people are complements to machines. The comparisons continue:

| *Traditional View* | *Sociotechnical View* |
| --- | --- |
| people as expendable spare parts | people as a resource to be developed |
| maximum task breakdown (division of labor) | optimum task grouping |
| narrow skills | multiple broad skills |
| autocratic management style | participative management styles |
| competition | collaboration |

Surprisingly, thus far, sociotechnical systems have not played a huge role in the contemporary workplace. They have been neglected for the same reasons we are just discovering W. Edwards Deming's principles of quality control, although the Japanese began practicing them some 30-odd years ago: If the prevailing paradigm precludes a (different) system of thought, people who espouse that system will probably not be heard. And even if they are heard, their principles will not be effectively implemented. But this too is changing; a recent management "fad" is the *self-managed work team* (SMWT), which has grown out of the sociotechnical systems school.[30]

**Table 13.2** Sociotechnical Principles

1. Variety and complexity are to be valued over the simplicity and routineness found in machine bureaucracies.

2. The work group, not the individual job holder, is the central unit of focus.

3. The sociotechnical work group is self-regulating (internally) rather than externally regulated by supervisors (a key feature of SMWT).

4. The individual becomes viewed as complementary to the machine rather than as an extension of it.

SOURCE: Extracted from Eric L. Trist, "The Sociotechnical Perspective," in *Perspectives on Organization Design and Behavior*, ed. A. H. Van de Ven and W. F. Joyce (New York: John Wiley, 1981), 22-23.

## Self-Managed Work Teams: The New Paradigm?

A self-managed work team is a work group allocated an overall task and given discretion over how the work is to be done. These groups are self-regulating and operate without direct supervision.[31] Workers are organized into teams of 5 to 15 employees, and the teams make routine decisions on equipment purchases, hiring, firing, vacations, quality, and interpersonal matters. In other words, traditional management functions are performed by the teams; these groups represent the transfer of authority *down* the hierarchy.

Predictably, the results of instituting SMWT have been impressive. At a General Mills cereal plant in Lodi, California, teams "schedule, operate and maintain machinery so effectively that the factory runs with no managers present during the night shift."[32] Since General Mills introduced SMWT at the plant, productivity has risen by up to 40%. Recent indications are that initial gains have now leveled off, however, and some problems, associated with the necessary paradigm shift by both workers and managers, have emerged.

Self-managed work teams challenge many of the core assumptions and expectations of industrial paradigm adherents. Supervisors and managers, long rewarded for effectively directing work and making key decisions, must suddenly learn and embrace the new role of facilitator, "cheerleader" (to use Peters and Waterman's term), and resource procurer with other parts of the organization (and elements of the external environment). Workers, on the other hand, have to develop risk-taking behaviors, decision-making abilities, and team skills after being conditioned to be individualistic, achievement-/competition-oriented, submissive, and obedient to authority. Paradigm shifts *are* rocky.

In summary, the sociotechnical systems approach acknowledges that demands from the external environment can compel changes in the technical subsystem; for instance, a new computer system becomes available for use that is more efficient than the currently used model. Likewise, changes in the external environment can cause changes in the social subsystem of an organization; for example, changing societal values and attitudes toward work can influence expectations on the job. Because the two are inextricably intertwined, it makes sense to adjust changes in one to changes in the other. There must be a synchronicity between the two subsystems in order for optimal work effectiveness to be achieved. A basic review of the literature in sociotechnical systems reveals a bias toward variety, challenging jobs, social support, collaboration and recognition, whole jobs (rather than division of labor), minimized external controls, and performance feedback on a timely basis.

---

## The Interaction of
## Culture and Technology

---

In his landmark work *Organizational Culture and Leadership,* Edgar Schein offers some insights as to how culture and technology interact. He notes:

> If the new technology is to succeed, those advocating it must recognize from the outset that the resistance to it is not to the technology *per se* but to the cultural change implications of its introduction. . . . the new technology brings with it its own occupational culture. Only when change is under way do managers realize that, with the new technology comes a whole new set of assumptions, values and behavior patterns.[33]

Let us look for a moment at data-processing technology. People who work in the data-processing "fraternity" tend to have their own vocabulary, their own values and traditions, their own vision of the importance of the field, and their own perspective on how the technology should be used, none of which may match the languages, perspectives, and norms of the groups that will be using the technology.[34] Occupations tend to build their practices, values, and role self-images around their technologies. Data-processing people, for example, tend to be left-brain linear/rational/sequential types, convergent in their thinking processes, output oriented, compulsive, precise, and with low tolerance for ambiguity; therefore, they are likely to clash with users who do not possess these personality traits.

An organization that is successful because of a given technology also tends to develop its identity around that technology. Therefore, if the technology changes in a substantial fashion, the organization must redefine itself in ways that involve deep cultural assumptions about "who we are," "why we do what we do," and so on. One of the most powerful aspects of an organization's culture is the status system that evolves from the possession of key items of information or critical skills (the aforementioned *sapiential authority*). With the introduction of data-processing technology, for instance, power shifts around; people who had no power suddenly have access to some. Because they sense these implications, current power holders may resist the new technology.

Therefore, because the collective paradigm has created and maintained the old technology, the new technology will be alien to those paradigmatic assumptions and beliefs. A clash of cultures is inevitable; the old culture, with its myths, norms, roles, and expectations, will naturally resist the inevitable reshaping of those invisible factors to accommodate the new technology. The successful introduction of any new technology must be seen as a problem of blending two or more organizational subcultures and/or changing the dominant organizational culture.[35]

---

## Technology and the
## Postindustrial Paradigm

---

The transformational approach assumes that both technology and structure are caused by the collective paradigm, and, as the paradigm shifts, we can expect new structures and new technologies. This is in fact occurring. The matrix and organic structures, with their dependence on personal maturity, are starting to appear, and the emerging dominant technology of the postindustrial era—electronic information processing and communications—is making an impact on virtually every organization.

The transformational perspective is this: Technologies are a direct reflection of the consciousness of those who produce them. Because these technologies were all developed under a self-centered, effect-dominated paradigm, they will necessarily be destructive in nature, because they were created with a limited perspective of the whole. As the shift to a whole-centered paradigm begins to gain momentum, technologies will naturally emerge that will be life enhancing and blended with the larger whole.

A technological "discovery," according to transformational theory, becomes manifest only when the changes in consciousness that can produce it are in place. Thus new technologies in communications and information processing are manifest expressions of the possibilities inherent in the emerging paradigm. They are also perfectly suited for the key job of today: *fully integrating the firm into its environmental context*, that is, the larger whole in which it is embedded. Morgan has an interesting view of this:

> Information technology—in the form of microcomputing, electronic communication, and robotics—has the capacity to transform the nature and structure of many organizations and the nature and life cycles of their products and services. Organizations that fail to get "on board" and to reap the potential benefits will find the competition passing them by. The technology is leading us into a new age in which completely new styles of organization and new managerial competencies will come into their own.[36]

## How New Technologies
## Are Affecting Organizations and Work Flow

New information technologies are radically transforming organizational structure and strategy. When the General Motors environmental advisory staff made a commitment to use information technologies to integrate staff planning and to make the sharing of information more timely and consistent, it found three significant organizational changes occurred, apparently as a result of the new technology:

> First, staff members found themselves using a much more elaborate network of communication that included both personal contacts and task-related interactions. More information was being processed than before, and, perhaps more significantly, task-relevant communication became more focused, personal contacts developed between members newly linked with the system, and the new network tied together people with complementary skills and common problems.
>
> The second change occurred in the use and purpose of the organization's hierarchy. Power based on hierarchical position was replaced by power based on competency (sapiential authority) as demonstrated throughout the system. Centers of competence became more obvious as the technology allowed performance to become more visible. . . . While these practices

did not remove the formal hierarchy, *task performance was no longer dependent on hierarchical channels.* A less formal, more spontaneous system was used for getting information.

Finally, the jobs of members became more flexible and the time available for getting work done increased. Routine tasks became eliminated for professionals, taken over by clerks. Jobs were "enriched," i.e., made more complex and rewarding.[37]

In other words, the new technology allowed for reciprocal interdependency among the parts of the organization, which in turn flourishes in an organic structure rather than a bureaucratic one.

## Implications of Technological Demassification

Alvin Toffler, in his best-seller *The Third Wave*, speaks of a state "beyond mass production."[38] Using Hewlett-Packard as an example, he describes a company where status and hierarchy are much less important than in a traditional bureaucracy, and where informal dress, loose culture, and flexible hours are the norm. He offers Hewlett-Packard as a prototype of the new corporation, one that does not make large, mass-production runs of a standardized product, but, rather, makes "short runs of partially or completely customized products."[39]

Toffler cites an analyst in *Critique* (a Soviet journal) who states that whereas the less highly developed countries (those with GNP of between U.S. $1,000-2,000 per capita per annum) concentrate on mass-produced manufacturing, the most highly developed countries concentrate on the export of short-run manufactured goods depending on highly skilled labor and high research costs, such as computers, specialized machinery, aircraft, automated production systems, high-technology paints, pharmaceutical products, and high-technology polymers and plastics.[40] Toffler calls this trend "demassification." The step beyond this, of course, is complete customization, the manufacture of one-of-a-kind products. In the near future, it will be no harder to custom manufacture with "flexible" manufacturing than it is to mass produce today (because of the availability of the new technologies of manufacturing). This is essentially custom tailoring on a high-tech basis. As some industries are moving from mass production to small-batch production, others will move beyond that into custom manufacture on a continuous-flow basis (Woodward's terminology).

Toffler notes that, whereas industrial era (he calls it "second wave") manufacturing is Cartesian (or Newtonian) in that products are broken

into pieces and assembled, the new paradigm (or "third wave") manufacturer will be post-Cartesian or holistic. He uses the example of the
wristwatch: In the "old days," wristwatches had hundreds of pieces, but
now solid-state watches can be made with no moving parts at all. Laser
technology also will be revolutionary in its application. We are integrating many more functions into fewer and fewer parts, substituting whole
subassemblies or assemblies for many discrete components.

Obviously, all this has organizational implications. In the industrial
era, work was organized into small, repetitive, and often sequential jobs
(division of labor) on the assumption that the parts make up the whole;
no allowance was made for synergy (the famous "2 + 2 = 5" effect). In
the industrial era we also had what Toffler calls a "factory-like caste
system." Under the current paradigm shift, he argues, "all the old
hierarchies and structures are soon to be reshuffled."[41] We will see the
decline of formal authority (and rise of sapiential authority), the development of self-managed work teams, more project/temporary team use,
and more structural fluidity and flexibility. Gareth Morgan notes:

> Managers of the future will have to become increasingly skilled in under-
> standing how computer-based intelligence can be used to develop new
> products and services and redesign existing ones. Products and services
> that are "smart," "multipurpose," "user driven," and capable of evolving
> in design point toward the future of many industries and services. The
> trends are already present in many areas of the economy; for example, in
> how microcomputing has transformed products like typewriters into word
> processors and banking and other financial services into automated trans-
> actions.[42]

## Entrepreneurs and the Electronic Cottage

New technology provides a physical means for linking together parts of
the whole. Through computer networking, an organization with offices
around the planet can be effectively and instantaneously integrated.
Computer networking technology is a "natural" integrator at the level of
the organizational form or structure. It also has spawned the now-common
practice of *telecommuting;* workers stay at home or travel short distances
to "satellite" offices and thereby avoid long commutes to a congested
central work area. Environmental constraints, overcrowding in cities,
and other "quality of life" issues make this option more appealing all
the time.

Toffler calls this the development of the "electronic cottage."[43] Satellite and neighborhood work centers are alternative remote work arrangements that are aided by communications/information technology. The satellite office is a relatively self-contained work center in a location physically separate from the central office and within easy driving distance of most unit employees. These employees are linked to the whole through telecommunications. As a result of such changes, employee autonomy will necessarily grow; it will be hard to supervise people closely if they aren't in the building. Centralization will be possible only through the facility of computer linkages or networks among telecommuters such as consultants, writers, brokers, and salespeople.

### Increased, Timely Managerial Information

Thanks to information products such as Executive Information Systems, managers can get real information in "real time." This means it is possible for a manager to get current information on inventories, receivables, payables, cash flow, and the like at any time of the day or night.

In the mid-1980's the right ingredients finally came together: powerful PCs and workstations that could shape masses of numbers into simple, colorful tables and charts; the touch screen and the mouse; interconnections that could weave a single network out of a company's different hardware and databases; and the software to turn it all into a system.[44]

Now, chief executive officers can, with the touch of a finger or the movement of a mouse, retrieve facts and figures that allow for decision making based on systemwide information. Executives get more information, and they get it faster.[45] The growth in the popularity of such technology reflects two dominant beliefs:

1. Executives are finally willing to admit that their organizations are *open systems* and, as such, need to be managed with more information about the whole organization and its environment.
2. The dependence on numbers and measurement (indicative of the old paradigm) is still strong. The reassuring nature of numbers still lulls us into a false sense that we actually know something.

Steven Jobs is using the new workstation developed by his company NeXT Computer Inc. to create a new organizational form. Through the use of this technology, Jobs is encouraging open communication among all the levels of his company. Matt Rothman notes:

In fostering this level of communication, Jobs figures NEXT [*sic*] has an edge . . . its own workstation. His management philosophy hinges on total disclosure within the company, and the machine is one of his tools. One sits on each employee's desk and is linked to a sophisticated electronic network. Jobs, himself, is so taken by its capabilities that he declares it will usher in what he calls the age of "interpersonal computing." As spreadsheets and desk top publishing distinguished the IBM PC and the Apple Macintosh, he claims NEXT's [*sic*] powerful messaging software is going to set his workstation apart in the 1990's. "It flattens out the hierarchy and lets more of the brains in our company participate in decisions," he says. "It absolutely revolutionized our company."[46]

This does not mean that all will use such technology to its full and positive potential. As Gareth Morgan states:

The new technology can be used to reinforce bureaucratic, "top down" styles of organization. But its true potential rests in promoting decentralization, network styles of management, and capacities for self-organization. The technology has a capacity to dissolve organizational hierarchies by creating smaller-scale, loosely coupled organizational units coordinated electronically, *where work units can remain separate yet integrated.* The technology facilitates new work designs that are flexible and self-organizing, where the network rather than the pyramid is the primary organizational form.

The technology will also transform interorganizational relations, dissolving rigid boundaries between separate organizations and creating more open patterns of interaction. This trend is vividly illustrated by the Just-in-Time (JIT) management systems, which, supported by sophisticated information technology, create new connections among suppliers, subcontractors, retailers, and customers. Organizations of the future are much more likely to form elements of a loosely coupled network of subcontracted relations, where boundaries are intermeshed rather than discrete.[47]

Not all jobs will be autonomous, however. The automation of the office and the factory, once a fantasy, is now a reality. There are similarities and differences between mechanized and computerized work.[48] Both types of work control the worker in a technological sense; that is, certain steps have to be done in a certain order. Also, the task characteristics tend to be narrow and specialized. Computerized work seems to be no more intrinsically motivating than mechanized work; the main difference is that, whereas mechanized work emphasizes the physical, computerized work stresses the mental (and the word *stress* is appropriate here).

**Vignette 1**

A small manufacturing facility in Colorado has recently converted to a computer management information and networking system in which each worker has a terminal and can input and retrieve data in such areas as customer files, accounts payable, accounts receivable, word processing, and order entry. This system has the potential for transforming how work is done in the organization. The company president, however, apparently operating from a Theory X orientation, sees the system as a means for him to keep tabs on his workers; he has had the system designed with a variety of safeguards and code words so that certain workers do not have access to certain information. Yet, at his desk, he has the capacity to monitor the work of all his employees. This is a perfect example of technology being used to support a certain mind-set and view of personal reality.

## The Integrating Power of the New Technology

A final point is that the new technology can practically act as the eyes and ears of the manager in this emerging age. It can allow the manager to move with the currents of change and to adapt to the ebbs and flows:

> As the process and structure of management have become more sophisticated and complex, one of the key developments has been the growing reliance on equally complex information systems as an aid to management. These information systems, whether they report on the external world (e.g., market surveys) or the internal workings of the company (e.g., inventory control), all serve an objectifying function.[49]

Realizing this, we sense that many new technologies will emerge in the near and medium-term future that will still bear the mark of self-centered will; yet we can see that, with the gathering momentum of the paradigm shift, people are beginning to experience themselves as part of a larger whole. Marshall McLuhan, with his notion of the "global village," warned us of this change. We are interdependent, irrevocably so. As this reality truly dawns on the self-centered mind, its assumptions and beliefs will begin to crack, and the integrating force of life itself will begin to be known in human experience.

## NOTES

1. Billy Joe Hodge and William P. Anthony, *Organization Theory* (3rd ed.) (Boston: Allyn & Bacon, 1988), 427.

2. See Charles Perrow, "A Framework for the Comparative Analysis of Organizations," *American Sociological Review* 32 (1967): 194-208.

3. See, for example, Frederick Herzberg, *Work and the Nature of Man* (New York: New American Library, 1973).

4. Pehr Gyllenhammar, "Volvo's Solution to the Blue Collar Blues," *Business and Society Review* (August 1973).

5. See Marilyn Goldstein, David Scholthauer, and Brain H. Kleiner, "Management on the Right Side of the Brain," *Personnel Journal* (November 1985): 40-45.

6. See, for example, Edward C. Whitmont, *Return of the Goddess* (New York: Crossroad, 1982); Robert A. Johnson, *She: Understanding Feminine Psychology* (New York: Perennial Library, 1977); Robert A. Johnson, *He: Understanding Masculine Psychology* (New York: Perennial Library, 1977); Robert A. Johnson, *We: The Psychology of Romantic Love* (San Francisco: Harper & Row, 1983).

7. See Charles Hampden-Turner, *Radical Man* (Cambridge, MA: Schenkman, 1970), especially chap. 1.

8. Gareth Morgan and Linda Smircich, "The Case for Qualitative Research," *Academy of Management Review* 5, no. 4 (1980).

9. See Joan Woodward, *Management and Technology* (Problems of Progress in Industry Series, No. 3) (London: Her Majesty's Stationery Office, 1958); Joan Woodward, *Industrial Organization: Theory and Practice* (London: Oxford University Press, 1965).

10. Edward Harvey, "Technology and the Structure of Organizations," *American Sociological Review* 32 (1968): 249.

11. William L. Zwerman, *New Perspectives on Organization Theory* (Westport, CT: Greenwood, 1970); James D. Thompson, *Organizations in Action* (New York: McGraw-Hill, 1967); Perrow, "A Framework for the Comparative Analysis."

12. David J. Hickson, D. S. Pugh, and Diana C. Pheysey, "Operations Technology and Organization Structure: An Empirical Reappraisal," *Administrative Science Quarterly* 14 (September 1969).

13. D. S. Pugh, D. J. Hickson, C. R. Hinings, and C. Turner, "The Context of Organization Structures," *Administrative Science Quarterly* 14 (March 1969).

14. Howard E. Aldrich, "Technology and Organization Structure: A Re-examination of the Findings of the Aston Group," *Administrative Science Quarterly* 17 (1972): 26-43.

15. Other studies have further clouded this issue. Child and Mansfield, using Woodward's scale, found a different pattern of variables but reached the same conclusion as the Aston Group; that is, "size has a much closer relationship to the aspects of structure measured than does technology." John Child and Roger Mansfield, "Technology, Size and Organization Structure," *Sociology* 6 (1972): 383. Another study that downplayed the effect of technology on structure was conducted by Negandhi and Reimann, who saw environmental concerns strongly related to structure. Anant R. Negandhi and Bernard C. Reimann, "Correlates of Decentralization: Closed and Open Systems Perspective," *Academy of Management Journal* 16 (1973). Finally, Khandwalla focused on the integration aspect of organizations and its relationship to technology. He proposed a model in which mass-production technology, in particular, is associated with decentralization and subsequent integration efforts. Pradip N. Khandwalla, "Mass Output Orientation of Operations Technology and Organization Structure," *Administrative Science Quarterly* 18 (March 1974).

16. Thompson, *Organizations in Action*.

17. Ibid., 17.

18. Charles Perrow, *Organizational Analysis: A Sociological View* (Belmont, CA: Wadsworth, 1970), 79-91.

19. Michael Withey, Richard Daft, and William H. Cooper, "Measures of Perrow's Work Unit Technology: An Empirical Assessment and a New Scale," *Academy of Management Journal* (March 1983): 59.

20. Robert Miles, *Macro Organizational Behavior* (Glenview, IL: Scott, Foresman, 1980): 78-83.

21. Ibid., 81.

22. Ibid., 82.

23. Jerald Hage and Michael Aiken, "Routine Technology, Social Structure and Organizational Goals," *Administrative Science Quarterly* 14 (September 1969).

24. Donald Gerwin, "Relationships Between Structure and Technology at the Organizational Job Levels," *Journal of Management Studies* (February 1979).

25. Ibid.

26. Andrew Van de Ven, Andre Delbecq, and Richard Koenig, Jr., "Determinants of Coordination Modes Within Organizations," *American Sociological Review* 40 (April 1976).

27. See Eric L. Trist, "The Sociotechnical Perspective," in *Perspectives on Organization Design and Behavior*, ed. A. H. Van de Ven and W. F. Joyce (New York: John Wiley, 1981).

28. Henry Ford II, quoted in Miles, *Macro Organizational Behavior*, 85.

29. See Trist, "The Sociotechnical Perspective," 53.

30. This literature is rich. See, for example, Peter Senge, "The Leaders' New Work: Building Learning Organizations," *Sloan Management Review* (Fall 1990): 7-23; Charles C. Manz and Henry P. Sims, Jr., "Leading Workers to Lead Themselves: The External Leadership of Self-Managing Work Teams," *Administrative Science Quarterly* 32 (1987): 106-128.

31. See David Buchanan, "Job Enrichment Is Dead; Long Live High Performance Work Design," *Personnel Management* (May 1987): 40.

32. Brian Dumaine, "Who Needs a Boss?" *Fortune*, May 7, 1990, 52. © 1990 Time Inc. All rights reserved. Used with permission.

33. Edgar H. Schein, *Organizational Culture and Leadership* (San Francisco: Jossey-Bass, 1985), 37. Used with permission from the publisher.

34. F. P. Brooks, Jr., *The Mythical Man-Month* (Reading, MA: Addison-Wesley, 1975); P. G. W. Keen, "Cognitive Style and Career Specialization," in *Organizational Careers: Some New Perspectives*, ed. J. Van Maanen (New York: John Wiley, 1977).

35. T. J. Allen, *Managing the Flow of Technology* (Cambridge: MIT Press, 1977).

36. Gareth Morgan, *Riding the Waves of Change* (San Francisco: Jossey-Bass, 1988), 9. Used with permission from the publisher.

37. Daniel Robey, *Designing Organizations* (2nd ed.) (Homewood, IL: Irwin, 1986), 500-501; emphasis added.

38. Alvin Toffler, *The Third Wave* (New York: Simon & Schuster, 1982), chaps. 15, 16.

39. Ibid., 181.

40. Ibid., 182.

41. Ibid., 187.

42. Morgan, *Riding the Waves of Change*, 9-10. Used with permission from the publisher.

43. Toffler, *The Third Wave*.

44. Jeremy Main, "At Last, Software CEO's Can Use," *Fortune*, March 13, 1989, 77. © 1989 Time Inc. All rights reserved. Used with permission.

45. See Mark Lewyn, "Computers Easing Workloads in More Executive Suites," *USA Today*, August 23, 1989, 2B.

46. Matt Rothman, "A Peek Inside the Black Box," *California Business* (April 1990): 33.

47. Morgan, *Riding the Waves of Change*, 10. Used with permission from the publisher.

48. See Robert E. Callahan, C. Patrick Fleenor, and Harry R. Knudson, *Understanding Organizational Behavior* (Columbus, OH: Charles E. Merrill, 1988), 19.

49. Peter Schwartz and James Ogilvy, *The Emergent Paradigm: Changing Patterns of Thought and Belief* (report issued by the Values and Lifestyles Program, April 1979), 23.

# 14 Organizational Size and Structure

*With increasing size comes complexity. As an organization grows, its operations and structure invariably become more difficult to manage. A manager's challenge thus becomes to balance the advantages of size with the limitations of complexity.*

(Billy Joe Hodge and William P. Anthony,
*Organization Theory*, 1988, p. 395)

---

**SUMMARY:** In this chapter we examine the relationship between organization size and organization structure. Size seems to be an important variable to consider in relationship to organization structure, a relationship that can be seen in terms of the dominant paradigm.

---

**W**hy do organizations grow? Primarily, they grow because, in order to continue their success, they need to add people to handle increasing business and to respond to the increasingly complex requirements of the external environment. As companies grow, they begin to need to pay attention to things they may have ignored before, such as market research, public relations, and new product development.

There seems to be an inevitability toward increasing bureaucratization with increasing size. An organization may begin as an organic, flexible unit with few work rules; informal, cooperative interrelationships; and a common, unifying purpose. But internal controls seem to become necessary as the growing organization begins to hire those who do not share the vision/purpose of the founders. At this point, the company begins to write job descriptions, organization charts, RRPP, and so forth.

# What Is Organizational Size?

There are a number of ways to measure the size of organizations. Share of market is one indicator; a firm that controls its market is considered large, whereas firms with a fraction of the market are thought of as small.[1] John Kimberly suggests that size has four components:

1. physical capacity of the organization (e.g., size of plant, or, in universities, office and classroom space)
2. personnel available to the organization (commonly used but ambiguous— who is in the organization? employees? part-timers? volunteers?)
3. organizational inputs and outputs (e.g., number of customers served [input] or sales volume [output])
4. discretionary resources available to the organization (wealth or net assets available for use)[2]

But is size—whether measured by gross revenues, the number of units sold last year, market share, the number of full-time employees, or assets—a factor that determines organizational structure?

# Organizational Size as a
# Causal Variable

Research seems to indicate that increase in organizational size is associated with the following structural characteristics:

- increased number of management levels (vertical differentiation)
- increased number of jobs and departments (horizontal differentiation)
- increased specialization of skills and functions
- increased formalization
- increased decentralization
- smaller percentage of top administrators
- increased percentage of technical and professional support staff
- increased percentage of clerical and maintenance support staff
- increased written communications and documentation[3]

Does size actually *cause* these structural characteristics? Researchers do not agree. Peter Blau, a major proponent of size as a determinant of structure, has studied the relationship between organizational size and differentiation.[4] His work suggests that an increase in organizational size will lead to the following:

1. an increase in the differentiation of organizational effort (i.e., further specialization of labor, more spatial dispersion of work sites, new departments and divisions, new levels in hierarchy)
2. more organizational subunits, larger size of individual subunits, and a wider managerial span of control
3. a higher ratio of administrators to nonadministrators

Other researchers concur. England's Aston Group, whose research was discussed in Chapter 13, found that of the seven primary influences on organizations, size was the greatest predictor of structure.[5] In a replication of those studies, John Child confirmed that size and structural complexity are related.[6] A newer study by Armandi gives general support for the Blau hypothesis.[7]

A dissenter, Howard Aldrich, reexamined the Aston data and argued that technology is the independent variable and size the dependent variable.[8] In other words, he saw that changes in structure were often brought on by changes in technology, which, in turn, caused changes in size. This is quite the opposite of the more common notion that size causes structure. The transformational assumption, of course, is that size, technology, and structure are *all* intervening variables of the dominant cause—the collective paradigm.

Studies seem to show that small organizations in the early stages of their life cycles tend to change structurally at different rates than do mature organizations. In other words, entrepreneurial organizations change much faster than mature organizations. Small organizations also seem to expand first in a horizontal direction, adding new positions, departments, or divisions, whereas mature organizations seem to expand by vertical differentiation, adding new levels in the hierarchy.

### The Argument for Size Causing Structure

The argument that size is a causal variable in the determination of organizational structure is widely accepted in organization theory literature.[9] As an organization increases in size, it is able to use specialists more effectively in a variety of areas. In fact, it can be argued that dynamic, turbulent environments actually necessitate increasing organizational complexity for an organization to meet the challenge of change.[10]

As the number of subunits increases, they are grouped around functional specialties, such as public relations, market research, and legal affairs. Because they have different time horizons, different languages or jargon, and different priorities or goals, the potential for conflicts among subunits increases. In response to the need for increased coordination and control, top executives typically attempt to achieve integration through structural changes. They impose standardized rules and procedures that increase formalization, reduce the demand on executives for routine decision making, and set the limits of worker discretion at lower levels.

In other words, executives can replace their decision making with rules, regulations, policies, and procedures. Workers then have little need to make discretionary choices because their parameters are specified for them. With the removal of the higher levels of decision making, the executive level can then concentrate on strategic matters and place the immediate supervisors in charge.

**Vignette 1**

McDonald's restaurants are organizations that are high in RRPP. If someone wants to rotate jobs and try his or her hand at making french fries (instead of shakes), the supervisor on duty may approve such a request, provided the rules, regulations, policies, and procedures are followed strictly. Decisions about operational changes fall into the supervisor's hands, and the executives have their requirements met through the standardized RRPP they have set and handed down.

## Decentralization, Formalization, and Size

Decentralization and formalization seem to reinforce each other. Formalization facilitates decentralization, and the need to decentralize seems to encourage more formalization. More levels of hierarchy are created to coordinate the ever more diverse subunits. The number of administrative, clerical, and professional personnel is also increased. By substituting an impersonal system of RRPP for personal supervision and control, the organization can grow in an orderly way, with top management retaining overall control but delegating specific decision making to lower levels.

**Vignette 2**

In some cases, decentralization can work with lower formalization. The Equitable, a New York-based insurance company, reduced its centralized meeting planning department of 22 to a core of 6, decentralizing the function among different departments.

"Decentralization is not all it is cracked up to be," says Carol Johnsen of the Equitable. Although the decentralized system works to the advantage of the corporation as a whole, it makes meeting planning less efficient. "We laugh about it a lot," Johnsen says. "For instance, I have made plans for the site inspection of a property, and, when I call them, they tell me someone from another department was just there." Decentralization has also diluted buying power. As the volume of meetings done at corporate has decreased, so has its power to negotiate with suppliers.

"Also, a lot of cross-training is lost," she says. "Agency people don't do Board of Directors meetings, my people don't do incentive meetings, and the result is we are not developing well rounded planners." But a plus is decreased formalization: "You know exactly who your clients are and you have easier access to them; when I'm dealing with a smaller meeting and charging back for services, there is no interference from other departments. . . . There is no one to tell me that corporate policy says you have to do this and that. If they (my department) are paying the bill, they get what they want. . . . The executives feel more in control of their meetings."

SOURCE: David Ghitelman, "When Planning Goes Corporate," *Meetings and Conventions*, 1988, 45. Used with permission.

---

## How Size Affects Structure:
## Aspects of the Size-Structure Relationship

A number of studies have attempted to relate the element of size to various structural components. Let us look at some of these in detail.

### Size and Complexity

Large organizations seem to show a definite pattern of greater complexity.[11] Complexity grows as the organization attempts to meet the various demands of external stakeholders, such as customers, suppliers, and the government. The need for additional specialties occurs more often in large organizations; new administrative departments are often created in response to problems of large size.[12] Large organizations can also add new jobs or departments at smaller proportionate expense than can small ones. Finally, as growth occurs, specialties are added and the existing departments become so large and differentiated that it is logical to split them off into new departments.[13]

Vertical complexity and spatial dispersion increase as organizations grow. As new departments are added, new levels of supervision are introduced to reduce the span of control. This vertical complexity allows each manager to supervise a smaller number of subordinates effectively. Spatial dispersion is created by the need to service different geographical locations; again, the emphasis is on dividing up the work and then integrating it through control and coordination mechanisms.

But not all research supports the relationship between size and complexity. Hall has found that geographic dispersion and the type of work being performed are more important factors than size for organizational complexity.[14] Child reports that the degree of formalization has a more direct relationship with complexity than does size, but size is a major predictor of decentralization.[15] Although there is no evidence that the two are directly related, Hall suggests that there is a reinforcing effect between complexity and size.

## Size and Delegation

The workload increases as an organization grows. To cope, managers either hire new people or begin to delegate duties to existing subordinates. Delegation involves assigning authority and responsibility for completion of tasks or projects to others, and requiring accountability. It can serve both as a means of accommodating organizational growth and as a way of developing the potential of subordinates, but it can get out of hand. As organizations become very large and complex, they may grow to a point where delegation is no longer the solution of choice. Today's biggest corporations are now just a third of their 1970s size,[16] in part because top management has decided that, rather than continuing to delegate work to existing personnel, it is better to subcontract work to outside agencies and organizations—a trend that appears to be catching on in many organizations.

Once delegation occurs, management must concern itself with integration, the coordination and control that must occur so that all the parts of the organization operate as one.[17] Lack of integration causes duplication of effort, cost overruns, poor morale, inefficiency, and a bloated bureaucracy. Under old-paradigm thinking, management must ensure that task differentiation and delegation are controlled if effectiveness is to be achieved.

As General Electric's CEO Jack Welch points out, delegation is an important technique in the 1990s:

> Simply doing more of what worked in the 1980's . . . the restructuring, the delayering, the mechanical, top-down measures that we took . . . will be too incremental. More than that, it will be too slow. The winners of the 1990's will be those who can develop a culture that allows them to move faster, communicate more clearly, and involve everyone in a focused effort to serve ever more demanding customers. . . . We've got to simplify and delegate more.[18]

Obviously, the more delegation is practiced, the more integration is needed as a form of organizational glue. One example of good integration is the Toyota *kanban*, the just-in-time inventory system.[19] Partly as a result of technology and partly through delegation, one Toyota assembly line can produce six different Toyota models without any slowdown or stoppage.

---

**Vignette 3**

The diseconomies of size and top-heavy administration can be seen at Dartmouth College, where tuition and room/board grew from $6,425 in 1977 to $18,400 in 1987—an increase of more than 300%. "A major reason," reports the *Hopkins Bulletin*, "has been an explosion in size of the college's bureaucracy, beginning in the 1970s. Now overseeing the 699 faculty members and 1,680 support personnel are 455 administrators! That is one administrator for every five faculty and nonfaculty employees. What's more, the college is about to add another administrative level at the top of the structure, immediately below the President."

SOURCE: *Hopkins Bulletin* 2 (November 1988): 2-3.

---

## Size and the Administrative Component

*Parkinson's Law* is a humorous treatise that suggests that "work expands to fill the time available for its completion," and that "there need be little or no relationship between the work to be done and the size of the staff to which it may be assigned."[20] This particular insight into bloated bureaucracies has spawned a great deal of attention to the

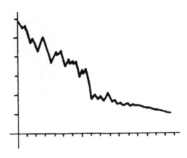

POT-SHOTS NO. 395

# CHEER UP!

THINGS MAY BE
GETTING WORSE
AT A SLOWER RATE.

*Ashleigh Brilliant*

question of size and its relationship to what is called the *administrative component.*

The "commonsense" hypothesis concerning this relationship would be that as size increases, the proportion of employees in the administrative component increases. Administrators and staff are primarily responsible for coordinating and controlling (integrating) the various units of the organization into a functioning whole. As the number of employees increases, so do the problems of integration. To achieve effective integration, the organization must allocate more resources— that is, increase the administrative component. Studies by Terrien and Mills, and by Hinings, confirm this hypothesis,[21] but more recent studies have found a negative relationship between size and the administrative component. These studies show that as the organization increases in size, the proportion of employees allocated to administration decreases. A study of Veterans Administration hospitals found the administrative component to decrease as the organization grew in size.[22]

Which is true? Blau and Schoenherr have shown that increasing size increases complexity, which in turn causes a larger administrative component, but increases in organization size also produce economies of scale (which allow the administrative component to be reduced relative to size).[23] In many organizations, the effects of economies of scale seem to exceed the effects of complexity, allowing for the administrative component to be of smaller *relative* size in larger organizations than in smaller ones. But at least one study has suggested that the economies-of-scale argument is potentially spurious.[24]

To reconcile this inconsistent research evidence, we must ask two questions:

1. *Is the relationship between size and the administrative component the same when the organization is growing as when it is declining?* Common sense would say no. When an organization is declining, more emphasis would probably be paid to goods-producing functions rather than support functions. One study found that office staff grew as the company grew, but pared down when decline began.[25]

2. *What is meant by administrative component?* Studies often conflict because they measure different things under the same rubric, such as the ratio between managers and employees, the proportion of line managers and their support staff to production personnel, staff (administrative component) and line, and all "support personnel in an organization."[26]

From our point of view, it seems reasonable to arrive at the following conclusions:

1. As size increases, the administrative component will grow to facilitate integration.

2. At some point in the growth curve, the proportion of administrative component to all employees will decline (the economies-of-scale argument).

3. The relationship may in fact be curvilinear. The administrative component may be greater for smaller and larger organizations than for those of moderate size.[27] At some point (where that may be is an empirical question), the diseconomies of size outweigh the economies and more support staff is required for integration. The point no doubt varies by industry, technology type, and other factors.


## Size and Centralization

As organizations grow, centralization becomes increasingly difficult to implement because "more is happening than any one individual can comprehend."[28] Many researchers seem to conclude that increasing size brings pressure for decentralization.[29] In fact, numerous studies have shown a negative relationship between increasing size and increasing centralization of decision making.[30]

Most small companies are centralized, but, as complexity increases, it becomes virtually impossible for one person to supervise all areas of concern, and delegation becomes a necessity. For example, Roger Smith, the CEO for General Motors Corporation, pushed routine decisions far down the corporate hierarchy; otherwise, GM's response to its market would be too slow.[31] Coupled with greater formalization, decentralization permits decisions to be made at lower levels without a loss of control.

An exception to this rule is the stubborn owner-manager. Even at the cost of increased ineffectiveness, some owner-managers will continue to exercise centralized control as size increases. Some large, financially successful companies are run this way, but employee turnover tends to be high, in part because senior executives see that they will always be followers, not leaders, and they have no incentive to stay.

---

**Vignette 4**

Charles Kyd tells this story: "Many companies pay for positions that were needed in the past but not in the present. Several years ago, for example, I was vice-president of finance for a small manufacturer in desperate need of a turnaround. To raise cash and cut costs, we sold our manufacturing plant and then purchased our product from private label manufacturers. With only 10 employees remaining in the company and no manufacturing plant, the firm didn't need a vice president of finance. So I fired myself."

SOURCE: Charles W. Kyd, "Waste Not, Want Not," *Inc.*, December 1987, 177-178. Reprinted with permission of *Inc.* Magazine. © December 1987 Goldhirsh Group, Inc.

---

## Size and Formalization

When an organization is small, its members generally come in contact with each other on a daily basis. Because they know each other so well, there seems to be little need for rules and procedures. For instance, when Celestial Seasonings had fewer than 100 employees, it had frequent companywide meetings, where everyone could have a say in determining company policy and direction. But once growth begins in earnest, informality seems inevitably to be replaced by structure and formality. Growth brings new people who don't know the original people, or don't share their passion for the organization and its purposes. It often brings geographic separation as well, and soon there are a lot of "strangers" working together.

**Vignette 5**

A company launched in a garage workshop grew until it employed more than 1,000 people. But employee turnover was high. The company spent thousands of dollars a year on executive recruiters to fill the frequently vacant top positions. On the advice of consultants, the president began to work with an organization development team to spread decision-making power to lower levels of the organization. However, he also sabotaged efforts by missing meetings and not complying with requests for information and documents. It was obvious that the president was not interested in allowing the leaders he had hired to actually lead.

Similarly, in a highly centralized $10 million-a-year manufacturing facility in California, all decisions must be approved by the president and an executive VP. This creates several problems: (a) When both are absent, everything comes to a halt, because people don't want to risk making decisions autonomously; (b) middle managers, with no de facto power to make decisions, have no command authority, and are ignored by their subordinates when they give orders; and (c) motivation is low because everyone is just following orders rather than being creative and exercising initiative.

SOURCE: Files of Renaissance Business Associates, Inc.

The use of rules, memos, and policy statements to substitute for personal contact becomes fact. This process facilitates decentralization because it adds an element of certainty to the decision-making process (i.e., it ensures that decisions are made within certain specified parameters). Apple Computer provides an example. Under the leadership of Steven Jobs and Steve Wozniak, the company was very informal and organic. But when John Sculley reorganized Apple upon his takeover, he took "long overdue action to formalize the company. Now, there are rules, strict financial controls, formal reporting relationships, and tough product development deadlines."[32]

The studies of the Aston Group, discussed in Chapter 13, support the conclusion that size affects formalization. Although Hall is somewhat more reticent to declare a strong relationship between the two, he does say:

> Relatively strong relationships exist between size and the formalization of the authority structure, the stipulation of penalties for rule violation in writing, and the orientation and in-service training procedures. A general association does exist to the extent that larger organizations tend to be

more formalized on the other indicators, even though the relationship is quite weak.[33]

In general, the larger the organization, the more formalized its behavior.[34] This formulation includes not only the written rules, regulations, policies, and procedures that a company employs to regularize behavior, but also unwritten RRPP, or cultural norms.

The purpose of formalization is to get people to behave in an organizationally acceptable mode, rather than use their own personal discretion to decide how to do things. Large organizations tend to formalize activities that occur often, so that each time they occur, the person involved will not have to "reinvent the wheel" to take appropriate action. Given management's desire to reduce confusion and regularize behavior, formalization seems a rational strategy to achieve these ends.

## Conclusions About Size and Structure

We can summarize the findings discussed in this section as follows. As an organization grows, there is a greater division of labor. With continued growth, coordination and control become a problem, so there is an increase in the number of levels of hierarchy and in delegation. With further growth, there is the continuing hiring of specialists and the institution of informal controls (formalization). There emerges a tendency to standardize routine operations.[35]

With growth comes a greater distance between top management and the rank and file (and between top management and the organization's clients). The administrative component grows, too. Morale begins to be

---

**Vignette 6**

During the early days of Ben & Jerry's Homemade Inc., it was a ritual to have "dinner with Ben and Jerry." However, a 1988 article in *Inc.* magazine indicated that close, family feelings were no longer the norm at the company. The company had grown to a size where rules and regulations became substitutes for individual discretion and shared purpose. An illustration of a symptom of this change is an event that occurred at a companywide meeting at which someone was to receive an award for merit. When the person's name was announced, a voice from the audience cried, "That person is no longer with the company!"

SOURCE: Files of Renaissance Business Associates, Inc.

---

a problem. Appropriate selection of qualified personnel becomes crucial to ensure that standards are maintained despite the distance between top management and the workers.

Henry Mintzberg, in his classic *The Structuring of Organizations*, offers these propositions:

1. The older the organization, the more formalized its behavior.
2. Structure reflects the age of the founding of the industry.
3. The larger the organization, the more elaborate the structure, that is, the more specialized its tasks, the more differentiated its units, and the more developed its administrative component.
4. The larger the organization, the larger the size of its average unit.
5. The larger the organization, the more formalized its behavior.[36]

---

## Size and the
## Stages of Organizational Development

---

Under the industrial paradigm, organizations develop in a rather predictable fashion. As they grow, they progress through several distinct developmental stages—stages that seem common to all public and private sector organizations alike. Not all organizations pass through the exact sequence in the exact order—and some fail before they can pass through all the stages—but the progression does seem to be rather typical and predictable.

A number of models of this growth cycle describe a series of structural transitions that occur as the organization adapts to different environmental contingencies. These "metamorphosis models" view growth not as a "smooth, continuous process but one marked by abrupt and discrete changes" in structures.[37]

We shall discuss the sequence in six discrete stages, using as the basis of our approach the work of Henry Mintzberg.[38] The six stages are as follows:

1. craft
2. entrepreneurialism
3. bureaucratic structure
4. divisionalized structure
5. matrix structure
6. mixed or organic structure

Movement through these stages might be jerky rather than smooth, and parts of an organization can be at one stage while other parts are at another.

Some organizations begin in the craft stage as "cottage industries" based in their founders' homes, and later pass into the entrepreneurial stage. Far more seem to begin in the entrepreneurial stage. The craft and entrepreneurial stages are characterized by undifferentiated, organic structures, collegial decision making, and general informality. As entrepreneurial organizations grow, they begin to differentiate and formalize, leading to the bureaucratic stage.

Further growth can lead to a market-based grouping of activities, or the divisionalized stage. Continued growth and the pressures of a turbulent marketplace will then drive some organizations to a fifth stage, the matrix stage, wherein an organic component is used for quick decision response and flexibility.

Finally, given the requisite worker maturity, turbulent environmental pressures, and nonroutine technology, the organization can pass into the final stage, the mixed or organic stage. This final stage is not included in Mintzberg's model. In this structure, the organization has virtually no hierarchy, little formalization, "whole jobs" (complete jobs, with the same worker beginning and finishing the job), worker flexibility, high personal responsibility, and a constantly changing structural arrangement to meets the needs of the moment. It can also include certain aspects still organized bureaucratically (e.g., departments with routine technologies such as long-linked or mediating). Each of the six stages is described in turn below.

*Stage 1: craft.* This stage is characterized by one informally organized group that has daily face-to-face communications, a natural division of labor (people do what they are good at doing), and frequent and expected job rotation. Coordination is effected by standardization of skills through apprenticeship. The administrative component is small, consisting of owners working right alongside the employees. There are few or no rules, little vertical differentiation, and little concern with job titles or status. The Celestial Seasonings tea company began as a craft structure. Corner service stations, most barbershops, and craft studios are organizations that usually stay at this stage.

*Stage 2: entrepreneurialism.* As creative entrepreneurs invent new products, organizations are started to facilitate the design, elaboration, testing, and eventual commercialization of those products. Because the entrepreneur makes most of the decisions and supervises the work of everyone else, this stage is marked by centralization, but the structure remains informal and organic, with no "middle management." Eventually, informal face-to-face communication becomes increasingly inadequate to facilitate integration. "The energies of group members, instead of being devoted to the primary task, are increasingly diverted to the task of holding the group together," notes E. J. Miller.[39] According to Mintzberg, "New levels of management must develop and direct supervision must be more relied upon for coordination."[40]

*Stage 3: bureaucratic structure.* Eventually, the informal, organic, entrepreneurial organization must begin to formalize its operations and decentralize its authority structure by adding a middle-management layer of vertical differentiation. Under our current paradigm, organizations that do not successfully make this transition eventually fail or are severely retarded in their growth.

Although entrepreneurial organizations with mature workers and well-articulated visions can continue for much longer with organic structure, most organizations have to get rid of the entrepreneur in order to make the transition to the bureaucratic stage. The owner-founder with strong ego involvement in the success of the firm wants to continue to make all the decisions, creating a bottleneck at just the wrong time in the company's growth. Job descriptions must be created where none existed, and previously casual reporting relationships must be formalized, especially with old-paradigm workers, who are looking for leaders to lead them (centralization) and directions to follow (formalization).

The shift from the organic or quasi-organic structure of the entrepreneurial stage to a bureaucratic one seems inevitable under the existing paradigm. This transition is typical of all types of organizations, public or private sector, manufacturing or service based:

> For example, the innovative psychiatric clinic gains a reputation and attracts both patients and personnel. Its novel techniques, created by one or a few people, are viewed as the reason for its success. Thus, the same techniques are prescribed for new personnel to follow. As a result, these techniques must be explicated and broken down into steps, and checkpoints must be provided along the way. Soon, the new approaches are frozen into convenient dogma, and the clinic has become a factory.[41]

*Stage 4: divisionalized structure.* This stage of growth sees the organization begin to expand into different markets, develop different products for regional needs, and the like. In order to coordinate these diverse activities, the organization must shift its structural configuration into a form that can control for each site or product line. It becomes imperative that the organization be divisionalized.[42]

The classic example of this structure is General Motors. Under its product divisionalization scheme, it has separate, relatively autonomous divisions for Chevrolet, Oldsmobile, Buick, Pontiac, and Cadillac cars. Each of these profit centers has a vice president who acts as a chief operating officer. The headquarters staff is charged with the responsibility of tying all of this together. Not all organizations reach this stage; many stay at Stage 3, the functional bureaucratic stage.

Here in this form we see a response to a special set of problems attendant to growth into different regions and with different products. Mintzberg says:

> Like the amoeba, the overgrown functional bureaucracy splits into distinct entities or divisions, each typically a . . . bureaucracy with its own operating core that serves its own market. The central "headquarters" coordinated their activities largely through an impersonal performance control system, and occupied itself with the introduction of new divisions to serve new markets and the deletion of old unsuccessful ones.[43]

Do all organizations eventually diversify into divisionalization? Clearly not, but there does seem to be an imperative based on market diversification, age, and size.[44] Research shows that, of these three, diversification is the important intermediate variable.[45] Divisionalization, then, seems to be, under the industrial paradigm, a logical consequence of aging and growth.

*Stage 5: matrix structure.* A number of large multinational corporations have found themselves with more than one market focus, such as product, geographic, functional, even technological. A decision to favor any focus, such as product, inevitably sacrifices the other foci. Therefore, as Stopford and Wells note:

> Some firms have found that none of the three global structures (area divisions, worldwide product divisions, or a mixture of product and area divisions) is entirely satisfactory. All three structures are based on the (classical) principle of unity of command: one man has sole responsibility for a specified part of the business and is accountable to a single superior officer. As a result, barriers to communication between divisions are high, and coordination of the activities of foreign subsidiaries in different divisions is difficult.[46]

In 1972, when *Managing the Multinational Enterprise* was published, Stopford and Wells noticed that some companies had tried to overcome these problems by creating new structures, characterized by "dual or multiple reporting relationships" and "worldwide product divisions and area divisions . . . with shared jurisdiction over the foreign subsidiaries."[47] Today, we recognize this then-nameless structure as a matrix.

The matrix structure combines the stability and predictability of the bureaucracy with the flexibility and speed of the organic structure. Dow Corning and Texas Instruments are good examples of companies employing the matrix structure.

*Stage 6: mixed or organic structure—the new-paradigm organization.* An organization begins with an organic form, and, if it reaches Stage 6, adopts it again. However, there are some important differences in this stage. In the Stage 1 structure, the glue that holds the organization together is the excitement of newness, the challenge of creating a company, and, most of all, the *transcendent vision of the founders.* By Stage 6, the company has grown to a large size and the mixed or organic structure is created by splitting up the larger company into smaller work units.[48] The smaller work units can consist of organic teams or they can have some of the attributes of a bureaucratic form, as required.

Flexibility is the major benefit of the Stage 6 organic form. Those working with nonroutine technologies in a turbulent environment will call for organic teams, whereas aspects of the company doing routine tasks may stick to the bureaucratic scheme. The structure of a true organic company will change as required. Dr. Raymond E. Miles, dean of the Business School at the University of California, Berkeley, seems to agree with this perspective:

> The linking of all this is that you cannot run an organization that's lean, highly adaptable, both deep and flexible if your theories of management are traditional or human relations. *You can't do it.* And you won't be able to put those together and couple them and uncouple them quickly *unless you are highly flexible in your thinking and basic theory beliefs.*[49]

Sound like utopia? It isn't. The single most important factor for this to occur is the ongoing paradigm shift. As a critical mass of mature, responsible employees is reached, the form will naturally emerge.

## The Critical Mass of Bigness

How big is big? At what point does an organic, free-form organization begin to calcify into a bureaucracy? At what point do additional employees have a minimal effect on the organization's structure? There are no hard-and-fast answers to these questions, but, in asking them, we get a closer look at the dynamics of the collective paradigm-structure interplay.

Once an organization reaches a certain point in size, it tends to be high in complexity, formalization, and decentralization. Each incremental addition of employees makes much less difference to the structural configuration than do additions at the earlier stages of growth. Some researchers have estimated that an organization population of between 1,500 and 2,000 employees is the stage when additional employees have little impact on structure.[50] So, for our purposes, we can call organizations with fewer than 1,500 employees "small." With a size larger than 2,000 employees, the organization seems to need to differentiate, integrate, and formalize to regularize work. (Actually, we have seen organizations with as few as 100 employees that are highly centralized or bureaucratized.) This shows the power and impact of the current industrial paradigm.

---

## A Paradigmatic View
## of the Size-Structure Relation

---

Let us examine in detail the metamodel as it relates to organizational size. As stated earlier, a small, entrepreneurial organization can be organic in its earlier stages, providing the following ingredients are present:

1. *a transcendent purpose or vision for the organization* that inspires loyalty and commitment to the organization
2. *psychological ownership of the company,* wherein the company's purposes become (or are aligned with) the individual's purposes
3. *a high level of maturity/personal responsibility of the organization members,* so that each member is willing to do what is necessary to get the job done, without regard to roles, job descriptions, and so on
4. *clear performance expectations* shared by all

In the exciting early days of a company with a transcendent or inspiring purpose, it is easy to find euphoria and high commitment to purpose. Apple Computer, People's Express, and Celestial Seasonings, for example, all were attempting to contribute something judged to be beneficial to the whole. Their original purpose had nothing to do with profits, return on investment, or the like; self-centered motives were pushed to the background. These purposes also reflected the passion of the founder as they brought their personal visions into organizational manifestation.

The magnetic quality of the transcendent vision will attract people who wish to offer their best to the joint venture. For a while, at least, the organization can continue its growth pattern with reasonably mature people; formalization and centralization are not required yet. Eventually, however, the organization must begin to hire people who do not share the vision (or who share it to a lesser degree). Inevitably, people are hired who have exclusively extrinsic motives—they are in it for the money, the prestige, the mobility, or whatever.

**Vignette 7**

There has been some evidence that not everyone at Ben & Jerry's Homemade Inc. shares the total purpose and vision of the founders. In a 1988 article in *Inc.*, a sales manager reportedly indicated that he thought the 5:1 ratio (the company's established policy of paying no one any more than five times the pay of the lowest-paid worker, a structural attempt to reduce the influence of status and hierarchy) was not fair. This manager felt that he should be making at least as much as those he was selling franchises to; to do this, he would have had to double his current salary. Here we see the dominant effect-oriented, addicted-to-externals paradigm alive and well. (It is interesting to note that although there has been some adjustment to the salary ratio in recent years, the salaries of Ben and Jerry and their managers are still far closer to those of their lowest-paid workers than would be found in almost any other corporation.)

When lack of alignment with purpose begins to happen, the glue that the vision and personal maturity provides begins to weaken, and external controls must be instituted to replace them (RRPP). If the dominance of internal, vision-inspired controls begins to fade, external controls must replace them; otherwise, anarchy will result. The same is true at the societal level: If we had a society made up of nothing but 100% responsible, loving people interested in consistently expressing the finest quality of character they were able to, we wouldn't need police, lawyers, security patrols, jails, or judges.

A society requires a control pattern. In the human, self-centered state, the control must come from internal sources (values, morality, ethics) or external sources (laws, courts, police, jails, fines). In the transformational perspective, control comes from the integrating quality of the design inherent in the whole; each one, aligned with the purposes of the whole, will naturally do what is required in each situation. In other words, the whole organizes the parts—a key transformational assumption.

If persons are willing to see themselves in terms of the larger picture and realize that their identities are much bigger than their roles in life, a new perspective begins to emerge. By consistently expressing the finest quality of character possible in each situation (i.e., qualities of helpfulness, compassion, inclusion, integrity), forgoing self-centered goals and motives, the transcendent view begins to come into focus. If each person in the organization is willing to do this consistently, there are *no* theoretical limits to the size of an organic organization.

## Size and the New Paradigm

In the industrial age, large size was an advantage because of economies of scale. But in turbulent environments, size is becoming a disadvantage. Management consultant Ennias E. Bergsma notes:

> The costs of size fall into three categories. First, as the pace of change in the environment accelerates, the inflexibility and complacency often bred in large enterprises become a major disadvantage. It's a bit like a large oil tanker trying to maneuver through waterways that become narrower, curved and filled with rapids. Second, the cost of complexity . . . all the difficult tradeoffs and increased sophistication necessary to manage the diversified enterprise . . . increases. Finally, the financial cost of the corporate center, both direct and indirect, can become a tax on the corporation's constituent businesses that outweighs its benefits.[51]

Small companies generate more jobs than big ones, and they can take credit for the most important technological innovations of recent years.

> "Virtually every innovation in computation since the mainframe—the microprocessor, personal computer, minicomputer, work station, supercomputer, and much software—has been started or commercialized by venture-backed, entrepreneurial companies," says Benjamin Rosen, a leading venture capitalist. "They have created millions of jobs. It's what has kept us alive in world competition."[52]

### Vignette 8

Two young hippies, Mo Siegel and John Hay, began producing herbal teas for sale to Boulder, Colorado, health food stores in the early 1970s. From their experience picking various herbs in the nearby Rocky Mountains, they had developed some tasty recipes. Mo and John, with the help of their wives, packaged the tea in bulk form and took it to health food stores in an old pickup truck. When their products proved to be popular in the local area, the two founders incorporated Celestial Seasonings with a $5,000 bank loan and $5,000 borrowed from a friend.

Within five years, the company was producing some 32 types of herbal teas and, thanks to shelf space in national supermarket chains such as Safeway, the general public was falling in love with Celestial Seasonings teas. Through these early years, the company had a loose, laid-back culture, with an emphasis on informality, participation, and even spirituality (a silent grace was said before each lunch in the cafeteria, for example). But as the company grew, the culture changed. No longer two men and their wives in a cottage industry, it was fast becoming "big business."

Outside management "experts" were brought in. Mo Siegel stopped reading metaphysical literature and began reading the works of Peter Drucker. The technology became assembly line (instead of small batch), and the whole system for acquiring, processing and packaging the herbs became complex. Newly hired people had no allegiance to the values and ethos of the old culture; formalization began to replace the company's small, friendly, participative culture. By the time it was purchased by Kraft, Inc., in 1984, it had become a bureaucracy.

Eventually it appeared that the tea company didn't fit with Kraft's corporate structure. Kraft was faced with two alternatives: integrate the tea as a brand name or sell the business. The Celestial president, Barnet Feinblum (who served as Celestial's vice president during the Siegel/Hay time with the company), began investigating ways to buy back the business, which was about to be sold to Lipton. On November 2, 1988, a group of Celestial managers and Vestar (an investment company) bought control of Celestial from Kraft, with Feinblum as CEO.

"I'm perfect for the company in its mid-size range," he noted when the buyback was complete. "Mo and John Hay (the co-founder) were perfect to start it, but the kind of management it takes to start a company is different than what it takes to run one. I'm the kind of manager that is more entrepreneurial than corporate, but I also have the training and discipline to run the business."

One of the buyout team's members called Feinblum's management style "participatory," based on the concept that the right hand needs to know what the left hand is doing. "At Kraft, we never had the big picture; we now feel that the more we tell people, the more they will do their jobs."

SOURCES: Sandra D. Atchison, "Kraft Is Celestial Seasonings' Cup of Tea," *Business Week,* July 28, 1976, 73; Nora Gallagher, "We Are More Aggressive Than Our Tea," *Across the Board,* July/August 1983; Eric Morgenthaler, "Herb Tea's Pioneer: From Hippie Origins to $16 Million a Year," *Wall Street Journal,*" May 6, 1981, 1-22; Nancy Nachman-Hunt, "A Celestial Story," *Boulder County Business Report* 8 (December 1988): 1-6.

As a result, companies are seeking to avoid the disadvantages of size in creative ways. For example:

> W. L. Gore and Associates is a company structured upon the principles of personal responsibility and self-management. Gore believes that "groups respond to recognized authority or to individual commitment. If you are going to have a lot of change in an organization, you better get a commitment. In the process, natural leaders will evolve." He also believes that people work better when they are in groups of no more than 200. This way, they can maintain an intimate, family atmosphere of communication. Thus, Gore's 4000 employees work in 30 small plants.
>
> In terms of operating efficiency, this decentralized plant system would seem suboptimal. But Gore maintains that creativity and productivity thrive in this small-plant atmosphere. Is this approach working? With an annual growth rate of 30-40%, it would seem that this approach has merit.[53]

Companies are also using *intrapreneurship* strategies to bolster innovation and responsiveness.[54] In what Peters and Waterman call "skunk works," a company purposefully creates small, autonomous units within the larger whole whose job it is to create, to innovate, without the stultifying effects of bureaucratic controls.[55] The 3M Corporation has become famous for this approach and is considered a model for innovation.[56] Intrapreneurship is a result of "America's biggest companies busily trying to find ways to infuse some of that entrepreneurial fervor into their comparatively staid veins."[57] However, corporations have found mixed success with this approach; basically, the problem is that "true entrepreneurs have a driving need for achievement, autonomy and aggression."[58] Intrapreneurs, although having more freedom than corporate types, still must report to someone in the larger bureaucracy.

No less an authority than the widely influential Peter Drucker of the Claremont Graduate School in Southern California has the following observation:

> The typical large business twenty years hence will have fewer than half the levels of management of its counterpart today, and no more than a third of its managers. In its structure, and in its management problems and concerns, it will bear little resemblance to the typical manufacturing company, circa 1950, which our textbooks still consider the norm. Instead, it is far more likely to resemble organizations that neither the practicing manager nor the management scholar pays much attention to today; the hospital, the university, the symphony orchestra. For like them, the typical organization will be *knowledge-based*, an organization largely composed of specialists who direct and discipline their own performance through

organized feedback from colleagues, customers, and headquarters. For this reason, it will be what I call an *information-based organization*.

Information technology demands the shift. . . . As advanced technology becomes more and more prevalent, we have to engage in analysis and diagnosis—that is, in "information"—even more extensively, or risk being swamped by the data we generate. . . . Information transforms a budget exercise into an analysis of policy. . . . Information is data endowed with relevance and purpose. Converting data into information thus requires knowledge. And knowledge, by definition, is specialized. So, information-based organizations will require far more specialists than the command-and-control companies we are accustomed to. . . . To remain competitive—maybe even to survive—businesses will have to convert themselves into organizations of knowledgeable specialists.[59]

## NOTES

1. Dennis S. Mileti, David F. Gillespie, and J. Eugene Haas, "Size and Structure in Complex Organizations," *Social Forces* 56 (September 1977).

2. John R. Kimberly, "Organizational Size and the Structuralist Perspective: A Review, Critique and a Proposal," *Administrative Science Quarterly* 21 (December 1976): 577-597.

3. See Richard L. Daft, *Organization Theory and Design* (2nd ed.) (New York: West, 1986), 184.

4. See, for example, Peter M. Blau, "The Hierarchy of Authority in Organizations," *American Journal of Sociology* 73 (January 1968); Peter M. Blau, "Decentralization in Bureaucracies," in *Power in Organizations*, ed. Mayer N. Zald (Nashville, TN: Vanderbilt University Press, 1970); Peter M. Blau, *The Organization of Academic Work* (New York: John Wiley, 1973); Peter M. Blau, Wolf Heydebrand, and Robert E. Stauffer, "The Structure of Small Bureaucracies," *American Sociological Review* 39 (April 1974).

5. D. S. Pugh, D. J. Hickson, C. R. Hinings, and C. Turner, "The Context of Organization Structures," *Administrative Science Quarterly* 13 (March 1969).

6. John Child, "Predicting and Understanding Organization Structure," *Administrative Science Quarterly* 18 (June 1973).

7. Barry Armandi, *Organizational Structure and Efficiency* (Washington, DC: University Press of America, 1981).

8. Howard E. Aldrich, "Technology and Organization Structure: A Re-examination of the Findings of the Aston Group," *Administrative Science Quarterly* 17 (1972): 26-43.

9. Peter M. Blau and Richard A. Schoenherr, *The Structure of Organizations* (New York: Basic Books, 1971).

10. See Paul Lawrence and Jay Lorsch, *Organizations and Environment* (Homewood, IL: Irwin, 1969).

11. See, for example, Robert Dewar and Jerald Hage, "Size, Technology, Complexity, and Structural Differentiation: Toward a Theoretical Synthesis," *Administrative Science Quarterly* 23 (1978): 111-136; Guy Geeraerts, "The Effects of Ownership on the Organization Structure of Small Firms," *Administrative Science Quarterly* 29 (June 1984); Cheng-Kuang Hsu, Robert M. Marsh, and Hiroshi Mannari, "An Examination of the Determinants of Organizational Structure," *American Journal of Sociology* 88, no. 5 (1983).

12. See Richard L. Daft and Patricia J. Bradshaw, "The Process of Horizontal Differentiation: Two Models," *Administrative Science Quarterly* 25 (December 1980).

13. See Blau, *The Organization of Academic Work*.

14. Richard H. Hall, *Organizations: Structures, Processes, and Outcomes* (4th ed.) (Englewood Cliffs, NJ: Prentice Hall, 1987).

15. Child, "Predicting and Understanding."

16. Amanda Bennett, "Growing Small: Big Firms Continue to Trim Their Staffs, 2 Tier Set-Up Emerges," *Wall Street Journal*, May 4, 1987.

17. Lawrence and Lorsch, *Organizations and Environment.*

18. John F. Welch, Jr., "Today's Leaders Look at Tomorrow," *Fortune*, March 26, 1990, 30. © 1990 Time Inc. All rights reserved. Reprinted with permission.

19. See Joel Dreyfuss, "Toyota Takes Off the Gloves," *Fortune*, December 22, 1986, 78.

20. C. Northcote Parkinson, *Parkinson's Law* (Boston: Houghton Mifflin, 1957), 33.

21. Frederic W. Terrien and Donald Mills, "The Effect of Changing Size Upon the Internal Structure of Organizations," *American Sociological Review* 20 (February 1955); Robin Hinings, Alan Bryman, and Bruce D. Foster, "Size and the Administrative Component in Churches" (working paper, University of Aston, Birmingham, England, 1972).

22. Theodore Anderson and Seymour Warkov, "Organizational Size and Functional Complexity: A Study of Administration in Hospitals," *American Sociological Review* 26 (February 1961).

23. Blau and Schoenherr, *The Structure of Organizations.*

24. Robert Coates and David E. Updegraff, "The Relationship Between Organizational Size and the Administrative Component of Banks," *Journal of Business* 46 (October 1973).

25. John E. Tsouderos, "Organizational Change in Terms of a Series of Selected Variables," *American Sociological Review* 20 (April 1955).

26. Child, "Predicting and Understanding," 329.

27. See Tsouderos, "Organizational Change"; J. Eugene Haas, Richard H. Hall, and Norman Johnson, "The Size of the Supportive Component in Organizations: A Multiorganizational Analysis," *Social Forces* 16 (October 1963).

28. Richard H. Hall, *Organizations: Structure and Process* (2nd ed.) (Englewood Cliffs, NJ: Prentice Hall, 1977), 184.

29. See Blau and Schoenherr, *The Structure of Organizations*; John Child and Roger Mansfield, "Technology, Size and Organization Structure," *Sociology* 6 (1972): 369-393; Pradip Khandwalla, "Mass Output Orientation of Operations Technology and Organization Structure," *Administrative Science Quarterly* 18 (March 1974).

30. See, for example, David J. Hickson, D. S. Pugh, and Diana C. Pheysey, "Operations Technology and Organization Structure: An Empirical Reappraisal," *Administrative Science Quarterly* 14 (September 1969); C. R. Hinings and G. L. Lee, "Dimensions of Organization Structure and Their Context: A Replication," *Sociology* 5 (January 1971); Khandwalla, "Mass Output Orientation."

31. Daft, *Organization Theory and Design*, 179.

32. Billy Joe Hodge and William P. Anthony, *Organization Theory* (3rd ed.) (Boston: Allyn & Bacon, 1988), 402.

33. Hall, *Organizations* (4th ed.), 103.

34. See Henry Mintzberg, *The Structuring of Organizations* (Englewood Cliffs, NJ: Prentice Hall, 1979), 233.

35. Pradip N. Khandwalla, *The Design of Organizations* (New York: Harcourt Brace Jovanovich, 1977), 295.

36. Mintzberg, *The Structuring of Organizations*, 227-235.

37. W. H. Starbuck, "Organizational Growth and Development," in *The Handbook of Organizations*, ed. J. G. March (Chicago: Rand McNally, 1965), 486.

38. Mintzberg, *The Structuring of Organizations*, 241-248.

39. E. J. Miller, "Technology, Territory and Time: The Internal Differentiation of Complex Production Systems," *Human Relations* 16 (1959): 249.

40. Mintzberg, *The Structuring of Organizations*, 242.

41. Charles Perrow, *Organizational Analysis: A Sociological View* (Belmont, CA: Wadsworth, 1970), 66.

42. See Lawrence and Lorsch, *Organizations and Environment.*

43. Mintzberg, *The Structuring of Organizations*, 246.

44. See J. M. Stopford and L. T. Wells, Jr., *Managing the Multinational Enterprise: Organization of the Firm and Ownership of the Subsidiaries* (New York: Basic Books, 1972), 72.

45. Mintzberg, *The Structuring of Organizations*, chap. 15.

46. Stopford and Wells, *Managing the Multinational Enterprise*, 27.

47. Ibid.

48. David J. Rachman and Michael M. Mescon, "A Structureless Organization?" in *Business Today* (5th ed.) (New York: Random House, 1987), 135.

49. Quoted in E. Leroy Plumlee, "A Visit With Raymond E. Miles," *Management Newsletter* (November 1990): 7; emphasis added.

50. Daft, *Organization Theory and Design,* 196; Daniel Robey, *Designing Organizations* (2nd ed.) (Homewood, IL: Irwin, 1986), 121.

51. Ennias E. Bergsma, "Managing Value: The New Corporate Strategy," *McKinsey Quarterly* (Winter 1989): 61. Used with permission.

52. Quoted in ibid.

53. Rachman and Mescon, "A Structureless Organization?" 135.

54. Gifford Pinchot, III, *Intrapreneuring: Why You Don't Have to Leave the Corporation to Become an Entrepreneur* (San Francisco: HarperCollins, 1986).

55. Thomas J. Peters and Robert H. Waterman, Jr., *In Search of Excellence: Lessons From America's Best-Run Companies* (New York: Harper & Row, 1982).

56. Rosabeth Moss Kanter, *The Change Masters: Innovation for Productivity in the American Corporation* (New York: Simon & Schuster, 1983).

57. Chris Lee and Ron Zemke, "Intrapreneuring: New Age Fiefdoms for Big Business?" *Training,* February 1985, 27.

58. Ibid., 28.

59. Peter F. Drucker, "The Coming of the New Organization," *Harvard Business Review* (January/ February 1988): 45.

# 15  Power, Politics, and Structure

*Something is radically wrong with the mind set that is being
used at work. People are using an overly rational approach that
implies more logic and objectivity than what actually exists. What
is taking place is far more personal, far more subjective, and far
more power oriented and political than most popular theories lead
one to expect. Managers control others far less than their words,
plans and actions imply. Systems and procedures are determined
far more by personality and hard-fought compromise than the
logical explanations used to describe and justify them would ever
lead one to believe.*

(Samuel A. Culbert and John J. McDonough,
*Radical Management*, 1985, p. 3)

**SUMMARY:** In this chapter, we examine power and politics in organizations.
The reader will recall that the coalition model of organizations, discussed in
Chapter 1, argues that organization design is the product of political factors
in the organization. In other words, the dominant coalition (the group with key
roles in the organizational decision-making process) produces the structure
and influences the process of the organization. This approach is compatible
with the metamodel. In this chapter we look at what power is, and how it is
traditionally used in organizations. We also look at how politics influences
organizations, and how the new paradigm will affect both factors.

For years, textbooks on management and organization virtually ignored what is arguably the dominant factor in organizational life:
political behavior as it relates to organizational power. Why was this

factor ignored? One answer is that under the industrial era assumption that organizations are rational, machinelike entities, irrational behavior (which indulging in politics clearly is) would be unthinkable. Yet managers know that politics is the single most important factor in organizational success (or failure) from a personal point of view. It should be self-evident that

> the *rational actor approach* often fails to predict or explain important aspects of organizational life. Frequently, individuals, groups, and organizations do not act in internally consistent ways. Public or explicit goals have little relation to what actually brings about behavior. The resulting patterns of behavior are therefore completely different than that which the utility maximizing models would predict.[1]

In other words, organizations do not operate as well-oiled machines, a clear assumption of the original scientific management designers.

No longer is the political approach ignored in the management literature. In fact, Culbert and McDonough note the following:

1. Everyone knows that individual self-interest dictates task selection and accomplishment.
2. Organizations do not allow individuals to acknowledge their self-interest (we are pretending to be rational!).
3. Personal goals are attained by *not* revealing one's self-interest (a corollary of 2, above).
4. There is a double standard of self-interests; people claim that when their actions match their self-interests it is mere coincidence, but that others doing the same is "unfair manipulation."
5. People say and behave in two different ways.
6. Self-interest motivates people in the pursuit of excellence.[2]

Increasingly, power is recognized as an extremely critical variable in organization design. Some argue that it is a contingency variable, at least as powerful in determining structure as size, environment, and technology.[3] Others see power as a useful "image of organization" or lens (paradigm) through which organizational reality can be viewed.[4] Power seems to be a primary ingredient in the formation and survival of organizations.[5] In fact, the formation of an organization has been described as a direct result of a person's desire for power or the things that power can provide; for example, "A person desiring power provides a viable idea system and gains power from that system by forming and operating an organization."[6]

### Vignette 1

A business school associate professor, newly hired in 1981 at a large Catholic university, decided to find out the criteria for promotion at that school. Operating from a "rational" perspective, the professor discovered that the criteria were, in order of importance: scholarly research and publications, teaching effectiveness, and community service (including service on committees at the school). Armed with this information, the professor began a calculated strategy for promotion by "holing up" in his office to write. This had the unintended consequence of making him seem aloof and distant to the other faculty; also, many of the senior faculty had not published, and they viewed his behavior as threatening to their prestige.

The professor also put a lot of effort into teaching innovations and into specific committee work and community involvement. After four years, he had arguably the best publishing record in the college, was voted "Outstanding Business Professor" by the graduating MBA class, and had numerous citations for volunteer work in the community.

Confident that he had done what he needed to do, he walked into the review committee meeting with keen anticipation. After a secret ballot, he discovered that his support was far from unanimous. In a divided faculty, he received approximately a two-thirds endorsement. Disappointed, he still felt he would be promoted. However, he was told by his dean that the dean would not support his candidacy for promotion. The dean explained that the last three recipients of promotions to full professor were "embarrassing to him," because they were viewed as weak candidates and he was politically forced to support them. This, he felt, put him in such a position that he wanted to support only candidates who clearly had the unanimous support of their departments. The professor was told he could pursue his case, but the dean would not support such an action.

Chastened, the professor withdrew his petition and immediately took a position at another university, at the rank of full professor. He had learned a valuable lesson in organizational politics.

## The Nature of Power and Authority

It is useful at the outset to distinguish between two terms that are often used interchangeably: *power* and *authority*. Every social relationship involves power. Power can be defined as the ability of one person or group to get another person or group to do something they wouldn't otherwise have done.[7] This rather commonsense definition can be represented simply as shown in Figure 15.1.

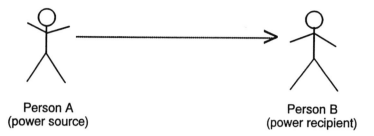

Person A                              Person B
(power source)                     (power recipient)

**Figure 15.1.** The Power Relationship

When a superior asks a subordinate to do something, or a teacher gives a study assignment, power is being exercised. Centralization, which we have discussed previously, is primarily about power; the power to make decisions is concentrated at the top of the hierarchy. Other definitions of power include the following:

1. the ability to influence others to carry out orders[8]
2. the ability to achieve goals or outcomes that power holders desire[9]
3. the ability of a person or department in an organization to influence other people to bring about desired outcomes[10]

Formal authority, on the other hand, is related to power but is narrower in scope. Authority is also a tool for achieving desired outcomes by using influence, but only within the confines of organizational hierarchy and reporting relationships. Basically, the organization bestows power on a legitimate officeholder (formal authority) in order to facilitate his or her getting the job done.

Organizational power can be exercised upward, downward, and horizontally; formal authority can be exercised only downward (vertical power). Formal authority is vested in the organizational position; this is also called *legitimate* or *positional power*. This authority is voluntarily accepted by subordinates and tends to flow down the hierarchy.[11] Informal authority, on the other hand, tends to come from such sources as expert knowledge and charisma.

## Types of Authority

Under the general category of formal authority, we find four subcategories: line authority, staff authority, functional authority (sometimes called functional staff authority), and operative authority.

### Vignette 2

There was no question that Barbara was competent: three years before, she had been hired as an executive vice president because of her ability to prepare long-term marketing analyses that were almost always on the money. She certainly knew more about market forces than her boss, Mike, who had an operations background. Therefore, she felt she didn't need as much input from him as did her coworker, Miranda, who had weekly meetings with Mike. To Barbara, those meetings seemed a waste of time. When she met with Mike, he would talk about everything but the project she was working on. He even suggested that Barbara spend time with the sales department. Didn't Mike realize that she had enough to do already?

Barbara was proud of the fact that she was an independent agent, and needed little assistance from other areas. Miranda, on the other hand, always seemed to be shuttling from one office to another. And whereas Barbara regularly worked through lunch so she could turn in top-notch reports, Miranda would often hand over important assignments to her assistant while she went out to lunch with people in sales. Because of her self-sufficiency and dedication, Barbara felt confident that she would step into Mike's job when he moved up. She was shocked when Miranda was promoted over her.

But Barbara had been blowing her own fuses all along: instead of accessing the many outlets available to her, Barbara had disconnected herself from the company's main power supply—and ended up short-circuiting her career.

SOURCE: Randi Blaun, "Plugging Into the Power Source," *Executive Female*, November/December 1988. Reprinted with permission from *Executive Female*, the official publication of the National Association for Female Executives (NAFE).

## Line Authority

Line authority—also called *managerial* or *positional* authority—is the bread and butter of organizational authority. It is the authority that is used to acquire, deploy, and control the resources needed to fulfill the organization's objectives. This authority represents the legitimation of influence within the organizational context; it has its roots in the legitimation of the organization in a larger society.

There is a collective agreement in consciousness that the holder of line authority has the right and the responsibility to give orders and enforce decisions with certain sanctions. Subordinates who defer to this authority are expected to follow the orders under penalty of sanction.

According to the parity principle, managerial authority should be commensurate with responsibility. No one should be asked to be respon-

POT-SHOTS NO. 947.

# EVERYTHING IS CONTROLLED BY A SMALL EVIL GROUP

## TO WHICH, UNFORTUNATELY, NOBODY I KNOW BELONGS.

*Ashleigh Brilliant*

sible for a given area unless that person has the means to secure cooperation and assistance from other elements in the organization, as required. This parity prevents the problems that arise when a manager is held responsible for a project's completion but lacks the authority to carry it out effectively. An example of such a dysfunctional situation is given in Vignette 3.

**Vignette 3**

In one case, a female administrator who was responsible to a male CEO had the responsibility of managing four department heads who refused to acknowledge her authority. The CEO failed to back up her authority, and the administrator was constantly bypassed in the decision process. She was finally fired because the CEO found that he was doing her job as well as his. He then hired someone else (a male) to fill the position and, this time, backed the person with his authority.

SOURCE: Files of Renaissance Business Associates, Inc.

## Staff Authority

Staff authority is primarily the authority to make recommendations and suggestions to line managers. It is generally exercised by professionals such as internal consultants, financial advisers, accountants, public relations experts, and lawyers, but it can be exercised by any organization member. The legitimacy of staff authority tends to depend on the perceived credibility of the advice giver. For example, the advice of a management consultant tends to be given more credence than that of a subordinate clerical person. Thus staff authority is possessed by everyone in the organization, but individuals might (a) choose not to exercise it or (b) be ignored if they do use it.[12]

## Functional Authority

Sometimes, staff authority tends to evolve into functional or situational authority. This hybrid of line and staff authority is essentially authority granted to a staff person that gives him or her line authority in certain situations only. Hodge and Johnson note, "Generally, it is delegated to a staff expert who is restricted rather severely in the areas of organizational structure and function in which it can be exercised. This expert is given the right to make binding decisions (an element of managerial authority) about a given function in the organization structure."[13] For example, a company president might give the personnel director the authority to make everyone in the organization take a personality test. By acting on the president's behalf on this project, the personnel director "borrows" the president's line authority to force compliance.

Situational or functional authority is usually granted after the staff subordinate gains the confidence of his or her superior in the given area of expertise. Then the staff person is given the right to make decisions within a limited area without the explicit prior approval of the line superior. This is a potent type of authority, less cumbersome and more efficient than staff authority. What is being offered is no longer advice, but a line-based order requiring compliance. Situational authority is often used in the arenas of management information systems, financial controls, and public relations.

## Operative Authority

According to Hodge and Anthony, "Operative authority is made up of two basic rights: the right to carry out responsibility and the right to

© ASHLEIGH BRILLIANT 1981.                    POT-SHOTS NO. 2188.

# WHY IS THERE ALWAYS SUCH A POWER STRUGGLE

## WITHIN THE MOVEMENT FOR PEACE AND FRIENDSHIP?

Ashleigh
Brilliant

determine, within reason, how and when it will be done."[14] This authority concerns the individual's right to make certain decisions about how he or she does the work. This right to work without undue supervision is commonly considered to apply to all members of the organization.[15]

There is a direct relationship between the amount of de facto operative authority present in an organization and the collective paradigm as it relates to trust of workers and centralization/formalization. In organizations with a Theory X mind-set, very little operative authority will be evident. In organizations that treat workers as mature adults, that operate from Theory Y, large amounts of this authority can be found.

---

## Power, Authority, and
## the Industrial Era Paradigm

---

The concepts of power and authority are deeply ingrained in our industrial era paradigm. Much of our socialization is focused on *teaching* obedience to authority. Beginning with our parents, various people and organizations (teachers, bosses, doctors, clergy, army sergeants) in our lives stress respect for authority.

To appreciate fully the ingrained nature of our power and authority mental "programming," one need only look at one of the classic social science experiments of the twentieth century: the Milgram experiments.[16] Stanley Milgram, a social psychologist and a European Jew, had always been disturbed, both personally and professionally, by what he saw as the peculiar behavior of the German people during World War II. He found it amazing that, during Hitler's reign of genocide against the Jews, there were very few instances of civil disobedience by average civilians against Nazi authority figures. People apparently just stood by and watched 6 million people being systematically slaughtered. And there are other infamous incidents of apparently blind obedience recorded in history, such as the My Lai massacre of the Vietnam era.

Is this a flaw in the human character? Why have people been so obedient to authority figures who clearly violated common standards of morality and decency? With these questions in mind, Milgram designed an experiment to discover why people obey authority and under what conditions they would actually disobey a legitimate authority figure. Given that he was a professor of psychology at Yale University at the time, he decided to initiate the experiment with students; he later replicated it with all mixes of subjects—older and younger people, men and women, different ethnic groups. The experiment has now been conducted hundreds of times, and the results vary minutely between groups—an indication of how pervasive the "programming" for obedience to authority is in the dominant paradigm.

## Design of the Milgram Experiment

Milgram's experiment proceeded in the following manner. A room was set up as depicted in Figure 15.2; there was a partition in the middle of the room with a one-way mirror looking into the side of the room in which sat a replica of an electric chair. This chair looked just like the ones used for execution of prisoners; it had a skull cap, wrist bands, and wires running everywhere. On the other side of the partition was a switchboard with toggle switches labeled "10 volts," "20 volts," and so on, all the way up to 450 volts. At the switchboard was a chair. There were three people involved in each session of the experiment: the subject; a confederate of the researcher, who appeared to the subject as another subject (the two would draw straws to see who would sit in the chair, and this was always rigged so that the confederate would "win"; that is, sit in the chair); and the legitimate authority figure (the researcher, complete with white lab coat and a name tag identifying him as "Dr.").

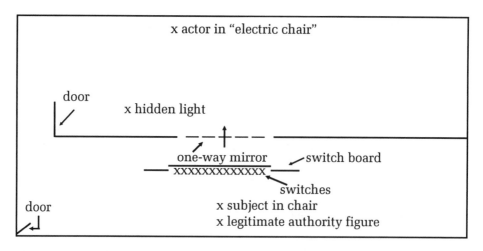

**Figure 15.2.** Physical Design of the Milgram Experiments (view from above)

The subject was told that this was to be a "learning experiment"; he or she was to use "aversive therapy," giving the other subject (the confederate) increasingly greater electric shocks each time that person (the confederate) made an error in reciting word pairs back to the subject (after the subject had read them in series of five). Actually, the experiment had nothing to do with learning. The experimental goal was to see if people would follow the orders of an authority figure to do something that is clearly morally questionable (if not outright wrong). How many people would actually shock total strangers just because someone in a lab coat told them to? Would some people refuse to do it on moral grounds? What were the variables at work here?

No electrical shock was actually administered. The switches were hooked to a partially hidden light on the confederate's side of the room; when a switch was thrown the light would go on, and the confederate would feign being shocked. Subsequent follow-up interviews showed that the subjects were convinced that the other person was being shocked when they threw the switches.

In this experimental situation, the only force requiring the subject to throw switches was the power of a perceived authority figure saying, "Please continue the experiment." The subjects received minimal stipends or payments for participating, but it was made clear that they could keep the money regardless of their decision to continue the experiment.

### The Hypotheses and Results

When he first formulated the experimental design, Milgram made the following hypotheses:

1. There would be a group of subjects (probably around 10%) who would not choose to participate (for various reasons).
2. The great majority of subjects (around 80%) would agree to start the experiment, but would drop out at some point when the stress of actually hurting another person would cause them to disobey the authority figure.
3. There would be a small group of subjects (around 10%) who would obey the authority figure and shock the confederate/subject all the way to 450 volts (the confederate, by the way, was instructed to keep making "mistakes" in the word pairs, so that the subject would have to continue "punishing" him or her).

Subjects who fell into the last group would be seen as the "neo-Nazi" faction, and it was Milgram's hope that their behavior would lead to some understanding of why the German people acted as they did. Was deep-seated sadism at work?

The results were shocking (pardon the pun), to say the least. Milgram found that more than 70% of subjects were willing to shock the other person all the way up to 450 volts! In subsequent replications of the experiment, the results were consistently within five percentage points of this result, revealing a remarkably uniform pattern. Far from being sadistic, these "normal" people would shock a total stranger, possibly risking that person's health (or even life), but the process was *not* enjoyable for them. Many subjects experienced extreme stress, resulting in headaches, nausea, and high blood pressure. To make matters worse, when the experiment was over and the subjects were told of the hoax, many were unable to deal with what had happened. When confronted with the evidence of their tendency toward what could be viewed as inhumanity, many became angry, and some suffered stress-related breakdowns and illnesses. This was viewed by many social scientists as a serious ethical problem with the research.[17]

## Personal Responsibility and Obedience

Why would these people harm an innocent person in such a way? What compelled them to do it? Milgram concluded that it was the power of the legitimate authority figure. The subjects simply assumed that the experimenter knew what he was doing. The pressure to do "as one is told" is extremely strong; it took a very strong person to defy the authority figure. There did seem to be a point in the process for virtually every subject where he or she turned around and confronted the authority figure, saying something like "I can't go on; I can't be responsible if he dies!" To this the authority figure would say, "Don't worry. I'll take complete responsibility. Please continue the experiment!" Then it was relatively easy to continue to the end; the subject was off the hook for the outcome of the experiment. Milgram summarizes his findings as follows:

1. We find a set of people carrying out their jobs and dominated by an administrative, rather than a moral, outlook.
2. Indeed, individuals involved make a distinction between hurting others as a matter of duty and the expression of personal feeling.
3. Individual values of loyalty, duty and discipline derive from the technical needs of the hierarchy. They are experienced as highly personal moral imperatives by the individual, but at the organizational level they are simply the technical preconditions for the maintenance of the larger system.
4. There is frequent modification of language so that the acts do not, at a verbal level, come into direct conflict with the verbal moral concepts that are part of every person's upbringing. Euphemisms come to dominate language . . . not frivolously, but as a means of guarding the person against the full moral implications of his acts.
5. Responsibility inevitably shifts upward in the mind of the subordinate. And, often there are requests for "authorization." Indeed, the repeated requests for authorization are always an early sign that the subordinate senses, at some level, the transgression of a moral rule is involved.
6. The actions are always justified in terms of a higher set of moral principles, and come to be seen as noble in the light of some high, ideological goal. For example, the destruction of the Jews in Germany was represented as a "hygienic process" against "Jewish vermin."[18] In the learning experiments, the justification was the advancement of scientific knowledge, or some similar explanation.
7. When the relationship between the subject and the authority remains intact, psychological adjustments come into play to ease the strain of carrying out immoral orders.
8. Obedience does not take the form of a dramatic confrontation of opposed wills or philosophies, but is embedded in a larger atmosphere where social relationships, career aspirations, and technical routines set the dominant tone. Typically, we do not find a heroic figure struggling with conscience, nor a pathological aggressive man ruthlessly exploiting a position of power, but a functionary who has been given a job to do, and who strives to *create an impression of competence in his work*.[19]

Milgram concludes with some sobering observations:

The behavior revealed in the experiments reported here is normal human behavior but revealed under conditions that show with particular clarity the danger to human survival inherent in our makeup. And what is it we have seen? Not aggression, for there is no anger, vindictiveness or hatred in those who shocked the victim. Men do become angry; they do act hatefully and explode with rage at others. But not here. Something far more dangerous is revealed; the capacity for man to *abandon his humanity, indeed, the inevitability that he do so, as he merges his unique personality into larger organizational structures.* . . . It is ironic that the virtues of loyalty, discipline and self-sacrifice that we value so highly in the individual are the very properties that create destructive organizational engines of war and bind men to malevolent systems of authority. Each individual possesses a conscience which to a greater or lesser degree serves to restrain the unimpeded flow of impulses destructive to others. *But, when he merges his person into an organizational structure, a new creature replaces autonomous man, unhindered by the limitations of individual morality, freed of humane inhibition, mindful only of the sanctions of authority.*[20]

---

**Vignette 4**

Just as self-centered humans are programmed to accept authority from legitimate figures, so are they willing to pass the buck to their bosses in terms of responsibility. If an employee can pass off responsibility to an authority figure, many illegal actions can be "justified," such as pirating software, making false declarations, plagiarism, copyright transgressions, and even phone tapping. "My boss told me to do it!" General William Westmoreland used this excuse (referring to President Johnson) to justify some of his actions in Vietnam.

---

Milgram's experimental revelations are disturbing. Such results could only happen from the identity of the separate ego-self. If identity is in the whole, there is no compulsion to do anything that would disturb or violate the inherent integrity of the whole. There is no need to be "liked" by the authority figure, or to feel pressure to do something that is clearly in violation of the welfare of the whole.

As a result of the aftereffects of Milgram's experiments on the subjects, there were many lawsuits filed, and the American Psychological Association now considers performing this experiment to be a violation of ethics. Yet we learned something very graphic from Milgram about the industrial era paradigm: We are all programmed to accept authority without questioning it, if the authority is perceived as legitimate. And, perhaps more important, we obey external authority because we accept the false identity of the ego-self (which needs the approval of superiors to feel competent).

This limited, separate creature will always be more important than some, and less important than others. This is why formal authority is the glue that holds the bureaucratic form together. Superiors tell subordinates what to do, and the subordinates comply. However, with the "knowledge worker" of today often having more expertise than his or her boss, legitimate authority tends to be undermined, as well as, therefore, the bureaucratic form itself. This erosion of formal authority is one of the symptoms of the breakdown of the dominant industrial paradigm.

---

## The Sources of
## Power in Organizations

---

A classic study by French and Raven shows at least five sources from which organizational "power brokers" can draw.[21] These sources can be used separately or combined; the combination of two or more power sources will necessarily enhance the power of the user. The five power sources can be labeled reward, coercive, legitimate, expert, and referent.

*Reward power.* This form of power comes from an individual's ability to dispense rewards in order to get another person or group to do something.[22] Examples include the ability to get someone a raise in pay, compensatory time off, a promotion, or a bonus. Obviously, the potency of the *actual* power exercised would depend on how much the recipient wants the reward offered. Also, the belief that the reward will actually be dispensed as a result of a given action is important. So, for maximum potency, a person using reward power will have to offer a desirable reward and convince the recipient that, by performing the required behavior, he or she is certain to receive the reward. Much as operant conditioning and Thorndike's *law of effect* would predict, rewarded behavior is more likely to be repeated in the future than is unrewarded behavior.

*Coercive power.* This type of power comes from the ability of the power holder to punish or deprive another person or group if the power holder's requests are not met.[23] This is the opposite of reward power, in a sense; in this case, conformity by the power recipient depends on the ability of the power holder to mete out punishment. Many managers will not hesitate to fire an employee (or dock his or her pay) if performance is not up to expectations. To be effective, coercive power depends on the definition of punishment (will the recipient perceive the outcome as punishing?), the probability that it will be used (if workers know that the boss always bluffs about punishment, it will have no impact), and the measurement of desired behavior (is it clear what is desired by the power holder?).

## Vignette 5

"Gil needs to move someone quickly into a regional sales job that entails being out of town about 60 percent of the time. Sharon is the most likely candidate. When Gil asked her to do it, he put a lot of pressure on her. His final comment was: 'Sharon, this is something I want you to do, and it will be good for your career here.' Sharon doesn't want the job because of the travel, but she feels coerced."

Managers have enormous power over subordinates and, to ensure that the power is not abused, management must balance the interests of the organization and its employees. This requires sensitivity.

SOURCE: "Coercion Undermines the Dignity of Subordinates," *Denver Post*, December 5, 1988, 4D.

*Legitimate power.* Also called *formal authority* or *positional power,* legitimate power is a subset of what Max Weber calls "rational/legal power." This power comes as a right of the office or position in the hierarchy. There is little or no question about whether its use is considered proper. Basically, this power is based in an agreement in the collective paradigm; all organizational members accept it as a given. The boss has the right to give orders and to expect them to be carried out. In Milgram's experiments, legitimate power was a major source of influence for the subjects.

## Vignette 6

"Alongside the case studies indicating union acceptance and recommendation of quality circles, there is also evidence of a quite contrary reaction: that in some companies, quality circles may be seen as a *threat to the power and influence of trade union shop stewards on the grounds that circle activity will inevitably result in a less cohesive union membership.*" Quality circles are the Japanese-inspired groups of workers that meet regularly to discuss and implement changes in their work patterns to increase productivity; the theory is that those who do the work know best how to do it.

SOURCE: W. G. Jones, "Quality's Vicious Circles," *Management Today,* March 1983, 97; emphasis added.

*Expert power.* Expert power comes from the presence of special skills or knowledge. For example, a doctor uses expert power to get patients to do certain things, such as exercise or take medication. This assumption on the part of the power recipient is that the "expert" knows more than he or she does, so the recipient had better conform. Evidence from the Milgram experiments suggests that expert power also plays a role in the conformity of subjects. For example, in the early 1960s, the first author was a systems analyst for large, mainframe computers. During that era, computers were not user-friendly, so his expertise was not widely shared and was seen to be arcane yet very necessary to organizational success. This gave him power. Successful use of expert power within its sphere of influence tends to increase or at least maintain its potency, whereas its use outside its prescribed area of appropriateness tends to weaken its strength.[24]

*Referent power.* This form of power comes from the recipient's identification with the power holder. An example of this is "hero worship." Many people who have this power might not even be consciously aware of it. If a person reveres or highly admires/respects another person, that would make it likely that he or she might obey an order or request from the revered one. This is related to (but slightly different from) *charismatic power* (influence based on personality). John F. Kennedy, Vince Lombardi, and Ronald Reagan are often mentioned in this vein.

All of the five sources of power are available within the organizational context. Power, the ability to influence without the sole sanction of the organization, is a force that managers must acknowledge and recognize. Obviously, legitimate power uses the organizational sanction, but the others may be independent of it.

## The Exercise of Power Within Organizations

Exercise of power can lead to one of two outcomes: conformity/compliance or disobedience/conflict. The latter will be discussed in Chapter 19. Conformity, or acquiescence to the requests of the power holder, comes in two forms: behavioral conformity and attitudinal conformity.

*Behavioral conformity* occurs when the power recipient agrees to behave in ways indicated by the power holder, but does not necessarily agree with or like the idea—as in, "I'll do it, but I don't have to like it!"

Sometimes, all the power holder needs is behavioral conformity; prison guards do not care if inmates like the idea of getting back into their cells, they just want them to do it.

When *attitudinal conformity* is present, not only does the power recipient agree to do what is asked, but he or she has the belief that it is the right thing to do. From a manager's viewpoint, attitudinal conformity is preferred most of the time. In the Milgram experiments, many subjects reported that they conformed because they assumed the experimenters knew what they were doing, but they didn't necessarily think it was right (behavioral conformity). However, there were undoubtedly other subjects who thought the stated goals of the research (to learn about the use of aversive therapy in learning outcomes) were worthwhile, and this agreement yielded attitudinal conformity.

One interesting piece of research has shown how the different sources of power are related to the types of conformity.[25] As one might expect, coercive power has been shown to be overwhelmingly associated with behavioral conformity; also, reward power elicits primarily behavioral conformity. Depending on who the authority figure is, legitimate power can elicit either behavioral or attitudinal conformity. Expert and referent power tend to elicit attitudinal conformity, so managers should be concerned with cultivating these sources of power. A powerful manager, then, would be one who, with a given level of legitimate power, is seen as an expert in his or her field and who is respected (even revered) by subordinates.

## Horizontal Power Relationships

Horizontal relationships are those that exist between individuals or groups at approximately the same organizational level. As soon as one of the parties in such a dynamic begins to try to influence others, a power relationship exists. Typically, horizontal power pertains to relationships across departments. Each department makes a unique contribution to organizational success, and, inevitably, some departments are viewed as more important than others. In a study of 14 industrial firms, Perrow found that in most firms, sales had the most power. In some firms, production was the most powerful.[26]

These differences of power come into play in decisions about such issues as budget allocations, staffing, output quotas, and personnel priorities. All horizontal power relationships essentially fall into three categories: staff-line relationships, professional-organizational relationships, and cliques.[27]

## Staff-Line Relationships

Staff-line relationships often give rise to staff-line conflict.[28] Generally, the younger, better-educated, more academically oriented (newly minted MBAs?), and better-dressed staff tend to look down on the older (lower-middle-class?) line managers, who in turn see the staff people as young, impulsive, and lacking any real appreciation for what it takes to run a business.

In this power relationship, each side uses a different source of power to advance its interests. From a strict organizational standpoint (legitimate power), the line people hold the upper hand. Staff has one major function: to *advise* line managers on problems related to their staff expertise. In order for the two sides to work together, the staff must secure some cooperation from the line. Even though they must play a somewhat subservient role to the line, staff people try to influence line managers with their expert power. The result is that line people tend to see staff people as encroaching on their domain, even though they need staff expertise. The staff resents the line, and vice versa.[29] Vignette 7 provides an example of a horizontal power relationship involving some struggle between line and staff.

**Vignette 7**

In a large printing firm, two rival cousins feuded constantly. The college-educated head of the staff support bristled over being dependent upon his blue-collar cousin (the line manager). No printing job could be processed without the cooperation of the line. The personality problem between the two men was never far below the surface; finally, after a team-building intervention by an organizational consultant, the two decided to put the company's goals and future direction ahead of their petty rivalry.

SOURCE: Files of Renaissance Business Associates, Inc.

## Professional-Organizational Relationships

This is similar to the line-staff dynamic just discussed. However, the organizational counterpart usually is a former professional (e.g., an engineer or a lawyer) who has been promoted into management (e.g., an executive position). The modern executive is usually well educated and is likely to show the same kinds of values as the professional,[30] so the professional will likely be supervised and evaluated by a former colleague who has been promoted into the ranks of management. On the organization chart the two will appear to be at the same level, because they are professional colleagues; yet the professional-organizational dichotomy can create conflict.

If the organization attempts to exercise legitimate power through the hierarchy, the professional will tend to resist it. If the organization gives control to the professional, it will lose the ability to ensure that the professional's contribution is organizationally enhancing. This dilemma is usually resolved by letting professionals supervise themselves, but with a fellow professional (called a research administrator) there to supervise the overall effort. Also, many organizations develop "dual ladder" promotion systems, whereby the professional can be promoted without joining the ranks of management. Although the levels are equal from an organization chart perspective, everyone in the organization knows that the organizational ladder is where the "real power" is.[31]

There is often tension between the organization and the professional. The professional typically feels that the organization's rules and regulations are there to thwart him or her. The members of the organization may view the professional as too theoretical and impractical, "hopelessly out of touch with what is really important to the organization."[32] However, these lateral relationships are on the increase, because many organizations are moving to project management or matrix structures. Therefore, conflict resolution in these relationships becomes of central importance.

## Cliques

The final type of lateral relationship is the organizational clique, a coalition formed with the purpose of gaining something for the members involved (the collective self-interest, if you will). *Horizontal defensive cliques* form when the members band together to thwart a real or imagined threat from another part of the organization (at the same level). The *horizontal aggressive clique* forms to push for a specific purpose, perhaps to halt expansionary efforts of another clique at the same level. Hall offers this view:

> Dalton's analysis tends to lead one to view organizations as a "bewildering mosaic of swiftly changing and conflicting cliques, which cut across departmental and traditional loyalties. . . ."[33] While this view is warranted as a check on an overly formalistic view of organizations, it is an overreaction. Cliques would not form if there were not a common base for interaction or if there were not already interaction among members. Rather

than being random, *clique formation obviously begins from the established organizational order and then becomes variations from that order.* The fact that these cliques can form vertically or horizontally and represent personal and subunit interests reflects the constant interplay of the power variables within the organization.[34]

---

## Vertical Power Relationships

---

The formal hierarchy provides power to the incumbents of the top echelons. The top people are responsible for the entire organization and its success or failure, so they have authority commensurate with that responsibility. The *chain of command,* a term used often in the military, reaches its apex in the top positions. Top managers make the strategic decisions for the organization, and they allocate resources to achieve organizational objectives. The formal structure reflects these facts:

> The design of an organization, its structure, is first and foremost the system of control and authority by which the organization is governed. In the organizational structure, decision discretion is allocated to various positions and the distribution of formal authority is established. Furthermore, by establishing the pattern of prescribed communication and reporting requirements, the structure provides some participants with more and better information and more central locations in the communications network. . . . Thus, organizational structures create formal power and authority by designating certain persons to do certain tasks and make certain decisions, and create informal power through the effect on communication and information structures within the organization. Organization structure is a picture of the governance of the organization and a determinant of who controls and decides organizational activities.[35]

The organization structure confers a great deal of formal authority on senior executives. Top managers get their power from this source (formal position in the organization) as well as from other sources.[36]

### Control of Resources

Top managers have control over resources that are necessary for the various aspects of the organization to accomplish their missions. The allocation of such resources has both strategic and power dimensions. Resources can be used to reward certain behaviors and to punish others.[37] The allocation of resources creates a dependency relationship, which in turn confers power. If a department is dependent on a senior executive for authorization before spending money or beginning a major project, this means the department must act to please the executive or risk losing the resource. Compliance then is gained by the strategic allocation of resources of all kinds—information, capital, equipment, people, and other resources.

## Control of Lower-Level Decisions

Top managers actually control the premises for lower-level decisions. "In one sense, the top managers make big decisions while the lower level managers make small decisions."[38] For example, top managers set the large goals for which the company is striving, the types of products to make or services to offer, from whom supplies and raw materials are to be purchased, and what customers to pursue. One way they control decisions is through the control of information. *Vertical communication* means that only the information top management wants sent down through the hierarchy gets sent. Typically, downward communication has to do with guidelines for lower-level managerial behavior, policies, procedures, goals, and the like.

## Centrality

Top managers not only have power by virtue of their position, but, through the appointment of key executives in strategic places in the hierarchy, they build networks of influence. In this way, they get access to information about what is happening throughout the organization and are able to coordinate the activities of others effectively.[39] By surrounding themselves with loyal managers they know and can easily control, top managers increase their overall power.

Top managers form coalitions that increase their power; in fact, if top managers do not build such coalitions, and rely solely on positional authority, they are playing with fire. When Semon Knudsen was hired by Henry Ford to run Ford Motor Company, Knudsen relied on his formal authority alone. By not forming coalitions with Lee Iacocca and others of power in the company, he set himself up for his eventual termination by Henry Ford.[40]

Network centrality enables people to gain power simply because their positions allow them to integrate other functions or reduce organizational dependencies.[41] Who has centrality does not depend on luck, but on the organization's strategy and what is critical to the organization at any given point in time, such as problems and crises.

The closer an individual is to the source of formal authority in the organization (e.g., the CEO), the more power that person will have. In fact, network centrality often determines who emerges as the CEO of a company. If the critical contingencies facing an organization are production related, expect a production person to rise to the top; the same goes for marketing or financial contingencies. In fact, it can be argued that those holding power in an organization will often "invent" problems they can handle so that they can prove their value to the organization.[42]

## Strategic Choice

John Child was the first to introduce the idea that power is actually a key variable in the determination of structure, at least as strong as technology, environment, and size.[43] Since then, Pfeffer and others have extended his basic thesis:

1. Decision makers have more autonomy than the defenders of the environment/technology/size theories will admit.
2. Rather than maximizing effectiveness, power holders "satisfice"; that is, they select structures that meet the minimal requirements of effectiveness, while maintaining their power base.
3. Organizations will, whenever possible, use their power to manipulate their environments to their advantage.
4. According to the theory of "enactment," strategic choices will reflect the *perception of external environmental forces*, rather than objective reality.[44]

According to strategic choice theory, power holders have a degree of discretionary choice when it comes to organizational decision making. They will choose a structure that will maximize their power, not necessarily one that will maximize the organization's effectiveness at the same time.

## Uncertainty or Instability

It has been shown that unstable or uncertain environmental/organizational contingencies can enhance power holders' power if they can respond effectively (or, at least, they are perceived to respond effectively). A characteristic of the industrial era paradigm is a strong bias for certainty and predictability. Also, as we have mentioned, there is a bias toward leaders telling followers what to do. These two factors give power holders leverage in times of flux, when followers are looking for someone to save them. Hence instability is typically a legitimate power enhancer.

## Information Control

Those who control the information in an organization have enhanced and broadened power. Information access, especially under norms of secrecy, can be a prime source of power enhancement, for both upper- and lower-level participants. However, network centrality often gives access to information that helps reduce uncertainty or gives a strategic advantage in some way. The *dominant coalition* (those in positions of legitimate power and their associates) can often control information as a way of maintaining or strengthening their power base:

> It is difficult to think of situations in which goals are so congruent, or the facts are so clear cut that judgement and compromise are not involved. What is rational from one point of view is irrational from another. Organizations are political systems, coalitions of interests, and rationality is defined only with respect to unitary and consistent orderings of preferences.[45]

### Vignette 8

A newspaper article from 1988 notes: "It is a dirty little secret in Washington reporting that many insider-style news nuggets are mined from the second and third level political appointees. *But their relatively low rank should not be equated with lack of power.* More often than not, they are the people who control the paper flow from bureaucrats below to big shots above. By framing the agenda, they get to make policy simply by deciding what options a president might see or might not see."

SOURCE: Andrew J. Glass, "Titles Belie True Power of 'Worker Bees,' " *Loveland Daily Reporter-Herald* (Colorado), November 14, 1988, 2; emphasis added. Used with permission from Associated Press.

## Lower-Order Participant Power

One cannot omit from a discussion of power in organizations the question of lower-order participant power. All of us have known secretaries, word processors, computer programmers, and even typists who have exercised power well beyond their formal authority and gotten away with it. How can they do that? What are their sources of power?

People at lower levels of the organization obtain their power from a variety of sources.[46] Some are based in the personalities of the power exercisers, and some come from their strategic positions in the organization. For example, a person can have power through the strength of his or her *persuasion and manipulation*.[47] Sometimes an attractive or seductive lower-level supervisor can gain inordinate access to the boss's ear, for instance. Persuasion is the most frequent type of upward influence attempted in organizations.[48] Manipulation differs from persuasion in that, in the manipulative mode, the motives for persuading the formal power holder to do something are hidden from view.

Exposure to powerful people and the ability to nurture friendships with them can provide lower-level persons with *access to power* and also, perhaps, *access to information*. This relates to strategic location in the organization; as centrality helps managers to enhance their power base, it helps the lower-level employee, too.

**Vignette 9**

Carl Smith had worked for a growing young manufacturer of chemical products and accessories for the motorboat industry since the owner had a retail store on the south side of town. In those days, it was a struggle to survive. Now, the company was growing at 30% per year, and the CEO had rewarded Carl with a first-line supervisory job, even though Carl didn't have a high school education.

From time to time, the various vice presidents of the company had run-ins with Carl, because he had a nasty temper and was a bit insecure about his position (given his lack of education and formal job knowledge). However, he was reassured regularly by the boss that he was a "valued member of the team." Gradually, Carl got the feeling that he wouldn't be fired no matter what, and he became bolder in his expressions of defiance to the vice presidents. At this point, the vice presidents went to the CEO with the demand that he get rid of Carl, but their pleas fell on deaf ears. The CEO was loyal to Carl, who had been with him since the early days of the business. Carl's power was secure.

*Physical location* can also be important. An office close to the company president's is a symbolic as well as a factual advantage for power enhancement. A person who is physically close to the boss is perceived as part of the "inner circle" and thought to be privy to information that could enhance a power position. "Central location lets the person be visible to key people and become part of the interaction networks. Likewise, certain positions are in the flow of organizational information."[49]

*Specialized expertise* is yet another source of lower-level participant power. Sometimes, a person takes on a difficult task and, in the process of doing it, acquires specialized knowledge that makes him or her indispensable to the organization. For instance, a person in a clerical position may gain power by being the only one in the organization who knows how to perform a particular operation. "Expert power" is common today in the computer software area. A clerical person who knows how to use certain software can be perceived as indispensable. An example of how this power can be used is provided in Vignette 10.

**Vignette 10**

Marie, a clerical worker, became disenchanted with the company she worked for and quit, knowing that her successor would have great difficulty with the billing and receivables software. Marie gave Anne, her replacement, only cursory training before she left.

Anne was at a standstill in her work when the company contracted for Marie to return as a "consultant." This Marie did, but her training of Anne was still rudimentary; she didn't divulge any of the shortcuts she had learned for operating the program with optimal efficiency. Anne gained knowledge for herself about the program only through costly phone calls to the software support office. Marie's intransigence cost the company dearly.

Lower participants can also form *coalitions* to increase their power, banding together to get certain concessions from top management. Even *rules* can be used by lower participants to exercise power. By strict adherence to rules, lower-level participants can really hold things up in an organization. This strategy is very hard for formal power holders to counteract; a boss cannot really criticize subordinates if they point out that they are "just following the rules." For example, the mail clerk who has been told not to take mail after 10:30 a.m. can refuse an important package at 10:32, thereby requiring an expensive courier to make a trip to the post office.

Finally, sheer *hard work* or *extra effort* often can gain a person some influence. Sociologist David Mechanic uses the example of university departmental secretaries, who can have power to make decisions about the purchase and allocation of supplies, the allocation of their services, the scheduling of classes, and at times, the disposition of student complaints. Such control may at times lead to sanctions against a professor by polite reluctance to furnish supplies, ignoring the professor's preferences for the scheduling of classes, and giving others preference in the allocation of services.[50]

People who demonstrate initiative and a good work ethic are often rewarded with influence; power accumulation is often associated with the amount of effort and interest displayed.

**Vignette 11**

Sally Jones was new to the company, a manufacturer of chemicals and accessories to the motorboat industry. She was a gung ho, hard-charging single woman who was placed under the supervision of an older man who had a heart problem and was erratic in his attendance. Sally was often in the CEO's office to talk about her plans, goals, and strategies. Because the CEO was concerned about the productivity of her department (the mass-merchandising sales area), he saw her as a possible future replacement for the older man.

All of this was not lost on the incumbent manager. However, as his productivity had fallen off dramatically with the onset of his health problems, he felt he had no way to defend his position. Sally continued to build up her case with the CEO, even in the face of damaging rumors that she was a drug user. The CEO liked her initiative and her spunk; in fact, her style reminded him of his own. The older man was increasingly left out of important decisions that affected his department, and the CEO turned to Sally.

## A Transformational Look at Power

From the industrial era paradigm perspective (and any other self-centered paradigm, for that matter), power is seen as essential to organizational survival. From this perspective, organizations have tremendous potential for satisfying self-centered human needs, and power becomes social energy that does the organization's work by transforming individual desires into cooperative activities for the benefit of the whole organization.

The continuing success of an organization requires organizational power holders to maintain enough power to direct individuals into the achievement of organizational goals. In fact, "power is required to inaugurate an association in the first place, to guarantee its continuance, and to enforce its norms. . . . circumstances require continual adjustments of the structure of every association . . . and it is power that sustains it through these transitions."[51]

The key to the maintenance of power imbalances (a hierarchy of power) lies in the phenomenon of the addiction to externals. People are interested in the external trappings of power because, in the absence of true meaning in life (the meaning that comes naturally from being identified with the larger whole), they try to make up or invent legitimate meanings, such as to be the president of a company, to be rich, or to have other people fear or respect them. Notice that many of the reasons people pursue power have to do with self-interest or self-aggrandizement. Notice also that this imbalance preserves competition, aggressive attitudes, and feelings of loss when power wanes.

By adopting an identity as part of the larger whole with a specific purpose in that context, feelings of insecurity and the apparent need for externally based power automatically disappear. There is no "position" to protect, no need for status or meaning. If you *are* meaning, you do not have to make up a reason to have meaning. And, perhaps more important, you cannot lose your meaning if that is who you are (a differentiated aspect of the larger whole); however, if your meaning is tied up in status or formal authority (transitory at best), you will be insecure and will struggle to maintain it (or acquire it). An example of a person's negating status as a form of meaning is given in Vignette 12.

---

**Vignette 12**

Actor George C. Scott stunned many people when he refused to accept the 1970 Academy Award for best actor for his work in the film *Patton*. When Scott was nominated for the Oscar, he wired the Academy of Motion Picture Arts and Sciences to request that his name be withdrawn from the list of nominees. "I mean no offense to the Academy," he explained, "I simply do not wish to be involved." Despite his request, he was nominated and was indeed voted best actor, but he refused to take the award. Later, he said, "Life isn't a race, and because it is not a race, I don't consider myself in competition with my fellow actors for awards and recognition."

SOURCE: *Parade Magazine*, February 12, 1989, 1.

## The Political Dimension in Organizations

Politics is rampant in most bureaucratic organizations. Jeffrey Pfeffer defines organizational politics as "those activities taken within organizations to acquire, develop, and use power and other resources to obtain one's preferred outcomes in a situation where there is uncertainty or dissensus about choices."[52] Robert Miles defines politics as "processes whereby differentiated and interdependent individuals or interest groups exercise whatever power they can gather to influence the goals, criteria, and processes used in organizational decision making *to advance their own interests.*"[53]

Both of these authors thus view as *political* in nature essentially any exercise of power within an organization the purpose of which is to advance the ideas, strategies, goals, positions, or causes of the power wielder. From the political model of organization, we see decisions made from power (and the needs of the power holders) rather than from a "rational" perspective that sees decisions as the result of natural rational processes to further the goals, objectives, and strategies of the organization.

This implies a dual reality in organizations. On the one hand, there is a common assumption of rational behavior and decision making. Under this assumption, organizational subunits (and their decision makers) direct their efforts toward some superordinate organizational goal (e.g., profit maximization, market share, revenue maximization). In reality, many do agree about overall corporate goals, but they may differ dramatically about means to attain them. The fact is that purely rational conditions rarely exist.

On the other hand is the existence of political behaviors and decision making. *Careerism* is a good example of behavior from people responding not just to organizational goals, but to their own perceived needs for survival and promotion. This is where "patronage" comes in; the existing power holders give rewards to their loyal underlings, and mentor or guide their careers. Also, subunit differentiation leads to the development of specialized skills and expertise, which allows for greater influence of the subunit in organizational affairs. In the political model, organizations are collections of political groups, with the CEO playing the role of power broker.[54] This, in turn, leads to bargaining and negotiating among competing coalitions or interest groups.

As different groups attempt to consolidate their power in the organization, they form coalitions, groups of people informally bound together by a common interest in furthering some mutual goals or aims. At any given time in an organization there is a dominant coalition, that group of people who have a decisive influence on critical organizational decisions.

The bottom line to all this is that, unless organizational goals and criteria are universally shared among all participants in the organization, the use of power and influence in the pursuit of special interests instead of universal interests is inevitable.[55] Pfeffer notes that "in some way, the relative weighing of the various demands and criteria must be determined. Since there is no way of rationalizing away the dissensus, political strength within the coalition comes to determine which criteria, which preferences are to prevail."[56]

Even though it is widespread in bureaucratic organizations, politics is viewed as a negative thing and is therefore conducted unobtrusively.[57] There seem to be a "frontstage" and a "backstage" to politics; when with their own coalitions, members will talk openly about their vested interests and various intrigues in the "smoke-filled rooms" of backstage. However, they put on different faces for the organization (frontstage). When a group wants to get behind a particular proposal, it is always "for the good of the organization," never because it will really help that group.[58] The idea is to be self-centered without appearing to be so. The goal must always be framed in terms of organizational interests; blatantly ambitious, self-absorbed people are generally rejected by the organization.

At least three tactics are used in operating politically without appearing obtrusive:

1. *Selective use of objective criteria:* Interest groups will push for the use of criteria that will benefit their cause (e.g., in a school, teaching measurement criteria are pushed by faculty who love to teach and are good at it).
2. *Use of legitimate decision procedures:* Committees are used to put the stamp of legitimacy on any action that the group wants to take.
3. *Secrecy:* Political coalitions can benefit from the withholding of valuable information. For example, secrecy of pay and bonus information allows the dominant coalition to selectively reward its allies.[59]

Who can argue with so-called objective criteria? Or with the decision of a legitimately formed and commissioned group? Or with the withholding of certain information (after all, if everyone knew some things, this would create conflict)?

## Political Behavior and External Control

Pfeffer and others have argued that political behavior and the question of who governs an organization is often determined by this criterion: which group or coalition can most effectively transact with various key constituencies in the external environment of the organization. This also is a factor in the design of structure. "A number of power factors enter into the design of a structure, notably the presence of outside control of the organization, the personal needs of its various members, and the fashion of the day, embedded in the culture in which the organization finds itself."[60] Mintzberg posits the following hypotheses:

1. The greater the external control of the organization, the more centralized and formalized its structure.
2. The power needs of the members tend to generate structures that are overly centralized.[61]

Outside control of an organization, whether from government agencies, regulatory boards, or dependence on external suppliers, tends to concentrate decision-making power at the top of the organization. It also tends to reinforce a great reliance on rules, regulations, policies, and procedures. Mintzberg adds: "The two most effective means to control an organization from the outside are (1) to hold its most powerful decision maker—namely its chief executive officer—responsible for its actions, and (2) to impose clearly defined standards on it. The first centralizes the structure; the second formalizes it."[62] In fact, Dill has noted:

Business firms have traditionally been more unabashedly authoritarian than many other kinds of organizations. Both in ideology and in practice, the main locus of formal power starts with the owner-manager; even now in companies with diffuse and relatively powerless ownership, power lies with the top executives. Strong central control is assumed to be necessary in order to achieve the focusing of action, the coordination of effort, the means of conflict resolution, and the control of results that are required to deal effectively with the organization's external environment.[63]

In other words, external control tends to force the organization into being especially careful about its actions. Because it has to justify its behavior to outsiders, it tends to be overly cautious, resulting in high centralization and/or high formalization. In addition, responsibility to an external locus of control necessitates centralization for more accountability. In summary, the ability to deal successfully with an element of the external environment gives political power to that person or group (usually, but not always, the dominant coalition).

## Politics and Organizational Commitment

To succeed, an organization must have at least some degree of commitment from its members. Commitment has three components: satisfaction, identification, and involvement.[64] In other words, the employee must be satisfied with his or her job role, status in the organization, job content, and context. The employee must also identify with the organization; the organization's goals must be, at least to some degree, the individual's goals. Finally, the individual must be involved in the organization; informal relationships, friendships, and after-work groups all play a role in this.

When people are committed to the organization, they are more willing to be directed and controlled by their bosses. In other words, they will follow direction willingly lest they lose their membership. Also, when they perceive their personal goals and the goals of the organization to be congruent, they allow power to be used on them. They become more compliant. Members who are committed will tend to overlook what they don't like and emphasize what they do. Also, members who participate actively in decision making in the organization feel a sense of commitment and are more willing to subordinate their interests to those of the overall organization.

Chester Barnard, one of the pioneers of classical management theory, sums it up with his concept of the "zone of indifference."[65] The narrower the zone, the less commitment to the organization and the more difficult it is to control subordinates. The wider the zone, the greater the commitment and the more easily employees are controlled. Managers can then expand their degree of influence by increasing the commitment levels of their subordinates. They can do this by creating an atmosphere of mutual trust and agreement on goals, by allowing genuine participation on decision making, and by fostering identification with the organization.

In summary, political power can definitely be enhanced through the increase of commitment to organizational goals and objectives. It is to the benefit of the power elite that members be committed to the organization and its goals, because this increases both their power and their longevity as power holders.

## A Transformational Look at Politics

Under the crumbling industrial era paradigm, political skills are a necessity, because the people under that paradigm take their identity and raison d'être from their job role. How much status do I have? How can I get more? How do I compare with others? How can I get to the top and create meaning for myself in life? These are all questions born of the insecurity inherent in the old paradigm.

Under the new paradigm, where whole-centeredness rather than self-centeredness is the norm, politics will be far less important. People will naturally, with identity in the whole, seek to complement others in noncompetitive ways.

## Power and Control in the New Paradigm

The top-down, autocratic model of management worked well in an earlier time of lower personal expectations and educational levels, but it is less suitable for today's business environment. The purpose of the obedience-to-authority aspect of the current paradigm is to ensure compliance from subordinates, even if it is obvious that the "superiors" don't know what they are doing. In the military, unquestioning obedience is an essential attribute; given that the hierarchical, bureaucratic organization that has dominated the industrial age was modeled after the military organization, it has seemed to follow that *positional power* was the route to achieve compliance. However, the more knowledge-based a society becomes, the more impotent a power system based on mere position becomes.

In the knowledge-based organizations of the present and future, sapiential authority, authority that springs from what one knows, will be the source of power, replacing positional or formal authority.[66] Sapiential authority can come from technical knowledge—so that, in an organic work team, the leader is, at any point in time, the person whose expertise is most relevant to that part of the cycle in the collaborative effort—or it can be authority based in personal maturity. It will be common to defer naturally to those with greater degrees of spiritual authority; those whose lives have been exemplary in the expression of integrity and consistency will be increasingly valued as sources of wisdom, knowledge, and experience in how to accommodate the creative processes of life.

Executive power will also change, as Schwartz and Ogilvy note:

In the (conventional) model of the executive, there is a command and control hierarchy. That control is the exercise of hypothetical power, both inside and outside the corporation. Yet, if one were to ask senior executives whether they feel powerful, most would probably say "no." More and more, a complex of constraints restrains the dimensions of their control. If power is the ability to carry out intention, i.e., having your intentions realized, *then power is an increasingly elusive phenomenon.*

Perhaps we might do better to speak of impacts. A decision may indeed produce noticeable results, but these often have little to do with what was intended. Rather than control or power, it may be more useful in the emerging context to speak of the concept of *influence*. Influence connotes a multiplicity of causes for any desired effect. The successful executive may be the one who has the sensitivity to identify that multiplicity of forces, and then, like the adept at *aikido* (a Japanese martial art based on harmony and flow), helps guide these forces to a more desirable outcome.[67]

Obviously, the emerging paradigm is taking us away from the industrial era's emphasis on prediction and control through the exercise of externally applied power. We find, under the new paradigm, more of a desire to blend with the whole, to influence people and situations gently toward preferred outcomes, rather than to force them autocratically. This, of course, is more an art than a science, and the practitioners of such artistry exercise power in a radically new way.

## NOTES

1. Michael L. Tushman and David A. Nadler, "Implications of Political Models of Organization," in *Perspectives on Behavior in Organizations*, ed. J. R. Hackman, E. Lawler, and Larry W. Porter (New York: McGraw-Hill, 1977), 179.

2. Samuel A. Culbert and John J. McDonough, *Radical Management* (New York: Free Press, 1985), 6-7.

3. See, e.g., Stephen P. Robbins, *Organization Theory* (2nd ed.) (Englewood Cliffs, NJ: Prentice Hall, 1987), 176.

4. Gareth Morgan, *Images of Organization* (Beverly Hills, CA: Sage, 1986).

5. See, for example, R. Carzo and J. N. Yanouzas, *Formal Organizations: A Systems Approach* (Homewood, IL: Irwin, 1967); Richard H. Hall, *Organizations: Structures, Processes, and Outcomes* (4th ed.) (Englewood Cliffs, NJ: Prentice Hall, 1987); Amitai Etzioni, *A Comparative Analysis of Complex Organizations* (New York: Free Press, 1961).

6. H. G. Hicks and C. R. Gullet, *Organization: Theory and Behavior* (New York: McGraw-Hill, 1975), 261.

7. See Robert Dahl, "The Concept of Power," *Behavioral Science* 2 (1957): 202-203.

8. See, for example, Michael Korda, *Power: How to Get It, How to Use It* (New York: Random House, 1975); Robert J. Ringer, *Winning Through Intimidation* (New York: Fawcett, 1973).

9. Gerald R. Salancik and Jeffrey Pfeffer, "The Bases and Uses of Power in Organizational Decision Making: The Case of the University," *Administrative Science Quarterly* 20 (September 1975).

10. Richard L. Daft, *Organization Theory and Design* (2nd ed.) (New York: West, 1986), 385.

11. Ibid.

12. Billy Joe Hodge and William P. Anthony, *Organization Theory* (3rd ed.) (Boston: Allyn & Bacon, 1988), 522.

13. Ibid., 253.

14. Ibid., 525.

15. Billy Joe Hodge and Henry J. Johnson, *Management and Organizational Behavior* (New York: John Wiley, 1970), 143-144.

16. Stanley Milgram, *Obedience to Authority: An Experimental View* (New York: Harper & Row, 1974).

17. Ibid., app. I.

18. Ralph Hillberg, *The Destruction of the European Jews* (Chicago: Quadrangle, 1961).

19. Milgram, *Obedience to Authority,* 186-187. Selected excerpt from *Obedience to Authority* by Stanley Milgram. Copyright © 1974 by Stanley Milgram. Reprinted by permission of HarperCollins Publishers, Inc.

20. Ibid., 188; emphasis added.

21. John R. P. French, Jr., and Bertrand Raven, "The Basis of Social Power," in *Group Dynamics* (3rd ed.), ed. Dorwin Cartwright and Alvin Zander (New York: Harper & Row, 1968), 259-269.

22. B. H. Raven, "Social Influence and Power," in *Current Studies in Social Psychology,* ed. I. D. Steiner and M. Fishbein (New York: Holt, Rinehart & Winston, 1965), 374.

23. B. H. Raven, "Legitimate Power, Coercive Power, and Observability in Social Influence," *Sociometry* 21 (1958): 83-97.

24. Arnold S. Tannenbaum, "Control in Organizations," *Administrative Science Quarterly* 7 (September 1962): 236-237.

25. Donald I. Warren, "Power, Visibility and Conformity in Formal Organizations," *American Sociological Review* 33 (1968): 961.

26. Charles Perrow, "Departmental Power and Perspective in Industrial Firms," in *Power in Organizations,* ed. Mayer N. Zald (Nashville, TN: Vanderbilt University Press, 1970), 59-89.

27. Richard H. Hall, *Organizations: Structure and Process* (2nd ed.) (Englewood Cliffs, NJ: Prentice Hall, 1977), 216-219.

28. See Melville Dalton, *Men Who Manage* (New York: John Wiley, 1959), 71-109.

29. Hall, *Organizations* (2nd ed.), 216.

30. Renato Taguiri, "Value Orientations and the Relationship of Managers and Scientists," *Administrative Science Quarterly* 10 (June 1965): 39-51.

31. See R. Richard Ritti and G. Ray Funkhouser, *The Ropes to Skip and the Ropes to Know* (3rd ed.) (New York: John Wiley, 1987).

32. Ibid., 218.

33. Nicos P. Mouzelis, *Organization and Bureaucracy* (Chicago: Aldine, 1968), 159.

34. Hall, *Organizations* (2nd ed.), 219; emphasis added.

35. Jeffrey Pfeffer, "The Micropolitics of Organizations," in *Environments and Organizations,* ed. Marshall W. Meyer et al. (San Francisco: Jossey-Bass, 1978), 29.

36. See Daft, *Organization Theory and Design,* 386-388.

37. French and Raven, "The Basis of Social Power."

38. Daft, *Organization Theory and Design,* 386.

39. W. Graham Astley and Paramjit S. Sachdeva, "Structural Sources of Intraorganizational Power: A Theoretical Synthesis," *Academy of Management Review* 9, no. 2 (1984): 104-113.

40. For a full description of the drama, see the case "The Ford Motor Company" (available from the Intercollegiate Clearing House, Harvard University, Cambridge, MA).

41. Robbins, *Organization Theory,* 192.

42. Jeffrey Pfeffer, "Power and Resource Allocation in Organizations," in *New Directions in Organizational Behavior,* ed. Barry M. Staw and Gerald Salancik (Chicago: St. Clair, 1977), 257.

43. John Child, "Organization Structure, Environment, and Performance: The Role of the Strategic Choice," *Sociology* (January 1972): 1-22; Derek S. Pugh, "The Management of Organization Structures: Does Context Determine Form?" *Organizational Dynamics* (Spring 1973): 19-34.

44. Child, "Organization Structure."

45. Jeffrey Pfeffer, *Organizational Design* (Arlington Heights, IL: AHM, 1978), 11-12.

46. Daft, *Organization Theory and Design,* 391.

47. See Warren K. Schilit and Edwin A. Locke, "A Study of Upward Influence in Organizations," *Administrative Science Quarterly* 23 (December 1978): 304-316; Richard T. Mowday, "The Exercise of Upward Influence in Organizations," *Administrative Science Quarterly* 23 (June 1978): 137-156.

48. Schilit and Locke, "A Study of Upward Influence."

49. Daft, *Organization Theory and Design.*

50. David Mechanic, "Sources of Power of Lower Participants in Complex Organizations," *Administrative Science Quarterly* 7 (December 1962): 353.

51. Robert Bierstedt, "An Analysis of Social Power," *American Sociological Review* 15 (1950): 246.

52. Jeffrey Pfeffer, *Power in Organizations* (Marshfield, MA: Pitman, 1981), 7.

53. Robert H. Miles, *Macro Organizational Behavior* (Glenview, IL: Scott, Foresman, 1980), 154; emphasis added.

54. Ibid.

55. Ibid., 160.

56. Jeffrey Pfeffer, "Power and Resource Allocation," 239.

57. Miles, *Macro Organizational Behavior,* 161.

58. Tom Burns, "Micropolitics: Mechanism of Institutional Change," *Administrative Science Quarterly* 6 (1961): 260.

59. Pfeffer, "Power and Resource Allocation," 241-248.

60. Henry Mintzberg, *The Structuring of Organizations* (Englewood Cliffs, NJ: Prentice Hall, 1979), 288.

61. Ibid., 288-290.

62. Ibid., 289.

63. William R. Dill, "Business Organizations," in *Handbook of Organizations,* ed. J. G. March (Chicago: Rand McNally, 1965), 1097.

64. James G. Houghland and James R. Wood, "Control in Organizations and the Commitment of Members," *Social Forces* 59, no. 1 (1980): 92.

65. Chester Barnard, *The Functions of the Executive* (Cambridge, MA: Harvard University Press, 1938).

66. Robert Theobald, *An Alternative Future for America II* (Chicago: Swallow, 1970).

67. Peter Schwartz and James Ogilvy, *The Emergent Paradigm: Changing Patterns of Thought and Belief* (report issued by the Values and Lifestyles Program, April 1979), 22; emphasis added.

# 16 Strategy and Structure

*Following Chandler, in 1972, I saw the decentralized product-division structure as the solution to the problem of managing diversity. The headquarters unit, freed from the responsibility of day-to-day operations, could formulate long-term strategies and set overall policy. But today I am increasingly sensitive to the un-anticipated side effects of this structure; the financial orientation it imposes on general management, the way planning systems in large firms drive out subtlety, and the lure of exciting large-scale acquisitions and mergers to senior managers suffering the ennui of a move from an operating job to a headquarters position.*

(Richard P. Rumelt,
*Strategy, Structure and*
*Economic Performance*, 1986, p. ix)

*An organization is both an articulated purpose and an established mechanism for achieving it. Most organizations engage in an on-going process of evaluating their purposes, questioning, verifying, and redefining the manner in which they interact with their en-vironments. Effective organizations carve out and maintain a viable market for their goods or services. Ineffective organizations fail at their market alignment task.*

*Organizations must also constantly modify and refine the mech-anism by which they achieve their purposes, rearranging their structure of roles and relationships and their decision-making and control processes. Efficient organizations establish mechanisms that complement their market strategy. Inefficient organizations struggle with these structure and process mechanisms.*

(Raymond E. Miles and Charles Snow,
*Organizational Strategy, Structure, and*
*Process*, 1978, p. 3)

**SUMMARY:** In this chapter we address the relationship between the strategy an organization chooses to pursue in order to achieve its objectives and the structure it uses to support that strategy. We look at this relationship from the perspective of the traditional paradigm and through the lens of the transformational paradigm.

Under the traditional approach to creating strategy, a company first analyzed its own strengths and weaknesses, and then turned to the environment to discover opportunities it could exploit. To arrive at a final strategy, it chose a product or service that presented the best match between the company's strengths and the environment's needs and opportunities. But this approach to strategy is not wearing well. As new challenges and opportunities demand faster, more precise strategic responses from a company, the old way is proving too slow and too restricted to just the top decision makers. In this chapter, we look at the old approach and juxtapose it against the new one, in both cases looking at how strategic decisions affect structural decisions.

The first researcher to uncover a relationship between a company's strategy and the structure it developed to pursue its business was Alfred Chandler of the Harvard Business School. We discuss his work below.

## Strategy/Structure Research

Alfred Chandler defined strategy as "the determination of the basic long-term goals and objectives of the enterprise and the adoption of courses of action and the allocation of resources necessary for carrying out these goals."[1] In his now-classic study of 100 U.S. firms from 1909 to 1959, he found that a pattern emerged. An organization typically began with a simple structure and a single product line. It specialized in what it did best: manufacturing and selling a single product. To do this successfully, a company used a centralized, simple structure to execute a narrowly focused strategy. At this early stage, Chandler concluded, the most efficient structure for this simple type of organization was high centralization, low formalization, and low complexity.

However, as the organization grew, Chandler noted, "a new strategy required a new or at least refashioned structure if the enlarged enterprise was to operate effectively."[2] The organization tended to develop a more elaborate strategy, usually focused on vertical integration. Typically, it would try to expand its activities within the same industry.

This increased activity with several products tends to require more interdependence within the organization, and, therefore, a need for increased organizational complexity (and increased integration efforts). Chandler saw that many firms adopted *functional structures* that allowed for a continuation of centralized control as well as differentiation into functional specialties.

As they became even more successful, firms tended to develop product diversification strategies, wherein a number of different products (not necessarily for the same customers) were developed. Firms became quite large, and the centralized functional organizations became inadequate for the task of coordinating across units making radically different products. Hence the *divisional structure* was born, with its emphasis on accountability, decentralization, and the efficient allocation of functional resources.

Chandler's work has found many supporters, most notably Richard P. Rumelt, who writes:

> When an industrial corporation decides to diversify its product line, it is making a strategic decision whose consequences may alter the fundamental nature of the firm and may involve as well a substantial redeployment of resources and a redirection of human energy. Diversification, however, is neither a goal nor a plan; each firm that diversifies must choose the types of businesses it will enter, the degree to which it will build on past strengths and competencies or require the development of new ones, and the total amount of diversity that is appropriate. There is no single strategy of diversification.[3]

Rumelt studied a sample of 246 firms from the Fortune 500 in each of three time periods: 1949, 1959, 1969. Between 1949 and 1969, most of the largest Fortune 500 companies became significantly diversified and adopted product-division structures. His study produced several conclusions:

1.  The greater the diversification of the firm, the more likely it was to have a multidivisional structure.
2.  The likelihood (with only two exceptions) that a firm had a multidivisional structure increased with time for all strategies.

3. Combined with a definite positive association between diversification and divisionalization was a secular trend toward divisionalization that affected firms in all strategic categories.

---

**Vignette 1**

A West Coast manufacturer of products for the waterbed industry began in the early 1970s as a manufacturer of a chemical designed to eliminate bacteria growth in waterbed mattresses. With a single product, the company used a simple structure, with everyone reporting to the CEO. As the company began to grow with the burgeoning waterbed industry, the CEO began an aggressive research and development program to come up with companion products for the chemical.

New products began to appear in quick succession. The company began making other chemical products (such as one to eliminate odor in waterbeds) plus waterbed hoses, drain and fill kits, patch kits (for leaks in the beds), and mattress heater and liners. Demand for the products began to soar and a functional structure emerged, again centralized, with the CEO providing overall direction.

The company now manufactures and/or distributes hundreds of products for the waterbed industry, as well as products for other industries, such as fabric protectant, futon mattresses, and other products. The CEO still uses a centralized functional structure that he has modified by using "product champions" to bring new products to the market and keep them moving. At some point, he no doubt will adopt a divisionalized structure, especially as his international sales continue to grow.

---

Chandler's original research led to increased inquiry into the strategy-structure link, most notably by Drucker, Thompson, Lawrence and Lorsch, Perrow, Galbraith, Miles and Snow, and Rumelt.[4] Chandler was essentially saying that *structure follows strategy*. But, although there does seem to be some validity to this assumption, the relationship is not so simple.

## Do Strategic Choices Shape Structure?

One can make the argument that an organization's strategic choices concerning its *perceived environment* play a role in shaping the structure and process of the organization. In Mintzberg's view, strategy is a pattern of major and minor decisions that redirect the organization's resources toward environmental opportunities (and away from threats) and toward possible changes in domain (areas of operation) in the future.[5] The popular strategic choice perspective introduced by Child, discussed in Chapter 15, recognizes that the major decisions an organization makes serve to define its relationship with its broader external environment.[6]

Top management has the opportunity and the requirement "to view the organization as a total system, a collection of people, structures and processes that must be effectively aligned with the organization's external environment."[7] This implies quite a range of freedom for organizational decision makers to define the organization's relationship with its environment. An extreme view is the *population ecology perspective* (mentioned in Chapter 12), from which the environment is seen as a limiting factor that will permit the success (even survival) of only those organizations that conform to its requirements.

## Do Structure and Process Constrain Strategy?

A complementary view is the notion that, once an organization has developed a particular strategy-structure-environment relationship, it tends to be locked into that configuration and "may have difficulty pursuing activities outside its normal scope of operations."[8] This fits our earlier discussion of selective perception, the tendency to see only what is contained within the parameters of a given paradigm. Cyert and March found that managers searched only in the "neighborhood of familiar alternatives" for solutions to problems.[9] March and Simon, in their noted discourse on "bounded rationality," point out that managers are limited in their ability to make rational decisions and therefore seek to "satisfice"; that is, once rules, regulations, policies, and procedures are in place, these provide boundaries and guidelines for areas of rational decisions.[10]

Fouraker and Stopford found that diversified organizations made up of autonomous divisions are more likely and able to move quickly into foreign operations than are centralized, functional organizations.[11]

The combined research of Drucker, Chandler, and Perrow shows, among many other things, that *structure tends to follow strategy and that the two must be properly aligned for an organization to be effective.* Other researchers have shown that structure may constrain strategy; in many instances an organization cannot change strategy until it implements changes in structure.[12]

## Industrial Paradigm Adaptive Strategies

There are a diversity of organizational strategies present under the current paradigm. Each is aimed at reducing uncertainty, handling resource dependency, and so forth. Some strategies are adopted by a single organization, others by a group of organizations acting in concert. For example, Robey's *proprietary strategies* are strategies "undertaken by the individual organization acting independently."[13] They include location, product differentiation, pricing policy, inventory policy, public relations, and vertical integration.

*Location.* One choice an organization has is the location of its facilities. For example, locating a chocolate factory in a rural area can help to smooth out labor demands. More factory workers are needed during the winter, the peak season for chocolate and a low-activity time for farming, and then many workers can be free for farming and other activities during the other months of the year. Also, foreign plant location is a good strategy for serving foreign markets with local labor, which yields political goodwill and cheap labor rates.

*Product differentiation.* This marketing strategy, in which minor product differences are introduced, is used to convince consumers that they are buying something "new." In spite of questionable ethics, this seems to be an effective strategy for creating the image of innovation where very little actual product change has occurred. It maintains the strength of an established market while creating the impression of continued product improvements. Also, product differentiation is often used to "segment" a market into low-end, medium-end, and high-end products.

*Pricing policy.* Another proprietary strategy is to lower the price of a product drastically to drive out competition. Lower prices usually mean higher volume, and perhaps the creation of brand loyalty. Once a customer has tried a lower-priced product and is satisfied with it, he or she will tend to stay with it. An example of this strategy is the "loss leader" approach. A company will offer one of its products at cost or very little profit in order to get consumers to try it. Sometimes retail stores will do this just to get customers to come in; the hope is that they will also buy some full-price items during the same shopping trip.

**Vignette 2**

A manufacturer of chemical products for the furniture industry places an unchanged formula of one of its products in new packaging that emphasizes "new and improved" on the front. In addition, the company puts the same chemical formula into products designed for different applications in other industries; all are the same product technically, but they are perceived as different products. Furthermore, through a *private branding strategy,* the same chemical formula is sold under a different company name.

*Inventory policy.* Sometimes organizations will carry unusually high levels of inventory to protect themselves against fluctuations in supply and demand. The lower the ability to predict supply and demand (resource uncertainty), the larger the inventories must be.

*Public relations.* Sometimes an organization will pursue a public relations strategy aimed at creating a favorable image of the organization in the mind of the public. An example of this is the "institutional advertising" done by the oil industry during the late 1970s and early 1980s, when oil company profits were widely considered to be "obscene." Also, companies that have been suspected of polluting rivers have used advertisements touting their concern for the environment.

*Vertical integration.* This is another strategy whereby a company acquires suppliers (to ensure raw material availability) and/or retailers (to ensure control over customer markets). Auto companies have used this strategy quite regularly, buying up automobile parts manufacturers and auto dealerships. The company described in Vignette 3 is pursuing vertical integration.

**Vignette 3**

A medium-sized California manufacturer of products for the waterbed industry and fabric protectant markets has recently purchased several computer-driven injection molding machines to ensure a supply of plastic bottles for its waterbed chemicals, parts for waterbed fill kits, and other products in their line.

What Robey labels "cooperative strategies" call for "groups of organizations to find joint means of managing their shared environment."[14] The hybrid transorganizational form of organization, discussed in Chapter 11, is one such strategy. Others include the following:

- *Contracts:* Companies can enter into specific agreements with other organizations for the purpose of pursuing collaborative activities. These binding agreements typically exist for a limited time period and for specific reasons.
- *Choosing boards of directors:* The phenomenon of *interlocking directorates* is a very common industrial strategy. Members of different organizations can serve on each other's boards, thereby ensuring some cooperation and collaboration. The term *co-optation* is used to describe the process whereby one organization places outside members on its board for strategic reasons.
- *Joint ventures:* These are very common in situations where a great deal of risk is being undertaken (as a way of spreading the risk and marshaling large amounts of capital and human resources). Oil companies commonly enter into such arrangements to explore new fields, refine their products, or test new technologies that are unproven, economically speaking (e.g., coal gasification, the experimental method of extracting natural gas from coal). Joint ventures can allow for control over raw materials and distribution of products and services, elimination of competitors (through co-opting them into the venture agreement), and the aforementioned pooling of risk.
- *Mergers:* Mergers involve the intermingling of assets and the creation of a new entity where two existed previously. "Merger mania" was the catchphrase of the 1980s under Republican leadership, which allowed antitrust regulations to be interpreted broadly. Control of resources and elimination of competition are seen as the two strongest reasons for mergers, but the balancing of risk and potential profit in a leveraged buyout are also potent reasons.[15]

## Environment, Strategy, and Structure

As Figure 16.1 illustrates, organizational decision makers in the industrial paradigm design a *strategy* in response to the perceived opportunities and constraints of the so-called external environment. Conventional wisdom suggests that an organization that does not adapt to changing environmental circumstances can find itself out of business in a hurry.

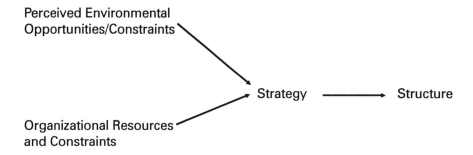

**Figure 16.1.** The Environment-Strategy-Structure Link

## Organizational Adaptation
## to Today's Environment

*Strategic management,* the name often given to the approach to managing that establishes "formal linkages between the external elements of the organization and internal decision-making or resource allocation functions," follows a fairly common pattern.[16] This pattern has the following stages:

1. assessing the external environment
2. formulating the organization purpose, philosophy, mission, and key goals
3. making major choices as to a particular set of long-term objectives and grand strategies needed to achieve them
4. developing short-range objectives and allocating resources to achieve them
5. designing organizational structures and systems to achieve the goals[17]

One definition of *strategic management* is "the process of adapting the organization to its environment to better accomplish organizational purpose and to sustain the organization's long-term viability by enhancing the value of its products and/or services."[18] *Strategic decisions* are those key decisions that tie the organization's mission and purpose to its environmental opportunities and constraints; they are long-term decisions that have a major impact on the organization.

Until fairly recently, many organizational theories have been based on the assumption that organizations respond in rather predictable ways

POT-SHOTS NO. 1662. ©ASHLEIGH BRILLIANT 1980.

**LOOK HOW OFTEN THE UNEXPECTED HAPPENS~**

**AND YET WE STILL NEVER EXPECT IT!**

*Ashleigh Brilliant*

to their environments, shaping their strategies and behaviors to meet market and other demands. As a result, researchers have looked for ways in which environmental factors shape organizational behavior. But two theories have challenged the assumption that the environment is passively "out there," waiting to be perceived. The *strategic choice perspective* discussed by Child (see Chapter 15) calls for a recognition of the dynamic interchange between the organization and its environment; that is, the perception of the environment causes certain strategic moves that, in turn, appear to affect the environment and either validate or serve to modify the strategic choice. More important, perhaps, is Weick's groundbreaking work on *enactment,* which is discussed in depth in the appendix to this volume.[19] Weick argues that organizations do not passively respond to their environments, but, rather, enact (create) them through a series of choices regarding resource allocation, market domain, technologies, products, and so on.

The range of possibilities is actually theoretically limited only by people's imaginations (which are constrained by the assumptions of the dominant paradigm), although Miles and Snow argue that the type of environment an organization can enact is constrained by existing knowledge about alternative organizational forms and managers' beliefs about how people can and should be managed.[20]

---

## The Emerging
## Transformational Strategic View

---

Today, the environment is no longer perceived as a passive entity "out there"—and the neat and tidy strategic management approach no longer seems to fit the realities of the world we live in.[21] Morgan writes:

> Managers and their organizations are confronting wave upon wave of change in the form of new technologies, markets, forms of competition, social relations, forms of organization and management, ideas and beliefs, and so on. Wherever one looks, one sees a new wave coming. And it is vitally important that managers accept this as a fundamental aspect of their reality, rise to the challenge, and learn to ride or moderate these waves with accomplishment.[22]

In the same vein, Vaill notes:

> Twenty years ago, Emery and Trist said that, in turbulent environments, "the ground itself is moving." This image captures the change in context; indeed, it suggests that contexts themselves have destabilized to the point where we can no longer assume that the basic structure of the context surrounding a situation will hold still long enough to make a planned course of action feasible. At least that is the way it feels; more and more, executives cannot count on the presence of markets, the availability of technologies, the likely actions of competitors (foreign and domestic), and of legislators and regulatory bodies, or the reactions of their employees, of their families, and, indeed, of their own bodies and minds to the kinds of actions they are contemplating.
>
> This is what I mean by a destabilized context: things one used to be able to take for granted, treat as relatively given, can no longer be viewed that way. In a destabilized context, you cannot know exactly what your problems are![23]

The metaphors used by these two authors (Vaill's "permanent white water" and Morgan's "riding the waves of change") point to a reality in which all the conventional rules have been suspended and a new sea of change and instability has been substituted. This is our current reality. How, then, does an organization adapt to an environment that is seemingly unstable and unpredictable? What is "strategy" in a world that is apparently out of control?

## A Transformational Perspective
## on Strategy/Structure

In the self-centered, "effect" state of the industrial paradigm, the organization seeks to "manage" its environment through strategic decisions that either *decrease uncertainty* (such as buying a competitor or a supplier) or *increase predictability* (influencing customers, hiring an ex-Pentagon general to help "market" products to the federal government, long-term contracts).

Under the old paradigm, strategic decisions are made from a perspective that is narrowed by organizational or personal self-centeredness. These decisions take into account only those factors that can be seen from the egocentric perspective; however, we know from systems theory that *everything affects everything else,* and strategic decisions that might bring apparent short-term gains can cause immense long-term damage.

In the context in which we have used it, the term *strategy* has an inherent self-centered bias. Strategies that have emerged in the industrial era have focused on the same self-centered human principle: How can we maximize our wealth?

Because our measurement system for success in business (profit-and-loss statements, balance sheets, cash-flow statements) has emphasized economic factors only, strategies have always emphasized what seemed "good" for the welfare of the firm and have ignored the implications of those actions for other parts of the whole. As firms attempt to maximize their wealth without recognizing any need to consider the external costs of their operations, they have used a simple equation as a measuring stick: revenues minus costs equals profits. Under this system, there are two ways to increase profits. The first is to increase revenues. In a self-centered paradigm, this can include strategies such as misleading packaging and advertising, subliminal advertising, and media campaigns emphasizing the fears and needs of self-centered consumers. The second way is to decrease costs. In the self-centered paradigm, this can include hiring unskilled labor for critical jobs, illegal dumping of waste products, using substandard or lower-priced materials, ignoring the need for quality, and utilizing unsafe work practices. Both types of strategies obscure any concern for the needs of the whole.

In the relatively stable and predictable world of the industrial era, when many people were experiencing an increase in external, material well-being, these external effects of self-centered activity were ignored. But now, in the "white-water rapids" of the new age, a new approach to strategy is needed, one that will consider the whole in deliberations about where the organization is to go.

## Creating Strategy in the New Paradigm

Peter Vaill states that "the problem for consciousness in the world of permanent white water is to stay sufficiently open yet sufficiently centered to handle the surprises, puzzles, contradictions, and absurdities that the modern world presents." It is important to "keep consciousness open to the variety and complexity it is immersed in without casting it loose completely from its moorings of familiar thoughts, feelings and values."[24] To do this, Vaill suggests three approaches:

1. *Working collectively smarter:* This approach implies remaining in touch with those around us, their ideas and their energy. We need to stay connected with our environmental factors (this is the second part of the creative process).

2. *Working reflectively smarter:* This approach requires us to reconsider what the world is presenting to us, to examine the grounds on which an idea rests and the assumptions that must hold true if the proposal is to work as planned. Reflection is the capacity to "notice oneself noticing," that is, to step back and notice one's mind and its assumptions relative to the various projects and plans with which one is involved.

3. *Working spiritually smarter:* This approach means paying more attention to one's inner voice, one's spiritual qualities, feelings, insights, and yearnings. It is to reach more deeply into oneself for what is unquestionably authentic. It is to attune oneself to those truths one considers timeless and unassailable, the deepest principles one knows.[25]

Schwartz and Ogilvy add the following insights:

One of the critical functions of management is planning. In the old management paradigm, planning required prediction and control; predicting future conditions and controlling the organization's behavior to realize those objectives. Having already abandoned control in favor of influence, what of prediction? Donald Michael, in his book, *On Learning to Plan and Planning to Learn*, suggests that planning ought to be conceived of as *learning*, which in his terms means "error embracing." Specifically, error embracing means an openness to a multiplicity of interpretations and theories. Furthermore, a good manager is one who facilitates error embracing in others and in the structure of the organization.[26]

The inescapable conclusion is that strategy must be flexible, open to change, if momentary conditions imply a shift in the flow of life's workings. Rigid goals will yield to vision/purpose as a focus for strategic decisions; purpose will no doubt still include an emphasis on effectiveness, but will also emphasize the balancing of stakeholder interests and the interests of the firm. "Thus, it is likely that profit and growth will migrate from the top of a hierarchy of goals into a more complex relationship of a heterarchical sort; two goals among others in a mutually reinforcing system."[27]

## The Role of Vision

For an organization to integrate effectively, a strategy must flow from its vision/purpose. Noel Tichy and Mary Anne Devanna talk about the transformational process as though it were a "three-act play":

- Act I: Recognizing the Need for Revitalization
- Act II: Creating a New Vision
- Act III: Institutionalizing Change[28]

Basically, Tichy and Devanna see the primary leadership goal of today as the challenging of the status quo (by recognizing early warning signs of stagnation), helping to articulate a new vision of where the organization is to go in the future, and helping to create a change-compatible culture.

Many contemporary writers have discussed the importance of vision to an organization.[29] Hickman and Silva see vision as "creating the future"; more specifically, they see it as "a mental journey from the known to the unknown, creating the future from a montage of current facts, hopes, dreams, dangers and opportunities."[30] And in a study of 90 top leaders, Warren Bennis came to realize that all of them shared a common trait: a compelling vision about their work.[31]

But even though many "new age" management consultants are talking about the importance of vision, very few see it for the truly creative act it is. Hickman and Silva, for example, see vision as derived from *the current circumstance* (e.g., current facts, hopes). In our view, vision *must* transcend the current circumstance. It is basically a dream, a hoped-for manifestation of our highest individual and collective purpose. As such, it pulls us to the future.[32] According to management consultant Robert Fritz:

> In order to generate real vision, the vision itself must be conceived independent of the circumstances. The vision must also be conceived without reference to the apparent possibility or impossibility of its accomplishment. Since most people have been trained to think in terms of responding appropriately to circumstances, the unfortunate policy of limiting what one wants to what seems realistic and possible forms a common counter-creative habit. It is actually astonishing to discover how little ability most people have simply to describe what they want to create. And yet, the premier creative act is to conceive of what one wants to create. Real vision is the conceptual crystallization of a result a creator wants to bring into reality.[33]

> Most people ask, "Why?" People of vision ask, "Why not?"
>
> —adapted from a quote by George Bernard Shaw

Vision, then, is a mental construct of some desired future state; however, as Fritz points out, if it is limited by the current circumstances or self-limiting beliefs, values, and so on, the vision will be small. Fritz goes on to say: "Every professional creator either consciously or intuitively thoroughly understands the principle of how a creator conceives of a vision . . . *the creator simply makes up the vision.*"[34]

Vaill issues a useful caveat to all this enthusiasm about vision and purpose. He sees the "purposing" process as essential to the success of an organization. By this, he means "that continuous stream of actions by an organization's formal leadership that has the effect of inducing clarity, consensus, and commitment regarding the organization's basic purposes."[35] However, that alone will not suffice:

> What is still missing are the core values of the person who would do this thing I am calling purposing. What is it the person deeply *cares* about? What is it that *matters?* What does the person have genuine, spontaneous, unrehearsed, unmodulated and unhomogenized energy for? What is at the core of the person's *being?*
>
> To the extent that attempts to state vision and mission and introduce vitality are conducted *apart* from these basic qualities of the executive's character, *to that extent the mission will not take hold, the vision will just be an abstract and impersonal dream, and there will not be the vitality that is needed to set a complex organizational process in motion.* Instead, fear will be the main engine of vitality. People will do their jobs well enough to avoid getting fired even though they do not know the broader mission and purpose.[36]

## Identity and Vision

Vaill introduces an important point here: Unless the individuals of the organization have the personal maturity, integrity, deep personal passion for the truth of life, and 100% responsibility to carry forward the vision of the firm, all of the "vision-driven" strategy being talked about these days is just so much fad. The first step is to ensure that the organization has a vision that is transcendent and inspiring. If this is in place, then mature, responsible people will naturally align with that purpose and give it life.

But the identity of the person creating the vision determines whether the vision is able to do its job. If the separate human ego, trapped in fear and shame, tries to make up a vision, it will necessarily be self-serving in terms of perceived threat or enhancement to self. However, in true identity, one is a creator, and the vision that emerges from alignment with the larger whole and its creative processes will necessarily produce creative, harmonious results. In other words, vision is an important element of a transformative strategy—but only if it emerges from true or spiritual identity.

In the self-centered context, vision is just another "artificial integrator" along the lines of goals, rules and regulations, and the hierarchical order. But accompanied by a recognition of the end of the self-centered state, vision *is* important. If vision is to be ultimately effective, however, it must spring from an intimate connection with the larger order of things.

**Vignette 4**

A purpose, to be really empowering, must have some "juice" behind it. It must excite the deepest passions of the people in the organization. Read the following two organizational purpose statements:

- To provide responsive automation expertise and cost-effective automated services to the organization and its clients
- To *excel* in providing responsive automation *leadership*, expertise, and cost-effective automated services and facilities to the organization and its clients

Notice that the first of these does not inspire; it is rational and precise, but bland. Creation of this statement took two days at an executive retreat; the second one crystallized in about an hour after the senior VP could no longer hold back and, apologizing for "dominating" the process, pleaded for some passion in the purpose. He got it. Strategy, flowing from a transcendent purpose, will naturally produce organizational effectiveness.

SOURCE: Peter B. Vaill, "Executive Development as Spiritual Development," in *Appreciative Management and Leadership*, ed. Suresh Srivastva and David L. Cooperrider (San Francisco: Jossey-Bass, 1990), 8-9. Used with permission.

---

## A Changing
## Managerial Mind-Set

---

Many authors are openly calling for a new mind-set (paradigm) for managing in the new world we have created.[37] It is increasingly recognized that

> managers of the future will have to develop their leadership skills. In particular, they will have to view leadership as a "framing" and "bridging" process that can energize and focus the efforts of employees in ways that resonate with the challenges and demands of the wider environment. This process requires many competencies, especially those that enable the leader to create or *find the vision, shared understanding or sense of identity* that can unite people in pursuit of relevant challenges; and to find means of communicating that vision in a way that makes it actionable.
>
> Managers of the future must pay attention to skills that increase their power to communicate, to create shared understanding, to inspire, and to empower others to take on leadership roles. The leader of the future will not always lead from the front; in times of uncertainty, a significant part of a leader's role rests in finding ways of unlocking the ideas and energies of others. He or she must articulate a relevant sense of direction, while broadening ownership of the leadership process so that others are also encouraged to bring forth their ideas and thus influence the direction that the organization actually takes.[38]

The leader's mind-set must change from that of *cop, enforcer, authority* to one of *enabler, visionary, empowerer,* and *developer.*[39] Leaders must move from the "leader lead and followers follow" mind-set to one in which they ask, How can we collectively create a future that is aligned with the larger picture (of which we are an integral part)? We must move, to complete the paradigm shift, from seeing vision and participation as just "improved" integrators (over the mechanistic ones) to a realization that true vision comes from only one source: true identity.

One responsibility of the new leader is to pursue the "purposing" process outlined by Vaill in his book *Managing as a Performing Art* (1989). Five "values clarification" questions, each in a different strategic area, can help a manager uncover, create, and maintain a sense of purpose:

1. *Economic:* Where is gross revenue going to come from and what is the "bottom line" going to be? What are the economic priorities of the organization?

2. *Technological:* How is the organization going to do what it does? What are its choices of method?

3. *Communal:* What kind of community does the organization want to be? What does it want its members to feel and to receive as a result of being affiliated with the organization?

4. *Sociopolitical:* What kind of citizen does the organization want to be in its environment? What kinds of relationships does the organization want to have with its various constituencies?

5. *Transcendental:* What does the organization want to mean at a deeper level to those who work in it and do business with it?

This process of values clarification is a step toward the ultimate shift into the state of connection with the source of life, and perhaps serves as a useful bridge to that state.

The value of a clearly articulated vision in an organizational context is this: "As the leader crystallizes the vision with greater additive clarity, more and more people can see it, support it, align with it, contribute to it, add to it, and join in its final creation."[40]

---

## Strategy and Structure:
## A Summary

---

The strategic orientation of an organization clearly affects the structure it employs to achieve that strategy. But this relationship is subordinate to the more central relationship: Both strategy and structure are created by (and sustained by) the dominant collective paradigm.

Diversified strategies, designed to cope with complex and turbulent environments, tend to use divisionalized structures or, if the organization is small enough, organic structures. On the other hand, simple, narrowly focused strategies (e.g., a single product line) tend to use centralized, mechanistic forms to implement the strategies. Tomorrow's world will certainly be even more complex and dynamic than today's; therefore, diversified strategies and organic structures seem likely.

In the industrial paradigm, the term *strategy* has come to imply a set of actions designed to manifest some future objective; the implication is that the company knows what it should be doing. But, for an organization that recognizes it is part of a larger whole, strategy becomes the sensing of where it fits in the larger picture and how it might effectively play its role in that picture. The manipulative strategies of the old paradigm, with their emphasis on "getting," are replaced by "giving, serving" attitudes.

In a skein of thought similar to that found in Tom Peters's work, Hickman and Silva argue that *locating, attracting, and holding customers are the purposes of strategic thinking.*[41] Both Peters and Hickman and Silva recommend that the arrogant stance of "We know what customers want" be replaced by a responsive, proactive strategy that satisfies customers' needs. What could the organization provide that would be nurturing and uplifting to the larger picture? How might it be of service to the larger whole? These are the strategic questions that are crucial in new-paradigm thinking. Structurally, these new strategies will no doubt result in smaller, organic units that are flexible, adaptive, and connected in networks that will provide useful products and services for the larger whole.

If we redefine *strategy* as the conscious alignment of an organization with the larger whole of life by listening and sensing how it might most effectively play its role in the processes of the whole, then we have an approach that can work. This type of strategy would most probably create an organic structure that is flexible, adaptive, and reinforcing of personal maturity.

A final note on new-paradigm strategies must include a word about the growing emphasis on a *collaborative* rather than *competitive* attitude. Hickman and Silva say that three fundamental forces are driving this trend:

1. the increasing cost, complexity, and risk of developing new technologies
2. the globalization of markets, leading companies to seek partners who can help them crack foreign markets
3. the emergence of powerful competitors[42]

Atomistic, Darwinian competition is increasingly seen for what it is: out of step with current realities. More and more, companies are seeing that "we are all in this together," and global strategic alliances, joint ventures, and partnerships are flourishing as never before.[43]

## NOTES

1. Alfred D. Chandler, Jr., *Strategy and Structure* (Cambridge: MIT Press, 1962), 13.
2. Ibid., 15.
3. Richard P. Rumelt, *Strategy, Structure and Economic Performance* (Boston: Harvard Business School Press, 1986), 1.
4. See, for example, Peter F. Drucker, *Management: Tasks, Responsibilities and Practices* (New York: Harper & Row, 1974); Paul R. Lawrence and Jay W. Lorsch, *Organization and Environment: Managing Differentiation and Integration* (Boston: Harvard Business School, Division of Research, 1967); James D. Thompson, *Organizations in Action* (New York: McGraw-Hill, 1967); Jay Galbraith, *Designing Complex Organizations* (Reading, MA: Addison-Wesley, 1973); Charles Perrow, "A Framework for the Comparative Analysis of Organizations," *American Sociological Review* 32 (1967):

194-208; Raymond E. Miles and Charles C. Snow, *Organizational Strategy, Structure, and Process* (New York: McGraw-Hill, 1978); Rumelt, *Strategy, Structure.*

5. Henry Mintzberg, "Patterns in Strategy Formulation" (working paper, McGill University, Faculty of Management, 1976).

6. John Child, *Organization: A Guide to Problems and Practice* (2nd ed.) (London: Harper & Row, 1984).

7. Miles and Snow, *Organizational Strategy,* 6.

8. Ibid., 7.

9. Richard Cyert and James March, *A Behavioral Theory of the Firm* (Englewood Cliffs, NJ: Prentice Hall, 1963).

10. James G. March and Herbert A. Simon, *Organizations* (New York: John Wiley, 1958).

11. L. E. Fouraker and J. M. Stopford, "Organizational Structure and the Multinational Strategy," *Administrative Science Quarterly* 12 (March 1968).

12. Miles and Snow, *Organizational Strategy,* 8.

13. Daniel Robey, *Designing Organizations* (2nd ed.) (Homewood, IL: Irwin, 1986), 325-331.

14. Ibid., 331-339.

15. Jeffrey Pfeffer, "Merger as a Response to Organizational Interdependence," *Administrative Science Quarterly* 17 (1972): 382-394.

16. William R. Boulton, William M. Lindsay, Stephen G. Franklin, and Leslie W. Rue, "Strategic Planning: Determining the Impact of Environmental Characteristics and Uncertainty," *Academy of Management Journal* 25 (September 1982): 501.

17. See John A. Pearce II and Richard B. Robinson, Jr., *Strategic Management* (Homewood, IL: Irwin, 1982), 4-5; Leslie W. Rue and Phyllis C. Holland, *Strategic Management* (New York: McGraw-Hill, 1986), 4-20.

18. Billy Joe Hodge and William P. Anthony, *Organization Theory* (3rd ed.) (Boston: Allyn & Bacon, 1988), 239.

19. Karl Weick, *The Social Psychology of Organizing* (Reading, MA: Addison-Wesley, 1969).

20. Miles and Snow, *Organizational Strategy,* 6.

21. See, for example, Gareth Morgan, *Riding the Waves of Change* (San Francisco: Jossey-Bass, 1988); Peter B. Vaill, *Managing as a Performing Art: New Ideas for a World of Chaotic Change* (San Francisco: Jossey-Bass, 1989).

22. Morgan, *Riding the Waves of Change,* xii. Used with permission from the publisher.

23. Vaill, *Managing as a Performing Art,* 3.

24. Ibid., 29-30.

25. Ibid., 29-31.

26. Peter Schwartz and James Ogilvy, *The Emergent Paradigm: Changing Patterns of Thought and Belief* (report issued by the Values and Lifestyles Program, April 1979), 21.

27. Ibid., 25.

28. Noel M. Tichy and Mary Anne Devanna, *The Transformational Leader* (New York: John Wiley, 1986), 5-6.

29. See, for example, William B. Joiner, "Leadership for Organizational Learning"; Dennis T. Jaffe, Cynthia D. Scott, and Esther M. Orioli, "Visionary Leadership: Moving a Company From Burnout to Inspired Performance"; Willis Harman, "Transformed Leadership: Two Contrasting Concepts"; Harrison Owen, "Leadership by Indirection"; Robert Fritz, "The Leader as Creator"; Dick Richards and Sarah Engel, "After the Vision: Suggestions to Corporate Visionaries and Vision Champions"; all in *Transforming Leadership: From Vision to Results,* ed. John D. Adams (Alexandria, VA: Miles River, 1986).

30. Craig R. Hickman and Michael A. Silva, *Creating Excellence* (New York: New American Library, 1984), 151.

31. Warren Bennis, *On Becoming a Leader* (Reading, MA: Addison-Wesley, 1989).

32. For a complete discussion of "future pull," see George Land and Beth Jarman, *Breakpoint and Beyond: Mastering the Future Today* (New York: Harper Business, 1992), chap. 9.

33. Fritz, "The Leader as Creator," 174-175.

34. Ibid., 174; emphasis added.

35. Peter B. Vaill, "The Purposing of High Performance Systems," *Organizational Dynamics* (Autumn 1982): 325.

36. Peter B. Vaill, "Executive Development as Spiritual Development," in *Appreciative Management and Leadership*, ed. Suresh Srivastva and David L. Cooperrider (San Francisco: Jossey-Bass, 1989), 326; emphasis added. Used with permission.

37. See, for example, Vaill, *Managing as a Performing Art*; Morgan, *Riding the Waves of Change*; Tichy and Devanna, *The Transformational Leader*; Hickman and Silva, *Creating Excellence*; James O'Toole, *Vanguard Management* (Garden City, NY: Doubleday, 1985); Alan Raymond, *Management in the Third Wave* (Glenview, IL: Scott, Foresman, 1986).

38. Morgan, *Riding the Waves of Change*, 6-7. Used with permission from the publisher.

39. See Thomas J. Peters and Robert H. Waterman, Jr., *In Search of Excellence: Lessons From America's Best-Run Companies* (New York: Harper & Row, 1982).

40. Fritz, "The Leader as Creator," 175.

41. Hickman and Silva, *Creating Excellence*, 46-48.

42. Ibid., 46.

43. John A. Byrne, "The Virtual Corporation," *Business Week*, February 8, 1993, 37-41; David Limerick and Bert Cunnington, *Managing the New Organisation: A Blueprint for Networks and Strategic Alliances* (Chatsworth, NSW, Australia: Business and Professional Publishing, 1993).

**PART IV**

■ THE PROCESSES
OF ORGANIZATION

# 17  The Organizational Life Cycle

*New organizations are continually being created in both the public
and private sectors. New business firms, new public agencies, new
consumer advocate groups . . . the list is nearly endless . . . are
formed with great frequency. But, just as the rates of formation are
high, so, apparently are the rates of demise. The rates of failure of
small businesses are legendary. . . . The point is that when one
views the population of organizations, one sees demographic
changes. These demographic changes reflect, in the aggregate,
the fact of birth, life and death among organizations.*
(John R. Kimberly, Robert H. Miles, and Associates,
*The Organizational Life Cycle*, 1980, pp. 2-3)

---

**SUMMARY:** In this chapter, we examine the creation, growth, and decline of
organizations through the lenses of several models of the organizational life
cycle, a metaphor based on the biological model of growth and evolution.
Under this model, all organizations are understood to begin with their creation, to then pass through an early developmental stage and various stages
of growth, and then to stagnate and decline (unless there is an intervention
to forestall or prevent this). We will examine how this research fits with the
assumptions of the metamodel of organization.

---

## The Growth and
## Development of Organizations

---

Every organization seems to pass through a cycle on its way to maturity. Early research suggested that a *biological metaphor* could be used

to explain how a company is born, grows, and eventually decays and/or dies. One of the pioneers in this field was Mason Haire, a social psychologist whose article "Biological Models and Empirical Histories in the Growth of Organizations" supported the idea that organizations followed biological growth curves.[1] Haire was the first to identify a primary component related to organizational stagnation or demise: that the administrative component in large organizations can grow to unwieldy proportions. "Just as there is an absolute limit to the size of a physical structure, such as a bridge, there is an absolute limit beyond which an organization cannot support its own operations," he pointed out.[2]

Other researchers have since provided some support for the biological analogy, although J. W. Gardner adds an important disclaimer:

> Like people and plants, organizations have a life cycle. They have a green and supple youth, a time of flourishing strength and a gnarled old age. . . . But organizations differ from people and plants in that their cycle isn't even approximately predictable. An organization can go from youth to old age in two or three decades, or it may last for centuries. Most important, it may go through a period of stagnation and then revive. In short, decline is not inevitable.[3]

There is now some agreement that the biological metaphor is limited; organizations don't have to decay and die.[4] Also:

> Organizations do not follow predictable biosocial stages of development. They share some common properties with biological systems . . . for example, they are born, they import energy, transform it and produce an output, and are differentiated and functionally specialized. However, they also have unique capacities such as negentropy and go through changes that are explained more by such factors as environmental threats, opportunities, size and technology than by unfolding maturational processes. Organizations are not easily categorized by such labels as "childhood," "adolescence," and so on. The laws of social systems are not the same as those of biological systems.[5]

But without doubt, an organization grows, changes, and requires continuous nourishment for survival; otherwise, it may die. Some, especially small, businesses die even before they have progressed through the cycle. Some estimates hold that four out of five small businesses will not survive to their fifth year, largely because of underfinancing, poor management, unfavorable economic conditions, fickle consumer demands, and a variety of other factors. According to Freeman, Carroll, and Hannan:

New organizations suffer from a *liability of newness,* a greater risk of failure than older organizations, because they depend on the cooperation of strangers, have low levels of legitimacy, and are unable to compete effectively against established organizations. . . . New organizations of a new form are more likely to fail than new organizations with an established form. As time passes, structures stabilize and ties with environments become durable, causing death rates to fall for organizations with both common and innovative forms.[6]

Organizations that do prosper evolve through a number of transitions, successfully addressing a particular set of problems or challenges that comes with each stage. This *life-cycle approach* has some key assumptions:

1. There are distinct stages through which organizations must proceed.
2. The stages follow a consistent pattern.
3. The transitions from stage to stage are predictable rather than random occurrences.

In many organizations, decline does seem to set in eventually. Much of organizational research and practice in the past 30 years has addressed this problem, which seems to be signaled by *increasing bureaucratization and stagnation.*

In the following pages, we review five of the most widely respected life-cycle models, with an eye toward their unique perspectives and lessons for organizational transformation. The models have some similarities, yet they are different enough to be a useful source of inquiry into the nature of organizational growth and development.

## The Greiner Model

Larry E. Greiner has developed a model in which

growing organizations move through five distinguishable phases of development, each of which contains a relatively calm period of growth that ends with a management crisis. . . . since each phase is strongly influenced by the previous one, a management with a sense of its own organization's history can anticipate and prepare for the next developmental crisis.[7]

The basic theme of this work is that the future of an organization may be determined less by outside forces than by the organization's history. This notion is in direct contradiction to Chandler's assertion that a company's strategy (and its resultant structure) is a product of outside market opportunities and forces.

Greiner's theory is based on two discrete yet interdependent phenomena:

1. *evolution:* prolonged periods of growth and expansion in which there are no major upheavals in organizational practices
2. *revolution:* the periods of substantial turmoil in organizational life

Figure 17.1 depicts this process.

Greiner uses five key dimensions in his model:

1. age of the organization
2. size of the organization
3. stages of evolution
4. stages of revolution
5. growth rate of the industry

Basically, Greiner sees the evolutionary and revolutionary cycles to be the same regardless of the size or age of the company; however, low-, medium-, and high-growth companies have cycles that occur over different time horizons and, obviously, high-growth companies get bigger more quickly than do low- or medium-growth companies.

With reference to age, Greiner argues that management problems and principles are "rooted in time."[8] A particular structural component (e.g., decentralization) may have meaning at one time in an organization's life, but not at another time. Also, he sees that managerial *attitudes* tend to become institutionalized; not only do they become more predictable over time, they become "fossilized," or hard to change.

As we have noted previously, increased size tends to bring on problems of coordination, interdependence, multiplying levels and horizontal differentiation, and so on. Also, growth rate plays a role; in high-growth industries, "evolution can be prolonged, and revolution delayed, when profits come easily."[9] Revolutions do seem to be much more severe when the market turns down and profit opportunities shrink.

In examining the Greiner model's five specific phases of evolution and revolution, keep in mind that each evolutionary period has a specific management style used to sustain growth, and each revolutionary period has a dominant management problem that must be solved before the next evolutionary stage can start. Also, each phase is both an *effect* of the previous phase and a *cause* of the next phase.

*Phase 1: creativity.* A young organization grows and thrives because of energetic, committed leadership and resourceful employees. Everyone has the "vision" in this phase. Communication is

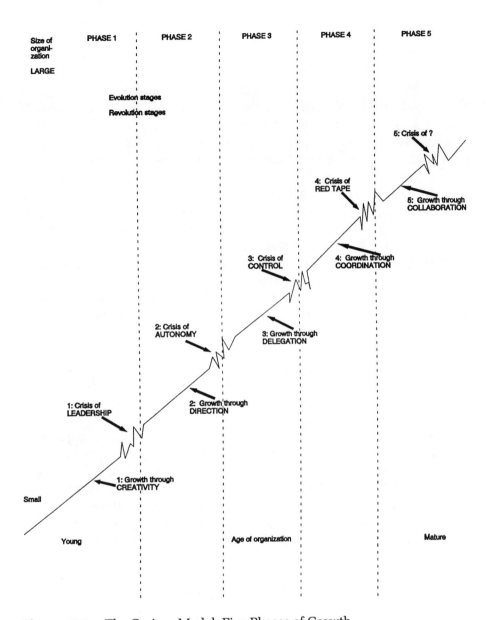

**Figure 17.1.** The Greiner Model: Five Phases of Growth

SOURCE: Larry E. Greiner, "Evolution and Revolution as Organizations Grow," *Harvard Business Review* 50 (July-August 1972): 39. Reprinted by permission of *Harvard Business Review*. Copyright © 1972 by the President and Fellows of Harvard College, all rights reserved.

frequent and face-to-face. Feedback is immediate, and most work long hours in a "labor of love." However, at a certain point, along comes a *leadership crisis*. The owner-founder may have technical competence but very little management expertise. Specific skills in people management, motivation, financial management, manufacturing, and the like are needed. In many small companies, the owner-manager is the barrier to growth for this very reason. So who is to lead the company out of this crisis?

*Phase 2: direction.* Companies that survive the first crisis hire a capable business manager and things run smoothly for a while. Usually, a functional structure is established, reporting requirements set, a hierarchy developed, and specialists hired. Communications become more formal and accounting/financial control systems are installed. Then comes the *autonomy crisis.* Lower-level employees find themselves restricted by cumbersome bureaucratic red tape and long for the good old days. They begin to feel torn between following procedures and taking initiative on their own (they generally are closer to the market than top management and very often know more of what is needed). What is clearly needed is delegation; however, managers who are used to giving orders often find it hard to empower others to take on responsibility. So the company must begin to decentralize.

*Phase 3: delegation.* The successes of this phase build on the advantages of decentralization. Specifically, profit centers are set up, authority and responsibility are delegated, with appropriate accountability, management by exception becomes the rule, and so on. This stage is very useful for the expansion of the company, as people are given relative freedom to spread their wings. However, this leads inevitably to a *control crisis.* Top executives begin to sense that they are losing control over things; freedom "becomes a parochial attitude."[10] Some companies attempt a return to centralized management, which is often a disaster. So the company must learn to coordinate.

*Phase 4: coordination.* This phase includes the use of formal systems for achieving greater levels of coordination or *integration,* for example, the conversion to a product or geographic structure, formal planning procedures, staff additions to facilitate coordination, and centralized data processing/management information systems. However, all this inevitably leads to a red-tape crisis. The proliferation of systems eventually builds a bridge between line and staff managers, and between headquarters and the field. This signals the need for the next revolution.

*Phase 5: collaboration.* This phase involves the initiation of project teams, greater interpersonal collaboration, team building, greater spontaneity in management, problem-solving task forces, and so on.

Social control, personal responsibility, and self-discipline take the place of formal control systems. The company mission and philosophy become increasingly important. Headquarters staff are reduced and red tape is eliminated where possible. This leads to the *???* *crisis.* Greiner speculates that the next crisis will be one that could be called *psychological saturation.* By this, he means that employees grow weary and burned out by the pressure of teamwork and the constant demand for innovative solutions.[11] He suggests:

> The phase 5 revolution will be resolved by new structures and programs that allow employees to periodically rest, reflect, and revitalize themselves. We may even see companies with dual organization structures: a "habit" structure for getting the daily work done, and a "reflective" structure for stimulating perspective and personal enrichment. Employees could then move back and forth between the two structures as their energies dissipated and refueled.[12]

Greiner goes on to suggest some managerial strategies for dealing with each of the crises discussed above. These are summarized in Table 17.1. Greiner cautions managers to remember the following guidelines:

1. Know where you are in the developmental sequence.
2. Recognize the limited range of solutions.
3. Realize that solutions breed new problems.

## The Lewin Change Model

The Lewin change model provides an interesting way to look at the problem of organizational change as it relates to the crises Greiner addresses.[13] Developed in the late 1940s, Lewin's model is based on the notion that changes in organizations are caused by changes in the magnitude, direction, and/or absolute number of factors that facilitate change (driving forces); by changes in the factors that oppose change (restraining forces); or both. This relationship is represented pictorially in Figure 17.2.

The process of change, according to Lewin, has three phases:

1. *unfreezing:* the upsetting of the balance between driving and restraining forces
2. *moving:* an increase in driving forces or reduction of restraining forces
3. *refreezing:* the establishment of a new equilibrium between driving and restraining forces

**Table 17.1**    Organizational Practices Corresponding to the Five Phases

| Category | Phase 1 | Phase 2 | Phase 3 | Phase 4 | Phase 5 |
|---|---|---|---|---|---|
| Management focus | make and sell | efficiency of operations | expansion of market | consolidation of organization | problem solving and innovation |
| Organization structures | informal | centralized and functional | decentralized and geographic | line staff and product groups | matrix of teams |
| Top management style | individualistic and entrepreneurial | directive | delegative | watchdog | participative |
| Control system | market results | standards and cost centers | reports and profit centers | plant and investment centers | mutual goal setting |
| Management reward emphasis | ownership | salary and merit increases | individual bonus | profit sharing and stock options | team bonus |

SOURCE: Larry E. Greiner, "Evolution and Revolution as Organizations Grow," *Harvard Business Review* 50 (July-August 1972): 45. Reprinted by permission of *Harvard Business Review.* Copyright © 1972 by the President and Fellows of Harvard College, all rights reserved.

Thus the evolutionary period in Greiner's model would be a time of relative equilibrium between the two forces, and a revolutionary crisis would be precipitated by an imbalance. Presumably, if the organization resists the changes demanded by the imbalance, organizational stagnation or worse would be the outcome.

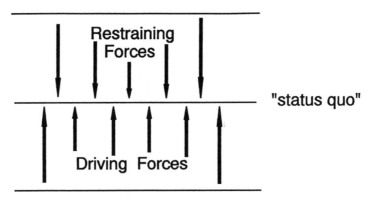

**Figure 17.2.**    Lewin's Force-Field Analysis

The driving forces may also be called *forces for change.* Pressures for change arise when there is a discrepancy between the desired (or potential) level of functioning of the organization and the actual state of functioning. That is, "a motive force for change occurs in 'discrepant situations,' in cases of a difference between stimulus and a person's 'internal anchors' of attitudes, perceptions or whatever."[14] In other words, a critical mass of people in the organization see the need for change because of internal and/or external factors relating to the organization.

Some of the internal factors that may encourage change are as follows:

1. favorable experiences with changes in the past
2. changes or reordering of organizational goals
3. strikes, low productivity, and/or rising costs
4. differences between personal and organizational goals
5. the presence of innovators or "change agents"
6. unfavorable organizational climate
7. resistance to authority
8. other situations involving conflict[15]

External factors that can lead to change include the following:

1. changes in knowledge or technology
2. ideological and cultural changes
3. ecological pressures
4. demographics of the population
5. the distribution of political power
6. general economic conditions[16]

Restraining forces, or forces for stability, include a variety of personal and systemic sources of resistance.[17] Personal resistance comes from individuals' perceptions that change will threaten the status quo or will likely bring consequences they judge to be personally unfavorable. Systemic resistance includes resource limitations, constraints on behavior, vested interests, accumulation of official constraints on behavior, sunk costs ("We have so much invested in this!"), interorganizational agreements, and the like.

So, to make sure the organization comes through the *revolutionary crisis* successfully, the manager needs to ensure that the driving forces for change are greater than the restraining forces preventing it. The Lewin change model also predicts that it is better to reduce restraining forces than to try to beef up driving forces. (Increasing driving forces can have the unintended consequence of encouraging more resistance—that is, increasing restraining forces.)

## The Cameron and Whetton Model

The Cameron and Whetton model is similar to the Greiner model, with some exceptions.[18] These authors represent the organizational life cycle with another five-stage model:

1. *The entrepreneurial stage:* The organization is in its infancy. There is low formalization, goals are not clearly spelled out, and creativity/hard work is strong.

2. *The collectivity stage:* This stage solidifies the gains of the prior stage with a clear mission and more hard work.

3. *The formalization and control stage:* Now the organization begins to formalize its structure. Innovation is deemphasized and rules, regulations, policies, and procedures are emphasized. Decisions are centralized and increasingly conservative; that is, they need to be justified from a pragmatic, dollars-and-cents point of view. Roles are formalized, reporting relationships specified, and accountability tied down.

4. *The elaboration-of-structure stage:* The organization now diversifies its markets and searches for new growth opportunities. The structure becomes more decentralized and complex.

5. *The decline stage:* Because of declining productivity, shrinking markets, obsolete technology, excessive competition, or the like, the organization begins to find the demand for its products shrinking. Management looks for new ways to revive the company. Turnover among key personnel increases, as does conflict in the organization. Decision making becomes centralized as new leadership wrestles with the decline.

Figure 17.3 is a representation of this life cycle.

## The Ainsworth-Land Model

The life-cycle model developed by George Ainsworth-Land, vice chairman of Wilson Learning Systems, Inc., is similar to the others, but it also has some important differences.[19] Figure 17.4 is a pictorial representation of the model.

In Phase I of this model (the entrepreneurial or formative stage), the task is to create "a pattern that works." In other words, from one's set of beliefs, attitudes, and values (paradigm), come up with a formulation that produces a desired set of results. This pattern is usually articulated by a leader (the founder), and a small cadre of people who believe in the leader and/or the company march forward with continued success.

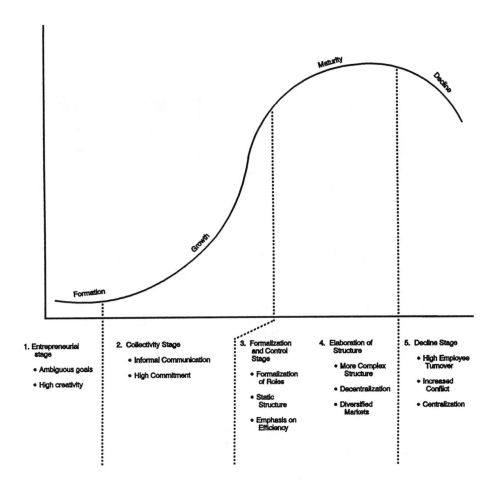

**Figure 17.3.** Organizational Life Cycle

SOURCE: Kim Cameron and David A. Whetton, "Perceptions of Organizational Effectiveness Over Organizational Life Cycles," *Administrative Science Quarterly* 26 (1981): 527. © 1988 by Cornell University. 0001-8392/88/3302-0 177/$1.00.

Usually, there is very little formalization at this stage, and a lot of frequent, face-to-face contact is the norm.

In Phase II (the administrative or normative stage), the developmental task is to refine, apply, and extend the pattern that works. In other words, "If it ain't broke, don't fix it!" Here, the collective paradigm becomes very rigid. The systems are formalized, hierarchy is elaborated, and formal relationships spring up to replace the informal, collegial atmosphere of the formative stage. The organization, in the latter stages of this phase, develops independence from the leader, and a full-fledged bureaucracy is in place. Profits continue to rise and the company seems to be able to do no wrong. Matthew Juechter makes some interesting observations about Phase II:

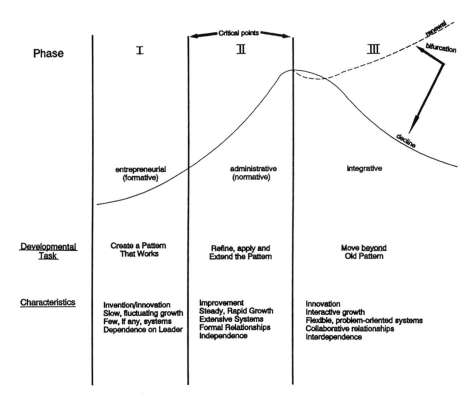

**Figure 17.4.**   Ainsworth-Land Life-Cycle Model

SOURCE: Lynda Lawrence, "Phase Change: Larry Wilson on Selling in a Brave New World," special report, *Training*, February Suppl. 1988, 11-14. Reprinted with permission from the FEB SUPPL. 1988 issue of TRAINING Magazine. Copyright © 1988. Lakewood Publications, Minneapolis, MN. All rights reserved. Not for resale.

Life in a Phase II organization goes something like this. You're welcomed with a standard speech by the CEO and the standard orientation program. You are given the policies and procedures manual. You are told where to sit, what your title will be, and what your job description will be. Someone comes along some six months later and, if you have done the things in your job description, you'll probably get a standard raise.

The good thing about working for Phase II organizations is that it's very hard to screw up. The bad thing is there's very little opportunity to grow or to create. Command and control organizations are set up so that most of the thinking goes on at the very top. *It's assumed that a small group will run things—usually about 6% of the whole organization.* The rest are told, "Be loyal. Do your job."

If you agree with the assumptions of a Phase II organization, what does that mean *for a person's spirit?* Where are the opportunities for adventure, joy, risk, making a difference and—at the very highest level—*for having some connection with your true nature and spirit?* Is it any wonder that people are ready to bust out of the building at 4 o'clock, leap into their RV's and take off to the woods to recapture some of who they are—the precious part for which they aren't being paid?[20]

Then, in Phase III, something radically different happens. The old pattern no longer works. What is required here is a paradigm shift; the organization must move beyond old patterns and develop new ones more fitting with the existing circumstances of the moment. The management styles that were successful in Phase II are no longer successful. The short-term political behavior that was very successful in Phase II no longer works. The left-brain, analytic approach of the administrative phase is suddenly incomplete. The choice, then, in Phase III, is to break completely with the past and allow a new *vision* and *pattern that works* to emerge. The reader should note that a "bifurcation" (Ainsworth-Land's term) occurs at the end of Phase II; the organization can either go down (remaining a "cash cow" for some time) or it can renew itself and begin another life cycle. But, to renew, it must create a new pattern.

## The Tichy Model

Noel Tichy's model is similar to Greiner's in one respect: Both emphasize the necessity for organizations to solve basic problems at various stages in the cycle.[21] Tichy argues:

> Organizations have three interrelated cycles. These cycles are not based on maturational processes but on the dynamics of social systems surviving and making adjustments in various contexts. Organizations must make cyclical adjustments over time. These adjustments come about as the organization attempts to resolve three basic ongoing dilemmas.
>   The first dilemma is the *technical design problem*. Here, the organization faces a production design problem; that is, social and technical resources must be arranged so that the organization produces some desired output. The second is the *political allocation problem* or, in other words, the problem of allocating power and resources. The uses to which the organization will be put, as well as who will reap the benefits from the organization, must be determined. The third is the *ideological or cultural mix problem*. As social tools, organizations are held together by normative glue, that is, by the sharing of certain important beliefs by its members. Hence, the organization must determine what values need to be held by what people.[22]

Tichy goes on to say that these problems are never totally resolved, and that, at different points in time, each of them comes up for resolution. These areas are conceptualized in cyclical terms, and the cycles may overlap or reinforce each other (a peak indicates a high need for adjustment and a valley means a smooth, nonproblematic time for that cycle). This is depicted in Figure 17.5. Each cycle requires a different set of problem-solving strategies and has its own type of uncertainty. Organizational health, according to Tichy, is directly related to an organization's ability to deal with the "problem cycles."

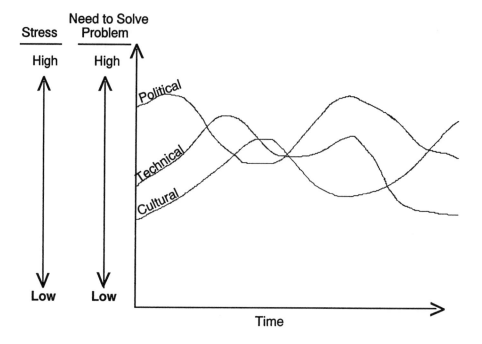

**Figure 17.5.** Organizational Cycles

SOURCE: Noel M. Tichy, "Problem Cycles in Organizations and the Management of Change," in *The Organizational Life Cycle: Issues in the Creation, Transformation and Decline of Organizations,* ed. John R. Kimberly, Robert H. Miles, and Associates (San Francisco: Jossey-Bass, 1980), 165. Used with permission from the publisher.

## Gareth Morgan's Critique of the Life-Cycle Approach

In his critique of the whole "organization as organism" approach, Gareth Morgan points out that the organismic metaphor has been a useful lens through which to view organizations, one that has produced a number of strengths:[23]

1. It emphasizes the relationship between the organization and its environment, something ignored by earlier mechanical theories.
2. By asserting that the management of organizations can be improved by systematic attention to the "needs" that must be satisfied if the organization is to survive, the metaphor focuses on survival as a process rather than a unitary goal.
3. By identifying different "species" of organizations, it acknowledges that there are many ways to design an organization, including bureaucratic, matrix, organic, and other newer "species" of structure.
4. It stresses the virtue of organic forms of organization, applauding their much higher levels of innovation.

5. It makes important contributions by focusing on "ecology" and interorganizational issues.

But, because every metaphor (paradigm) is incomplete, a way of
seeing is also a way of *not* seeing. According to Morgan, the major
limitations of this approach are as follows:

1. We are led to view organizations and their environments in a way that is
   far too concrete. Although organisms live in a natural world, they are
   creations of the mind, and their shape and structure is much more fragile
   and tentative than that of a material organism. Also, by stressing an
   organization's need to "adapt" to its environment or that environment's
   ability to "select" organizations that are to survive, the metaphor fails to
   recognize that organizations "are active agents with others in constructing
   that world."[24]
2. The organismic metaphor is limited by its assumption of "functional
   unity." Unlike the human body, whose organs all work together to achieve
   homeostasis or balance, organizations in the "effect" or self-centered
   world rarely have functional unity. It must be created or integrated
   "artificially."
3. The metaphor may become an ideology, as functional unity cannot be
   achieved in the "effect" state.

## The Industrial Era
## Paradigm and Growth

The industrial era made organizational, technological, and economic
growth into an unquestioned "good."[25] In fact, organizational growth
seems to be a requirement in the dominant survival needs of particular
organizations. Pfeffer puts it this way:

> Not only is survival a generally agreed-upon objective, so is the growth of
> the organization. Organizational growth increases the chances of the
> organization's survival. Large organizations are not permitted to go out of
> business like small organizations. They have constituencies and an impact
> that provides them, because of their size, with claims on society's re-
> sources necessary for their continuation.
> While small, "mom and pop" stores open and close continually, large
> organizations, such as Lockheed, are kept operating even with extraordi-
> nary measures. This is because the failure of a small organization has limited
> impact, but the failure or closing of a large organization has greater impact,
> and therefore is more likely to be prevented by political intervention.

In addition to increasing the organization's capacity for survival, growth provides two other advantages. First, growth usually means that there are more resources to be divided up among the participants. More resources means that, instead of as much conflict over the division of resources, all participants can get more out of a steadily increasing pool of resources. Conflict is less likely under conditions of constant organizational expansion. . . . Organizational growth also provides the organization with more power with respect to other organizations and groups in its environment. . . . Size provides some measure of power, other things being equal, in a system of organizations. This power, of course, can be used to extract more resources from the environment, to be shared among participants, and to further organizational growth and survival.[26]

But a host of social, environmental, and economic problems is making us reassess our progrowth stance. Today, growth is being questioned as never before. This is why the transformational perspective asks questions such as these:

- Is growth balanced?
- Is growth in keeping with the needs of the larger whole?
- What are the side effects of growth? Are they sufficiently deleterious to bring continued growth into question?

One of the biggest problems in talking about a paradigm shift is that solutions to current problems are conceptualized in terms of the old paradigm, because that is what we know to be "reality." That makes it difficult to speak of a world without growth as we know it, because our current economic system demands growth for the organization (or the society) to "succeed."

Growth has implied, in the current paradigm, the need for large organizations to achieve economies of scale and financial leverage. And, to be sure, mergers and consolidations continue apace, with the result being that large bureaucratic organizations are very much alive. However, a countertrend is also gaining momentum; this takes the form of entrepreneurship and intrapreneurship.[27] There is a strong trend toward the formation of new business units.

It could be hypothesized that the surge in both entrepreneurship and intrapreneurship is the *result* of the paradigm shift; as such, this surge represents symptoms of the larger compulsion toward balance, wholeness, work with intrinsic meaning, and structural integrity.

Willis Harman has glimpsed this larger compulsion toward wholeness and balance:

It is important to remind ourselves that there is no need, ever, for a society to limit productiveness and growth in human terms. As Erich Fromm expresses it in *Man for Himself,* "Productiveness is man's ability to use his powers and to realize the potentialities inherent in him." The resolution of the growth dilemma lies in the creation of a society which is highly productive in human terms, which fosters individual growth and development, but which is frugal of material resources. A guiding principle is "do more with less." In a frugal society:

1. An ethic of frugality and ecological harmony would replace the consumption-and-waste ethic of industrial society.
2. Human energy and social resources would be devoted largely to creating meaningful individual lives and a humane society, and far less to those kinds of technological achievements that are wasteful of human resources.
3. Evolutionary change would occur, but growth in a material sense would be slow.
4. Technology would be very sophisticated but would conserve energy and raw materials and would be small in scale.
5. Production units (e.g., farms, factories) would tend to be small and self-sufficient.[28]

Of course, a core question must then be asked: How might this utopian view be realized? The industrial society's appetite for consumer goods would seem to make Harman's ideas wishful thinking. Harman begins to address the problem when he says, "The feasibility of the creation of such a society depends on the successful resolution of a dilemma involving the need for meaningful work—*for there must be some other operative measure of worth in the society to augment or replace goods production and acquisition.*"[29]

Actually, the "problem" is much broader than meaningful work; it resides in the question of *personal meaning* itself. Much has been written about "man's search for meaning."[30] This existential quest has been initiated by many of us at one time or another; many just give up and settle for survival. One author argues that excessive materialism is the result of this search for a sense of identity.[31] As we have pointed out, a person who lacks an intrinsic sense of worth will endeavor to create a false sense of security and identity through external things—material goods and job titles. Most people have so little sense of a personal purpose beyond mere survival (or a glorified job title) that they pursue materialism to quell the empty feeling inside.[32]

The transformational perspective on the problem of growth (and its related subproblems) is centered on this question of identity. It says that each of us is an aspect of life. A person has things, but those things are not the person. Each of us is part of the motivating force of the cosmos, a differentiated aspect of the creative power of the universe. That is no small thing. With this identity, a person doesn't need to grow in wealth, status, or material possessions to be impressive or to gain power. Identification with the whole brings security and a sharp reduction in materialism, pollution, power struggles, and other aspects of "human nature" for which there seem to be no solutions.

Organic organizations can be created and sustained only by people who have a large, transcendent sense of personal purpose and who really know who they are (transcendent personal identity). As we have noted, this personal maturity will be the key to the organizational structures of the future.

## Organizational Decline and Death

Why do organizations eventually seem to decline and/or die? One of the characteristics of open systems is *negative entropy*. Entropy is the tendency of systems to run down; negative entropy is the ability of open systems to maintain themselves by importing energy from the external environment to try to offset entropic effects. In other words, without a concerted effort by the organizational system to forestall decline, it will happen. There appear to be several reasons for this.

*Organizational atrophy.*[33] When organizations grow older, they often seem to get "fat"; they lose their lean, competitive edge. Inefficiency sets in, and the organization begins to rest on its laurels. Gareth Morgan calls this being "trapped by success."[34] Responses get slower, and competitors begin to dominate the market. A subcategory under this cause is the well-documented *resistance to change* phenomenon we mentioned in Chapter 10.[35] Equally likely on the personal and the organizational level, it occurs because immature people create rigid and inflexible organizational forms. According to Chris Argyris, the most prominent culprit of such self-defeating behavior is the traditional bureaucratic form. He and others believe that the on-slaught of increasing competition and technological change will spell the end of bureaucracy.[36]

*Environmental vulnerability.*[37] Vulnerability reflects the organiza-tion's probable inability to succeed in its environment. A small organization that lacks financial resources and stable market position will be vulnerable to changing consumer tastes and the economic health of the larger society. An organization that is no longer perceived as producing something useful for the larger society—such as cigarette manufacturers and the makers of other unsafe products today—is made vulnerable by this loss of legitimacy.[38] Organizational "slack" (spare resources) is often needed to cope with the problem of vulnerability.

*Environmental entropy.*[39] If the resources of the environment are insufficient to support the organization, the organization has to either scale down its operations or redefine its operational domain. When external resources are not growing, an organization has to divide up a constant or shrinking pie. Organizations faced with a stagnating economy or a flat market will inevitably decline unless they make the necessary adjustments.[40]

---

**Vignette 1**

A sales engineer for General Electric with a background in hydraulic engineering was offered a job with a new intrapreneurial venture within GE. He was to direct the marketing effort for silicon carbide, a new product devised in the GE labs. This product has unusual properties: It can withstand very high temperatures for long periods of time without breaking down.

Senior executives at GE recognized the market potential for such a product in the oil-field industry (drill bits, machinery, and so on) and started the company to develop the product and find markets for it. The GE executives recognized that to do this within the confines of the existing bureaucracy would be time-consuming, laborious and, most of all, inefficient. So this new, five-person grouping (made up of GE employees) was to create a company. The group was given a budget of $5 million and five years to develop the product and form a freestanding company.

The start-up was good; because the project had the blessings of corporate staff, access to funds was relatively easy. Things were moving along well when the oil industry collapsed. With the product's primary market bottoming out and no new prospects in other markets readily apparent, the intrapreneurship effort was abandoned, and the members of the group were all offered jobs back in the GE hierarchy.

---

## An Antidote to Decline:
## Organizational Adaptability

---

Because an organization is an open system—dependent on other groups and organizations in its domain for input acquisition and output disposal—it must be able to *adapt* to changing circumstances. In fact, the most frequently expressed reason for organizational demise is an inability to adapt to an increasingly turbulent external environment. In one sense, external forces seem to place claims on an organization.[41] The organization's survival seems to be dependent on the following:

1. the occurrence of fortunate events, such as technological advances, whereby the scarce resources attainable by the organization can be spread across more of the claims that are placed on it
2. the ability of the organization to forecast the strength that the various environmental forces will have in enforcing their claims on the organization
3. the ability of the organization to find new patterns of activity (Ainsworth-Land's Phase III, Argyris and Schön's Model II learning—see below) that will adequately meet emergent claims on them

Adaptability is far and away the most critical issue in organizational survival. Short-run environmental fluctuations may be tolerable without flexibility, but flexibility to long-run environmental conditions is necessary for survival.[42] It is widely accepted that the environment of the future will be even more turbulent than today's. If this does occur, many authors agree that the organization's quick and accurate response to environmental changes will account for a large share of its successful continuation.[43]

Because, as Karl Weick argues, the environment in which the organization operates is an "enacted" environment, boundary role players will be accurate in perceiving that environment only to the extent that their perception is not grossly distorted by the organizational "theory-in-use," or dominant paradigm.[44] Adaptability can be severely limited by the blinders of inappropriate value/belief/attitude systems. The perceived environment is what is acted on by decision makers. Because an accurate perception of environmental changes is necessary for adaptability and survival, "reality testing" of executive perceptions by multiple measures may be critical to survival. Some companies already do this informally with their boundary role personnel. In fact, Joel Barker, in his popular video *Discovering the Future: The Business of Paradigms,* claims that "paradigm flexibility" is the most important management skill for the future.[45]

Stephen Robbins looks for the necessary prerequisites of adaptability under the premise that *survival requires change.*[46] He assumes that many organizations do not see environmental changes because they are shielded by their own complacency. The U.S. automobile industry is a good example. Given this problem, Robbins sees conflict as valuable to an organization in that existing assumptions, prejudices, and so on can be brought up for review and challenged, leading presumably to a more proactive stance with regard to coming changes in the environment. Some authors view adaptation as an evolutionary trend. Others, like Greiner, see evolution combined with periodic "revolutionary shifts" (stormy, critical periods of growth and change) as leading to adaptation. One author relates three possible states that an organization can adopt with respect to its environment:

1. *Homeostasis:* The internal and external forces exerting pressure on the organization are in equilibrium.
2. *Adaptation:* Passive change or evolution occurs in this state.
3. *Radical change:* This occurs when evolutionary change is not sufficient to keep the organization alive and competitive.[47]

Broadly speaking, there seem to be two schools of thought regarding adaptation: One could be called the *forecasting/planning* school and the other the *manage-the-environment* school. Some authors see adaptation as a by-product of good planning and forecasting. If the organization does its boundary role work well, it should know of major environmental shifts in time to mobilize organizational resources. This approach assumes that the role of the organization is to adapt to whatever changes the environment offers. The other view, more deterministic in nature, is receiving more attention of late.[48] This is a predictable outcome of a reactionary, "effect-oriented" paradigm.

This approach argues that an organization should fully exploit its environment by gaining some degree of control over it, thus helping to shape the organization's future role in a "designed" environment. Ackoff, in particular, talks of his "adaptivizing" philosophy, which pushes beyond responsiveness, readiness, or compliance into shaping the environment to suit the organization's own ends.[49] Price fixing, lobbying, and market division arrangements/cartels are all attempts to do this, and many are acknowledged as having undesirable side effects. An extreme but not necessarily singular example of manipulating the environment is presented in Vignette 2.

**Vignette 2**

In 1988, ecologist Francisco Mendes of Xapuri, Brazil, was murdered. Mendes was shot to death outside his home because he angered ranchers/businessmen (who profit from the development of the jungle) with his fight to protect the Amazon jungle. In this case, businesspeople self-centeredly altered their environment (by killing Mendes) to protect their short-term profits.

SOURCE: "Brazil Murder Nearly Solved," *Denver Post International*, December 31, 1988.

The transformational perspective transcends both of these old-paradigm approaches. According to this approach, the *whole organizes the parts.* In other words, the organizational environment is a larger whole within which the organization finds itself. This automatically eliminates the manipulative manage-the-environment approach. Who could possibly know or anticipate all of the possible ramifications of such manipulation (given that everything is connected to everything else)? Although it might be possible to produce seemingly pleasing results in the short term for the organization, one would be hard-pressed to guarantee the long-term benefits of such an interventionist strategy.

However, there are things to be done. An organization doesn't just "flow along" with its environment. Here is where vision or transcendent purpose comes in. The basic reason for the existence of an organization is to *add something creative to the larger whole.* Profits are *not* the raison d'être of private organizations, as many believe. Organizations exist to serve the purposes of the larger whole by providing goods or services in effective and responsible ways. They are to discern how to do that: It may be by changing a product line, modifying service offerings, or something entirely different. The point is that the strategy must come from this purpose; a *giving* rather than a *getting* posture. Here is the transcendent perspective in action.

Adaptation and survival are natural by-products of looking to see how to be of service. An organization must keep in touch with environmental trends and changes, to be sure; the work of boundary role incumbents is crucial in this regard. However, the information so gathered is not used to exploit the environment; rather, it is used to ask the creative question: How might we change to accommodate the changes being brought to us from the environment? Here is true adaptability and ultimate success in a dynamic world.

### Organizational Learning and Renewal

It has been recognized that, in order for an organization to move out of the "stuckness" of mature bureaucracy, there needs to be a way for it to learn how to be new. Harrison Owen writes:

> There was a time when the prime business of business was to make a profit. There is now a prior, prime business which is to become an effective learning community. Not that product and profit are no longer important, but *without continued learning, they will no longer be possible.* Hence, the strange thought: the business of business is learning . . . and all else follows.
>
> Present and emergent events have radically altered the conditions under which business will be done. It is a new game with new rules which demand new approaches. The alternatives are not thinkable, unless going out of business is an option. Not only are the conditions new, but the time available for adaptation is diminishing on the same exponential curve which describes the advance of technology. Under the circumstances, life-long learning is no longer a fringe benefit to be enjoyed by the few. It is the critical difference between success and failure.[50]

A widely accepted and quoted theory of organizational learning has been developed by Argyris and Schön, whose definition of learning, in essence, relates to the occurrence of productive (as opposed to defensive) reasoning in organizations.[51] *Productive reasoning*, by their definition, is marked by the absence of defensiveness, willingness to combine advocacy and inquiry, and willingness to make statements that are both disconfirmable and open to being tested. *Defensive reasoning* lacks these qualities, and that, according to Argyris and Schön, is what limits learning.[52]

Argyris and Schön define *learning* as the "ability to detect and correct error." They define an *error* as a mismatch between intention and outcome; in other words, "Things didn't work as we wanted them to." Argyris and Schön identify two types of error detection: single-loop learning and double-loop learning. *Single-loop learning* involves improving the strategies used to reach a certain goal, but does not question the norms and values that underlie the strategies themselves. For example, a factory might try to better its production quotas by improving its just-in-time efficiency, or a financial services company might alter its marketing strategy to obtain higher market visibility by cutting back on newspaper advertisements/television expenditures (after learning that its potential clients watched television and didn't read newspapers). Improving the JIT system, in the first example, might increase efficiency. New information about its market might help the financial services company alter its marketing strategy. In these examples, the strategies are different, but the goal remains fixed.

In contrast, *double-loop learning* questions the fundamental assumptions and values within which a company might be operating. For example, a company that was founded on a particular vision may find that its philosophy is no longer viable in its current market environment. A company that began in industrial components and had a long tradition of success in that market (Phase II of Ainsworth-Land) might then have "forward integrated" into consumer products. Because of a sluggish component market, the company's profit may be largely coming from the consumer business, suggesting that the company should divest its original business. This could cause considerable conflict within the company, between those who feel the business "should be" an industrial components business, and those who feel the profitability and success of the company depend on the ability to relinquish an albatross division and free up resources for innovation and investment in newer areas. This dilemma, caused by a conflict in values, might force the organization to redefine itself. Double-loop learning thus involves change in the underlying norms that govern the company, and not merely the strategies needed to achieve some agreed-on goal set.

Argyris and Schön define *organizational learning* as the ability to perform double-loop learning regularly. This correlates directly with the theory of personal maturity/100% responsibility presented in this book; mature employees will be able to spot gaps between their intention and their behavior and close them without becoming defensive. For example, John brings to Ed's attention that Ed had committed to open and honest communications with him. However, Ed omitted essential information in a recent letter to John. Ed can accept this feedback without defensiveness, or he can continue to say one thing and do another. The self-esteem of mature employees will allow for resilient behavior and for the ability to self-diagnose in a creative way. A learning organization, then, is able to expand the kinds of errors it is able to address, and the processes it uses to address them, until it is able to deal easily and continuously with the fundamental problems it might be facing. In a recent book, Peter Senge fully explores the implications of creating a learning organization.[53]

This theory of organizational learning accounts for important dimensions in the ways in which people operate in group settings. Argyris and Schön describe two kinds of "behavioral worlds" that are the results of individual learning styles found in two fundamentally different models of reasoning and the values/strategies associated with them. They identify defensive reasoning as Model I and productive reasoning as Model II. Generally, Model I prevents double-loop learning and Model II describes it. Argyris and Schön note that as they can predict the kinds of learning that go on when individuals operate with Model I theory-in-use, they can also predict the kinds of interactions that result when people use Model II theories-in-use (or paradigm). *Espoused theory* involves concepts that conform to the paradigm's ideas of *good* values and beliefs. There is often a gap between what people say (espoused theory) and what they do (theory-in-use). Similarly, Argyris and Schön predict the kinds of learning that go on within Model I and Model II organizational settings.

### Model I

Model I settings are characterized by a climate of protectionism and reluctance to perform joint inquiry into problems. In such a setting, defensive routines tend to dictate behavior. Limited learning systems contain primary and secondary inhibiting loops. *Primary inhibiting loops* lead to unawareness of double-loop learning, dysfunctional group and intergroup dynamics, dysfunctional organizational norms and activities (e.g., games of deception), "lose-lose" conflict resolution, and "brittle learning systems." Model I governing variables remain in control in these settings, and errors tend *not* to be corrected. Cover-ups and blaming are the order of the day. This leads to further disguising (*secondary inhibiting loops*) and further limits to double-loop learning. These are the conditions of double binds, in which one loses no matter what one does.

This "no-win" element is a predictable consequence of limited learning systems. There are thus a series of dynamic behaviors that function in the climate of a Model I world that first directly inhibit double-loop learning and then set up conditions such that anything that would threaten the values governing the theory-in-use are in some way suppressed. There is a self-fulfilling and self-protecting pattern to this kind of behavior within organizations. Argyris and Schön argue that this kind of interaction is in fact very common in the organizational world.[54] It obviously leads to rigidity, defensiveness, and inability to learn.

### Model II

In contrast, a Model II behavioral world has characteristics that enable double-loop learning to occur. The nature of the behavioral pattern, according to Argyris and Schön, is different. In this setting, information is met with Model II theories-in-use, which leads to a particular type of error detection and diagnosis of error as an incongruity between organizational espoused theory and reality.

This is the optimal system in the "effect" paradigm. People are open to suspending their commitment to their worldview and open to changing it based on need. There is a state of opposition of ideas and people as a new level of clarity about underlying issues surfaces. The organization then institutes a new set of governing variables or an attempt to practice espoused theory, which increases the likelihood of double-loop learning.

## What Does It Mean for an Organization to Learn?

There are numerous, differing conceptualizations of the term *organizational learning*.[55] Some writers, for example, see learning as a way of making the organization's history understandable. Others use the term in a normative sense, to describe what *should* be done to increase organizational effectiveness. Still others have difficulty defining the word *learning* when it is used to describe an entity that acts as a unit. They see organizations as a number of related individuals and treat the term *organization* only as a metaphor. Finally, some writers believe these entities are more than the sum of their parts and can be said to "learn."[56]

Shrivastava suggests that four principal categories summarize research in this area:

1. *Adaptation:* Learning is done with respect to the outside environment, readjusting goals, attention rules, and search rules.
2. *Shared meanings:* This involves shared assumptions and theories-in-use, and learning is seen as a change in theories-in-use.
3. *Knowledge base development:* This is the process of development of knowledge about action-outcome relations.
4. *Institutionalized learning effects:* This refers to the learning curve effect as it extends into decision-making areas.

Shrivastava further suggests that one may synthesize the organizational learning literature into several themes:

1. Organizational learning is an organizational process and not an individual process, where this process is influenced by a broad set of social, political, and structural variables.
2. Organizational learning is closely linked with actual organizational experience.
3. Outcomes of learning are organizationally shared and problem-solving heuristics stemming from it are used.
4. Learning involves fundamental change in the theories-in-use (paradigm) of decision makers.
5. Learning occurs at several levels of the organization.

6. Learning is institutionalized into systems that include "the formal and informal mechanisms of management information sharing, planning, and control."[57]

So, what do we make of all this? First and foremost, it is important to recognize that the organization is a macro entity in and of itself. It has a life, a history, and a learning curve. However, it is made up of individuals, and considering the macro perspective without an appreciation of the micro elements that compose that whole is dangerous. A transformational leader can change the culture, and thereby the theories-in-use, of an organization; this is a key to the metamodel.[58] It is also useful to note that a leader, in the transformational sense, does not have to be the *formal* leader. The process by which transformational leadership occurs has three stages: *revitalization* (recognizing the need for change), *creating a new vision* (and Model II culture), and *institutionalizing change* (Model II implemented and rewarded).[59] Without the transformational perspective, the same old habits of thought and behavior will continue to be tried, with the result of increasing frustration and conflict.

## Senge's Perspective on Organizational Learning

Peter Senge, director of the Organizational Learning Project at MIT and author of the best-selling *The Fifth Discipline,* has some interesting ideas about how to create a "learning organization." The first step is to initiate an organizationwide *paradigm shift;* Senge asks, "Are we prisoners of the system or prisoners of our own thinking?"[60] He argues for *systems thinking,* or beginning to see problems in archetypal ways (what he calls "nature's templates"). Every organizational problem, from this perspective, is part of a larger system, and to solve it one must take into account the system dynamics. Here we see wholes within wholes, the transformational view. Leverage in problem solving comes only from seeing the interconnectedness of all things in the organization.

Senge then talks about the "core disciplines" of the learning organization. First, he discusses *personal mastery.* This is what we are calling 100% personal responsibility (the "cause" state). Then he talks about *mental models,* the equivalent of our concept of *paradigm.* Next is *shared vision,* which we have argued is the glue that holds the organic structure together. Finally, he discusses *team learning,* where a culture built around Model II (double-loop) learning is developed.

Here we see the successful organization of the future. Each person is empowered to express his or her unique contribution to the whole in a context where personal growth and organizational excellence are *both* encouraged. Everyone is fully aware of his or her implicit assumptions and belief systems, and a climate of constant inquiry leads to what Barker calls "paradigm flexibility."[61] The shared vision is inspiring, transcendent, and it captures the heart of the organization, galvanizing commitment and a results orientation. All work together harmoniously, putting aside ego and personality differences in the striving toward that vision. Finally, everyone understands the organizational system, its inherent dynamics, and the part he or she plays in the larger whole.

Can you imagine such an organization? Can you see how different it would be from today's effect-oriented, Model I hierarchies? Can you now see why today's bureaucracies are dinosaurs, as Rosabeth Moss Kanter has called them?[62]

## NOTES

1. Mason Haire, "Biological Models and Empirical Histories in the Growth of Organizations," in *Modern Organization Theory*, ed. Mason Haire (New York: John Wiley, 1959), 272-306.

2. Ibid.; quoted in John H. Jackson and Cyril P. Morgan, *Organization Theory: A Macro Perspective for Management* (Englewood Cliffs, NJ: Prentice Hall, 1978), 355.

3. J. W. Gardner, "How to Prevent Organizational Dry Rot," *Harper's*, October 1965, 20. Copyright © 1965 by *Harper's Magazine*. All rights reserved. Reprinted from the October issue by special permission.

4. See John R. Kimberly, "The Life Cycle Analogy and the Study of Organizations: Introduction," in *The Organizational Life Cycle: Issues in the Creation, Transformation and Decline of Organizations*, ed. John R. Kimberly, Robert H. Miles, and Associates (San Francisco: Jossey-Bass, 1980), 6-9.

5. Noel M. Tichy, "Problem Cycles in Organizations and the Management of Change," in *The Organizational Life Cycle: Issues in the Creation, Transformation and Decline of Organizations*, ed. John R. Kimberly, Robert H. Miles, and Associates (San Francisco: Jossey-Bass, 1980), 164-165.

6. John Freeman, Glenn R. Carroll, and Michael T. Hannan, "The Liability of Newness: Age Dependence in Organizational Death Rates," *American Sociological Review* 48 (October 1983): 692.

7. Larry E. Greiner, "Evolution and Revolution as Organizations Grow," *Harvard Business Review* 50 (July-August 1972): 37.

8. Ibid., 39.

9. Ibid., 40.

10. Ibid., 43.

11. Ibid.

12. Ibid., 44.

13. See Kenneth D. Benne and M. Birnbaum, "Principles of Changing," in *The Planning of Change*, ed. Kenneth D. Benne, Warren Bennis, and Robert Chin (New York: Holt, Rinehart & Winston, 1969), 328-335.

14. Robert T. Golembiewski, *Renewing Organizations: The Laboratory Approach to Planned Change* (Itasca, IL: F. E. Peacock, 1972), 101.

15. See, for example, A. S. King, "Expectation Effects in Organizational Change," *Administrative Science Quarterly* 19 (June 1974); Jerald Hage and Michael Aiken, *Social Change in Complex Organizations* (New York: Random House, 1970); James V. Clark, "A Healthy Organization," in *The Planning of Change*, ed. Kenneth D. Benne, Warren Bennis, and Robert Chin (New York: Holt, Rinehart & Winston, 1969), 282-297; Herbert Kauffman, *The Limits of Organizational Change* (Huntsville: University of Alabama Press, 1971); Larry E. Greiner, "Patterns of Organizational Change," in *Organizational Structuring*, ed. H. Eric Frank (London: McGraw-Hill, 1971).

16. Jackson and Morgan, *Organization Theory*, 360.

17. Ibid., 361.

18. Kim S. Cameron and David A. Whetton, "Models of the Organizational Life Cycle: Applications to Higher Education," *Research in Higher Education* 5 (June 1983): 211-224.

19. See, for example, Larry Wilson, *Changing the Game: The New Way to Sell* (New York: Simon & Schuster, 1987); Lynda Lawrence, "Phase Change: Larry Wilson on Selling in a Brave New World," special report, *Training*, February Suppl. 1988, 11-14; George Ainsworth-Land, *Grow or Die* (New York; Wilson Learning Systems, 1986).

20. Matthew Juechter, "Bringing Spirit Back to the Workplace," *Training and Development Journal* (September 1988): 36-37; emphasis added.

21. Tichy, "Problem Cycles in Organizations."

22. Ibid., 165.

23. Gareth Morgan, *Images of Organization* (Beverly Hills, CA: Sage, 1986), 71-76.

24. Ibid., 74.

25. Willis Harman, *An Incomplete Guide to the Future* (San Francisco: San Francisco Book, 1976).

26. Jeffrey Pfeffer, *Organizational Design* (Arlington Heights, IL: AHM, 1978), 114-115.

27. See, for example, Karl H. Vesper, *Entrepreneurship and National Policy* (Chicago: Heller Institute for Small Business Policy Papers, 1983); Chris Lee and Ron Zemke, "Intrapreneuring: New Age Fiefdoms for Big Business?" *Training*, January 1985.

28. Harman, *An Incomplete Guide*, 49.

29. Ibid.; emphasis added.

30. See Viktor E. Frankel, *Man's Search for Meaning* (New York: Pocket Books, 1984).

31. See Philip Slater, *The Pursuit of Loneliness* (Boston: Beacon, 1970).

32. Ibid.

33. Richard L. Daft, *Organization Theory and Design* (2nd ed.) (New York: West, 1986), 193.

34. Morgan, *Images of Organization*, 201.

35. Alton C. Barnett and Thomas A. Sayer, *Changing Organizational Behavior* (Englewood Cliffs, NJ: Prentice Hall, 1973), 375-434.

36. Besides Chris Argyris, those who believe this include Warren Bennis, Paul Spencer and Cyril Sofer, and John W. Gardner.

37. Daft, *Organization Theory and Design*, 193.

38. An organization can enhance its legitimacy by adhering to society's norms, by convincing society that its view is better, or by using an already legitimate symbol to transfer legitimacy to the organization. For more, see John Dowling and Jeffrey Pfeffer, "Organizational Legitimacy: Social Values and Organizational Behavior," *Pacific Sociological Review* 18 (1975): 122-136.

39. Daft, *Organization Theory and Design*, 193.

40. See, for example, David A. Whetton, "Sources, Responses, and Effects of Organizational Decline," in *The Organizational Life Cycle: Issues in the Creation, Transformation and Decline of Organizations*, ed. John R. Kimberly, Robert H. Miles, and Associates (San Francisco: Jossey-Bass, 1980), 342-374; David A. Whetton, "Organizational Decline: A Neglected Topic in Organizational Science," *Academy of Management Review* 5 (1980): 577-588; Kim Cameron and Raymond Zammuto, "Matching Managerial Strategies to Conditions of Decline," *Human Resource Management* 22 (1983): 359-375.

41. William J. Gore, *Administrative Decision Making: A Heuristic Model* (New York: John Wiley, 1964), 23.

42. Louis C. Schroeter, *Organizational Elan* (New York: American Management Association, 1970), 87.

43. See, for example, Harold Leavitt, Lawrence Pinfield, and Eugene Webb, eds., *Organizations of the Future: Interactions With the Environment* (New York: Praeger, 1974), 22.

44. Karl Weick, *The Social Psychology of Organizing* (Reading, MA: Addison-Wesley, 1969).

45. Joel Barker, *Discovering the Future: The Business of Paradigms* (2nd ed.), videotape (Burnsville, MN: Charthouse Learning Corporation, 1991).

46. Stephen P. Robbins, *Managing Organizational Conflict: A Nontraditional Approach* (Englewood Cliffs, NJ: Prentice Hall, 1974).

47. Gerald J. Skibbins, *Organizational Evolution: A Program for Managing Radical Change* (New York: AMACOM, 1974), 8-9.

48. See, for example, Mary P. Mott, Harold B. Repinsky, John Riner, and Karl E. Weick, "The Research Team and Its Organizational Environment," in *Studies on Behavior in Organizations: A*

*Research Symposium,* ed. Raymond V. Bowers (Athens: University of Georgia Press, 1966); Russell Ackoff, *A Concept of Corporate Planning* (New York: Wiley Interscience, 1970).

49. Ackoff, *A Concept of Corporate Planning.*

50. Harrison Owen, "The Business of Business Is Learning" (occasional paper, H. H. Owen, July 1989), 1.

51. Chris Argyris and Donald Schön, *Organizational Learning* (Reading, MA: Addison-Wesley, 1978); see also William N. Isaacs, "Testing the Theory of Action Approach to Organizational Learning" (Ph.D. diss., University of Oxford, Lincoln College, 1993). Much of the following description of Argyris and Schön's model is extracted from Isaacs's dissertation proposal.

52. This is the distinction between Model I and Model II thinking, as described by Argyris and Schön.

53. Peter M. Senge, *The Fifth Discipline: The Art and Practice of the Learning Organization* (Garden City, NY: Doubleday, 1990).

54. Isaacs says, "This is a theory of constructive and destructive behavior patterns. It is a shift from closed defensive interactions to open, mutually self-reliant interactions. It is a theory about interaction patterns in particular and a description of learning. It uses descriptive words to point to a logical type shift problem, which neither really defines what exactly it is or how to produce it. These words thus have an existential quality to them." Dissertation proposal, p. 4; see note 51, above.

55. Paul Shrivastava, "A Typology of Organizational Learning Systems," *Journal of Management Studies* 20, no. 1 (1983).

56. See, for example, Karl Weick, *The Social Psychology of Organizing* (Reading, MA: Addison-Wesley, 1969).

57. Shrivastava, "A Typology of Organizational Learning Systems," 17.

58. Noel M. Tichy and Mary Anne Devanna, *The Transformational Leader* (New York: John Wiley, 1986).

59. Ibid., ix.

60. Senge, *The Fifth Discipline,* chap. 3.

61. Barker, *Discovering the Future.*

62. Rosabeth Moss Kanter, *When Giants Learn to Dance* (New York: Simon & Schuster, 1989).

# 18 Organizational Culture

*While we know about culture, the great need of many companies
to "manage" their culture, to create "excellent" cultures and to
"change" cultures that stand in the way of strategic directions has
corrupted that knowledge. No doubt many trainers and consultants
have already been asked to provide "culture audits." Certainly, there
is a ready market for lectures, demonstrations and exercises that
show management how to create the right kind of organizational
culture.* It is as if managements are saying to us: "Hey, this culture
stuff might be a useful new management tool for improving productivity, quality of work life, and helping us regain our competitive
edge."

> (Edgar H. Schein, "What You Need to Know About
> Organizational Culture," *Training and Development Journal*,
> January 1986, p. 30; emphasis added)

*Why do so many people build their lives around distinct concepts of
work and leisure, follow rigid routines five or six days a week, live in
one place and work in another, wear uniforms, defer to authority, and
spend so much time in a single spot performing a single set of activities? To an outsider, daily life in an organizational society is full of
peculiar beliefs, routines, and rituals that identify it as a distinctive
cultural life when compared to that of more traditional societies.*

> (Gareth Morgan, *Images of Organization*,
> 1986, pp. 112-113)

---

**SUMMARY:** The concept of corporate culture, the newest of the management
fads, is de facto evidence of the paradigm shift into a postindustrial world.
The surge of interest in culture means that, finally, management is becoming
interested in the invisible aspects of organization, such as shared systems of
belief, attitudes, and values. In fact, notes Edgar Schein, if we "take culture
seriously, we will help the manager recognize that cultural assumptions
dominate managerial decisions about strategy, *structure* and systems . . . not
just about style and people."[1]

---

**A**lthough many chapters in this book juxtapose the "new" and the "traditional" approaches to organization theory topics, considerations of culture are such a new-paradigm enterprise that this kind of comparison is not possible. The current interest in shared belief, attitude, and value systems is indicative of the paradigm shift. Suddenly, it would seem, we are more interested in the invisible factors of organization than we are in the more traditional organization charts, accountability relationships, and job descriptions.

A decade has passed since Stanley Davis, then a Harvard professor, first coined the term "corporate culture," which, to him, meant the unwritten codes of conduct that seem to govern the workplace.[2] Since then, many books have been written, seminars given, and speeches delivered on the subject—all without a generally agreed-on definition of what corporate culture is. Without such agreement, it is hard to operationalize a measure or develop parameters of how "strong" or "weak" a given culture is, or how it may be changing.

Reimann and Wiener have attempted to *operationalize* the definition of culture in order to measure it. They define corporate culture as follows:

> The pattern of core values which are widely shared by members of the organization. In this definition, culture is viewed as a variable, spanning a continuum ranging from "no culture," when no common, normative beliefs are shared by a significant number of members, to a "strong" culture, where a number of key values are widely shared. In this definition, then, the fact that members hold internalized normative beliefs or values does not, by itself, indicate the existence of a culture in the organization. Only when these beliefs are broadly shared by members can a strong corporate culture exist.[3]

If the key to the concept's definition is the degree to which core values are internalized by the organization's members, then a logical way to measure the strength of the culture is to measure members' *level of commitment* to the organization. *Commitment* is defined as the "totality of internalized normative pressures to act in a way that meets organizational goals and interests."[4] In a strong culture, a large majority of members experience strong commitment to the organization.

---

## Common Elements of Culture

---

Despite the disparity in definitions of corporate culture, there are some common elements.

*Shared values.* First, most authors agree that corporate culture involves shared values, or social ideals or normative beliefs about proper behavior in various situations ("how we do things around here"). The strength of a culture has to do with the degree to which these shared values have been internalized by organizational members; this is often called "psychological ownership" of the values or "buying into" the dominant value system.

*Belief systems.* Organizational cultures are influenced by two types of beliefs: guiding beliefs and daily beliefs.[5] The loftier *guiding beliefs* give direction to practical, nitty-gritty *daily beliefs*. A common problem in companies is that daily beliefs are not congruent with overarching guiding beliefs.[6]

*Cultural artifacts.* Many popular definitions list such symbolic artifacts of culture as rituals, rites, myths, norms, folkways, symbols, legends, heroes, and ceremonies and claim they make up the culture itself. Newer treatments of the subject now agree, however, that an organization's rituals, myths, stories, and so on are the *effects* of culture, not culture itself. Actually, these artifacts form a system "of support and maintenance for the set of prevailing beliefs."[7] As the visible expression of the culture, they are the effect of the central cause, the shared or collective paradigm.

*Cultural strength.* There also seems to be an inherent bias in the literature that a "strong" culture, one characterized by widespread and strong normative guides to behavior, is somehow better than a "weak" culture, which has virtually no common values or beliefs held by a significant number of organizational members. This is an appealing message, but there seems to be little empirical support for such a generalization. To begin with, a strong culture doesn't have to be positive; negative or destructive values can be widely held ("Don't take any risks here or you'll get your head chopped off!") in a strong culture. In fact, many of the strong-culture companies that Peters and Waterman declared excellent in their *In Search of Excellence* in 1982 subsequently stumbled in the marketplace, although many argued that their declines were caused by environmental factors that were essentially unrelated to culture strength.[8]

Culture, then, is the unwritten, taken-for-granted, feeling part of the organization. The purpose of corporate culture is to provide members with a sense of identity and to generate members' commitment to beliefs and values that are larger than themselves. Culture also enhances the stability of the organization and provides members with understanding that can help them make sense out of organizational events and activities.[9]

To summarize thus far, this definition fits well with the metamodel: "Corporate culture consists of a system of shared values (what is important) and beliefs (how things work around here) that interact to form norms of behavior (how we should do things around here), strategy and structure."[10] However, we hasten to add that *culture* as it is defined here is actually a *subset* of the *collective paradigm*, which, in the metamodel, creates the organizational structure and process. The culture consists of the beliefs, attitudes, and values *particular to the organization itself;* the collective paradigm includes that but also has beliefs, attitudes, and values about all other aspects of living—authority relationships, dependency issues, definitions of what is important in life, and so on. So, technically speaking, the organizational culture is a *subset* of the collective paradigm.

---

## Dimensions of Culture

---

Several authors have attempted to formulate typologies of corporate cultures in order to identify different kinds of cultures and determine the cultural dimensions that contribute to successful strategy formulation and implementation. We examine a number of these below.

### The Deal and Kennedy Typology

In *Corporate Cultures*, Terrence Deal and Allan Kennedy use two dimensions to categorize four types of cultures:

1. the degree of risk associated with the company's activities
2. the speed at which the companies or their employees get feedback on whether decisions or strategies are successful[11]

The four generic types are as follows:

1. "Bet your company," a culture in which high-risk decisions are commonplace. These decisions, which often lead to scientific breakthroughs, often place the future of the company at risk (hence the name) and have quite long feedback loops (that is, it is impossible to know if the bet was successful for a while).

| Degree of Risk | | Speed of Feedback: Slow | Speed of Feedback: Fast |
|---|---|---|---|
| | High | Bet Your Company | Tough Guy/Macho |
| | Low | Process | Work Hard/ Play Hard |

**Figure 18.1.** Generic Culture Types

SOURCE: Terrence E. Deal and Allen A. Kennedy, *Corporate Cultures: The Rites and Rituals of Corporate Life* (Adapted from pp. 107-108) (Reading, MA: Addison-Wesley, 1982). © 1982 by Addison-Wesley Publishing Company, Inc. Reprinted by permission of the publisher.

2. "Tough guy/macho," an individualistic culture offering high risks, high rewards, and quick feedback. The computer industry, Xerox, McDonald's, and most news and entertainment media companies are examples.
3. "Work hard/play hard," a culture type very common in the Silicon Valley of California. This culture is typically team oriented, with group goals, low risks, and quick feedback.
4. "Process," a culture found in government, some insurance companies, and utilities. This focuses on orderly process and has low risk and slow feedback.

These types are displayed in Figure 18.1.

## The Reimann and Wiener Typology

Deal and Kennedy's typology has come under criticism on several fronts. Reimann and Wiener find that Deal and Kennedy's dimensions have the following shortcomings:

1. They are difficult to measure.
2. They focus on the characteristics of the executive decision-making situation rather than culture or organizational values.
3. They depend on the external market environment faced by the firm in question and would be of little use for the study of the relationship between corporate cultures and such variables as environmental change or successful strategy implementation.
4. They are not independent of each other, because degree of risk and speed of feedback are often related.

5. They imply a strong tendency for a certain dominant type of culture to be successful in a particular type of industry.[12]

Reimann and Wiener define culture in terms of shared values, expressed in a two-dimensional matrix. The first dimension concerns the focus and content of the core values; the second is based on the source from which the values are derived. Dimension 1 is broken into two cells:

1. *functional:* values focusing on organizational goals, functions, or styles of operation, as in "Service is our business!" or "Quality is Job 1."
2. *elitist:* values focusing on the status or superiority of the organization's members or products, such as "We are the best!" or "Our products are clearly better!"

The values of the organization may come from two distinct sources. First is *organizational tradition,* which is passed from one generation to another through multiple role models or "prime movers."[13] Second is *charismatic leadership.* Whether organization members accept or internalize charismatically derived values depends on their personal identification with this leader. At NeXT Computer Inc., for instance, it is clear that the charisma of Steve Jobs is the company's unifying force. This is a "great man" culture.

Reimann and Wiener's typology is illustrated in Figure 18.2. The *strategic* culture focuses on functional values and is rooted in the organization's traditions (e.g., Caterpillar Tractor, IBM, Dana Corporation). The *chauvinistic* culture has an elitist value orientation rooted in a strong, charismatic leader (e.g., Route 128 high-tech firms in Boston and such Silicon Valley companies as NeXT and Apple Computer). The "entrepreneurial" culture is based on a charismatic leader who espouses functional, rather than elitist, values (e.g., Ford, McDonald's, Disney). Finally, the *exclusive* culture has elitist values rooted in tradition (e.g., hospitals, universities, and research labs).

One advantage to this particular approach is the focus on values. Values form the essence of the raison d'être or philosophy of the organization. They serve as guidelines for behavior and give direction to the organization. They also serve as guidelines for political success in the organization; for example, when high sales are important, those who sell will succeed. In this way, values define how far and how fast a person will rise in a company.[14]

Alert political players will study the rituals in their organizations and assign values to those rituals. In some organizations, for example, missing a staff meeting is a faux pas (e.g., in a process culture), whereas in others it is a sign that one's work is keeping one busy (e.g., in a

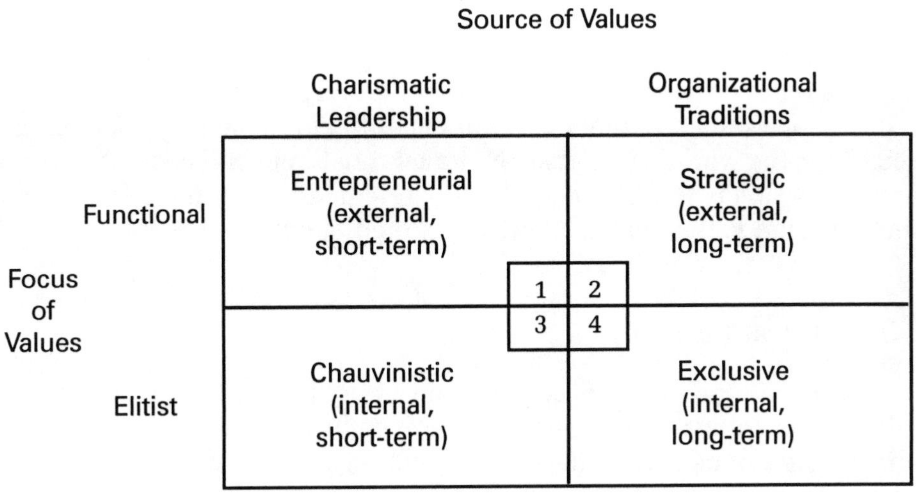

Source of Values

| | Charismatic Leadership | Organizational Traditions |
|---|---|---|
| **Functional** | Entrepreneurial (external, short-term) | Strategic (external, long-term) |
| | 1 \| 2 | |
| | 3 \| 4 | |
| **Elitist** | Chauvinistic (internal, short-term) | Exclusive (internal, long-term) |

Focus of Values

**Figure 18.2.** Generic Corporate Cultures Based on Source and Focus of Shared Values

SOURCE: Bernard C. Reimann and Yoash Wiener, "Corporate Culture: Avoiding the Elitist Trap," *Business Horizons* (March-April 1988): 39. Copyright © 1988 by the Foundation for the School of Business at Indiana University. Used with permission.

bet-your-company culture). In many cultures, employees are expected to take work home; as a result, adept corporate politicians are always seen leaving with briefcases, even if all they carry is the daily newspaper. The myths, rituals, and ceremonies observed in an organization are all created by the dominant values, beliefs, and attitudes in the organization's culture.

## Edgar Schein's Work on Culture

Writer/researcher Edgar Schein thinks that the whole idea of stereotyping total cultures into general types is a mistake:

> Simply put, we have not studied enough organizations to argue that cultures fall into types.
>
> From experience, I've concluded that every organization has its own particular pattern of assumptions about the world. We would be better served if we tried to represent it accurately instead of looking for a type into which to classify it. . . . If we don't know yet how to describe the subtleties of culture, how can we possibly talk of culture types?[15]

Schein raises an interesting question relating to the dominant industrial paradigm. The reader will recall that one of the core assumptions in this paradigm concerns *adherence to quantitative measurement.* By classifying things into typologies or putting them into neat categories, we create the illusion that we "know something" and, thereby, we can reduce uncertainty and increase predictability (and our level of feeling secure) in the world. Of course, the transformational perspective would argue that this is the false ego identity, oriented to external symbols of meaning and value, that is so intent on prediction and control.

## A Cultural Lexicon

Any discussion of organizational culture will include some concern with norms, folkways, mores, languages, symbols, ceremonies and rites, and myths. Let us define these terms before we go any further.

1. *Norms:* Standards of behavior to which people in the culture are expected to adhere. Any organization has an intricate set of norms. Some, such as respecting the chain of command, are obvious; others require discernment, such as knowing what clothes to wear to certain company functions.
2. *Folkways:* The customary, habitual ways in which people act in a given culture. Most often, these are unconscious ritual acts, such as shaking hands when meeting, pulling out chairs for women, and arriving early (or late) for meetings.
3. *Mores:* A subclass of folkways that must be followed, not because they are polite, but because they are important to the organization's function and survival. Mores distinguish between "right" and "wrong" behavior in the culture; for example, cheating on expense accounts may be forbidden.
4. *Languages:* Jargon or terminology that may be incomprehensible to outsiders. Internal communication can often be gibberish to the uninitiated— for example: "Exercise on the following and let RVO see the documented, corrected retrieval mechanism."
5. *Symbols:* Things or events that have special meaning in a given culture, communicating certain unspoken messages. For example, getting an office with a window or being seated close to the CEO at meetings can be symbolic. In a real sense, ceremonies, rites, and stories are symbols of deeply held values in the culture.[16]
6. *Ceremonies and rites:* Elaborate, planned events held to celebrate organizational values. Usually, these are dramatic in nature so that they reinforce specific cultural values, creating a bond of shared understanding and anointing cultural heroes and heroines. A gala ceremony to introduce a new college president and the annual picnic and awards party sponsored by Ben & Jerry's stockholders are examples.
7. *Myths:* Frequently told stories about the organization, based on true or imaginary events. These narratives are often shared among employees and told to newcomers.

---

## How Culture Is Analyzed

---

Researchers and business practitioners have latched onto culture as a way of regaining control and profitability and/or explaining success and failure in an increasingly complex and treacherous international marketplace. Many articles and books have appeared on the *measurement* of culture, the *management* of culture, and the *changing* of culture.[17]

Before a culture can be changed, it must be analyzed. Harry C. Miller, professor and chair of the Department of Educational Leadership at Southern Illinois University, has developed a "forecast" for deciphering an organization's culture.[18] This process tells about a given company's daily culture, whether or not people's expectations are being met there, and what it would be like to work for that company. The three-step process, based on a weather-forecasting analogy, is as follows:

1. *Trade winds:* The organization's purpose. People are brought together and actions coordinated to achieve some purpose; objectives are established, priorities determined, and resources allocated. (Is the purpose being actualized?)

2. *Temperature:* The hotness or coldness of morale relative to each person's perception of work. "Hot" individuals feel good about what is happening in the organization (Are people keen about their work?) and "cold" individuals don't feel okay about their work and the organization.

3. *Ceiling level:* The level of desire, commitment, and energy for organizational goals. This seems to depend on the organization's history, traditions, and norms. (Do people feel the sky's the limit, or do they feel constrained?)

This measure indicates the fit between the prevailing culture and individual values and needs. If the employees adopt the values of the prevailing culture, the climate is said to be "good"; if not, the climate is "poor" and morale, motivation, and productivity are expected to drop. Surveys such as this one help identify a culture's climate or point the way to new policies, procedures, and norms for a more effective culture, but they do not determine whether the culture lives up to its stated beliefs and principles.

Kilmann and Saxton have developed the Culture Gap Survey to measure a company's existing culture and identify the difference between that and the "desired" culture (this is the "culture gap").[19] In constructing the survey, Kilmann and Saxton collected more than 400 norms from managers of some 25 organizations. The survey contains 28 norm pairs such as the following:

(a) Share information only when it benefits your own group.
(b) Share information to help the organization make better choices.[20]

Survey respondents (employees) choose one statement in each norm pair in two ways: first, according to the pressures the work group puts on its members (actual norms), and second, according to which norms they feel *should* (a value-laden term) be operating in order to promote high performance and morale (which are presumably desired outcomes). Any gap between the two is explained by variances in task support norms, task innovation norms, social relationship norms, and personal freedom norms.[21] The greater the gap, the greater the likelihood that current norms create an ineffective culture.

Edgar Schein has developed a 10-step "culture audit" based on his consulting experiences:

1. *Entry and focus on surprises:* The consultant enters the group and begins to "feel" the existing culture and watches for "surprises."
2. *Systematic observation and checking:* The consultant checks to see if surprises really are that.
3. *Locating a motivated insider:* The consultant tries to find an "insider," that is, someone familiar with the culture, who can evaluate it.
4. *Revealing the surprises, puzzlements, and hunches:* In a candid way, the consultant reveals his or her data to the insider for validation.
5. *Joint exploration to find explanations:* Together, the consultant and the insider attempt to fit observations with guiding beliefs, attitudes, and values to explain behavior.
6. *Formalizing hypotheses:* The two collaborate to form hypotheses about the culture based on the data; these become a model of the culture.
7. *Systematic checking and consolidation:* Using the understanding gained thus far, the consultant gets more data from questionnaires, interviews, and so on.
8. *Pushing to the level of assumptions:* Once the hypotheses are validated (or not), the consultant derives cultural assumptions and sees how they affect what the members see and do and believe.
9. *Perpetual recalibration:* The model of culture is fine-tuned through testing on other insiders to see if it actually reveals the underlying assumptions of the culture.
10. *Formal written description:* The consultant reduces the model to writing and shows it around. The written form is kept current over time.[22]

## The Creation and Change
## of Organizational Cultures

In a sense, we can say that people working in factories and offices in Detroit, Leningrad, Liverpool, Paris, Tokyo and Toronto all belong to the same industrial culture. They are all members of the same organizational society. Their work and life experience seems to be qualitatively different from those of individuals living in more traditional societies dominated by domestic systems of production. If nothing else, modern office and factory workers share basic expectations and skills that allow organizations to operate on a day-to-day basis. Though we often regard the routine of organizational life as just that, routine, it does in point of fact rest on numerous skillful accomplishments. Being a factory or office worker calls on a depth of knowledge and cultural practice which, as members of an organizational society, we tend to take for granted.

However, though all modern (industrial) societies have much in common, it would be a mistake to dismiss cross-national differences in cultures as being of little significance. The course of history has fashioned many variations in national social characteristics and views of the meaning of life, and in national styles and philosophies of management. The recent success of Japan, the decline of industrial Britain, the fame of American enterprise, and the distinctive characteristics of many other organizational societies are crucially linked with the cultural contexts in which they have evolved.[23]

Although Gareth Morgan points out that "many of the major cultural similarities and differences in the world today are *occupational rather than national,*" an organization's culture may still be strongly influenced by the "host" country and its cultural parameters and assumptions.[24] Thus American managers have had little success in transplanting Japanese management principles (based on a cultural bias toward group effort, cooperation, and teamwork) into American companies, which are embedded in a strongly individualistic, achievement-oriented societal culture.

Over these larger cultural beliefs are laid the particular cultural beliefs, attitudes, and values of the organization. As Morgan notes, "Organizations are mini-societies that have their own distinctive pattern of culture and subculture."[25] Different organizational cultures form around varying corporate purposes, founder styles, industry norms of behavior, and environmental contingencies (e.g., competition). Given these critical variables, a culture begins to form.

Critical incidents shape organizational cultures. Surviving in the "darkest days," landing a big contract against heavy odds, and developing a leading-edge product in record time are examples of critical incidents. These incidents give rise to "heroes."[26] If Sally Smith sells 2 million widgets a month for a year, and is then promoted to senior VP, she becomes a hero. She actualized the value of sales success and showed how adopting the value can lead to personal advancement. Hero stories and other incidents become the folklore and mythology of the organization.

But the public and private faces of the organization can be, and often are, very different. For example, in a culture with a motto such as "We grow friends," people may seem to be polite and gracious, willing to cooperate, and able to function as "one big happy family." Yet behind this friendly exterior may be a norm of conflict reduction that ensures that meetings are superficial and ritualistic, discussions are never heated, and any undercurrent of conflict is always glossed over. In such a "fragmented" culture, the emphasis on the desirability of harmony can have the effect of driving conflict "underground."[27]

Also, *subcultures* that exist within the dominant culture may be created along the way. For example, a manufacturing concern can have a subculture of top management made up of eastern U.S., white, Anglo-Saxon Protestant males, a subculture of upwardly mobile "yuppie" middle managers, and a subculture of blue-collar union types. All of these subcultures can have shared paradigms that are radically different from one another.

## Culture: A Social Learning Process

Culture is formed out of a social learning process. Specifically, culture creates learned behavior that followers are taught through primarily explicit leadership functions.[28] A founder creates a culture from a preconceived cultural paradigm; the organization then learns about this paradigm. This learning is based on both positive reinforcement (repeating what works) and avoidance learning (avoiding painful experiences). Peters and Waterman, in *In Search of Excellence*, place considerable importance on positive reinforcement. They note that successful organizations seem to find appropriate ways to reward and motivate their employees so that they feel "part of a winner" or that they are winners themselves.[29]

In cultural learning, the organization must face the problem of not having a common language and conceptual system or a common set of rules for relating to the environment and to each other. A coherent corporate culture solves both these problems. Once people in an organization learn a set of assumptions, beliefs, and values that work to handle internal and external contingencies, the anxiety related to uncertainty and stimulus overload is reduced. This is why cultures resist change; a stable culture produces predictability and a feeling of safety.

Of course, the transformational perspective would argue that people in the egocentric, "effect" state want the security of norms, codes of conduct, and the like so that they can know what is expected of them, get rewarded, and avoid pain. The fact that a culture becomes "a source of identity" further explains why people are reluctant even to discuss changing cultural assumptions.[30]

## Maintaining the Culture

Just as we unconsciously create our world with our paradigmatic "filters" and assume that this is the way things are, so, through its culture, does an organization enact a shared reality. This shared reality is maintained by existing cultural artifacts:

> Organizational structure, rules, policies, goals, missions, job descriptions, and standardized operating procedures perform an interpretive function. For they act as primary points of reference for the way people think about and make sense of the contexts in which they work. Though typically viewed as among the more objective characteristics of an organization, an enactment view emphasizes that they are cultural artifacts that help shape the ongoing reality within an organization.[31]

Cultures are maintained partly by group processes. The human need to be accepted, in the egocentric, effect state, drives us to adhere to group norms and unwritten rules of behavior. Breaking these rules brings punishment, whereas following them brings rewards. It is this system of reward and punishment that shapes behavior. The more cohesive the organization, the more influence it may exert over an individual.[32]

Cultures are also maintained through constant reinforcement of core values and beliefs, as well as through the hiring and socializing of people who "fit in" with the existing culture, and the removal of members who deviate.

One author in the transformational literature says that culture is maintained by *spirit:*

> Culture is the dynamic field within which the spirit of man assumes its shape and gets the job done. In the powerful, well-formed cultures, the spirit is strong and tasks are accomplished with dispatch. But when the culture (dynamic field) becomes weak, flaccid and incoherent, the spirit loses its intention and direction. So, if our intention is to insure that the spirit of a particular organization is adequate to the task at hand, and to those tasks just over the horizon, our area of operation will be the culture of the organization.[33]

**Vignette 1**

A business school professor was quite successful in a midwestern university whose culture stressed individual initiative. He was used to arranging his own classroom space, ordering his own audiovisual equipment, and so on. Thus when he moved to a small private college in California, he continued to act this way.

At his new school, when he went to the scheduling person in administration to arrange a classroom for his audiovisual requirements, he was roundly criticized by his colleagues for being "disruptive." What he discovered was that *this* culture was team oriented and procedure driven: "Everyone has to follow procedure." There was a specific procedure to follow to get a classroom assigned—he needed to request in writing what he wanted and the dean would then forward the request to the scheduling person—and he had violated the cultural norm. He had not been "mentored" properly (i.e., told by a veteran of the culture of the prevailing norms), and had failed to grasp this essence of the new culture.

One and a half years later, stories were still being told about his "transgressions." The effects of breaches of cultural norms sometimes linger for a while.

**Vignette 2**

In 1989, Ben & Jerry's Homemade Inc. faced some tough decisions. The values on which the company were founded were being tested by vocal members of the new management team. These new people were "growth oriented"; Ben and Jerry wanted to keep the "family culture" that they had begun with. It could go either way: It could move toward a formalized, bureaucratic structure with a "businesslike" culture, or it could remain the free-spirited, open culture that Ben and Jerry loved. When we last checked in with Ben and Jerry, this market-driven company was becoming more bureaucratic with rapid growth.

SOURCE: Interview with Ben & Jerry's cofounder Jerry Greenfield, conducted by T. Elaine Gagné.

Cultures are also maintained by myth, ritual, and ceremony. Myth and ritual are two sides of the same coin, which Owen calls *mythos*.[34] The myth is the "likely story" that gives shape and focus to the spirit of the organization, and makes everything make sense.[35] Mythos may be defined as "a likely story arising from the life experience of the group, through which they come to experience their past, present and potential."[36] Ceremony is simply a formal ritual of recognition in which cultural values are reinforced and validated.

Thus the culture is maintained by the "story" and it doesn't matter if the story is factually true or not. As the stories are told, they tend to improve with the telling, and, in so doing, become firmly embedded, culturally speaking:

> Mythos images spirit in an organization in such a way that we not only learn about that spirit, but, in addition, may experience the presence of that spirit in immediate, palpable ways. The true function (work) of mythos is to say the unsayable, to express the ineffable, and, most importantly, to bring the participant into an immediate, self-validating relationship with Spirit in the organization. A tall order, to be sure, but a commonplace experience if we stop to think about it . . . for mythos does what any good story does as a matter of course.[37]

It is this "ineffable," "unsayable" aspect of culture that resists the left-brained, analytic approach of the industrial paradigm. One of the pioneers in the work on the corporate culture phenomenon, Terry Deal, says: "Culture ideas have taken me to a realm where it is a little easier for me to understand what goes on around me, *even when I am not able or willing to control it.* Symbolism gives me the ability to be out of control comfortably."[38]

**Vignette 3**

In a study on competition, it was discovered that medical student interns hid their mistakes, because they knew only a small percentage of all the students would pass. The competition was keen, and they did everything they could to stay in the program. When the rule that demanded the failing of a certain percentage of students was lifted, the atmosphere in the hospital became lighter. The students' performance actually improved, because the anxiety level was reduced, there was less stress, and the students were not afraid to ask questions.

## Changing the Culture

As an organization changes and grows through its life cycle, its culture needs to change as well to meet new realities. Even a positive culture can become dysfunctional if ignored.

A corporate culture should be changed if its guiding beliefs are inadequate to meet present and future competitive needs. Stated differently: When a corporation's initial beliefs and values are no longer assets to the company, culture change is indicated. For example, Xerox has gone through three different types of cultures during its life.[39] The first was created under Joseph Wilson, an entrepreneur who was CEO of Xerox from 1961 to 1968. Under Wilson, Xerox had a typical entrepreneurial environment, with an informal, risk-taking culture. Virtually everyone knew everyone else, and this made for a highly motivated workforce. C. Peter McCollough took over as CEO in 1968, and began the era of professional management. Growth led to bureaucratic controls; the culture became formal, with many "turf battles" and layers of "watchdog" managers. This culture of risk aversion and bureaupathic behavior hindered new product development. In 1982, David Kearns took over as CEO. Kearns trimmed Xerox down, stressed quality, and delegated power downward in the organization. Rules and policies became less important, and the innovative spirit returned somewhat.[40]

A culture that prevents a company from addressing competitive pressures or adapting to changing economic contingencies can lead to stagnation and demise. Pepsico faced that problem. Pepsi's cultural emphasis has changed from passivity to aggressiveness; once, the company was content to be "Number 2," offering Pepsi as a cheaper alternative to Coke. But today, as a new Pepsico employee quickly learns, beating Coke is the path to success. Pepsi marketing now takes on Coke directly; in recent years, consumers have been asked explicitly to compare the tastes of the two colas.

This direct confrontation is reflected inside the company as well. Managers are pitted against each other for market share, to work harder and to wring more profit out of their businesses. Because winning is a key value at Pepsico, losing has its penalties. Employees feel the pressure of this culture. Employees who do not succeed are history; even the company picnic thrives on competitive team sports.[41] Managers change jobs often and the atmosphere is "go-go," success at any cost.

If success is beating the competition, then Pepsico's culture change has been successful. But a culture may sometimes need to change for quality-of-life reasons instead. At one point, managers from TRW Systems, Inc., a California aerospace company, attended a sensitivity training course because the growing competitiveness of their field had made their corporate culture more competitive:

> What if the antenna engineer hits a snag in his calculations but refuses to confess the trouble for fear it will damage his chances for promotion? What if he spends a lot of energy defending a mistake once it came to light? What

if he felt resentment towards a colleague who offered help? Obviously, the man would suffer. So would the company.[42]

Although the training attempted to increase self-awareness of trust, expressiveness, caring, empathy, and tolerance for differences, it failed. Once the managers returned to their old culture, their personal success still depended on their adopting the old norms.

## Embedded, "Hard-to-Change" Cultures

It seems to be difficult to change a culture once it is embedded. For example, board members of the now-defunct Falcon Computer tried to create a new culture, an "ideal" culture, in the boardroom. Lacking little overt knowledge of their company's existing culture, they created a document called "Falcon Values," which was filled with ideals that did not match up with the realities of the existing culture—and so were largely ignored by the organizational membership. This lack of congruence between the "Falcon Values" and the existing culture at Falcon led to speculation that the document itself may have been one cause of the company's demise.[43]

Often, difficulties with change begin at the top. A founder's stated values always have an impact on the culture—but his or her *behavior* sends out the clearest signal of what is expected of employees.

---

**Vignette 4**

A small manufacturing facility in the eastern United States is run by a person who wants all decisions centralized. In the company's infancy, the CEO allegedly trusted some people he shouldn't have, and he got burned. Now he is reluctant to trust his employees, and wants all decisions funneled through him or his executive vice president. This is the classic, self-fulfilling Theory X perspective.

His reaction is certainly understandable, but his actions send confusing messages. He tells his employees that he wants them to make decisions in their areas of responsibility, but when they do and they make what are deemed to be "mistakes," the CEO comes down hard on them. So although his spoken values are for teamwork, cooperation, and delegation, his behavior has produced a company with a powerless middle management and employees who expend a great deal of effort to "please" him. Hence the political infighting is intense, as everyone vies for the boss's ear and his stamp of approval.

---

Problems always arise when stated values do not correspond with actual or reinforced values. For example, when innovation and risk taking are the stated values, but mistakes are ridiculed and/or punished, employees will not take risks or come up with new ideas; the resulting culture values playing it safe and pleasing the boss. A feeling of distrust between management and the employees is the by-product.

Ineffective cultures are often created by what Chris Argyris calls "skilled incompetence," or behavior whereby "managers use practiced routine behavior (skill) to produce what they do not intend (incompetence)."[44] In other words, managers develop what he calls "defensive routines," actions or policies designed to avoid surprise, embarrassment, or threat. These managers are excellent communicators, but in their attempt to smooth over conflict and avoid potentially embarrassing situations, they say what they think others want to hear.

One company Argyris discusses was trying to hammer out a strategic plan. Meeting after meeting, the executives worked cordially, yet nothing emerged in the way of a consensus. Argyris concludes:

> How can skillful actions be counterproductive? When we are skillful, we usually produce what we intend. So, in a sense, did the executives. In this case, the skilled behavior—the spontaneous and automatic responses— was meant to avoid upset and conflict at the meetings. The unintended by-products are what cause trouble. Because the executives don't say what they really mean or test the assumptions they really hold, their skills inhibit the resolution of the important intellectual issues embedded in developing the strategy. Thus the meetings end with only lists and no decisions.[45]

An example of a case in which skillful actions were counterproductive is presented in Vignette 5.

Defensive routines are widespread in ineffective cultures. Many people are afraid to say what they really want to, and many say what they think others want to hear. The result is many mixed messages, such as, "Be innovative and take risks; but be careful." Defensive routines are systemic in nature, in that most people in a company adhere to them. People come and go in the organization, but the defensive routines stay intact. In fact, Argyris says there are four "easy steps to chaos (mixed messages)":

1. *Design a clearly ambiguous message,* such as "Go, but just go so far." Not defining "far" covers the speaker as well as the receiver. The receiver clearly understands the ambiguity and imprecision, but is afraid a request for more clarity will be seen as a sign of immaturity, stupidity, or inexperience. And the receiver may need an "out" someday, so the receivers don't want "far" defined any better than the senders do.

**Vignette 5**

A not-for-profit organization in Colorado was considering a new telephone answering system. The board of this organization was so intent on being skillful at communicating and getting along that it overlooked the fact that their current and projected needs did not warrant the expensive system they were considering.

Those who saw this basic point did not say anything for fear of being considered obstacles to peaceful decision making (this is what Irving Janis calls "groupthink"). The system was voted in. When one board member (who had missed the decision meeting) saw the meeting minutes, he asked, "Why are we doing this? Our setup doesn't warrant this technology. We can do the same job for a fraction of the cost with a different solution." A second board member then spoke in an informal way about the matter to the president of the board. The issue was reopened, and the decision was changed.

SOURCE: Files of Renaissance Business Associates, Inc.

2. *Ignore any inconsistencies in the message.* When people send mixed messages, they do it spontaneously, with no sign the messages are mixed. To show that would be seen as a sign of weakness.

3. *Make the ambiguity and inconsistency in the message undiscussable.* The whole point of sending a mixed message is to avoid dealing with the situation straight on. The sender doesn't want the ambiguity exposed. To challenge the clarity of the sender is to imply that the sender is duplicitous—not a likely thing for a subordinate to do.

4. *Make the undiscussability also undiscussable.* Make the message in a setting that is not conducive to open inquiry, such as a large meeting.[46]

## How Culture Can Be Changed

If a legion of defensive routines is working to prevent change, then how does change happen? There seems to be consensus that *true culture change must begin at the top,* because leadership initially creates cultural norms and boundaries.[47] With top-management commitment, several strategies can be used successfully to create more effective cultures.

Sometimes, executives need to shake up the status quo enough to make employees open up to new ways of doing and saying things. Mergers often provide the impetus for such change. Facing potential conflict between the different cultures of two companies, a merged

**Vignette 6**

A new recruit at a prestigious law firm was keen on listening well and doing a fine job. During a weekly staff meeting, the firm's founder prefaced a question with "I really want you to think about this question and be honest in your answers."

The new recruit did not understand the question (which was really not presented very clearly) and asked for clarification. But before she could finish her request, a senior partner jumped in and changed the subject. The conversation bewildered the new associate; it seemed to go nowhere and was full of praise for the founder. Later, the new person learned the unspoken rule: *Never question the founder on anything, regardless of what he might say.*

SOURCE: Files of Renaissance Business Associates, Inc.

**Vignette 7**

The CEO of a large manufacturing company sends a photocopy of a seven-page article from the *Academy of Management Review* titled "Managerial Subordination" to the vice president in charge of personnel. Attached to the copy is a note that says, "Ralph, please *exercise on this* at your earliest opportunity. Marsh." Ralph sends the article to his assistant, Sheila, with the note, "Sheila, let's exercise on this. Ralph."

The process continues down the chain of command until it can go no lower. Ted gets the article with the note, "Ted, I'd like you to exercise on this. This is something Mr. Marsh wants now." This is basically a corporate ritual in which lower participants get their exercise. No one knows what Marsh means by "exercise on this," but, for fear of looking stupid or, worse, insubordinate, they don't ask.

SOURCE: "Don't Ask," in R. Richard Ritti and G. Ray Funkhouser, *The Ropes to Skip and the Ropes to Know* (3rd ed.) (New York: John Wiley, 1987), 213-215.

organization can create a new, joint culture. To create this new "partnership," several steps can be taken:

1. Create a new, single culture that is appropriate for all the entities that have become part of the merged organization. Define its purpose, what it stands for, why it exists.

**Vignette 8**

A human resource vice president sent to a colleague in another company a list of self-help courses purported to promote effectiveness in the workplace. Included in the listing were such courses as "How to Bonsai Your Pet" and "How to Turn Your Family Room Into a Garage." When the VP visited her friend's office, she noticed the list in memo form on the desk of one of her friend's subordinates. It appeared that her friend had only glanced at the list casually and passed it along for routing. If the friend had read the list with any care, it would have been clear to her that it never should have been routed. The whole affair caused quite a chuckle at the expense of the person who routed it.

2. Define norms, myths, rituals, and ceremonies that will enhance unity of spirit, results orientation, and cohesiveness.
3. Be willing to not know. In managing culture, what matters is asking the right questions, not in providing ready-made answers.[48]

One innovative way to defeat the defensive routines that prevent conflictual situations and block cultural change is to use Argyris's "how to become unskilled" approach.[49] To uncover defensive routines and begin to make beliefs and operating assumptions more conscious in an organization, leaders can take some specific steps:

1. Arrange a two-day retreat session for all managers.
2. At the retreat, have everyone write up cases relating to problems they face at work.
3. Have the group solve each case, assuming they could talk to whomever they wished. Next, have participants explore what they would *actually* say in each case (plus their guesses as to the responses of the persons they would talk to) as well as what they would *like to* say (along with their thought and feelings).

Working on such cases can produce vivid examples of skilled incompetence. But by uncovering these hidden assumptions, feelings, and thoughts, executives can become more conscious and a norm of openness can develop whereby the culture shifts dramatically.[50]

Schein makes some interesting observations about the whole process of culture change:

If trainers and OD (organizational development) consultants get serious about culture change, then they must base their work on correct conceptual models of what the change process involves. It will require a period of unfreezing that includes the pain of disconfirmation. . . . old assumptions no longer work. OD consultants must provide psychological safety, communicating the possibility of bearing the temporary anxiety of giving up the old assumptions while new ones are learned. Leadership is critical at this stage; it requires strength to help the group cope with and not avoid anxiety. Leaders not only develop and articulate new visions but they create trust. They help the members of the group survive the anxieties that accompany transitions. . . .

Should trainers and consultants attempt to be change agents in this sense or should they limit their role to helping those in power be clearer in their own thinking? Leaders do have to change cultures if their vision tells them that to stay the course threatens extinction. But, in producing such change, in using their power and vision to produce anxiety and start a new learning process, leaders have to take the responsibility both for the process and for the ultimate outcomes. Are consultants and trainers who advocate certain kinds of cultures really prepared to accept this kind of responsibility?[51]

The idea of "changing a culture" is fraught with difficulty. Who is to say how a culture *should* be? A consultant? The employees? The management? Also, cultures are not created overnight. If they have been reinforced over time, they tend to become entrenched and resistant to change efforts.[52] Finally, if it is easy to define what a "good" culture is and it is easy to change a "bad" culture, why don't more organizations have good cultures? If organizations could "install" a culture such as that at IBM, McDonald's, or Xerox, wouldn't they do it? Just because one can describe a culture doesn't mean one can change it.

## What Is an Effective Culture?

Earlier in this chapter, we pointed out that a strong culture is not necessarily an effective one. In fact, cultures seem to range on a continuum from effective to ineffective in the following way:

1. *Reactive organizations* just react to environmental changes or internal changes; they meet challenge with action (*Do something!*) and always seem to be struggling to keep up.
2. *Responsive organizations* are responsive to their own needs, their customers' needs, and changing environmental needs. They are satisfactory in stable environments but tend to get defensive in dynamic circumstances.

3. *Proactive organizations* have an analytic quality about them such that they try to anticipate emerging trends, market changes, and the like so that they can adapt accordingly. Their capacity for self-criticism and environmental assessment keeps them on top of things.

4. *Interactive organizations* are vision based and function as a whole. The interactive organization perceives itself in its connectedness as opposed to its several parts. "Whereas the pro-active organization approached itself in an analytical, reductionistic fashion, seeking to identify problems that may be isolated, fixed or replaced, the interactive organization approaches itself as a totality in which parts may be arbitrarily identified as discrete entities, but ultimately make no sense or have separate existence apart from the whole."[53] Vision and whole-centeredness are the keys.

5. *Inspired organizations* are the equivalent of "self-actualized" organizations. Beginning with the narrow particularity of the reactive organization, spirit is transformed through responsiveness, proactivity, and interactivity. At each stage, the constraints of form and structure becomes of less consequence, whereas the possibility for the full expression of spirit in time and space increases. Yet, even at the interactive level, form and structure are important and constraining considerations. The inspired level brings the possibility of *going beyond these constraints.*[54]

If cultural behavior by leaders is consistent with spoken values, if the culture enhances the strategic direction of the organization, and if the culture allows for individual expression and creativity, that culture is likely to be *effective.*

## Creating Culture in the New Paradigm

A transformational definition of an effective culture might be as follows: a culture in which the organization plays its part in the larger whole, changing as needed with the changing cycles of the creative process, of which it is a part. In a real sense, this is independent of judgments of "good" and "bad." The keys to an effective and healthy culture seem to include the following:

- a leader who sets the tone for culture formation and culture change
- an ability to recognize and play the organization's part in the larger whole (this is usually measured first by survival and then by profitability in the long term)
- frequent self-examination, to determine whether the organization's assumptions, values, and operating beliefs are still valid

Deal and Kennedy make some normative statements about what they call the ideal, "atomized" culture of the future.[55] They think a new kind of corporate culture may be emerging. The "atomized organization," with an emphasis on small size and flexibility of work units, is basically a "no boss" business (i.e., it has no one with direct formal authority).[56] This culture is much as one would expect attendant to an organic organization. Its features include a *highly productive workforce*, with a high mean educational level and high pay (white-collar, flexible, less job dependent, interested in self-actualization); and *smaller work units* (10-20 people maximum), each unit having control of its own destiny (autonomy) economically and managerially.

Deal and Kennedy see this culture as being strong within the work unit as well as within the larger organization.[57] They cite four reasons:

1. Workers will be more effective if they feel in control of their destinies.
2. Peer group pressure seems to be a motivating factor within the group, creating cohesion.
3. Cultural bonds are stronger with high cohesion and autonomy.
4. Communications technology and electronic data processing will increase work unit effectiveness.[58]

Organization culture can help a manager understand what binds people together in the workplace. It can also be an important tool for changing an organization's strategy, for strategy and culture are intimately connected. Where the company wants to go in the future is linked to values, as is its cultural underpinning. The two must be compatible.

With a knowledge of culture, managers can design ceremonies, symbols, and rituals to emphasize new beliefs, attitudes, and values that are to be shared (or to reinforce old ones) and use stories and myths to create new, life-affirming values (or to reinforce old ones). One example of someone who does this is Jim Treybig of Tandem Computers. Through a number of ceremonies and stories, he has defined and reinforced a culture that seems to fit the strategy of the firm. For instance, at 4:00 p.m. every Friday afternoon the employee beer bust is in full swing.[59] Another event is the "incredible hunk" contest, in which female employees vote for their favorite males. Fun prevails, yet the work ethic is strong. Through his culture's rituals, Treybig seeks to express "five cardinal rules":

1. All people are good.
2. People, workers, management, and company are all the same thing (a holistic perspective?).
3. Every single person in the company must understand the essence of the business.
4. Every employee must benefit from the company's success.
5. Leaders must create an environment where all of the above can happen.[60]

# Conclusion

Culture can be a powerful tool for transformation, or it can reinforce rigidity and skilled incompetence. The key to its function seems to lie in the *conscious awareness* of the culture's participants. The degree to which hidden assumptions, beliefs, and values are subject to constant inquiry and scrutiny is critical. Powerful, effective cultures have a norm whereby *all* assumptions are continually examined for workability and utility.

Consultant Brian Hall, an Episcopal priest, has spent some 30 years developing and refining a values inventory that can be used by organizations to create cultures based on their highest values.[61] Hall and his company are assisting major corporations in changing cultures and developing leaders with value orientations that can keep them moving, changing, and developing. Culture change as a transformational tool is here to stay.

## NOTES

1. Edgar H. Schein, "What You Need to Know About Organizational Culture," *Training and Development Journal* (January 1986): 31. Reprinted with permission (see copyright notice, p. 194).

2. Stanley M. Davis, *Managing Corporate Culture* (Cambridge, MA: Ballinger, 1984); cited in Paul McCracken, "Changing the Code," *Changing Times*, September 10, 1985, 64.

3. Bernard C. Reimann and Yoash Wiener, "A Typology of 'Generic' Corporate Cultures" (paper presented to the Business Policy and Planning Division at the annual meeting of the Academy of Management, Chicago, August 1986), 4.

4. Yoash Wiener, "Commitment in Organizations: A Normative View," *Academy of Management Review* 7, no. 1 (1982): 424.

5. Davis, *Managing Corporate Culture*, 3.

6. Ibid.

7. Reimann and Wiener, "A Typology," 4.

8. See Thomas J. Peters and Robert H. Waterman, Jr., *In Search of Excellence: Lessons From America's Best-Run Companies* (New York: Harper & Row, 1982); "Who's Excellent Now?" *Business Week*, November 5, 1984, 76-78.

9. Linda Smircich, "Concepts of Culture and Organizational Analysis," *Administrative Science Quarterly* 28 (December 1983); see also Peters and Waterman, *In Search of Excellence*.

10. John M. Ivancevich and Michael T. Matteson, *Organizational Behavior and Management* (Plano, TX: Business Publications, 1987), 29.

11. Terrence E. Deal and Allan A. Kennedy, *Corporate Cultures: The Rites and Rituals of Corporate Life* (Reading, MA: Addison-Wesley, 1982), 107.

12. Reimann and Wiener, "A Typology," 7.

13. Rosabeth Moss Kanter, *The Change Masters: Innovation for Productivity in the American Corporation* (New York: Simon & Schuster, 1983).

14. Deal and Kennedy, *Corporate Cultures*, 21-36.

15. Schein, "What You Need to Know," 31.

16. Robert C. Ford, Barry Armandi, and Cherrill P. Heaton, *Organization Theory: An Integrative Approach* (New York: Harper & Row, 1988), 455-456.

17. See, for example, Schein, "What You Need to Know"; Ralph H. Kilmann, Mary J. Saxton, Roy Serpa, and Associates, *Gaining Control of the Corporate Culture* (San Francisco: Jossey-Bass,

1986); Davis, *Managing Corporate Culture;* Gareth Morgan, *Riding the Waves of Change* (San Francisco: Jossey-Bass, 1988); Kanter, *The Change Masters.*

18. Harry C. Miller, "Forecasting the Weather and Controlling the Organizational Climate," *Vital Speeches,* August 1980, 610-612.

19. Kilmann et al., *Gaining Control.*

20. Ibid., 66.

21. Ibid.

22. Edgar H. Schein, *Organizational Culture and Leadership* (San Francisco: Jossey-Bass, 1985), 114-119. Used with permission from the publisher.

23. Gareth Morgan, *Images of Organization* (Beverly Hills, CA: Sage, 1986), 113-114.

24. Ibid.

25. Ibid., 121.

26. Deal and Kennedy, *Corporate Cultures.*

27. Morgan, *Riding the Waves of Change,* 122.

28. William G. Tierney, review of *Organizational Culture and Leadership,* by Edgar H. Schein, *Academy of Management Review* (April 1986): 677.

29. Peters and Waterman, *In Search of Excellence.*

30. Ibid.

31. Ibid., 132.

32. Kilmann et al., *Gaining Control,* 62-68.

33. Harrison Owen, "Leadership by Indirection," in *Transforming Leadership: From Vision to Results,* ed. John D. Adams (Alexandria, VA: Miles River, 1986), 115.

34. Harrison Owen, *Spirit: Transformation and Development in Organizations* (Potomac, MD: Abbott, 1987), 12.

35. See C. J. Jung, *Symbols of Transformation* (Princeton, NJ: Princeton University Press, 1956).

36. Owen, *Spirit,* 15.

37. Ibid., 22.

38. Terrence E. Deal, *Research on Culture* (New York: ASTD, 1986); quoted in Schein, "What You Need to Know," 32; emphasis added.

39. John Byrne, "Culture Shock at Xerox," *Business Week,* June 22, 1987, 106-108.

40. Ibid.

41. Richard L. Daft, *Organization Theory and Design* (2nd ed.) (New York: West, 1986), 487.

42. John Poppy, "It's OK to Cry at the Office," *Look,* July 9, 1988, 67.

43. Ibid.

44. Chris Argyris, *Overcoming Organizational Defenses* (Boston: Allyn & Bacon, 1990); quoted in Fred Kofman and Peter M. Senge, "Communities of Commitment: The Heart of Learning Organizations," *Organizational Dynamics* (Fall 1993): 9.

45. Argyris, *Overcoming Organizational Defenses,* 75.

46. Ibid., 76.

47. Schein, *Organizational Culture and Leadership.*

48. Morty Lefkbe, "Why So Many Mergers Fail," *Fortune,* July 20, 1987, 113-114.

49. Argyris, *Overcoming Organizational Defenses,* 77.

50. Ibid.

51. Schein, "What You Need to Know," 32.

52. Stephen P. Robbins, *Organization Theory: Structure, Design, and Applications* (2nd ed.) (Englewood Cliffs, NJ: Prentice Hall, 1987), 369-370.

53. Ibid., 51.

54. Ibid., 47-53.

55. Deal and Kennedy, *Corporate Cultures,* 177-185.

56. Ibid., 177.

57. Ibid., 182-183.

58. Ibid., 184.

59. Daft, *Organization Theory and Design,* 491.

60. Myron Magnet, "Managing by Mystique at Tandem," *Fortune,* June 28, 1982, 84-91.

61. Brian T. Hall, *The Genesis Effect* (New York: Paulist Press, 1986).

# 19   Structural Conflict in Organizations

> *Organizational conflict is something we all experience more or less on a day-to-day basis as we attempt to perform our roles and manage our careers in complex organizations. In fact, the inevitability of conflict is assured by forces residing both inside and outside our organizations. The hard design choices involving structures, technologies, and tasks needed to accomplish the mission of the organization often create and reinforce differences in the operations, goals and orientations between organizational members and subunits. Moreover, the external environment of organizations sometimes changes in ways that necessitate a reshuffling of priorities and resource allocations among internal subunits and stimulate shifts in the balance of power and patterns of influence between them.*
>
> (Robert H. Miles,
> *Macro Organizational Behavior,* 1980, p. 120)

---

**SUMMARY:** A key industrial era assumption about conflict is that it is inevitable. Most work in this area starts with that assumption and discusses strategies for resolving it, at best, in a "win-win" manner. Few suggest that a state could exist in which conflict is transcended. In this chapter, we review the major work in this area by traditional researchers and scholars, and then present a transformational perspective that gives the parameters for a conflict-free state.

---

Everyone in organizations has had, at one time or another, direct experience with organizational conflict. Usually, it centers around some group wanting something that another group has (or wants also).

POT-SHOTS NO. 3691.

**REASONABLE PEOPLE CAN HAVE REASONABLE DIFFERENCES OF OPINION,**

**SO LONG AS NOTHING REALLY IMPORTANT IS AT STAKE.**

Opinions about conflict range from the notion that it is *bad* (dysfunctional) to the belief that it can be *good* (functional). In this chapter, we focus on structural conflict, that is, conflict that originates as a result of structure or process variables inherent in the organizational design itself. So-called personality conflicts (people just not liking each other) are typically a micro organizational behavior topic, and are dealt with elsewhere (in micro organizational behavior texts, among other places).

---

## Defining Structural Conflict

---

*Structural conflict* refers to disputes or disagreements between units of organizations, not simply between individual organization members. Miles views conflict as "a condition that is manifested when the goal-oriented intentional behaviors of members of one unit or a coalition of units result in blocked goal-directed behaviors and expectations of members of other organizational units."[1] Hodge and Anthony state that "conflict occurs when two or more individuals or groups that have opposing goals, ideas, philosophies, or orientations confront each other in some way. They might oppose each other by vying for resources, support, etc., to ensure that their position prevails."[2] A brief overview yields the following definitions of conflict:

1. a struggle over values and claims to scarce status, power, and resources in which the aims of the opponents are to neutralize, injure, or eliminate their rivals[3]
2. a type of behavior that occurs when two or more parties are in opposition or in battle as a result of perceived relative deprivation from the activities of or interacting with another person or group[4]
3. overt behavior arising out of a process in which one unit seeks the advancement of its relationship with the others; advancement must result from determined action, not fortuitous circumstance[5]
4. the process that begins when one party perceives that the other has frustrated, or is about to frustrate, some concern of his or hers[6]

According to Robbins, there are a number of *common themes* found in conflict situations:

1. Conflict must be perceived by the parties to the conflict. It takes two to make a fight.
2. Opposition, blockage (of a goal), and scarcity crop up consistently.
3. The parties to the conflict have interests or goals that appear to them to be in conflict (the perception issue again).
4. *Intent* comes into play where blocking behavior is concerned; is it intentional or merely a result of "fortuitous circumstances"?
5. Signs of overt struggle must usually be present for a situation to be recognized as conflict.[7]

Robbins supplies his definition of conflict: "a process in which an effort is purposely made by A to offset the efforts of B by some form of blocking that will result in frustrating B in attaining her goals or furthering her interests."[8] A highly publicized instance of intraorganizational conflict is described in Vignette 1.

## Types of Structural Conflict

There are two general types of structural conflict: horizontal and vertical.[9] *Horizontal conflict* occurs between two groups at the same level of the organizational hierarchy, such as the classic disputes between line and staff units, or the frequent rifts between parallel departments—sales and production, for example—that occur as a result of horizontal differentiation. *Vertical conflict* arises from differences in hierarchical level. Conflict can arise over differences in control, philosophy, wages,

**Vignette 1**

In 1985, at Apple Computer, Steve Wozniak, one of the company's founders, had invented the hot-selling Apple II computer. Wozniak's creation became the backbone of Apple's sales. Wozniak's partner and Apple's cofounder, Steven Jobs, was strongly focused on product development and was heading up the Mac project, the development of the now-famous Macintosh PC, which was to compete directly with the IBM PC and be Apple's "product of the future."

A conflict situation arose from the attention being lavished on the Mac project; while Mac Division employees watched Jobs's presentation of the new computer from front-row seats in the auditorium, the Apple II people watched on closed-circuit TV sets in another room. Clearly, in Jobs's view, the Apple II was old hat and the Mac was the future of the company; the differential treatment the two groups received caused Wozniak to resign and the morale of the Apple II personnel to plummet. A great deal of internal conflict ensued.

SOURCES: Deborah C. Wise and Geoffrey C. Lewis, "A Split That's Sapping Morale at Apple," *Business Week*, March 11, 1985, 106-107; Edward Nee, "Sculley Confirms Rift With Jobs," *Electronic News*, July 29, 1985, 22.

© BRILLIANT ENTERPRISES 1974.                              POT-SHOTS NO. 581

IT CAN'T
MAKE THINGS
ANY WORSE.

scarce resources, psychological distance, and goals. For instance, a company headquarters staff often finds itself in conflict with its geographically dispersed regional offices. Management can conflict with workers; in fact, the rise of trade unionism was seemingly caused by such conflict. Franchisers can conflict with franchisees; for example, the head office of McDonald's can want to impose uniform standards of restaurant design on the Des Moines, Iowa, restaurant, and the local franchisee might think a different design would attract more customers. A good example of vertical conflict is presented in Vignette 2.

---

**Vignette 2**

In 1981-1982, the Professional Air Traffic Controller's Organization (PATCO) undertook what became an infamous strike. With a high level of internal cohesion, PATCO's members decided to strike for higher wages and better working conditions. Counting on the fact that the job of air traffic controller is recognized as extremely stressful and crucial to the safety of the air traffic system, the leaders of the union were almost arrogant in their demands.

However, President Reagan, through Secretary of Transportation Drew Lewis, told PATCO officials that their strike was illegal, and that it would be broken regardless of cost. PATCO officials assumed that Reagan was bluffing, but they miscalculated. Their emotional commitment to solidarity outweighed any thought of compromise with the "enemy," in this case the federal government. So, as they say, the rest is history. Reagan broke the union with wide public support, and the controllers found themselves without jobs.

SOURCES: Paul Galloway, "Negotiating Consultant Says Air Controllers Can't Win Strike," *Houston Chronicle*, August 25, 1981; Harry Bernstein, "Union Misjudged Government," *Houston Chronicle*, September 4, 1981.

---

"Of peer conflicts, conflict of agenda is the most serious. Achievement of goals is the reason for the existence of most supervisory and managerial employees. On the peer level, when those personal and professional agendas come into conflict, disaster looms."

— Mary Jean Parson, "The Peer Conflict," *Supervisory Management*, May 1986, 25.

POT-SHOTS NO. 212

**ALL I WANT IS**

**A LITTLE MORE**

**THAN I'LL**

**EVER GET.**

© BRILLIANT ENTERPRISES 1970

Ashleigh Brilliant

## Stages of Conflict

Conflict episodes seem to proceed in a predictable pattern. Louis Pondy argues that all structural conflict passes through five stages:

1. *Latent stage:* This stage is characterized by the conditions or antecedents of conflict (described below). These conditions constitute the context from which conflict might spring.
2. *Perceived conflict stage:* This occurs when one or more of the parties perceives the potential for conflict. Some call this the *cognitive aspect of the conflict,* because a mental appreciation of a symptom of conflict is noted here.
3. *Felt stage:* This is the stage when emotions are aroused, hostility is felt, and defenses come into play.
4. *Manifest conflict stage:* This is when behavior of a conflictual nature puts in an appearance. The behavior can take the form of catty remarks, apathy, or overt aggression.
5. *Conflict aftermath:* This is the stage after the overt conflict has manifested, and it can be resolution or a recycling of the incident into a new latent phase (for more conflict).[10]

---

## Antecedents to
## Organizational Conflict

---

Actual conflict seems to arise, in the dominant industrial paradigm, out of latent or potential conflict. In other words, there are situations that can potentially lead to conflict as a result of structural arrangement.

### Horizontal Differentiation

Horizontal differentiation is always a potential source of conflict, because different departments, functions, committees, and other groupings tend to have different attributes, concepts, priorities, and goals. Lawrence and Lorsch have identified four ways in which differentiation is reflected:

1. the manager's goal orientation
2. the time orientation (short- or long-term)
3. the interpersonal orientation
4. the formality of structural arrangements[11]

POT-SHOTS NO. 176.

IT'S NOT FAIR THE WAY YOU KEEP RETALIATING

AGAINST MY UNPROVOKED ATTACKS.

Ashleigh Brilliant

© BRILLIANT ENTERPRISES 1970.

POT-SHOTS NO. 187

I'LL LISTEN TO YOUR
UNREASONABLE
DEMANDS

*Ashleigh
Brilliant*

IF YOU'LL
CONSIDER MY
UNACCEPTABLE OFFER.

©BRILLIANT ENTERPRISES 1970.

For example, a marketing department's goal is sales volume, whereas production's is cost-efficiency. Marketing's time orientation is long-run sales, whereas production's is short-run output. Marketing is people oriented, whereas production is task oriented, and the production department's structural arrangements tend to be much more mechanical than marketing's.

Individuals in each department create their own realities according to their identification with these dimensions—and so from the perspective of the combatants, conflict is a perfectly justified response to "those people in that other department."

## Task Interdependence

Conflict is also possible when one unit is dependent on another for resources, materials, or information. *Pooled interdependence*—such as that found in banks or savings and loans, whose departments are relatively independent—does not often lead to conflict. *Sequential interdependence*—as in the mass-production assembly line—has more potential for conflict, because steps in the work must be accomplished in sequential fashion. *Reciprocal interdependence* has the highest potential for conflict, because constant interaction and mutual adjustment are required for the production process itself. Conflict results in any of these types of interdependency when the coordinating mechanisms become taxed and fail to produce the degree of cooperation required.[12]

**Table 19.1** Interdependence and Coordinating Mechanisms

| Interdependence | Coordinating Mechanisms |
| --- | --- |
| Pooled | RRPP<br>standardization<br>formal authority |
| Sequential | RRPP<br>standardization<br>schedules/plans |
| Reciprocal | RRPP<br>standardization<br>schedules<br>mutual adjustment<br>sapiential authority |

NOTE: RRPP = rules, regulations, policies, and procedures.

### Resource Scarcity

Whenever different units must share common resources, the potential for conflict exists. Resources such as money, space, equipment, personnel, time, and critical information are often fought over. For example, at universities it is not unusual for business schools to be in conflict with

POT-SHOTS NO. 1078.

YES, BUT
EVERY TIME I TRY
TO SEE THINGS YOUR WAY,

I GET
A HEADACHE.

*Ashleigh Brilliant*

© BRILLIANT ENTERPRISES 1977.

liberal arts schools over the allocation of resources; business schools argue that they are the cash cows for their universities (given their high enrollments and tuition revenue generated), whereas the liberal arts people argue for the validity of their offerings as part of a balanced curriculum (even though they don't have the enrollments), the high cost of their individualized instruction approaches, and so on.

In industry, research and development will argue for money on the basis of presumed future payoffs; production will argue in terms of current fiscal needs. Union-management relations is an obvious example of potential vertical conflict over scarce resources. After all expenses are subtracted from revenues generated, the surplus can be distributed to owners, retained in the company for capital needs, or given as bonuses or wage increases to the workers.

Obviously, there are implications beyond mere survival in winning the competition over scarce resources. One's prestige is enhanced when one gains control over resources, and this affects power distribution. Thus managers may submit inflated budget requirements in the knowledge that, even if they get only 80% of what they ask for, it will still be more than other departments receive.

### Goal Incompatibility

The operative goals of each department reflect the actual desired end states the department is trying to actualize or create for itself. Kochan,

Huber, and Cummings assert that goal incompatibility is probably the biggest single source of intergroup conflict.[13] The achievement of one department's goal (e.g., the highest actual sales for the sales department) can interfere with the achievement of another department's goal (e.g., quality of product for the production department). Other examples of goal conflict between marketing and manufacturing include the following:

1. Marketers want product variety for their customers, whereas manufacturing wants long, economical production runs of a few products.
2. Marketers want fast delivery times for their customers, whereas manufacturing wants regular, scheduled production, with no "custom" products.
3. Marketers want good quality at low cost to their customers, whereas manufacturers want good quality despite the cost.[14]

### Uncertainty

In stable times, departments can carve out their turf and negotiate their resources in predictable ways. However, when times are turbulent and new problems are arising constantly, departments may be faced with virtually constant renegotiation.[15] Each group has to sort out how new problems are to be handled, and, given task interdependencies, most likely the solutions will involve several departments. At least one study has shown clearly that nonroutine problems create more conflict than do routine ones.[16]

© BRILLIANT ENTERPRISES 1968                                     POT-SHOTS NO. 91

*Ashleigh Brilliant*

USE YOUR OWN JUDGMENT

THEN DO AS I SAY

POT-SHOTS NO. 1328.

THE MORE WE DISAGREE, THE MORE CHANCE THERE IS THAT AT LEAST ONE OF US IS RIGHT

© BRILLIANT ENTERPRISES 1977

## Low Formalization

Rules, regulations, policies, and procedures provide a conflict-reducing function, in that they can always be referred to in adjudication of a dispute. A high degree of RRPP tends to minimize ambiguity or uncertainty. Standardized role definitions make interactions more programmed and less subject to misinterpretation. With high formalization, opportunities for "misunderstandings" diminish; with low formalization, the opportunity for jurisdictional disputes increases.

## Differences in Rewards and Evaluation Criteria

The more reward systems and evaluation criteria tend to emphasize individual departmental performance, the more conflict will flourish. For example, sales departments tend to be rewarded for maximizing sales, whereas production departments are rewarded for long, economical runs. Sales departments often try to convince credit departments (which are rewarded for minimizing losses) to give delinquent customers "one more chance" before declaring them unworthy of credit. Line and staff units have different evaluation criteria, too. Staff departments tend to emphasize change, because they are paid to recommend it. Line people, on the other hand, want stability and predictability; not only do they not want change, they often can't see the rationale for disturbing the status quo.

## Jurisdictional Ambiguities

Ambiguities in the definitions of work domains (who is responsible for what) tend to escalate the potential for conflict. Such lack of clarity over jurisdiction encourages "victimized" units to engage in offensive tactics to get even. Lack of accountability over responsibilities leads to confusion in rewarding and evaluating people, too. Bickering and blame can become common if exact responsibilities over a joint project, for example, are not clearly understood. Ambiguity over the means to specified ends can also create problems.

## Communication Barriers

Communication deficiencies can take many forms. Geographic dispersion—offices in different cities or even different countries—can cause problems. Different training, socialization, and languages inherent to different departments can cause conflict. Sometimes, units in an organization are situated in such a way that they are out of the loop, failing to get information in a timely or accurate way. Finally, work groups that are not in the regular, main flow of work (e.g., shift workers) sometimes are ignored or discriminated against in communication patterns.

## Status Inconsistencies

Conflict can appear in a situation where two groups have unequal status in the organization. Line and staff units are a classic example. Staff units are expected to understand the problems of line personnel, get along with the line, promote their ideas and recommendations to the line and, in general, justify their existence, whereas the line units have no such obligations.[17] Depending on the organization, different departments have differing degrees of prestige and credibility. For example, until fairly recently, personnel departments and public relations functions were low-status units; in fact, personnel units often got the weakest members of the organization (who couldn't work anywhere else) because "anybody can work with people."

Serious conflict problems can arise when a low-status unit is required to report to top management on the activities of a higher-status unit. For example, staff units charged with the inspection of another unit's output can endanger the rewards for the higher-status unit. Litterer notes:

> The inspector is hired to find errors, but errors are someone else's output. Therefore, every time the inspector finds an error justifying his position's

existence and opening the opportunity for praise and reward, someone else is losing. The latter's output is shown to be inadequate and his rewards are endangered.[18]

---

"A classic management strain is that of the strongly entrepreneurial and successful worker with management. One example of this is when Merrill Lynch Realty agreed to end their seven-year relationship with top-producer ($33 million in sales in 1987) Olivia Decker. Because of her success, the 39-year-old Ms. Decker had carte blanche from her boss to maintain her own schedule and design her own advertising campaigns and brochures. She decided to leave because 'my boss liked to control what I did. I didn't feel like I had to consult her, but she did.'"

— William Celis III, "Agent's Split With Merrill Lynch Realty Spotlights Classic Management Strains," *Wall Street Journal,* December 6, 1988, B2. Reprinted by permission of *Wall Street Journal,* © 1988 Dow Jones & Company, Inc. All rights reserved worldwide.

---

## Cultural Antecedents

Conflict between groups often arises because each group, seeking to maintain its identity based on shared beliefs, attitudes, and values, compares itself with other groups in the organization and differentiates itself by opposing other groups' initiatives. Intergroup comparison, conflict, or competition actually serves to maintain intragroup culture.[19] This process of the formation of subcultures is similar to what Lawrence and Lorsch describe as differentiation into the various functional parts of the organization.[20]

When sales and production departments have trouble talking to each other, the problem can be viewed as an *intercultural* one. The same can be said of labor-management negotiations. Edgar Schein points out that because "each group in the negotiation has developed a culture of its own," the cultures may not "overlap enough to make mutual understanding possible."[21] An instance of conflict based in cultural antecedents is presented in Vignette 3.

Martin and Siehl describe three types of organizational subcultures, one of which is likely to produce conflict:

1. an *enhancing* subculture, in which adherence to the dominant organizational culture would be fervently supported; similar to a "cheerleader/ apologist" grouping

**Vignette 3**

Sanyo Manufacturing Company, a Japanese conglomerate, located a U.S. plant in Forrest City, Arkansas. The Japanese management style, heavily influenced by Japan's dominant culture, emphasizes sacrifice for the whole, teamwork, quality, and harmony. The American culture, which emphasizes competition and individualism, came into sharp focus through the American union representing the Arkansas workforce. The union desired traditional American benefits—seniority, wages, and benefits based upon individual performance, and so on—and this cultural rift finally resulted in an acrimonious 21-day strike in 1985.

SOURCE: Billy Joe Hodge and William P. Anthony, *Organization Theory* (3rd ed.) (Boston: Allyn & Bacon, 1988), 575.

2. an *orthogonal* subculture, which embraces the dominant core values along with a separate set of nonconflicting values and beliefs peculiar to themselves
3. the *counterculture*, which espouses a set of beliefs, attitudes, and values in direct opposition to the dominant culture

The probability and level of conflict between the dominant culture and the counterculture seems to depend on the strength of the two cultures, their internal cohesion, and their inclination to engage in conflictual behavior.[22]

---

## Differing Views of Conflict

---

From the point of view of the industrial paradigm, there are two basic views of conflict. The first is the *traditional* view: that conflict is bad and should be avoided. The second, the *modern* or *interactionist* view, is that conflict can be functional—that is, that conflict can perform beneficial services for the organization. A third view, from the transformational perspective, argues that conflict is not, in fact, inevitable; that is, there is a perspective that can be adopted that allows for the transcendence of conflict.

"Japan is experiencing a change in their here-to-fore tranquil labor and management relations in the wake of their booming economy. These tranquil relations are relatively new following the 25 years after World War II. It wasn't until the early 1970's that there were significant changes in labor-management relations which have subsequently been credited with Japan's ability to compete successfully in the global economy. . . . The system of cooperative labor relations, with the most favorable of economic backdrops, has been nourished by both management and labor and has helped to sustain unprecedented prosperity.

"However, Japan may be pricing itself out of a labor market that sees competition from China, South Korea, and Singapore. Japanese employers consequently find it hard to go to the bargaining table in the same spirit of cooperation that marked earlier years of negotiation. The resultant pressures upon both management and labor must inevitably pervade the talks and could result in discord not seen in Japan for many years."

— Jay S. Siegel, "Japan's Growing Labor Pains," *Wall Street Journal*, December 19, 1988, A14. Reprinted with permission of The Wall Street Journal © 1988 Dow Jones & Company, Inc. All rights reserved.

© BRILLIANT ENTERPRISES 1971

POT-SHOTS NO. 281

# AGREE WITH ME NOW:

# IT WILL SAVE SO MUCH TIME.

## The Traditional View

The traditional view of conflict assumes that conflict is bad. As Robbins and others have pointed out, "anticonflict values permeate our society."[23] Under the current paradigm, conflict is taken to be an indicator that things are not right, and many people prefer the appearance of agreement and cooperation to overt conflict. We are uncomfortable with disagreement because it implies that things might need to change.

With the addiction-to-externals phenomenon firmly in place, people get their psychological well-being from predictable circumstances; conflict can mean change, and maybe even unpredictable change! The famous psychologist Abraham Maslow once noted that there generally exists "a fear of conflict, of disagreement, of hostility, antagonism, enmity. There is much stress on getting along with other people, even if you don't like them."[24] According to Maslow:

> We are inculcated with anticonflict values from childhood, and, as a result, most of us grow up with mores that sanction unquestioned authority [the obedience-to-authority feature of the industrial paradigm]. Disagreement is considered unacceptable; all conflicts are bad. . . . We live in a society that has been built on anticonflict values. Parents in the home, teachers and administrators in schools, teachings of the church, and authority figures in social groups all traditionally reinforce the belief that disagreement breeds discontent, which acts to dissolve common ties and leads eventually to the destruction of the system. . . . Our desire for consensus and agreement appears to influence us more than the desire for effective performance.[25]

Daniel Robey points out that our fear of conflict and disagreement is reflected in management attitudes toward conflict:

> In the classical school, bureaucratic theory deals with conflict by emphasizing rules and hierarchy to govern behavior, much like rules and referees in a sporting event keep conflict from getting out of hand. Bureaucracy depends upon the acceptance of rules and of management authority as legitimate. The human relations approach also implies that conflict in organizations is bad and should be eliminated. However, in human relations, the key is to develop mutual understanding and trust between conflicting parties. Hostile attitudes are changed through a variety of training experiences, counseling, and third party interventions. Emphasis is on communications and trust, in hopes that the parties will see that working together is more productive than working at cross-purposes.[26]

The human relations approach, in and of itself, has an optimistic view of human nature, seeing people as receptive to appeals to the common

© ASHLEIGH BRILLIANT 1981.

POT-SHOTS NO. 2074.

**HOW COULD THERE EVER POSSIBLY BE ANY CONFLICT BETWEEN MY PRIVATE INTERESTS AND THE PUBLIC GOOD?**

good.[27] The overriding assumption is that people can rise up to a level where conflict can be avoided. But, factually speaking, the industrial paradigm, with its dominant values of competition, status, and "winning," tends to guarantee conflict.

Overall, however, the traditional view sees conflict as something that must be eliminated at all costs. The assumption is that, *if conflict does exist, a top priority is to get rid of it.* It is the manager's role to reduce tensions and calm the waters. However, more modern researchers in the field of conflict see this repression, or sweeping under the rug, of conflict as essentially unhealthy.

### The Modern or Interactionist View

According to this view, an organization totally devoid of conflict would be stagnant, uncreative, and unresponsive. The interactionist viewpoint is that *conflict can be functional;* that is, it can provide some unique benefits for the organization. For example, conflict can be a signal for needed change. Lawrence and Lorsch argue that some level of conflict between departments can have beneficial effects.[28] When competing departments vie over scarce resources, it can serve to unify each of the departments, leading to greater internal cohesion. Conflict can help to generate new ideas and new ways of doing things. It can also bring into question organizational goals and strategies; this can lead to a healthy review of vision or direction.

Conflict can be an "energizer"; in other words, conflict can get the organization or department moving again, after a period of "stuckness." It also serves as a thermostat, a regulator, whereby management can see areas that need attention. It can sharpen issues for in-depth examination. Conflict can also serve as a power-balancing mechanism; one author argues that "the most effective prerequisite for preventing struggle, the exact knowledge of the comparative strength of the two parties, is very often only attainable by the actual fighting out of the conflict."[29] Conflict can lead to greater group linkages (in collaborative liaisons against a common "enemy") and better-defined group identities and boundaries.

But not all conflict is good. Some conflicts *are* destructive and have no useful purpose. Destructive conflict reduces cooperation and teamwork, produces violence and enmity, destroys the status quo without offering a constructive substitute, and leads to disintegration.[30] According to the interactionist view, the manager's job is to create a context where conflict can be expressed in a healthy way, but is not allowed to run to destructive extremes. Obviously, this requires that managers adopt new values and attitudes, so that they can see conflict as a source of energy and innovation, rather than only as a destructive force.[31]

POT-SHOTS NO. 1510.

IF YOU CAN'T GO AROUND IT, OVER IT, OR THROUGH IT, YOU HAD BETTER NEGOTIATE WITH IT.

Ashleigh Brilliant

© ASHLEIGH BRILLIANT 1978

© ASHLEIGH BRILLIANT 1980

POT-SHOTS NO. 1676.

LOOK OUT!

YOU'RE STEPPING ON MY VALUES!

Ashleigh Brilliant

## The Transformational View

The transformational view is radically different from the other two, in that it does not assume that conflict is necessary or inevitable. However, the transformational view acknowledges that, in the current self-centered paradigm of the industrial era, conflict is inevitable. Conflict, from the transformational viewpoint, is the result of *attachment* or *loyalty* to something. Attachment or loyalty can occur at three distinct levels of human function:

1. *The physical level:* As children we become attached to our favorite stuffed animals or dolls; as we mature, we become attached to our friends, our parents, our BMWs, and so on. Attachment or loyalty to a material thing means that if someone else wants that same thing, the potential for conflict exists. Also, and perhaps more important, if we are attached to something, that thing becomes important to our identity (or how we define ourselves and our worth). Especially in a world where the consensual agreement is in so-called scarce resources (the science of economics is based on that assumption), the possibility for conflict at the physical level is high.

2. *The level of the mind:* Ideas, beliefs, attitudes, values, philosophies, and even religions are all based on *concepts*. People become loyal to or attached to their own ideas, beliefs, and values, and, thinking they have the "truth" in a given situation, are willing to do battle with any others who might disagree. Identity is also a factor here; we are prone to defining ourselves

in terms of the ideas we hold dear, and are reluctant to allow them to be challenged. For example, if a person's religious affiliation gives him meaning and status, then he may be willing to fight anyone who tries to challenge it.

3. *The level of spiritual reality:* When identity is truly in the spirit of life itself, conflict can be transcended. When one's identity is here, one is, by definition, infinite; there is no scarcity and, therefore, nothing to have conflict over.

What does this mean in practical, organizational terms? First, we must stop reacting automatically to environmental circumstances. Roger Harrison notes: "Thought is seen as the source of outer reality. We create reality through thought. Thus, we need not struggle with things-as-they-are. Instead, we may change our mode of perception and thus the quality of our experience."[32] This means we should disentangle ourselves from the level of external form, and take 100% responsibility for the world that we create. We must refuse to react, blame, criticize, or resent, even if our minds tell us that we are justified and our emotions churn violently. Remember, if your identity is in your physical form, then if your body feels bad, *you* feel bad. If your identity is in your feelings and you have a sad feeling, *you* are sad. If your identity is in your beliefs and those beliefs are challenged, *you* are threatened.

© ASHLEIGH BRILLIANT 1985.   POT-SHOTS NO. 3839

SHAME ON OUR OPPONENTS

FOR USING THE SAME DESPICABLE METHODS WE OURSELVES HAVE ALWAYS USED WHEN NECESSARY.

Ashleigh Brilliant

If we can stop our automatic reactions, we can then proceed through a four-step creative process:[33]

- *Step 1: Stillness—the internal state of quiet mind and emotion.* This is not necessarily the absence of external chaos but rather the art of being still regardless of the external state, much as an athlete would be prior to the start of an athletic event. It is out of this stillness that the next three steps flow.

- *Step 2: Connection*[34]—*honoring the relation to the important factors in the situation.* This includes connection to tangible as well as intangible factors such as other people's perspectives, machines, and one's own attitude regarding the situation. Before appropriate action can be taken, it is important to be aware of the current circumstance just as it *is* rather than how it *should* be.

- *Step 3: Action*—pro-*action* rather than re-*action* is what is required here. The first (pro-action) is based on an internal source of control; the second (re-action) is the knee-jerk reaction to the circumstance; i.e., the circumstance is in control.

- *Step 4: Creation—the difference between creation and results is the mastery of the person moving through the first three steps of the creative process. Anyone can achieve results, but only the master can infuse his or her artistry in such a way that results evolve into creation.*

When we stop reacting to (and being polarized by) externals, we begin a process wherein our capacities of mind and emotion begin to settle down from their self-centered, fear-based striving and become available for our use in true identity. Just the opposite happens each time we allow ourselves to be gripped by "justified" reactions; those reactions strengthen the polarity into the external world and increase the emotional upset, which effectively prevents alignment with the ongoing creative process.

When we find our identities truly in the spirit of life consistently, we will not be party to conflict. This does not mean we will be cheery-faced automatons. We will act and move as needed in any situation. Sometimes we will be firm, sometimes light. People around us, mired in the self-centered, addictive state, will often be engaged in conflictual situations. They may try to draw us into their dramas, but we will always have the choice: Do we remain faithful to our true identity and express our highest qualities of character, or do we sink into the addictive state of self-centered human nature and react to our circumstances? The whole question of conflict dissolves if we are not willing to participate! By rising above the level where conflict can exist (the level of attachment to things, ideas, feelings), we can remain attuned to the creative process and flow with its inherent rhythms (with no reactivity).

©ASHLEIGH BRILLIANT 1983.  POT-SHOTS NO. 2914.

**BUT IF I YIELD TO YOUR REASONABLE DEMANDS, I'LL NEVER BE SAFE FROM YOUR REASONABLE DEMANDS AGAIN.**

---

### Review of the Creative Process[35]

| Being Aspect | Achieving Aspect |
|---|---|
| 1. stillness | 3. action |
| 2. connection | 4. creation |

---

## Traditional Conflict Resolution Strategies

---

Conflict resolution approaches can be divided into three categories: win-lose, lose-lose, and win-win.

### Win-Lose

The win-lose strategy is based on the dominance of one group over another: The strong group wins, and the weak group loses. From the perspective of the winning group, this is a fine approach. From the point of view of the losers, it is not satisfactory; resentment, get-even strategies, and withdrawal are common results for the losing side. Other strategies that often result in win-lose outcomes are as follows:

1. use of power and/or authority (suppression)
2. smoothing (the use of consoling, affective language to restore peaceful relations)
3. avoidance (in which one party to the conflict simply ignores what has happened and leaves the field of potential conflict)
4. co-optation (the merging of a weaker hostile group into the larger and stronger group, e.g., corporate mergers)

### Lose-Lose

Lose-lose outcomes are the result of the stubbornness and intransigence of the two parties to the conflict. For example, in the PATCO strike described in Vignette 2, the union lost its identity and members lost their jobs, and the government and the public lost as well, experiencing delays at airports, increased fears about flying safety, and increased cost and time delays necessitated by having to train new air traffic controllers.

## Win-Win

In a win-win scenario, both sides come away feeling they have won. This does not mean that both got all they wanted, but it does mean that both feel the final resolution is acceptable. Various win-win strategies have some features in common; they begin by acknowledging the differences between the groups, but then they focus on *areas of agreement* (and the expansion of those) and *mutual benefits to be gained by settlement.* Some strategies that can yield win-win solutions include the following:

1. *confrontation and cooperation,* in which the conflict is faced squarely and dealt with based on facts rather than emotions (although emotions are certainly not ignored)[36]
2. *democratic process,* which uses full participation in airing differences and seeking joint solutions to create greater "ownership" of the final resolution
3. *third-party intervention,* in which a trained conflict resolution specialist helps conflicting groups arrive at a win-win outcome
4. *superordinate goal,* which frames the "problem" in a larger context (e.g., organizational survival) to persuade warring parties to settle
5. *the mini-max approach,*[37] which requires that parties to the bargaining ask four questions prior to entering the negotiations:

> What is the minimum I can accept?
> What is the maximum I can ask for without getting laughed out of the room?
> What is the maximum I can give away?
> What is the least I can offer without being laughed out of the room?[38]

A number of what Robert H. Miles calls "generic strategies" can also be used to achieve win-win outcomes.[39] In each case, part of the situation is "altered" so that the conflict can be reframed in a manner that encourages resolution.

## Altering the Context

This set of approaches focuses on altering the structural characteristics of the situation to achieve resolution. The larger context of a conflict includes the technology employed by the organization, environmental factors, the size of the organization, internal political factors, and the strategy the organization chooses to implement. For example, task interdependencies and status inconsistencies are often the result of work-flow design. Also, work layout can produce communications barriers and increase jurisdictional ambiguities.

One common way to resolve context disputes is to use an "integrator" or a third-party negotiator who can hear both sides of the dispute and offer creative suggestions for win-win resolution. Similar to this is the use of a *coordinator*. If the accounting and engineering departments of a firm are in conflict, it can be helpful to hire an individual with both engineering and accounting background, so that person can have empathy with both sides.

Under conditions of high task interdependency (e.g., sequential or reciprocal interdependencies), *decoupling* is often used. In a manufacturing unit, that may mean introducing buffer stocks so that one unit doesn't have to depend as much on the other. Another approach to the same end is to *make each work unit self-sufficient*. For example, to avoid conflict over course content, many business schools offer their own courses in mathematics, even though the math department typically offers the same or similar courses.

Still another approach is to institutionalize *grievance systems*. For example, the U.S. Army has the Inspector General group, the purpose of which is to investigate and adjudicate disputes. A final example of altering the context is to create a *buffer unit between the conflicting parties*. One function of middle management in companies is to buffer possible conflicts between lower levels and top management.

## Altering the Issue in Dispute

This approach is also called *issue control*. The idea is to take a large issue over which there is disagreement and "fractionate" it into smaller issues, so that there is more likelihood of agreement.[40] The Middle Eastern peace negotiators have been using this strategy for some time. "Separate the people from the problem" is an example of fractionating the issue; in other words, ask two conflicting parties to focus on the problem but separate themselves emotionally from identification with it by concentrating on the facts and practical solutions. Taking a position (defending a point of view) makes for tougher conflict resolution.[41]

Fractionating also makes it possible for one party to concede on a small issue without feeling that he or she has lost the contest. Piecemeal settlement recognizes that everything cannot be done immediately and that a slow, sequential approach allows for more compromise and win-win outcomes. Also, by fractionating a large issue, the precedent-setting implications become smaller; negotiators are often nervous about "giving in" because they fear the implications for the future. But, for smaller "stakes," people are more willing to be flexible.

## Altering the Relationship Directly

This approach seeks to alter the way in which the conflicting parties interact. The strategies range from total separation of the parties to intense interaction, depending on what is needed in the situation. These techniques can be used in conjunction with changes in the larger structural context or "issue control."

The first strategy is to create a cooling-off period by *separating the units physically,* moving one unit to another floor, another building, or another town. This is useful when task interdependency is low and speed in solving the conflict is of the essence. The second approach is to *allow interaction in only those areas (superordinate goals) where agreement already exists.* Compelling goals that are appealing to both units in the conflict (e.g., opportunities for higher unit productivity) can be very useful. A third approach is to *use integrators to help units to work together* on a common project while maintaining their separate identities. The level of interaction can be moderate here, and is controlled by the integrator so that potentially volatile areas can be sidestepped.

A fourth approach is to *use direct negotiators* (e.g., allies, agents, judges, or mediators) to resolve disputes. These third parties can regulate the interaction between the combatants and focus on resolution. The fifth and final approach in this spectrum is to *require intense interaction between the parties.* In this way, issues can be openly confronted, dealt with almost continually through open meetings until resolution is complete.

## Altering the Individuals Involved

Sometimes the best strategy is to remove one or both of the conflicting parties through dismissal, transfer, or job rotation. Also, there are a variety of training techniques such as T-groups and sensitivity training (developed by the National Training Laboratories in Bethel, Maine) that are designed to increase individuals' empathy for others and willingness to see others' points of view. Team building, process interventions, and behavioral modification strategies also fall under this category.

## Conflict Resolution in the Postindustrial Age

Organisms develop through differentiation and integration. In differentiation, the parts take on unique characteristics that make them different from and independent from one another. These parts are unified and harmonized through integration.

> During the process of differentiation, each part develops its own purpose. Between parts and the whole, relationships of greater or lesser "alignment" and "attunement" come into being. When a resonant relationship (attunement) occurs among the parts, the organism experiences peace, love and mutual nurturance among its parts. When a part consciously chooses to serve the evolution of the whole, alignment occurs, enhancing the well-being of all parts of the organism.[42]

There are two ways to achieve integration in an organizational context. Under the industrial paradigm approach, top managers force compliance with "artificial integrators" such as RRPP, job descriptions, goals, and formal hierarchy to achieve organizational purposes such as profitability and growth. But under the postindustrial paradigm approach, organizations with low formalization, decentralization, and high complexity are integrated by mature people who take 100% responsibility for both their jobs and the organizational purpose, and articulate a clear vision/purpose that can inspire participants to "own" the organization.

The ingredients that will integrate postindustrial organizations of the future will are also the ones that will prevent or substantially reduce conflict in the new paradigm. These key elements are as follows:

- a strong sense of purpose
- a clearly articulated vision that can be communicated to (and owned by) all employees
- an ability to act as parts of an integrated whole, so that the organization remains in alignment and attunement with its vision
- a culture that supports 100% personal responsibility

As the paradigm shifts, leadership is increasingly recognized as a source of inspiration and vitality for an organization.[43] Leaders set the tone for cohesive organizations, and can articulate and communicate a vision and a set of values that can inspire workers to great heights of productivity, quality, and performance. In fact, many so-called theories of high-performing organizations include visionary leadership as a prerequisite.[44]

## Articulating a Vision

A company's most valuable potential resources—energetic, dedicated, and creative employees—are squandered in an environment of mistrust, rules, stifling procedures, and Theory X attitudes. Employees who work under a visionary leader report more involvement in their work, more personal power, and the presence of a welcoming attitude toward change.[45] The following summarizes this position:

> The key to developing inspired performance and an inspired organization lies in cultivating resources that lie within the person . . . deep resources of internal creativity, energy, commitment and work spirit. In promoting health and managing stress, people need to learn how to pay attention to their inner person. The visionary leader, as we call such a person, is a master of not just the external world, but of the skill of inner visioning, a process that involves focusing one's attention inward with the quiet expectancy that something important and relevant will emerge. . . . Inspired performers universally report that they regularly tune into themselves.[46]

What is meant by *vision?* Essentially, "vision is a mental journey from the known to the unknown, creating a future from a montage of current facts, hopes, dreams, dangers and opportunities."[47] Executives with clear vision invent excellent futures for their companies; those who lack it set their companies adrift in turbulent waters. Vignette 4 illustrates the power of a well-articulated vision.

**Vignette 4**

F. W. Woolworth and S. S. Kresge were at one time both retail giants. In the fall of 1982, Woolworth closed 336 of its Woolco stores, laid off 35,000 employees, and wrote off a $325 million loss. In contrast, during the same year, Kresge's K mart chain had $17 billion in sales. Both had the same mass-discounting concept; how were they different?

From the beginning, Kresge boldly launched its vision by opening its stores and quickly discounting everything from tires to refrigerators. Woolworth, on the other hand, without a clear vision, tentatively opened only half of the stores planned for California and scrapped the rest. One executive said, "We couldn't decide which way we wanted to go, variety, discount store, or medium priced, right from the start." Woolco never recovered. Said one competitor: "Woolco had a lot of potential that was never exploited. The people at K mart called them a sleeping giant. But they never woke up."

SOURCE: Craig R. Hickman and Michael A. Silva, *Creating Excellence* (New York: New American Library, 1984), 150-151.

Leaders must take responsibility for articulating a strong vision. Bennis and Nanus found that top leaders share a common trait; all have a compelling vision and dream about their work.[48] Vision results from a profound understanding of the organization and its environment, its members, and its potential. Vision serves to set a context for the mind, which in turn creates reality for the individual. Imagine the power, then, of a collective paradigmatic focus or emphasis on a desired future state. For example, Jack Welch of General Electric has stated that GE "must be the industry leader; it must be number one or number two in everything it does." This passion for excellence has created startling effectiveness. Peter Senge, in his brilliant work *The Fifth Discipline*, defines "visioning" as a crucial new-paradigm skill.[49]

### Communicating the Vision

Bennis and Nanus argue that one trait all good leaders share is the ability to "manage meaning."[50] By this, they mean that such leaders are able to articulate their visions using metaphor and imagery, rather than simply dry facts—as former President Reagan did when, in discussing the federal debt, he used the metaphor, "Think of a stack of $100 bills as high as the Empire State building." Visionary executives frequently talk about their philosophies, the corporate values and directions/ purposes they think will keep their companies successful.[51] They also do what Peters and Waterman called "MBWA," or management by walking around.[52] They are visible, constant reminders and reinforcers of key aspects of their visions. Managers who initiate spontaneous lunches, short speeches, and quiet talks all serve to solidify the vision in the consciousness of employees. Tichy and Devanna talk of the need for a three-stage approach to communicating the vision:

1. demonstrating one's commitment to the vision
2. having effective two-way communication
3. "getting people signed on to the mission," or seeking employee participation and involvement in the process[53]

Communicating the vision has to be a top priority. Jack Welch at GE has said:

> You can't say "I am at GE and therefore I am safe." GE is not your safety, your own competitive business is your safety, winning in your markets is safety. GE has no wall around it that can protect anything. . . . Candor is calling it as you see it . . . dealing with it, getting it up on the table . . . talking about it here with people who can do something about it, not people who can commiserate with you about it.[54]

Welch's no-nonsense language communicates the urgency of the mission and the depth of his commitment to it. It also demonstrates his strong commitment to values of competition, win-lose, and a "duel to the death" mentality. Therefore, it would be inaccurate to call Welch a new-paradigm leader. He does, however, understand the power of a compelling vision.

Robert Fritz has made some interesting observations about the power of vision.[55] He argues that the difference between current reality and the vision sets up a "structural tension" in the individual or organization; by holding true to the vision, the leader can bring it into manifestation. He notes:

> Structural tension, which is created by the discrepancy between current reality (the way things really are) and vision (what you truly want) is a senior force. . . . when you create structural tension by observing current reality and simultaneously holding the vision of what you want to create, enormous energy and power are generated, because the path of least resistance is to resolve the discrepancy between the two in favor of the vision.[56]

## Alignment and Attunement With the Vision

"Alignment occurs when organization members act as parts of an integrated whole, each finding the opportunity to express his or her true purpose through the organization's purpose."[57] The individual, in other words, finds a way to expand his or her purpose within the context of the organizational purpose. This does not imply a sacrifice on the part of the individual, in giving up any of his or her identity and purpose. Organizational alignment behind leadership with a compelling vision must involve the merging and blending of the individual's strength with that of the collective.

For this to work, the individual must sense the higher or transcendent nature of the vision; it must capture the individual's loyalty and commitment. A vision such as "improved return on investment for the stockholder" simply won't do. In fact, as Harrison points out, many writers on vision tend to ignore the dark side of human nature, which Rollo May calls the *daimonic*. The presence of this dark side is probably behind the distrust of collective motives. How many people trust the motives of American business?

Thus a compelling transcendent vision must be supported by values that elicit the highest qualities of human expression. Hitler proved the power of a compelling vision, too, but few would call that vision's underlying values transcendent. Many contemporary writers have addressed the intimate connection between values and vision.[58]

The fact that people can align with any quality of vision shows the inherent limitations of alignment. Harrison talks about *attunement*, "meaning a resonance or harmony among the parts of a system, and between the parts and the whole." He goes on:

> As the concept of alignment speaks to us of *will*, so that of attunement up the mysterious operations of *love* in organizations; the sense of empathy, understanding, caring, nurturance, and mutual support.
>
> Love . . . what a "closet" word it is in organizations! Far better to talk openly about those old shibboleths, sex, money and power than to speak of love. . . . Yet love is far too powerful to ever be truly exorcised. We find it everywhere if we but look. Love is evoked by beauty and by quality in the goods and services we provide. It is present in the comradeship of co-workers, in the relationship of mentor to mentee, in the loyalties between people which *transcend personal advantage*. Love is found in the high ideals of service and contribution which are articulated in the published values of many corporations. It speaks through our dedication to workmanship and excellence of performance.[59]

**Vignette 5**

Donald Peterson of Ford has this to say about trust: "Another thing I'd say is extremely important is to get along with people. . . . I think I've watched more people fail because they failed on that score than because of any other single factor. One of the things that went very wrong in American industry, certainly in our industry and certainly at Ford, was that we fell into a pattern where we didn't operate from a point of view of trust . . . a point of view of wanting to cooperate with each other. . . . It might be that we let the initial total confrontation philosophy of the labor movement lead us to live with that environment of confrontation *in which we simply didn't ask any of our hourly employees their opinions about anything.*"

Notice Mr. Peterson's willingness to take personal responsibility for Ford's problems in this area. Notice that he doesn't blame anyone, but rather looks for ways to integrate. We would suspect that this attitude has played a large role in Ford's success in recent years.

SOURCE: Gabe Werba, "From Farm Boy to Ford Chairman: Riding the Fast Track," interview with Donald E. Peterson, *Mensa Bulletin*, November 1985, 8; emphasis added.

How could conflict exist in a state of attunement, where everyone is integrated with the high purposes of the whole? How could self-centeredness thrive in a place of love and caring? How could an attitude of "getting" and a consciousness of scarcity flourish in an atmosphere of attunement with the spirit of life? The answer is, obviously, they could not. So, we argue for the creation of this atmosphere of attunement in organizations, rather than the creation of more sophisticated conflict resolution techniques.

Another way of saying this is that there is a level at which conflict becomes obsolete; this is the level of true identity, identity in source. Identity in one's mental concepts or philosophies, in one's personal possessions, in one's role or status, all lead to inevitable conflict. Identity in that one spirit that is animating the entire cosmos provides an integrating context from which all naturally blends as an organic whole. The one spirit is integrating everything anyway; only separated (in consciousness) human beings are unaware of this fact. So, as we rise to the transcendent level where oneness is a reality, we find our lives blended into the larger whole, and a sense of ease, satisfaction, and effectiveness becomes natural.

## NOTES

1. Robert H. Miles, *Macro Organizational Behavior* (Glenview, IL: Scott, Foresman, 1980), 122.

2. Billy Joe Hodge and William P. Anthony, *Organization Theory* (3rd ed.) (Boston: Allyn & Bacon, 1988), 563.

3. Lewis Coser, *The Functions of Social Conflict* (New York: Free Press, 1956).

4. Joseph Litterer, "Conflict in Organizations; A Re-examination," *Academy of Management Journal* 9, no. 2 (1966): 178-186.

5. Stuart M. Schmidt and Thomas A. Kochan, "Conflict: Toward Conceptual Clarity," *Administrative Science Quarterly* 13 (December 1972): 359-370.

6. Kenneth Thomas, "Conflict and Conflict Management," in *Handbook of Industrial and Organizational Psychology*, ed. Marvin D. Dunnette (Chicago: Rand McNally, 1976).

7. Stephen P. Robbins, *Organization Theory: Structure, Design, and Applications* (2nd ed.) (Englewood Cliffs, NJ: Prentice Hall, 1987), 333.

8. Ibid.

9. Richard L. Daft, *Organization Theory and Design* (3rd ed.) (New York: West, 1989), 445-447.

10. Louis R. Pondy, "Organizational Conflict: Concepts and Models," *Administrative Science Quarterly* 12 (September 1967): 296-320.

11. Paul R. Lawrence and Jay W. Lorsch, *Organization and Environment* (Homewood, IL: Irwin, 1969), 9-10.

12. Joseph L. C. Cheng, "Interdependence and Coordination in Organizations: A Role-Systems Analysis," *Academy of Management Journal* 26 (1983): 156-162.

13. Thomas A. Kochan, George P. Huber, and L. L. Cummings, "Determinants of Intraorganizational Conflict in Collective Bargaining in the Public Sector," *Administrative Science Quarterly* 20 (June 1975): 10-23.

14. Benson S. Shapiro, "Can Marketing and Manufacturing Coexist?" *Harvard Business Review* 55 (September-October 1977): 104-114.

15. Richard E. Walton and John M. Dutton, "The Management of Interdepartmental Conflict: A Model and Review," *Administrative Science Quarterly* 14 (June 1969): 73-84.

16. Daniel S. Cochran and Donald D. White, "Intraorganizational Conflict in the Hospital Purchasing Decision Making Process," *Academy of Management Journal* 24 (1981): 324-332.

17. Melville Dalton, *Men Who Manage* (New York: John Wiley, 1959).

18. Litterer, "Conflict in Organizations," 182

19. Muzafer Sherif et al., *Intergroup Conflict and Cooperation* (Norman, OK: University Book Exchange, 1961); Robert R. Blake and Jane S. Mouton, "Reactions to Intergroup Competition Under Win-Lose Conditions," *Management Science* 7 (1961): 420-435; Charles P. Alderfer, "Group and Intergroup Relations," in *Improving Life at Work*, ed. J. R. Hackman and J. L. Suttle (Santa Monica, CA: Goodyear, 1977).

20. Lawrence and Lorsch, *Organization and Environment;* cited by Edgar H. Schein, *Organizational Culture and Leadership* (San Francisco: Jossey-Bass, 1985), 39.

21. Ibid.

22. Joanne Martin and Coren Siehl, "Organizational Culture and Counterculture: An Uneasy Symbiosis," *Organizational Dynamics* 12, no. 2 (1983): 54-55.

23. Robbins, *Organization Theory*, 336.

24. Abraham Maslow, *Eupsychian Management* (Homewood, IL: Irwin, 1965), 185.

25. Ibid., 337-338.

26. Daniel Robey, *Designing Organizations* (2nd ed.) (Homewood, IL: Irwin, 1986), 177-178.

27. Donald Nightingale, "Conflict and Conflict Resolution," in *Organizational Behavior: Research and Issues*, ed. George Strauss, Raymond E. Miles, Charles C. Snow, and Robert Tannenbaum (Belmont, CA: Wadsworth, 1976), 143.

28. Lawrence and Lorsch, *Organization and Environment.*

29. Georg Simmel, *The Functions of Social Conflict* (New York: Free Press, 1955), 47-48.

30. Marvin Deutsch, "Productive and Destructive Conflict," *Journal of Social Issues* 25 (1969): 7-42.

31. William G. Scott, "Organization Theory: A Reassessment," *Academy of Management Journal* 17, no. 3 (1974): 242-254.

32. Roger Harrison, "Leadership and Strategy for a New Age," in *Transforming Work*, ed. John D. Adams (Alexandria, VA: Miles River, 1984), 98-99.

33. T. Elaine Gagné, *Enhancing Personal Effectiveness* (workbook) (Colorado Springs, CO: Renaissance Associates, 1984). Originally published by Gagné Associates (Epping, NH), 1981.

34. George Land and Beth Jarman devote a whole chapter in *Breakpoint and Beyond: Mastering the Future Today* (New York: Harper Business, 1992) to "the force of connecting"; according to them, "Growth, change, and ultimately evolution occur as individuals, organizations and society increase the depth of their relationships by continually broadening and strengthening their independent connections" (189).

35. See Gagné, *Enhancing Personal Effectiveness.*

36. Robert Fritz, *The Path of Least Resistance*, 591.

37. Fred E. Jandt and Paul Gillette, *Win-Win Negotiating* (New York: John Wiley, 1985), 199-228.

38. Ibid., 201.

39. Miles, *Macro Organizational Behavior*, 139-148.

40. Roger Fisher, "Fractionating Conflict," *Daedalus* (Summer 1964): 920-941; see also his later work in Roger Fisher and William Ury, *Getting to Yes: Negotiating Agreement Without Giving In* (New York: Penguin, 1981).

41. Fisher and Ury, *Getting to Yes.*

42. Harrison, "Leadership and Strategy," 99.

43. See, for example, Warren Bennis and Burt Nanus, *Leaders: The Strategies of Taking Charge* (New York: HarperCollins, 1985); John D. Adams, ed., *Transforming Leadership: From Vision to Results* (Alexandria, VA: Miles River, 1986); Noel M. Tichy and Mary Anne Devanna, *The Transformational Leader* (New York: John Wiley, 1986); Craig R. Hickman and Michael A. Silva, *Creating Excellence* (New York: New American Library, 1984).

44. See, for example, Linda Nelson and Frank L. Burns, "High Performance Programming: A Framework for Transforming Organizations," in *Transforming Work*, ed. John D. Adams (Alexandria, VA: Miles River, 1984). See also Dennis T. Jaffe, Cynthia D. Scott, and Esther M. Orioli, "Visionary Leadership: Moving a Company From Burnout to Inspired Performance"; and Dick Richards and Sarah Engel, "After the Vision: Suggestions to Corporate Visionaries and Vision Champions"; both in Adams, *Transforming Leadership.*

45. Suzanne Kosaba, "Stressful Life Events, Personality and Health," *Journal of Personality and Social Psychology* 37 (1979).

46. Jaffe et al., "Visionary Leadership," 96-97.

47. Hickman and Silva, *Creating Excellence*, 151.

48. Bennis and Nanus, *Leaders*.

49. Peter M. Senge, *The Fifth Discipline: The Art and Practice of the Learning Organization* (Garden City, NY: Doubleday, 1990).

50. Bennis and Nanus, *Leaders*.

51. Hickman and Silva, *Creating Excellence*, 158.

52. Thomas J. Peters and Robert H. Waterman, Jr., *In Search of Excellence: Lessons From America's Best-Run Companies* (New York: Harper & Row, 1982).

53. Tichy and Devanna, *The Transformational Leader*, 152.

54. Quoted in ibid., 125.

55. Fritz, *The Path of Least Resistance*, 59-78.

56. Ibid., 77-78.

57. Harrison, "Leadership and Strategy," 100.

58. See, for example, Brian T. Hall, *The Genesis Effect* (New York: Paulist Press, 1986).

59. Harrison, "Leadership and Strategy," 101.

# 20 Facilitating New-Paradigm Organizations

*Either you take charge of change, or change takes charge of you!*
(Robert V. Hatcher, Jr., chairman and CEO, Johnson & Higgins;
advertisement in *Wall Street Journal*, June 6, 1989, p. A3)

*Managers and their organizations are confronting wave upon wave
of change in the form of new technologies, markets, forms of competition, social relations, forms of organization and management,
ideas, beliefs, and so on. Wherever one looks, one sees a new wave
coming. And it is vitally important that managers accept this as a
fundamental aspect of their reality, rise to the challenge, and learn
to ride or moderate these waves with accomplishment. This will
require an approach to management and the development of
managerial competence that are proactive and future-oriented, so
that future challenges will be tackled with foresight and flexibility,
and managers and their organizations will be able to deal with
the opportunities created by the change, rather than allowing the
waves to sweep over them.*

(Gareth Morgan,
*Riding the Waves of Change*, 1988, p. xii)

---

**SUMMARY:** We now come to a consideration of how we might facilitate the emergence of new-paradigm organizations in our world. Obviously, the creative process of change will, by itself, eliminate those organizations that do not adapt to the new realities. However, in this chapter, we look at possible ways we might be actively involved in creating and nurturing organizations that bring out the best in all of us.

---

The goal of new-paradigm management is not to manipulate, but to "learn to ride or moderate [the waves of change] with accomplishment," as Gareth Morgan says. This means sensing which way things are naturally going in the cycles of the creative process, and consciously cooperating with those cycles. Sensing and cooperating are but two of the skills new-paradigm managers need to employ in order to create new-paradigm organizations. In this chapter, we explore the traits that are essential for facilitating a shift in the collective paradigm so that the resultant flexible, adaptive organization structure will be able to complement the needs of the society in which it is embedded.

Many consultants and others concerned with the transformation of the bureaucratic form have wondered *how* to facilitate such a shift. The consensus seems to be that the key players are organization leaders. Peter B. Vaill has used the expression being in the world with responsibility to indicate what he sees as the main job of the manager/leader.[1] This means, essentially, that the effective new-paradigm manager takes 100% responsibility for the world of his or her organization. Vaill has also said that "to a large extent, *executive development for leadership of modern organizations* is *spiritual development.*"[2]

Howard Schechter, a practicing organizational transformation consultant, has pinpointed the consultant's role in facilitating organizational change, and the leader's role is not much different:

Most important are the deep, underlying attitudes that organize one's life and work. The qualities of acceptance, love, non-attachment to outcome, and authenticity are the most important elements a (group) leader can bring to the work.

The key ingredient is acceptance; acceptance of the client as he/she is. Unchanged. Respecting the trust within each which has led to this place in the present moment; this creates the necessary conditions for change to occur. When I accept someone, I too am accepted. When the group accepts me, the opportunity for doing great things [is] present. There are deep roots which must be tapped to nourish and allow the quality of acceptance to bloom; a loving attitude toward one's Self and the client, and an attitude of non-attachment to the outcome of the work. To be accepting, I must be loving. No matter how different the client is from me, how different the values, how I look at work and at organizations, it is still possible to extend love to the spark of his/her divinity at his/her Center. It is to their Center, from my Center, that I try to connect with my clients.

Non-attachment to the results of one's work with a group is essential. If I am attached to an outcome—attached to the notion that a group must change in a certain direction, that the organization must become more effective, that the people must cooperate and communicate effectively— then I am not in a space of accepting and loving. . . . The group will move with me or without me. Like water in a stream, it will continue to flow. My image of a successful group and organizational work is a vision of a client as a branch moving in a stream. The branch flows along until it gets hung up in a tangle. My job as an organizational consultant and group worker is to step into the stream and work with the branch until it is free, allowing it to continue on its course. The purpose of our tools of intervention is to facilitate sculpting the organization in a way that allows it to re-enter the stream more focused and dynamic.[3]

The essential job of a leader facilitating a paradigm shift is to create a context wherein people can recognize their responsibility for their worlds and choose to take responsibility for them. Notice that people are not "forced" to mature; they are "awakened" to the possibility of conscious leadership in their world and invited to participate in that leadership. Also, the facilitator cannot have an "agenda"; if he or she explicitly wants someone to change, that person's natural human defensiveness will rise up and say, "No way!" The facilitator must accept people as they are, no strings attached.

Finally, the facilitator must be authentic. The facilitator must model behavior of 100% responsibility in order to invite others to join him or her. "In practice, authenticity means being one's Self first, and following rules, maps and models second. In this approach, the tools of intervention are in service of what is real for the group and the group leader in the moment."[4] We would argue that this is the accurate way for a facilitator to allow for a transformation within an organization, but other approaches have been prescribed.

## Transformational Models

The writing on the subject of organizational transformation has obviously been tinted by the values and biases of each writer. For example, one widely used model of transformation argues for building a new culture in the organization through "modeling behavior, rewards and recognition for 'appropriate behavior' [whatever that would be], training, commitment and allocation of resources, and interactions," all to support the consultant's (or the organization's) idea of what the organization should be *and how its members should behave.*[5] So, in viewing any proposed model of transformation, one should be aware of both the implicit and explicit assumptions underlying that model.

One widely used approach to facilitating a shift is through the use of *myth and ritual.*[6] Through this approach, the transformational consultant assists the organization in developing new myths, rituals, and ceremonies to tell a new organizational "story" that supports a more positive organization vision and purpose.

Still another model sees organizational transformation as proceeding through a cycle:

1. *Unconscious:* In this phase, the organization is silently building a readiness for change.
2. *Awakening:* Suddenly, the organization awakens to possibilities and problems inherent in its current situation. A message of needed change is synthesized from the unconnected bits in the organization's unconscious.
3. *Reordering:* This is a process of analyzing the current situation and challenging underlying patterns of assumption and belief.
4. *Translation:* This is the process of formulating a vision from the integration of information, metaphorical images, personal visions, and feelings connected to the unconscious, awakening, and reordering stages.
5. *Commitment:* The organization takes responsibility for implementation of the new design.
6. *Embodiment:* The task is to bring the vision into practical, day-to-day operations.
7. *Integration:* The necessary changes, structural and behavioral, are completed, instituted, and in operation. People are now functioning from a new paradigm.[7]

This model combines the elements of a true shift, but the facilitator still needs to be sure to maintain a value-monitored, hands-off approach. A similar model also sees the process as having seven stages:

1. *Fertilization:* The necessary precursor to paradigm reframing within an organization is the birth of a new paradigm outside of it; that is, new ideas, suppositions, assumptions, and beliefs must be emerging in the mass consciousness.
2. *Crisis:* The reframing process needs a catalyst (an event or series of events that cannot be addressed or explained using the existing paradigm) to begin its cycle toward fulfillment.
3. *Incubation:* Lag time is needed for the pressure to build, as old, tried-and-true approaches continue to fail.
4. *Diffusion:* For a new paradigm to become "systemically potent," it must claim widespread acceptance.
5. *Struggle for legitimacy:* To gain the power to determine policy and behavior, explain events, and so on, a new paradigm must compete with the organization's existing suppositions, ideas, beliefs, norms, concepts, and symbols.

**Table 20.1**   Cycles of a Paradigm Shift

| The Creative Process* | Buckley/Perkins | Nicoll |
|---|---|---|
| stillness | unconscious; awakening | fertilization |
| connection | reordering; translation | crisis; incubation |
| action | commitment; embodiment | diffusion; legitimacy; acceptance |
| creation | integration | legitimation |

*See T. Elaine Gagné, *Enhancing Personal Effectiveness* (workbook) (Colorado Springs, CO: Renaissance Associates, 1984). Originally published by Gagné Associates (Epping, NH), 1981.

6. *Politics of acceptance:* At some point, the new paradigm (with the potential for acceptance) gains a champion (or champions) who becomes a vocal advocate for its adoption.

7. *Legitimation:* The new paradigm becomes habitual and implicit in the thought processes and work routines of the members of the organization.[8]

Let us examine each of these models in light of the creative process of life, as laid out in Table 20.1. The valid models of organizational transformation share the basic ingredients of the creative cycles of life. The fundamental problem with self-centered consciousness is that an understanding of this creative process is obscured by the wants and demands of the ego. But this doesn't mean that the process itself is thwarted; it just continues to operate without the conscious participation of humans. So the process moves, we continue to create, but what is created thereby is distorted by our failure to align with the flow as it moves. We are so transfixed by the world of external forms that we don't sense what life is actually calling forth into creation; so ill effects continue to manifest and we struggle with them, thereby creating more ill effects.

A central essence of this problem is the question of *timing.* Outside the creative process, it is impossible to know exactly when to act and when not to. Linda Ackerman writes:

> In certain times, knowing *when to act* is a fine-tuned skill that assists the unfolding of events in an organization. People often react to an event by saying, "the timing is all wrong!" or "perfect timing!" The Greek words *kronos,* or clock time, and *kyros,* or right timing, illustrate this point effectively. *Kronos* provides the logical, organized sequencing of events so necessary to planning and implementing complex changes. *Kyros* requires knowing when to act, when the moment is high, and when not to act. To

be effective at this, the (flow state) manager senses the political climate, people's need for direction and their openness to change.[9]

In other words, one needs to *sense* when to act; this sense can come only when one is *still* inside, *connects* up with all the factors present in the situation (the above-mentioned political climate, people's need for direction, and readiness to change), and then *acts* appropriately. Only then does true *creation* occur.

---

## The Role of Integrity in Transformation

---

According to Webster, *integrity* means "completeness" or "wholeness." To say that something has integrity is to say that it is complete unto itself, nothing is left out. All the factors necessary for its creative function are in place. To operate with integrity means to operate with a sense of the larger whole in which one functions as an interconnected part.

Integrity is *not* the same thing as ethics. Ethics is the self-centered paradigm's attempt to force people to "be good," that is, to act in socially acceptable ways. Ethics involves codes of behavior, prescriptions of "shoulds" and "should nots"; integrity concerns operating to one's highest vision of complementing the whole *in the moment.* Ethics assumes that people are fundamentally flawed and need to have guidelines to be "good." Integrity assumes that people can align with life and can operate with 100% responsibility if they choose to do so.[10] Vaill clearly sees the distinction between ethics and integrity:

> I think it is a scandal that there should be so little discussion of [the spiritual condition of executives] in the mainstream of management education and development. At best, we tend to treat the subject as primarily a matter of ethics. The practice of any system of ethics, though, makes all kinds of assumptions about the spiritual condition of those who are going to be doing the practicing. I am genuinely embarrassed for myself and my colleagues that we should, by and large, *be leaving these deep questions of executive character unaddressed, all the while calling for new vision, vitality, and spirit in Western organizations.*[11]

A number of writers appreciate the centrality of integrity. Joiner calls "open integrity" one of the three basic challenges to organizational learning; by this he means "to integrate the action of different subgroups in a way that is consistent with the organization's purposes, yet respects the individuality and autonomy of each group."[12] James A. Ritscher writes:

> Having integrity in an organization creates an experience of soundness, robustness and vigor. An organization without integrity is like a rotten log; when you hit it, it gives a dull thump and goes limp. An organization with integrity is strong like a well-rooted tree. When an outside force attacks it, the organization can withstand the blows. It has springiness and resilience.
>
> What specifically is organizational integrity? It is the sum total of the integrity of each of the individuals in the organization. For each person, it is the tendency to do that which is praiseworthy, effective, and right, and avoid that which is reprehensible, ineffective and wrong. *In an organization with integrity, everyone shoulders their responsibilities, conducts their business in an upright way, and expects everyone else to do the same.*[13]

Lawrence Miller says this about integrity:

> Leadership requires followership and following is an act of trust, faith in the course of the leader, and that faith can be generated only if leaders act with integrity. . . . Of all the principles of the new leadership, it is integrity with which there can be no compromise. . . . Integrity is honesty and the consistent, responsible pursuit of a stated course of action. The person or organization that has integrity can be trusted. . . . Managers who demonstrate integrity know the larger purpose of their organization and are focused on long-term objectives. . . . Managers who are trusted do what they say they will do. . . . It is my experience that managers who inspire devotion have a dedication to a higher, sometimes mysterious, perhaps spiritual purpose.[14]

James O'Toole argues that "in exerting moral courage, Vanguard leaders not only lay the groundwork for the long-term success of their companies, they lay the foundation for the continued survival of corporate capitalism."[15] In other words, without *self-regulation through integrity*, capitalism is doomed. Actually, Adam Smith saw this in 1776 when he wrote the classic *The Wealth of Nations*; he saw integrity as an essential feature to moderate the excesses of human nature's tendency toward greed and avarice.

It is informative to note that *integrity* and *integration* come from the same root word. Integrity comes from our innate connection with the whole through the creative process of life itself. When we are still, we get the wisdom to know what to do, and when to do it; we call this *intuition* or *gut feeling*. If we consistently operate from this sensing of what is right and fitting in the moment, we will find our actions to be consistently life enhancing and creative.

---

## Creating an Integrity-Based Organization

---

How do we create an integrity-based organization? Several strategies come to mind. The most obvious one is *leader modeling*. If the leadership of an organization effectively and consistently models attitudes of caring, compassion, empowerment, clarity, and inquiry, other members of the organization will have "permission" to exhibit these behaviors as well. Also, as Peter Block discusses in *The Empowered Manager*, leaders, through coaching and counseling, can legitimate spiritual values and 100% personal responsibility.[16]

A key to making this work is a reward system that encourages innovation, cooperation, team spirit, concern for the whole, and complementarity. A central theme here is that fear-based consciousness has been around for millennia; it will take some time and some encouragement for people to develop the habit of living from their highest values and visions.

### Avenues of Spiritual Growth for Managers

Peter Vaill argues that true leaders are those who have achieved a state of spiritual maturity; that is, they have a sense of identity in the whole and not in the external world of *form*.[17] He postulates seven "avenues of spiritual development" for leaders (and, we might add, followers). We discuss these avenues in turn below.

*Toward embracing new values and the possibilities they imply, and the relativity of all values to each other.* By this, Vaill means that we need to begin to see shades of gray and let go of "either/or" ways of judging things. He argues that "the truly democratic spirit which is determined to hear all sides is, of course, anything but weak; in fact, it is tougher than the simplistic, single-valued posture."[18] What he is talking about is "largeness of spirit," the ability to encompass many divergent viewpoints and find the point of agreement in all of them.

Land and Jarman, in *Breakpoint and Beyond: Mastering the Future Today*, make this excellent observation:

> In a very basic sense, when we pay attention without judging, we can actually hear what others are saying. We listen to understand, not to evaluate; we don't offer advice unless it is sought; and we stop thinking we know what the other person means. Gerald Jampolsky has this to say about not judging others: Not judging is another way of letting go of fear and experiencing love. When we learn not to judge others—and totally

accept them and not want to change them—we can simultaneously learn to accept ourselves.[19]

*Toward a passionate reason.* Impartiality, says Michael Polanyi, is "nothing more than the vacancy of the mind."[20] Spirituality is wholehearted and wholeheaded, says Vaill; it is a "feeling and a practice of the wholeness of oneself and cannot entail the suppression of one part over the other." To be fully mature, we have to "make the most passionate and daring guesses, hypotheses, and conjectures we can, and attempt to refute them with the force of our intellect." Here, we would qualify Vaill's observation; the separated human intellect is not capable of discerning what is good and what is bad; however, the human mind, under the control of the spirit of the whole, is very capable of discerning the true reality in any situation.

*Toward the development of an open value system.* Values are seen as systems, all of them creating a whole point of view, and the mature individual would be open to shifting them as new realizations become apparent. Openness takes us out of our own value systems and into the systems of others. The "capacity to experience the spirit of another across the cultural gulf is a prerequisite for true intercultural understanding and valuing." Vaill goes on to say that "the various parts of the organization *are* a value system in addition to a system in structure and in communication."[21] In his popular video *Discovering the Future: The Business of Paradigms,* Joel Barker says that a crucial management skill of the future will be the ability to adopt new paradigms consciously as easily as one changes hats.[22]

*Toward spiritual development that is shared with others.* The fellowship aspect of spiritual development is mentioned here, that is, the nurturing result of friends in agreement working together for a larger purpose. Organizations have the potential to be *spiritual brotherhoods,* says Vaill, and in so doing, they could confront "the loneliness, disappointment, and pain of the modern organization, and [decide] that these conditions should not continue to rot the spirit of the organization and the people in it."[23]

Here we can see the value of David Bohm's work on dialogue.[24] Bohm sees thought as largely a collective phenomenon and, by engaging in dialogue (*not* discussion), groups and organizations can cocreate meaning. In dialogue, a group explores different issues from many points of view, with members suspending judgment and communicating their assumptions freely. The result is a free exploration of people's thoughts, opinions, and experiences that somehow ranges beyond their individual views into what could be called a group mind experience.[25] This is spiritual development in a very practical sense.

*Toward a new vocabulary and grammar of spirituality.* We need to be able to talk about spirituality without sounding preachy. The word itself has years of religious conditioning associated with it and, for some, this makes the subject emotionally charged (either positively or negatively). Also, the so-called New Age movement has made spirituality seem "cool" to talk about, and the risk of superficiality, dogmatism, and spiritual arrogance is high.

*Toward the appreciation of the spirit in larger and larger wholes.* Vaill says, "Thinking holistically and appreciating the 'big picture' are routinely mentioned as key qualities of the executive leader."[26] What we don't know much about, he argues, is *how* to do this. In this book, we have argued that spiritual maturity comes from honoring the creative process of life—in other words, by being still within oneself, by connecting with all the factors in one's circumstance and then acting out of that place of connection. As one consistently does this, the vision of the whole naturally expands; this is what we call *spiritual maturity.* Vaill seems to recognize this:

> Seeing the big picture then becomes instead a progressive process, a process of progressive transcendence of the limits of one's understanding and appreciation of what one is involved in. This progressive transcendence is, I think, the spiritual growth I have been talking about all along. By definition, the spiritual dimension is unlimited in scope. The 'higher consciousness' that has been intuited so often over the centuries may be just the attainment of a scope and richness of appreciation which goes beyond the ordinary.[27]

*Toward centering in the present.* This avenue underlies all the others. Organizational life is full of distractions that vie for one's attention and pull one out of the present moment. But the only time that is real is *now;* the past is only a memory trace held in consciousness, and the future is imaginary. All we really know is what is true *now,* in this present moment.

Eldon Mayo, one of the most famous management pioneers, gives us the notion of the "efficacy at the point of action."[28] Mayo argues that in paying attention, one balances one's awareness of what is going on outside oneself with what is going on inside oneself. Thoughts and feelings are inside; people and events they seem to cause are outside. Attention is the meeting of the two; in the here and now, we feel, think, and experience. Most of the thinking and feeling comes from the memory traces out of the past, so it is an acquired discipline just to "be" with something without the overlay of paradigmatic judgment and opinions.

Vaill concludes, "The present is the only door through which the eternal can enter our awareness."[29] We would concur, and furthermore we would argue that new, organic organizational structures with flexibility, adaptability, low political interaction, results orientation, and all the rest will come about only as spiritually mature people, bonded by a transcendent vision of possibility, stay in the present and do what comes to them to do. How do they do this? By respecting the creative cycles of life, being still, connecting with all the factors in their experience, and only *then* acting. What is thereby created is naturally blended with the purposes of the larger whole.

## Entering the Emerging Paradigm

As Willis Harman puts it:

What you believe determines what you perceive as reality. What you believe determines what you feel you can do about it. What you believe determines the exhilaration and joy you get out of life. Some beliefs are wholesome; others are definitely unwholesome. (Along the way, most of us pick up some unwholesome beliefs.)

Beliefs can be changed. A life that is constructed around an inadequate or erroneous set of basic beliefs will include a lot of problems and pain. If a society is guided by an inadequate or erroneous set of basic beliefs, it will tend to foster a great deal of human misery. At the level of society, too, beliefs can be changed.[30]

We have argued that *we attract circumstances to ourselves that create self-fulfilling prophecies*. It is true that erroneous beliefs can cause misery. It is true that a paradigm shift to more life-enhancing is desirable. The first step is with the individual. The operative question is this: Am I willing to allow self-centeredness to recede and the design of life to appear through me? The entire process begins here. We conclude with the words of Michael Brown, an organizational transformation consultant:

In quiet moments of reflection, when we long to know the meaning of our lives, or search for wisdom with which to guide our actions in the world, we often look toward the stars for inspiration. These celestial bodies fill us with a sense of mystery and wonder, even as their subtle luminescence fills the darkness of the night.

Countless stars, scattered through the heavens, form the constellations we observe, and their patterns suggest that there is an implicit order, or divine intelligence, which underlies reality. All life finds its origin in the dynamic interaction between solar energy, elements in space, and time. Because of this, all creation seems responsive, interrelated and alive. In the presence of the stars, we feel we are not really alone, and in this we find much comfort.

Each of us, in truth, is a unique expression of the universal order. We are children of the light. What, then, shall we do? Let us learn to share the essence of ourselves with one another, as do the radiant stars, and thus become with them luminous givers of life to all with whom we interact.[31]

## NOTES

1. Peter B. Vaill, "Process Wisdom for a New Age," in *Transforming Work*, ed. John D. Adams (Alexandria, VA: Miles River, 1984), 18-33.

2. Peter B. Vaill, "Executive Development as Spiritual Development," in *Appreciative Management & Leadership*, ed. Suresh Srivastva and David L. Cooperrider (San Francisco: Jossey-Bass, 1989), 324. This and all other quotes from Vaill's chapter are used with permission.

3. Howard Schechter, "What I've Learned About Group Work," *TWG (The Organizational Transformation Connection)* 12 (May 1989): 1-2.

4. Ibid., 2.

5. Robert F. Allen and Charlotte Kraft, "Transformations That Last: A Cultural Approach," in *Transforming Work*, ed. John D. Adams (Alexandria, VA: Miles River, 1984), 36-54.

6. See, for example, Chandra Stephens and Saul Eisen, "Myth, Transformation and the Change Agent"; and Harrison Owen, "Facilitating Organizational Transformation: The Uses of Myth and Ritual"; both in *Transforming Work*, ed. John D. Adams (Alexandria, VA: Miles River, 1984).

7. Karen Wilhelm Buckley and Dani Perkins, "Managing the Complexity of Organizational Transformation," in *Transforming Work*, ed. John D. Adams (Alexandria, VA: Miles River, 1984), 55-67.

8. David Nicoll, "Consulting to Organizational Transformations," in *Transforming Work*, ed. John D. Adams (Alexandria, VA: Miles River, 1984), 157-163.

9. Linda S. Ackerman, "The Flow State: A New View of Organizations and Managing," in *Transforming Work*, ed. John D. Adams (Alexandria, VA: Miles River, 1984), 132.

10. For a complete development of this argument, see David K. Banner, "Why Business Ethics Don't Work," *Administrative Radiology* 5 (March 1986): 44-57.

11. Vaill, "Executive Development as Spiritual Development," 324; emphasis added.

12. William B. Joiner, "Leadership for Organizational Learning," in *Transforming Leadership: From Vision to Results*, ed. John D. Adams (Alexandria, VA: Miles River, 1986), 45.

13. James A. Ritscher, "Spiritual Leadership," in *Transforming Leadership: From Vision to Results*, ed. John D. Adams (Alexandria, VA: Miles River, 1986), 76; emphasis added.

14. Lawrence M. Miller, *American Spirit: Visions of a New Corporate Culture* (New York: Warner, 1984), 136.

15. James O'Toole, *Vanguard Management* (Garden City, NY: Doubleday, 1985), 370.

16. Peter Block, *The Empowered Manager* (San Francisco: Jossey-Bass, 1990).

17. Vaill, "Executive Development as Spiritual Development," 22-47.

18. Ibid., 24.

19. George Land and Beth Jarman, *Breakpoint and Beyond: Mastering the Future Today* (New York: Harper Business, 1992), 205.

20. Michael Polanyi, *The Tacit Dimension* (Garden City, NY: Doubleday, 1967); quoted in Vaill, "Executive Development Is Spiritual Development," 25.

21. Vaill, "Executive Development as Spiritual Development," 341.

22. Joel Barker, *Discovering the Future: The Business of Paradigms* (2nd ed.), videotape (Burnsville, MN: Charthouse Learning Corporation, 1991).

23. Vaill, "Executive Development as Spiritual Development," 342.

24. See, on Bohm, William N. Isaacs, "Taking Flight: Dialogue, Collective Thinking and Dialogue," *Organizational Dynamics* (Fall 1993): 24-39; Peter M. Senge, *The Fifth Discipline: The Art and Practice of the Learning Organization* (Garden City, NY: Doubleday, 1990), 239.

25. Senge, *The Fifth Discipline,* 241.

26. Vaill, "Executive Development as Spiritual Development," 348.

27. Ibid., 42.

28. Eldon Mayo, "Hawthorne and the Western Electric Company," in *Organization Theory,* ed. D. S. Pugh (Middlesex, UK: Penguin, 1971); cited in ibid., 43.

29. Vaill, "Executive Development as Spiritual Development," 351.

30. Willis Harman, "Visions of Tomorrow: The Transformation Ahead, *OD Practitioner* 13 (February 1981): 1-10.

31. Michael H. Brown, "Look Toward the Stars," promotional brochure for Brown's consulting practice (December 1988).

# Appendix

How Organization Has Been Studied:
Theories That Have Led to the Metamodel

*The way we see it, the next wave of management thinking must
include a perspective that will make it possible for managers to
penetrate existing modes of reasoning to accomplish some things
that current rationalistic approaches do not permit. It will have to
be different because there is a class of high priority issues that
resist solution even though they are the subject of constant
managerial attention. Managers don't know how to switch tracks in
dealing with them and we suspect that the conventional way of
approaching these issues is a large part of why they resist solutions.*
(Samuel A. Culbert and John J. McDonough,
*Radical Management*, 1985, pp. 4-5)

**A** number of theorists have, over the past 25 years or so, offered useful
perspectives on organization and structure, perspectives that have
led us to the development of the metamodel of organization. This appendix examines some of the metamodel's more important precursors.

### Self-Fulfilling Prophecy:
### The Work of Douglas McGregor

One of the earliest theorists to recognize the role of assumptions about
people in determining managerial style was Douglas McGregor, author

> People will live up (or down) to what is believed about them
> and/or what they believe about themselves.

of the now classic *The Human Side of Enterprise*.[1] McGregor introduced
the idea that attitudes about workers held by managers will greatly
influence the managers' behavior toward workers. We discussed these
attitudes—dubbed Theory X and Theory Y—in Chapter 10.

One outstanding example of such self-fulfilling prophecy has been
provided by a now-famous study of prejudice initiated in 1968 by a
teacher, Jane Elliot, in Riceville, Iowa. Elliot divided her class into two
groups, according to the color of their eyes: blue eyes and brown eyes.
She determined the "value" of the groups; one day the blue eyes were
considered the bright ones and were treated in a privileged way, whereas
the brown eyes were treated as "dolts" and were relegated to less-privi-
leged status. Another day, Elliot would reverse that arbitrary value
system. She found that test scores varied significantly between the
groups within a 24-hour period. The highest scores were consistently
earned by the privileged group of the day.[2]

Some modern managers have enthusiastically used the principle of
the self-fulfilling prophecy (i.e., believe workers will perform well and
they will) only to be disappointed; these managers did not consider the
impact of the dominant paradigm. Under the dominant paradigm in the
industrial age, people are expected to need to be told what to do, or else
they will make mistakes. This expectation creates dependent and immature subordinates.[3] Thus the "enlightened" managers treated people
as mature, self-starting, capable adults, only to see these same people
act in immature ways. Why? Because the workers had grown up under
a paradigm that emphasizes top-down control and that assumes workers
to be lazy, unintelligent, and unmotivated. In the context of that paradigm, workers may see increased autonomy and responsibility as li-
cense. It takes a patient, consistent, savvy manager to deal with this
transitional stage.

In addition to the self-fulfilling prophecy of individuals, there also
appears to be a self-fulfilling organizational culture prophecy.[4] Research
suggests that the dominance (or strength) and coherence (how well it
"hangs together") of culture are qualities found in excellent companies.[5]
Warren Bennis, described as the "poet-philosopher-scholar of organizational life," says that "successful organizational leaders . . . are particularly aware of the need to change the company's culture or 'social
architecture' to fit in with its guiding vision. Less successful leaders
underestimate the influence of a corporation's culture."[6]

The culture (shared beliefs, attitudes, values, and assumptions) of a firm is important because it conveys the traditions, myths, values, and ethics of that firm to new members. The stronger the culture, the greater the self-fulfilling tendencies. Everyone at Hewlett-Packard, for instance, knows that he or she is expected to be innovative. Everyone at Procter & Gamble knows that product quality is the number-one priority. Well-run companies encourage and support people by sending and enhancing cultural messages about quality, excellence, and innovation.

The IBM philosophy, the Hewlett-Packard "way," and the Procter & Gamble assumptions about people are that if you label a person a winner then that person will act like a winner. These companies have developed and nurtured cultures that produce winners. Poorer-performing companies often have strong self-fulfilling cultural norms, too, but they are not positive. They usually focus on internal politics, "win-lose" battles, and the like, rather than on developing people.

---

## Karl Weick and Enactment

---

One of the earliest organization theorists who saw the role of the collective mind in creating organization was Karl Weick. In his seminal work *The Social Psychology of Organizing*, Weick introduced the term "enactment." His message can be summarized as follows: We do not construct reality out of theory, but out of experience. According to Weick, the essence of enactment can be found in these three statements:

1. Experience is not what happens to a person, but what the person does with what happens.
2. "Our so-called limitations . . . apply to faculties we don't apply. We don't discover what we can't achieve until we make an effort not to try."
3. Imagine that you are playing a game of charades and that you must act out the title of a movie. Imagine that you are given, as your title, the movie *Charade.* As the presenter, you probably would try to get outside of the present game and point to it, so that the observers would see that the answer is the very activity in which they are engaged. Alas, the observers are likely to miss this subtlety and instead shout words such as "pointing," "finger," "excited," "all of this," and so forth.[7]

Weick's basic point is that there is no such thing as experience until someone does something. What he means is that the manager (or anyone else) literally wades into a chaotic set of environmental stimuli and somehow, through action, attempts to "unrandomize" these data and impose order. As a result of this process, the environment gets "order," at least in the experience of the person. Experience is the consequence of activity.

Weick also speaks of the enactment of limitations, or the way people stop themselves through assumptions based on presumption, rather than action. Stated differently, they stop themselves from doing something based on their presumptions about what they think will happen rather than their *actual* experience. The worker who refuses to suggest changes, always commenting, "The boss would never go for that!" is a good example of this phenomenon. These self-limiting beliefs, barriers, and prohibitions then become prominent "things" in the environment. Weick goes on to say that, "even though organizations appear to be quite solid, in fact much of their substance may consist of spurious knowledge based on avoided tests."[8] He calls this "stunted enactment."

Through selective perception, the manager attends to some of his or her environment, ignores most of it, and collects information from others in it.[9] As a result, the manager's surroundings get sorted into various cause-effect assumptions and linkages, and appear to be more orderly. This is what Weick calls "organizational sense-making." He goes on to say that "we construct categories of things, we stereotype people, we segment things together to make order out of chaos. People in organizations try to sort the chaos into items, events, and parts which are then connected, threaded into sequences, serially ordered, and related."[10]

If the people in an organization, regardless of what the "boss" says, think that a project will fail, chances are that it will. The people involved fail to see that they themselves create and maintain the structure (effective or ineffective) of the organization. They, in these cases, are "victims" at the mercy of an entity called the organization because they have mistaken *effect* for *cause*.[11]

As Weick notes, the "stunted enactment," or self-limiting belief, is the actual cause of the stuckness, not the structure itself (which is the effect). For example, one firm that offered professional seminars went through a slump period. A single external report about the decline of seminars was circulated by one of the seminar division managers who wanted to change the company direction. The slump continued until the seminar program was a limping division of the company. This all happened at a time when the seminar business in general was continuing to boom.

Weick's central point is that organizational "realities" have subjective origins. This consensus about "what's so around here" limits behavior to the extent of these norms and conventions. Much of the current work on the relationship between the organization and its environment tends to downplay the extent to which the boundary between the two is blurred, and the extent to which organizations actually produce their environments through either enactment or stunted enactment.[12]

# Attribution Theory
## and the Paradigm

Originally conceived by Kelly, and developed by Staw, Jones and Harris, Bem, and many others, attribution theory has to do with the reasons (causality) a person uses to explain occurrences in his or her environment.[13] For example, if a coworker is irritable, an individual may infer that some occurrence such as a comment made about that coworker at a recent staff meeting is the cause of that irritability. Technically speaking, *attribution* refers to "the process of inferring or perceiving the dispositional features of entities in the environment."[14] Again, the perceiver is seen as trying to make sense out of an essentially random, chaotic environment by ascribing causality to various outcomes. Typically, this relates to the attribution of motives to individuals.

Research indicates that, typically, when asked to account for some action he or she has just taken, a person will explain the behavior as stemming from some aspect of his or her environment at the time of the action. Observers, on the other hand, tend to explain the same action as a result of some trait or motive of the actor. This is especially true when the situation is one of failure rather than success.[15] For example, a supervisor who has a higher-than-average rate of turnover among staff may attribute that turnover to low pay or poor working conditions, whereas an observer might see that the supervisor has difficulty communicating with staff.

In the industrial era paradigm, there is a strong tendency to take responsibility for desirable outcomes and to blame others (and/or the situation) for undesirable circumstances. Also, we tend to assume that others choose to put themselves where they are, whereas they themselves assume that factors outside themselves caused them to be there. The skyrocketing rate of litigation in the last decades of the twentieth century is one indication of this blaming syndrome. Vignette 1 presents a classic case of this phenomenon.

Attribution theory has important organizational implications. The dominant paradigm colors the perception according to the expectations of that paradigm. For example, one waning but still predominant thought pattern among men (and many women) is that women are basically emotional, passive, and nurturing. Comparative lists such as the following, about the differences in perceptions of men and women on the job, were widely distributed and discussed in the early 1980s:

- If a man cries, he's sensitive; if a woman cries, she's emotionally unstable.
- If a man speaks up for what he believes, he's assertive; if a woman speaks up, she's pushy.

- If a man plays racquetball in the middle of the day, he is being balanced;
  if a woman does that, she is pampering herself.

With these assumptions as a basis, we begin to treat people as though
the things we assume to be true about them are actually true. Because
of the dominant paradigm, people see what they expect to see and
interpret accordingly. Perceptual distortion and "filling in" provide
abundant support for our beliefs.[16]

---

**Vignette 1**

An overweight woman decided to sue her mother:

for negligent parenting. [The woman], who stands five feet, three inches
tall and weighs 217 pounds, alleges that her obesity resulted from her
mother's incessant preparation of high-fat, high-sugar foods throughout
[her] childhood. [She] also asserts that not only did her mother make her
obese as a child, but her mother shaped [her] adult tastes so that she is
addicted to fattening foods, especially chocolate eclairs, which her mother
baked every Saturday. [The woman] claims that she has tried exercise and
diet programs advertised on daytime television, but her appetite for
pastries and pasta has proven unalterable. [She] is asking for $1 million
for mental anguish, $1.4 million for the income she estimates she has lost
and will lose because her condition has prevented her from marrying and
thus having a second wage earner in the household, and $250,000 for the
extra groceries she has had to buy and will have to buy.

At a preliminary hearing the defendant, [the woman's] mother, re-
marked that her daughter's suit came to $12,211.98 a pound, which she
said was an excessive price even for prime beef.

SOURCE: Bob Devine, "You Have the Right to Sue: Goodbye Individual Responsibility, Welcome
to the Age of Absurd Litigation," *Frontier* [defunct airline magazine], March 1986, 63-64.

---

## Metaphors of Organization

A number of researchers have begun to investigate the effects of metaphors on how organizations and organization life are seen. This approach presumes that the theories and explanations of organizational
life are based on systems of belief that lead to our perceiving and

understanding organizations in distinct yet partial ways. The metaphor that is used implies a way of thinking or a way of seeing that influences the understanding of the world generally.

Metaphors exert a formative influence on science, on language, and on how we choose to express ourselves on a day-to-day basis, but they can tend to produce one-sided insights. In highlighting certain interpretations or explanations of reality, a particular metaphor can ignore or underplay other interpretations. Thus it is useful to look at organizations from the perspectives of several different metaphors. Gareth Morgan, in his excellent work *Images of Organization,* employs eight different metaphors for organization in order to illuminate different problems or attributes. Each emphasizes a different aspect of the organization:

1. The metaphor of "organizations as machines" underpins the development of the bureaucratic organization (emphasizing efficiency).
2. The metaphor of "organizations as organisms" focuses attention on understanding and managing organizational needs and environmental relations.
3. The metaphor of "organizations as brains" draws attention to the importance of information processing, learning, and intelligence.
4. The metaphor of "organizations as cultures" focuses on the shared values, beliefs, and patterns of meaning among organizational members.
5. The metaphor of "organizations as political systems" looks at the role of power and influence in organizations.
6. The metaphor of "organizations as psychic prisons" sees people as being trapped by their unconscious thoughts, ideas, and beliefs that confine them to alienating modes of interaction.
7. The metaphor of "organizations as flux and transformation" focuses on organizations as self-producing systems that create and change themselves in their own images.
8. The metaphor of "organizations as instruments of domination" pays attention to the potentially exploitive aspects of organization.[17]

This entire approach is grounded in the belief that organizations are complex entities, ambiguous and paradoxical. Seeing organizations through various lenses increases our possibility of actually understanding them.[18] Each of these lenses has associated with it a wealth of assumptions, beliefs, and other patterns of thought. These patterns most often operate at the level of the subconscious and conscious mind.

June Smith, brand director for Coors Light Beer in Golden, Colorado, used the metaphor of a softball team to motivate people from many departments to launch a new ad campaign. She used concepts she learned as a high school coach of a girls' championship baseball team. Within the context of "team," she stressed cooperation, competitive spirit, and confidence. The team approach worked for Smith in record time and won accolades from all the top executives at Coors.[19]

### The Role of the Subconscious/ Unconscious Mind

One of the most widely recognized social science discoveries in recent years is that most of our mental activity occurs in the subconscious realm.[20] It is as though our conscious mental activity is the visible tip of the iceberg, with subconscious activity the vastly larger part hidden from view. This subconscious and unconscious (to use Freud's terms) portion of the mind greatly influences what we see and how we see it. Harman notes:

> Among the other aspects of these phenomena, we know that the way we see the world is affected by suggestions that we've absorbed, hypnotically or otherwise; it's affected by our expectations; it's affected by our perceived needs. If we have to see the world in a certain way in order to feel comfortable, we tend to see it that way. If people who are important in our lives see it a certain way, we tend to see it the way they do. We can be badly fooled in the way we perceive the world. We can be fooled individually or we can be fooled as a tribe. We know this because other tribes see things differently, so somebody's being fooled![21]

Harman goes on to talk about some recent research findings relating to what is called "remote viewing," or seeing things in a geographically distant location from where you are:

> Why is this such a controversial area? Well, probably because, to a certain extent, scientists have made the same mistake with their models and metaphors that religious people have made with their theologies. That is, they put too much stock in them. You tend to treat these models as if they were real, as though that were the picture of reality in which you have personally invested yourself. And so you feel personally threatened when that picture of reality is threatened.
>
> Physicists have gotten very laid back about this, as you well know. They have certain models that fit certain kinds of data and then there are other kinds of data which require other models, other metaphors. It's not too troubling to recognize that reality is too rich for any particular model to describe it completely. So we may need some complementary models.[22]

Harman ends his discussion with a quote from an earlier work by John Lilly: "There are no known limits to the abilities of the human mind other than those imposed by our beliefs."[23] All metaphors are limited because they contain only partial views of reality.

## The Power and Influence Metaphor

In the early 1970s, a leading food manufacturer designed a new plant along lines of participative management. By mid-1977, reports indicated that the experiment was a success. Employee satisfaction was high, turnover was low, and the new system was credited with economic savings of approximately $1 million per year compared with traditional plants.

At the same time, however, reports filtering out of the company indicated that many of the key managers involved with the experiment had left, and that the experimental plant might be switched to a traditional system. As one ex-employee reported, "Economically, it was a success, but it became a power struggle. It was too threatening to too many people."[24] It's possible that traditional managers, operating on the assumption that workers should do what they are told, were deeply disturbed by the overt participation of "underlings."

The importance of power to organizational design was first recognized by March and Simon in their early work on organizations and popularized in recent years by Pfeffer and Salancik.[25] Essentially, this view holds that the rational approach (in which organizations are seen to be predictable, analyzable, and programmable) and the contingency approach (in which organization structure is seen as determined by technology, size, and environment) are fine, but incomplete.

An alternative to both of these approaches is the coalitional model of organizations. Essentially, this political perspective on organizations sees them as characterized by conflict, value differences, and bargaining. *Politics* here refers to the structure and process of the use of authority and power to effect definitions of goals, directions, and other major parameters of the organization.[26] The political perspective emphasizes, then, the view that decisions are not made rationally in organizations, but rather through compromise, accommodation, and bargaining. Although it may be more pleasant to imagine that organizations are rational entities, there is a great deal of empirical evidence that the reality is otherwise. Examples of how politics figures in the decision making of corporations are not hard to find. One of the classics is presented in Vignette 2.

**Vignette 2**

The story of the mid-1940s rise and fall of the Tucker automobile company is dramatized in the 1988 movie *Tucker: The Man and His Dream.* As the movie shows, the Tucker automobile company was run by a board of directors controlled by "Big Three" automaker influences and by related government political factions. The car design ideas of the Tucker's designer/inventor, Preston Tucker, were systematically sabotaged because the success of his company would cost other automobile companies billions of dollars. The Tucker company died after making only 50 cars.

Tucker's lack of success was not a failure of the product; in fact, some of Preston Tucker's innovations, such as putting the engine in the rear of the car, fuel injection, disc brakes, and seat belts, were later resurrected by other automakers. Indeed, the country at the time was very receptive to the Tucker, and it was considered by many to be superior to any of the competition (46 of those 50 cars were still roadworthy as of 1988). But Preston Tucker's attempts to introduce change in a market dominated by others more powerful than him were dangerous to the status quo; politics determined the fate of the Tucker company.

Political behavior is a direct result of the beliefs, attitudes, values, assumptions, and expectations of the political players. Different groups or subunits within an organization have different preferences for outcomes and the allocation of organizational resources. Subunits (also called cliques and coalitions) interact in specific ways to enhance their power vis-à-vis organizational decision making. For example, groups will attempt to control scarce resources or to manage uncertainty to enhance their power. Political power seems to go to the group that can manage the "critical contingencies" in the environment that are most closely tied to organizational success/failure.[27] In an interesting blend of the environmental approach to the determination of structure and the power perspective, Pfeffer and Salancik argue:

> For if you conclude, as we do, that the environment sets most of the structure influencing organizational outcomes and problems, and that power derives from the organization's activities that deal with those contingencies, then it is the environment that needs managing, not power. . . . The real trick to managing power in organizations is to ensure somehow that leaders cannot be unaware of the realities of their environments, and cannot avoid changing to deal with those realities.[28]

Pfeffer and Salancik have also discussed the "external control of organizations."[29] This means that forces outside the organization exert considerable power over it. These authors build the case that organizational environments affect and constrain organizations and that effective organizations are the ones structured to manage these external constraints. This approach is really an offshoot of the open systems school: Managers are seen appropriately as symbol makers, adapters to social constraints, and manipulators of their environments. Organizations are seen as coalitions of competing interests that face an environment of competing, frequently conflicting demands, and that need resources from the environment. Boundaries are defined in terms of control over activities, and effectiveness is defined in terms of survivability (the ability to attract and maintain resources). Pfeffer and Salancik then explore the "enactment" process (how organizations perceive their environments); here the collective paradigm comes into play full force.

## Implicit Theories
## of Organizational Design

*Implicit theories of organizing* explain how the ideas of organizational designers are translated into organizational structures. They also explain how organizational members respond to structural characteristics.[30] One can clearly see this process in action by comparing two radically different organizations, Ford Motor Company and General Motors. Clearly, the implicit organizing theory of Henry Ford led to a highly formalized (many rules and regulations) and centralized (power concentrated at the top) bureaucracy. On the other hand, the implicit organizing theory of Alfred Sloan created decentralized, autonomous divisions at GM. Another way to say this is that Sloan's dominant paradigm included beliefs, attitudes, and values that created decentralized, autonomous units (beliefs such as "People can be trusted," or "People can exercise initiative"). Ford's dominant paradigm perhaps included beliefs, attitudes, and values such as "People need to be controlled and led."

Attribution theory, discussed above, is actually a subset of implicit theory. Earlier researchers into the micro implications of implicit theory used the term "naive, implicit personality theory" to describe the manner in which a person assumes a causal relationship among the attributes of people he or she perceives.[31] More recently, Schneider has described an implicit personality theory as a set of assumptions one has about why people behave as they do.[32] Kelly argues that attribution theory "describes processes that operate as if the individual were motivated to attain a cognitive mastery of the causal structure of his environment."[33] He notes:

> Attribution processes are to be understood, not only as a means of providing an individual with a vertical view of his world, but as a means of encouraging and maintaining his effective exercise of control in that world. The purpose of causal analysis . . . the function it serves . . . is effective control. The attributor is not simply an attributor, a seeker after knowledge. His latent goal in gaining knowledge is that of the effective management of himself, and his environment. He is not a "pure" scientist, then, but an applied one.[34]

Kelly's use of the word "control" has two meanings here.[35] First, it refers to cognitive control, with people accepting implicit theories of causality because it helps them organize and understand their world. Kelly calls this "psychological epistemology," the process by which people "know" their world and know that they know. The second meaning relates to the maintenance and alteration of the physical environment. Here is where we can see the relationship between implicit theories and organizing/structure in organizations.

Implicit theories, then, are used in making causal assumptions about outcomes. We see someone behaving a certain way; we "explain" it through an implicit theory, then we "prove" the theory to ourselves because the person behaves that way (circular logic). And, as with the concept of the paradigm, implicit theories are seldom revised in the face of contrary evidence (until it becomes too uncomfortable to hold on to them). Transferring this theory to organizing, we see a formalized organization and we attribute a cause to that formalization (e.g., they don't trust people around here to do the job by themselves).

As with the paradigm concept, organizational structures that are based on implicit theories are likely to be highly rigid in character because the assumptions in the implicit theory are seldom tested by the holder.[36] So it would seem that implicit theories of organizing mediate organizational structures; that is, the theories are mediators of the empirical observables we call organizational structures.[37] Managers seem to "construct, rearrange, single out and demolish 'objective' features of their surroundings."[38]

Implicit theories of organizing are used by top management to design their organizations.[39] Also, the manner in which the organization member "fills in" with his or her prescribed role will depend upon his or her own implicit theory of organizing, not the designers'.[40] So, for example,

> "There is a written and unwritten law. The one by which we regulate our constitutions in our cities is the written law; that which arises from custom is the unwritten law."
>
> — Plato

the bureaucratic structure, with high centralization and formalization, is conceived by the designers but maintained by the participants. It is obvious, then, that when people complain about how the bureaucracy is "doing it to them" they are missing the point; they are doing it to themselves.

Implicit theories are the means by which organization members interpret structure; the interpretation of that structure, in turn, is the means by which the structural characteristics produce behavior in organizations; that is, implicit theories are the cognitive mechanisms that translate organizational structure into member behaviors.[41] These theories also serve as guides for interpreting organizational characteristics and as a glue to hold together the social fabric. It has been well established that individuals with common belief systems are likely to establish very strong social bonding;[42] for example, members of the same church often socialize together well.

Implicit theories of organizing, then, are a major component in the metamodel of the creation and maintenance of organizations.

## Corporate Culture: A Creation of the Collective Paradigm

In recent years, corporate culture has become a faddish topic in organizational considerations. Many seem to sense that this is a powerful tool for describing and changing organizations, yet there is very little consensus about just what it is. One common definition of *corporate culture* is that it is made up of the observed behavioral regularities that take place when people interact, such as the language used and rituals/myths of the organization.[43] Myths are those elements that express and explain organizational reality and attach meaning to it. They serve as tools that provide narratives to anchor the present to the past. Harrison Owen writes:

Myth is neither true nor false, but rather *behind* truth. . . . myth, in short, is the eyeglasses through which a given people perceive and interpret their world. . . . myth communicates the moving quality of the human Spirit as it seeks to becomes whatever it was supposed to be. . . . finally, myth doesn't just communicate *about* Spirit in its quest, but in some way manifests that Spirit in experiential terms; you can feel it. . . . it is common practice to speak about myth and ritual as if they were two separate things but that is not so, for ritual is simply putting the words of myth into form, motion and music. Myth and ritual are two sides of the same thing, which I call *mythos*.[44]

Rituals are the systematic and programmed routines of day-to-day life in the organization. In their more mundane manifestations, they show followers what kind of behavior is expected of them. In their extravagant form, called ceremonies, they provide visible and potent examples of what the company stands for.

More common elements considered to be part of culture include the following:

1. The feeling, climate, or atmosphere that is felt as one enters an organization (conveyed by the physical layout, the way people treat each other, and so on).[45]

2. The rules of the game, the "ropes" that a newcomer must learn to get along in the organization.[46]

3. The credo or philosophy that guides an organization in its approach to its employees, customers, and others.[47]

4. The dominant values expressed by an organization in its approach to marketing, finance, and so on.[48]

5. The norms that evolve in work groups, such as the concept of a "fair day's pay for a fair day's work."[49]

6. The stories and "folktales" that are used to convey organizational meaning, such as values, morals, information, and myths, vividly and convincingly to those inside and outside the organization. These are told and recalled in formal meetings and informal settings to validate tradition.[50]

7. The metaphors that serve as symbolic representations. We often refer to external organizational consultants as "organization doctors" or CEOs as "quarterbacks" who lead their teams to their goals. It is crucial to remember that metaphors compress complicated issues into understandable (yet simplified) images, and that they can affect our attitudes, beliefs, judgments, and actions.[51]

8. The "heroes and heroines" who personify the culture's values and provide role models for newcomers and outsiders. These are the people who shape values and educate others by personal example. They bring vision and alignment to organizations by creating memorable moments in organiza-

tional life. These memorable moments are the catalysts through which metaphors, stories, myths, and, ultimately, values are established.[52]

Edgar Schein's discussion of this subject contains the notion that all of these are the *effects* of culture; that is, they reflect the existence of culture but are not in themselves culture:

> The term "culture" should be reserved for the *deeper level of basic assumptions and beliefs* that are shared by members of an organization, that operate unconsciously, and that define in a basic "taken for granted" fashion an organization's view of itself and its environment. . . . culture should be viewed as a property of an independently defined stable social unit.
>
> That is, if one can demonstrate that a given set of people have shared a significant number of important experiences in the process of solving external and internal problems, one can assume that such common experiences have led them, over time, to a shared view of the world around them and their place in it. . . . culture, in this sense, is a learned product of group experience and is, therefore, to be found only where there is a definable group with a significant history. . . . To summarize, I will mean by culture—a pattern of basic assumptions—invented, discovered, or developed by a given group as it learns to cope with problems of external adaption and internal integration—that has worked well enough to be considered valid and, therefore, to be taught to new members as the correct way to perceive, think, and feel in relation to those problems.[53]

Culture, then, is a way of thinking that one learns when one becomes a member of a certain organization. One learns that "this is the way things are done around here," and makes decisions and behaves from these unconscious assumptions. For example, Rosabeth Moss Kanter and Barry Stein relate how some women moving into a predominantly male culture will behave accordingly:

> The culture that sometimes develops in male groups, involving drinking, off-color stories, and sexual innuendoes, can be a source of awkwardness and discomfort for the only woman, even one who can easily become "one of the boys." . . . Though occasionally tempted to retaliate, many women have learned that it is better not to compete with this culture. Said one: "If a woman told the same joke the men tell, it wouldn't go over too well. A clean joke would be like a wet blanket. So I don't tell jokes."[54]

Culture could be called a subset of the collective paradigm. That is, the culture of the organization is the *shared* beliefs, attitudes, values, assumptions, and expectations that guide participants in their everyday behaviors in the organization. This could be illustrated as shown in Figure A.1.

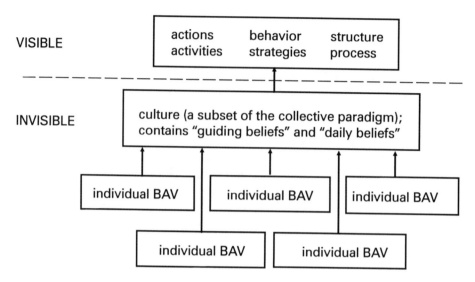

**Figure A.1.** The Relationship Between Individual Beliefs, Attitudes, and Values and Culture

NOTE: BAV = beliefs, attitudes, and values.


We can see some examples of the "collective paradigm" in action. In their excellent book *The Ropes to Skip and the Ropes to Know*, Ritti and Funkhouser talk about the "look of a winner":

> I was in New York for a week to go to this "systems procedures" seminar for all new plant people. One day it was really cold, windy, just miserable weather. The warmest thing I had was this old Army overcoat and head-gear. But I figured, what the hell, who cares what you look like for one day? . . . While we are waiting for the elevator, you can see (this old guy) giving me a fishy look, and finally he says, "*You* work for the Company?" I tell him I do, and then after a while he says, "Don't you think it's a bit risky to dress that way?" Now I am starting to get the picture. But even if I weren't, he gives it to me in detail as we ride up the elevator. "People in the Company don't dress that way," he says, "and if you ever want to get anywhere, son, you'd better think it over and change your ways."[55]

Ritti and Funkhouser go on to say that in a large organization, where people do not really know each other very well, people depend upon signals with agreed-upon meanings to interpret their world. People dress, act, and behave as part of gaining a subconscious agreement about their role or identity in the company. There are some exceptions to this rule, but they are usually exceptions only on the surface. In some "creative" jobs, for instance, such as advertising agency art director, people can get away with being "weird." In other words, the signal sent for that role is consistent with the role expectations.

Ritti and Funkhouser give another example from the point of view of a woman attending a corporate staff meeting. Every one of the vice presidents is there at the table with their pencils and yellow legal pads. The director arrives late ("power people" often do this), and sits down:

> Now at this point, and according to Company ritual, the host manager takes orders for coffee: "five black, two sugar only . . . ." Then he turns to me (a woman). *To me,* and says in this unctuous voice, "Would you get these for us, honey? The machine's down the hall to the left." Get these for us, honey?! Who the hell does he think he is? Why the hell should I get his lousy coffee? Just 'cause I'm the only lady in the room? I don't even drink the damn stuff!"[56]

As a pencil-wielding, yellow-pad-carrying female, she was understood to be filling the role of a secretary, willing to get the coffee, waiting to be told what to do, and with the primary job interest of pleasing male authority figures.[57] (Ritti and Funkhouser note that she could have avoided this problem by carrying an expensive leather briefcase and wearing a hat, sure signs of professional status.)

The following passage will clarify what all of this has to do with organizational structure:

> Many formal organizational structures arise as reflections of rationalized institutional rules. The elaboration of such rules in modern states and societies accounts in part for the expansion and increased complexity of formal organizational structures. Institutional rules function as myths which organizations incorporate, gaining legitimacy, resources, stability, and enhanced survival prospects.
>
> Organizations whose structures become isomorphic with the myths of the institutional environment—in contrast with those primarily structured by the demands of technical production and exchange—decrease internal coordination and control in order to maintain legitimacy. Structures are decoupled from each other and from ongoing activities. In place of coordination, inspection and evaluation, a logic of confidence and good faith is employed.[58]

In other words, organizations are compelled to incorporate the prevailing practices and concepts of work to increase their legitimacy and survival prospects. These practices and concepts function as powerful myths, and many organizations adopt them in a ceremonial manner. The formal structures of many organizations in society reflect the influence of these myths instead of the demands of the work. This results in loosely coupled activities, with bridged gaps between the formal structures and the work activities.

## Summary

All of the theories discussed above have led to the development of the metamodel of organization. One key aspect of transformational thinking is an explicit recognition of the power of thought. In the old paradigm, we have been much more interested in the level of visible, external forms; this is a natural outgrowth of the *effect* state. However, increasingly we are seeing that *everything is created by thought and feeling*. The theories addressed in this appendix, although developed in the dominant industrial paradigm, point to this perspective very clearly.

### DISCUSSION QUESTIONS

1. What are some mind-sets that affect how we think, feel, and act?
2. What are some of the "effects" of the culture in which you have been raised? That is, what reflects the existence of the culture but is not the culture itself?

### NOTES

1. Douglas McGregor, *The Human Side of Enterprise* (New York: McGraw-Hill, 1960).

2. Jane Elliot's experiment is documented in *A Class Divided* [videotape] (Washington, DC: PBS Video, 1985).

3. Chris Argyris, *Integrating the Individual and the Organization* (New York: John Wiley, 1968).

4. Thomas J. Peters and Robert H. Waterman, Jr., "How the Best-Run Companies Turn So-So Performers Into Big Winners," *Management Review* (November-December 1982): 9-16.

5. Thomas J. Peters and Nancy K. Austin, *The Passion for Excellence: The Leadership Difference* (New York: Random House, 1985).

6. In Warren Bennis and Burt Nanus, *Leaders: The Strategies of Taking Charge* (New York: HarperCollins, 1985); quoted in Norman Boucher, "In Search of Leadership," *New Age Journal* (October 1985): 52.

7. Karl E. Weick, "Enactment and Organizing," in *Perspectives on Behavior in Organizations*, ed. J. R. Hackman, E. Lawler, and L. W. Porter (New York: McGraw-Hill, 1983), 57; see also Karl E. Weick, *The Social Psychology of Organizing* (Reading, MA: Addison-Wesley, 1969).

8. Weick, "Enactment and Organizing," 59.

9. David Braybrooke, "The Mystery of Executive Success Re-examined," *Administrative Science Quarterly* 8 (1964): 533-560.

10. Weick, "Enactment and Organizing," 58.

11. G. Michael Durst, *Management by Responsibility* (Evanston, IL: Center for the Art of Living, 1982).

12. W. H. Starbuck, "Organizations and Their Environments," in *Handbook of Industrial and Organizational Psychology,* ed. M. D. Dunnette (Chicago: Rand McNally, 1976), 1070.

13. See, for example, Harold H. Kelly, "Attribution Theory in Social Psychology," in *Nebraska Symposium on Motivation* (Lincoln: University of Nebraska Press, 1967), 192-241.

14. Ibid., 193.

15. Lawrence S. Wrightsman, *Social Psychology* (2nd ed.) (Belmont, CA: Wadsworth, 1977), 100.

16. Barry M. Staw, "Attribution of the 'Causes' of Performance: A General Alternative Interpretation of Cross-Sectional Research on Organizations," *Organizational Behavior and Human Performance* 13 (1975): 414-442.

17. Gareth Morgan, *Images of Organization* (Beverly Hills, CA: Sage, 1986), 12-13.

18. See Gareth Morgan, "Opportunities Arising From Paradigm Diversity," *Administration & Society* 16 (November 1984); G. Burrell and Gareth Morgan, "Two Dimensions: Four Paradigms," in *Sociological Paradigms and Organizational Analysis,* ed. G. Burrell and Gareth Morgan (London: Heinemann, 1979); Douglas Berggren, "The Use and Abuse of Metaphor," *Yale University Review* (December 1962): 237-258.

19. Linda Heller, "The Competitive Edge: Sports Skills Can Help You Achieve Executive Success," *Executive Female,* January/February 1988, 24.

20. Willis Harman, "Visions of Tomorrow: The Transformation Ahead," *OD Practitioner* 13 (February 1981).

21. Ibid., 4-5.

22. Ibid., 7-8.

23. Ibid.; see also John Lilly, *The Center of the Cyclone* (New York: Bantam, 1968).

24. Michael L. Tushman and David A. Nadler, "Implications of Political Models of Organization," in *Perspectives on Behavior in Organizations,* ed. J. R. Hackman, E. Lawler, and L. W. Porter (New York: McGraw-Hill, 1983), 177.

25. See, for example, James G. March and Herbert A. Simon, *Organizations* (New York: John Wiley, 1958). Relevant works by Pfeffer and Salancik include Jeffrey Pfeffer and Gerald R. Salancik, "Organization Design: The Case for a Coalitional Model of Organizations"; and Jeffrey Pfeffer and Gerald R. Salancik, "Who Gets Power—and How They Hold On to It: A Contingency Model of Power"; both in *Perspectives on Behavior in Organizations,* ed. J. R. Hackman, E. Lawler, and L. W. Porter (New York: McGraw-Hill, 1983).

26. Tushman and Nadler, "Implications of Political Models," 179.

27. Pfeffer and Salancik, "Who Gets Power."

28. Ibid., 429.

29. Jeffrey Pfeffer and Gerald R. Salancik, *The External Control of Organizations* (New York: Harper & Row, 1978).

30. Arthur P. Brief and H. Kirk Downey, "Cognitive and Organizational Structures: A Conceptual Analysis of Implicit Organizing Theories," *Human Relations* 36 (1983): 1065.

31. J. S. Bruner and R. Tagiuri, "The Perception of People," in *Handbook of Social Psychology* (Vol. 2), ed. G. Lindzey (Reading, MA: Addison-Wesley, 1954).

32. D. J. Schneider, "Implicit Personality Theory: A Review," *Psychological Bulletin* 79, no. 3 (1973).

33. Kelly, "Attribution Theory," 193.

34. Harold H. Kelly, *Attribution in Social Interaction* (Morristown, NJ: General Learning, 1971), 220.

35. See Brief and Downey, "Cognitive and Organizational Structures," 1070.

36. Ibid., 1072.

37. Ibid., 1073.

38. Weick, "Enactment and Organizing," 164.

39. See, in this regard, Edgar H. Schein, *Organizational Culture and Leadership* (San Francisco: Jossey-Bass, 1985).

40. Brief and Downey, "Cognitive and Organizational Structures," 1075.

41. Ibid., 1076.

42. J. R. Terborg, C. Castonre, and J. A. Denino, "A Longitudinal Field Investigation of the Impact of Group Composition on Group Performance and Cohesiveness," *Journal of Personality and Social Psychology* 34, no. 5 (1976).

43.  Harrison Owen, "Facilitating Organizational Transformation: The Uses of Myth and Ritual," in *Transforming Work*, ed. John D. Adams (Alexandria, VA: Miles River, 1984); Erving Goffman, *The Presentation of Self in Everyday Life* (Garden City, NY: Doubleday, 1959); John Van Maanen, "The Self, the Situation, and the Rules of Interpersonal Relations" in *Essays in Interpersonal Dynamics*, ed. Warren Bennis et al. (Homewood, IL: Dorsey, 1979).

44.  Harrison Owen, *Spirit: Transformation and Development in Organizations* (Potomac, MD: Abbott, 1987), 11-12.

45.  Ronald Tagiuri and Gerald H. Litwin, eds., *Organizational Climate: Exploration of a Concept* (Boston: Harvard Graduate School of Business, Division of Research, 1968).

46.  Edgar Schein, "Organizational Socialization and the Profession of Management," *Industrial Management Review* 8, no. 1 (1966); Van Maanen, "The Self, the Situation"; R. Richard Ritti and G. Ray Funkhouser, *The Ropes to Skip and the Ropes to Know* (3rd ed.) (New York: John Wiley, 1987).

47.  William G. Ouchi, *Theory Z* (Reading, MA: Addison-Wesley, 1981); Richard T. Pascale and Anthony G. Athos, *The Art of Japanese Management* (New York: Simon & Schuster, 1981).

48.  Terrence E. Deal and Allan A. Kennedy, *Corporate Cultures: The Rites and Rituals of Corporate Life* (Reading, MA: Addison-Wesley, 1982).

49.  George Homans, *The Human Group* (New York: Harcourt, Brace, 1950).

50.  Joseph Rost, "Transforming Leadership: A Model for the Future" (paper presented at the annual meeting of the OD Network, October 15, 1985), 3.

51.  Ibid., 4.

52.  Ibid.

53.  Schein, *Organizational Culture and Leadership*, pp. 6-7. Used with permission from the publisher.

54.  Rosabeth Moss Kanter and Barry A. Stein, eds., *Life in Organizations: Workplaces as People Experience Them* (New York: Basic Books, 1979), 142.

55.  Ritti and Funkhouser, *The Ropes to Skip*, 24.

56.  Ibid., 41-42.

57.  Ibid., 43.

58.  John W. Meyer and Brian Rowan, "Institutionalized Organizations: Formal Structure as Myth and Ceremony," *American Journal of Sociology* 83 (1977): 340.

# Author Index

# Subject Index

# About the Authors

**David K. Banner** is the Napoleon Hill Professor of Leadership and former Director, Center for Management Development, School of Business and Public Administration, at the University of the Pacific in Stockton, California. Previously, he has served on the faculties of DePaul University, the University of New Brunswick, and the University of Houston. He has an undergraduate degree in mathematics/physics from The University of Texas at Arlington, a master's degree in human resource management from the University of Houston, and a master's degree in sociology as well as a Ph.D. in management from the Northwestern University Kellogg Graduate School of Management. He has authored or coauthored six books and many professional journal articles and conference papers on such topics as motivation, the relationship between work and leisure, delegation, organizational development, organization transformation, business ethics, integrity in business, and the foundations of leadership. He is one of the founding members of Renaissance Business Associates, Inc. He has consulted with a wide variety of public and private organizations in North America; some of his former clients include the Veterans Administration, General Electric (Canada), Blue Magic Products, Atlas-Copco, Metro State University (St. Paul, Nebraska), the President's Advisory Council on Minority Business Enterprise, and the Opportunity Funding Corporation. He is widely sought as a public speaker, organizational consultant, and adviser to management.

**T. Elaine Gagné** has been in the business/education field for more than 30 years. She has designed more than 40 corporate development programs, including presentations in Europe, South Africa, Australasia, and North America. She received national acclaim in adult education through the U.S. Department of Health, Education and Welfare. Her postdoctoral studies include work with Harvard University, the Institute of Management Consultants, the Four Fold Way (Dr. Angeles Arrien), and ongoing professional development in more than 20 workshops and seminars related to personal growth, human resource development, and business practice. She has authored two textbooks and five manuals/ handbooks for use in training programs. She is certified in the use and analysis of several psychological testing instruments, including the Center for Creative Leadership Benchmark program for managers, and is a certified Executive Coach. She is currently a Senior Associate with Renaissance Consulting Group, President of Renaissance Business Associates International, and a facilitator for the Covey Leadership Center Seminars.